Blockchain 2035

The Digital DNA of Internet 3.0

By

Jared Tate

Founder of the DigiByte Blockchain

Andrew Knapp

Founder and CEO of VESTi Inc.

Published by BlueShed LLC, A Blockchain Innovation Company.
Copyright © 2019 Jared Tate & Andrew Knapp, all rights reserved.

ISBN 978-0-578-47450-2

Published, October 28th 2019.
Cover art by Gandr&Kich

This book is dedicated to all the past, present, and future blockchain innovators and the entrepreneurs who will make ideas presented in this book (and more) a reality.

Table of Contents

PART I: THE BASICS 1
- INTRODUCTION: 1
- CHAPTER 1: OUR STORY & THE BIRTH OF DIGIBYTE 13
- CHAPTER 2: THE REVOLUTION IN OWNERSHIP 30
- CHAPTER 3: BLOCKCHAIN BASICS & TERMINOLOGY 50

PART II: THE PHILOSOPHY AND THE PHILOSOPHERS 74
- CHAPTER 4: BLOCKCHAIN, AN EVOLUTION OF APPLIED CRYPTOGRAPHY 75
- CHAPTER 5: BLOCKCHAIN IN THE SPECTRUM OF TIME AND TECHNOLOGY 94
- CHAPTER 6: BLOCKCHAIN, REBUILDING THE INTERNET & WEB 3.0 124
- CHAPTER 7: SECURING THE INTERNET OF THINGS ON A BLOCKCHAIN 135
- CHAPTER 8: BLOCKCHAIN RAILS FOR ARTIFICIAL INTELLIGENCE 158

PART III: THE APPLICATIONS 191
- CHAPTER 9: SURVEY OF EXISTING BLOCKCHAIN PROTOCOLS 192
- CHAPTER 10: SURVEY OF EXISTING BLOCKCHAIN PROJECTS 238
- CHAPTER 11: VETTING A NEW BLOCKCHAIN PROTOCOL OR PROJECT 268
- CHAPTER 12: FINANCIAL BLOCKCHAIN APPLICATIONS 288
- CHAPTER 13: GOVERNMENT BLOCKCHAIN APPLICATIONS 313
- CHAPTER 14: COMMERCIAL BLOCKCHAIN APPLICATIONS 345

PART IV: THE FUTURE 356
- CHAPTER 15: THE GRADUAL IMPLOSION OF THE UNBACKED FIAT SYSTEM 357
- CHAPTER 16: BLOCKCHAIN, THE NEW GEOPOLITICAL ARMS RACE 406
- CHAPTER 17: BLOCKCHAIN DEMOCRACY 460
- CHAPTER 18: THE QUANTUM LEAP 481
- EPILOGUE - INTRODUCING VESTI INC. 499
- ACKNOWLEDGMENTS 501

Part I: The Basics

Introduction

The blockchain stands to be among the most fundamental technological, sociological, and political innovations of the current era. It represents the next stage in the evolution of the internet that our world has come to so heavily rely upon, for everything from providing news and entertainment to streamlining logistics and finance. The existing internet has flattened the world, making information widely available and scalable in the same manner that Gutenberg's printing press made books cheaper and more available half a millennium ago.

Instead of working out of a dusty workshop in Mainz, the internet is a collective mass of cables, server farms, and billions of devices, all of which can effectively exchange and store information. This is not without its drawbacks - a significant second-order effect of this system is that the smooth transmission and consolidation of information has also led to massive data breaches and insecurity, endless copying of data that should have been kept private, and enormous hierarchies dominated by a few companies who have mastered the game in the markets that they dominate.

By 2035, blockchain will be more ubiquitous than quantum computing, as broadly used as the Internet of Things, and will reach maturity before any general AI does. The next evolution of the internet is now possible with the introduction of the blockchain.

For the very first time, we can recreate the uniqueness, decentralization, security, and continuity of critical data in a way that mirrors the way biological and physical nature preserves and procreate life across all species. Rather than the endless duplication of 'information technology,' the blockchain emulates how nature has been storing and transmitting information for over a billion years. Further, it follows the same physical laws that inspired countless advances in human technology in the past and enriches our means for systems to interact with each other.

Portable mechanical clocks improved our ability to navigate the globe by allowing sailors to judge longitude. The introduction of marine chronometers allowed users to judge their distance from a standard time (GMT), and thus measure how far they were from that based on a standardized understanding of the earth's rotation. To continue the analogy, this was possible because there was a new ontology - a new system of categories and rules - that sailors could readily use for a specific purpose.

Not only is tying a linear representation of time to the internet possible with blockchain – it is now possible to tie that linear progression to validate the existence of unique digital entities across several disciplines. Our ancestors won out over other competing species by their ability to adapt. Humans embody decentralization and diversity while retaining and communicating what we have learned to the next generation. This decentralization has enabled us to preserve valuable characteristics and information while adapting to the myriad of challenges we have encountered in our environment and history.

Human technology resembles biology in that the most robust systems have generally tended to overshadow weaker and less developed ones. Historically, the same rule went for culture, and the groups who best used and deployed new ideas gained the upper hand over those that did not. Technologies are an extension of this competitive biological process. We're confident that the most reliable and most decentralized blockchains will eventually win out, as they best embody these natural laws. As the technology finds its feet in the marketplace, those prepared to strike the balance between innovation and decentralization will be the biggest winners.

Just like powerful families, even within the strongest blockchains those chains are constantly forking, developing, iterating, and adapting, in ways that better enable them to provide value and survive in a competitive world. Today, blockchain technology is going through its adolescence, a time in which it is being evaluated and establishing just where it fits in the larger world.

The next stage, which will happen between the time we're writing this book and the year 2035, will not be without trials and tribulations. In most new industries, often, the first pioneers and innovators are overshadowed by upstart competitors and underdogs who answer the clunky innovations of those before them with a catchier product, a more robust business model, and viral growth. This progress will happen in the blockchain space, and many of the existing titans as we write this will be overcome by platforms that find more ideal use cases for the technology.

It took the internet 60 years to develop, and 30 of those years were spent to find its commercial roots and become the extension of human civilization that it is today. It is fitting to infer that we will look back on the year 2020 from 2035 in the same way that we now look back on 2004 from 2019 - before smartphones, YouTube, and Facebook changed our lives.

This timeframe is the origin of our title: Blockchain 2035, and our purpose in this book is to provide a helpful forecast for the pathways that this new technology might take as it comes into maturity.

The Root of the Biological Tech Stack: DNA

Imagine for a moment the DNA resting in every cell nucleus of your own body. That DNA embodies all the code that makes you, "you." We have billions of strands of DNA, composed of just 20 amino acids, strung in patterns not unlike words in every cell in our living bodies. These patterns detail every element of our physical embodiment, from our skin tone to the quality of our bones. Better yet, everything we eat has DNA - we're all part of a macro-organism that is bigger than us and helps us sustain our advanced brains by providing energy and building materials similar to our own bodies.

DNA is the decentralized blueprint that largely determines who you are and how you fit into the larger world as a biological organism, including some of the essential elements of our personalities and intellects. From DNA, your body has the necessary information to recreate not just organs but whole people through procreation.

To borrow from a claim cited early on in Max Tegmark's seminal recent book, *Life 3.0: Being Human in the Age of Artificial Intelligence*, our DNA represents the critical blueprint for creating and supporting a much more complex system, which is that of our conscious brains. Tegmark cites analysis that estimates the total information encoded in a given cell's DNA is roughly 1.6 gigabytes, which is an amazingly small number for how complex we are as organisms and how elaborate our minds are even in childhood.

By comparison, the same source estimates that the neural connections in our brains - which store all our memories, skills, habits, and impulses - store a whopping 100 terabytes. That 100TB of data represents our capacity for inherited knowledge and systems, which is a cornerstone of Tegmark's title.

In 'Life 1.0', bacteria existed as simple machines that follow predictable instincts that are hard-coded by their DNA.

In 'Life 2.0' (humans, to lesser degree primates and dolphins), this genetic code allows the ability to pass cognitive information down through use of symbols and language, in addition to the gifts of raw instinct.

In 'Life 3.0', AI adapts to its environment through the process of integrating new data and both information to and eventually update its hardware to an advanced state to improve to its environment.

We'll save the in-depth discussion of Blockchain and AI for Chapter 7, but the DNA metaphor applies to everything in this book. In the same way that the information gets efficiently encoded in DNA, blockchain will allow us to efficiently structure new data and systems. Additionally, it will give rise to the rules by which the internet of the future operates.

Users may produce and consume petabytes of data in the future, but the keys and rights to that data will get stored in tiny, unique key sets provided by one or more decentralized, worldwide blockchains. Users' online identity may be even smaller than their biological blueprint. For example, DigiByte's DigiAssets code uses just 80 bytes of data to describe a unique asset or access. If one compares DigiAssets to our biology, a user would need just over

21.6 billion distinct DigiAssets to equal the information density that their 1.6 gigabytes of DNA hold for an individual. Critical information stored in the blockchain will be substantially smaller than the large files that we use and interact with online.

The Great Bridge of Information

Often, we talk about the internet as a global infrastructure for the exchange of information, where information and value move around the globe at the speed of light. Just like the physical infrastructure in the towns and cities you and I live in, the foundation of the internet is built-in stacks, with each layer buried by newer and newer technology. Imagine the information superhighway as a bridge that crosses oceans, rivers, valleys, and streams. This bridge crosses national and physical boundaries built upon centuries of progress in science and engineering.

This bridge wasn't built all at once, and just like modern people paving over ancient Roman roads, there is old tech between our modern highway and bedrock. What you and I experience using the information superhighway is a state-of-the-art suspension bridge built with carbon fiber, awe-inspiring pillars, and supports that reach skyward, all with a smooth ride on synthetic pavement. High-speed magnetic trains rush below, and kids point from the cars at the hyperloop capsule that just rushed by past the speed of sound.

However, beneath this sleek exterior the bridge uses older technology - moving down a level, there are steel girders, rivets, and cables built in back in the industrial era. Below that are rusting iron supports no one has maintained in years, which are starting to show their age.

Deeper still, there are wooden beams, an abandoned railroad tunnel that hasn't seen traffic since the last century, and rusting black iron supports from when the bridge was built. Deeper still, we submerge ourselves in the ocean, going down to the pillars that connect our very modern bridge to ancient bedrock. These are concrete and brick supports poured long ago and covered in sea life. Maybe Jimmy Hoffa's resting place is somewhere down here, amidst all the rebar and forgotten stonework.

This stage reaches back to the early days of the information superhighway when the builders didn't know what was in store for this new technology, and what kind of load it would bear for society. Down here, you can see fissures in the concrete, places where the mortar has broken down, and bricks only stay in place because of the weight of the structure above them. We see situations where an earthquake or tsunami might damage the bridge and might break the ancient foundation of something we so cavalierly think of as high tech.

This analogy might seem silly, but it is how much of the modern internet is architected, on layers and layers without being fundamentally secure. We might still be able to drive down the highway unaware, but in truth, there are flaws deep below the surface that stand to threaten the way of life we have up top, whether that is due to a catastrophe or malicious action.

Web 1.0: Unstructured and Unsecured [No Encryption]

In Web 1.0, websites were generally static and not organized hierarchically - to go where you wanted, you had to know the URL and type it in, "http://www." and all. To use a general description, Web 1.0 was also unpermissioned - sites were presented as raw information, generally had inadequate security, and did not integrate a system of personal identity. The old New Yorker cartoon showing a dog at a desktop, captioned "on the internet; nobody knows you're a dog" embodies this era, an age where forums were ubiquitous but where the search, social, and commercial features we take for granted today were still in the future.

Web 2.0: Structured, Centralized, and Not Secure

Web 2.0's core characteristics are that it is hierarchical and tied to identity. What do we mean by that? Simply that, the "platforms" of Web 2.0 have provided means to make the user identifiable as an entity. This is the era of platforms like Google and Facebook which have redefined our online experience.

These platforms have created integrated 'walled gardens' where users are encouraged to enjoy the benefits of their systems, but these platforms have built on top of the old internet, without fixing its core insecurities. In some respects, these huge companies are leveraging these insecurities (such as dropping tracking pixels and cookies) to generate profits and influence. Google, Facebook, and their peers provide excellent software products free of overt charge because users pay with their data and the influence these platforms gain over them.

At a hardware level, the introduction of the iPhone and other smartphones have made personal computing not only ubiquitous but omnipresent and have extended this process much further into users' everyday lives than in the desktop-only Web 1.0 era. Web 2.0 is extremely hierarchical, with companies butting heads with nation-states and intelligence agencies for primacy over user data, often rebuffing democracies but appeasing authoritarian states when they have large enough markets.

These authoritarian states are in direct competition with US and European tech companies, as they have an incentive to not only emulate the West's hierarchical Web 2.0 systems, but to compete with the West in commercial, trade, and military terms, and control and surveil their populations through IT-based authoritarianism.

Many hold the opinion that tech giants, like Apple, Google, Amazon, and Facebook, are anti-competitive trusts that should be broken up by federal courts and state power. Moral and personal policy preferences aside, we think that in a world of Internet 2.0, this is unrealistic – as investor Peter Thiel often points out, no one wants to use the fourth best navigation app. Not all markets can sustain undifferentiated competition. All of these companies do something well enough that they have become the kings of their respective industries, and they have found themselves competing in fields where they all have an interest, but no party is dominant.

Witness the proliferation of "smart home" devices that all four companies have rolled out, in an attempt to be the default home AI system that is always listening. In short, existing Web 2.0 companies have expanded to the size of their container and are now forced to compete with each other in this hierarchical environment where dominance and control over the end user's data is the greatest prize.

This order is the critical flaw of Web 2.0, - that and by its hierarchical scheme, it is highly centralized. This arrangement necessitates vulnerabilities because it leverages the insecurity of the internet to effectuate its influence; further, it is leveraged - to track users across websites and to hoard user or company data as a means of analyzing private data and ultimately monetizing it.

Web 3.0: Decentralized and Secure

As a mark of evolution Web 3.0[1] will be both hierarchical and secure, which until the advent of the blockchain had remained an unsolved paradox. Hierarchy and structure are necessary elements of complexity, but complete centralization and insecurity aren't. There is no Google Search without Google Inc., no iPhone without Apple Computer, and no same-day delivery-of-any-good-you-can-imagine without Amazon.

The blockchain and Internet 3.0 is not about destroying or necessarily replacing these complex, centralized systems. It is about taking the most critical data that we use across these systems, including money, ownership, and identity, and securely decentralizing them so that the user - and not a group of competing corporate entities, controls. Some companies will fare better than others.

Blockchain Revolution

Believe it or not, this revolution has already started. As of this writing the blockchain has been around for ten years, and its non-monetary uses are becoming increasingly well recognized, with major tech giants and consultancies claiming patents for open-source technology that they hope to leverage on their platforms.

---

[1] Here we use Web and Internet 3.0 more or less interchangeably. We chose Internet 3.0 for our title because we mean to capture both the network itself, as well as the hardware, institutions, nation-states, and everything else connected to the internet, rather than just the searchable web, the deep web, and the "dark web." The internet is more fundamental than the web.

As forms of user identity and ownership become more important, people opt for more decentralized platforms and more explicit ownership of their data. This result doesn't mean that Web 2.0 and prior companies will disappear or cease to function, but they will have to compete with systems that are qualitatively superior to their own in terms of security and user control. There are natural limits to people and companies tolerance of the drawbacks and tradeoffs in the existing system, and blockchain opens the technological landscape for solutions that get around these limitations.

Imagine for a second that every single strand of DNA in your body, everything about you, was centrally located in the tip of your right index finger. Now imagine that one night, you are slicing limes for a cocktail, and you accidentally slip and slice the end of your finger-tip off! You would quickly be in a perilous situation. Not only would you no longer be able to heal, since your body would have no blueprint to direct the healing process for your finger, but the rest of your body would quickly wither and die.

This analogy sounds fanciful, but it is precisely how the internet and most computer systems function today. All around us are central points of failure which are vulnerable to accidents and disasters, both in terms of accidental deletion as well as unintentional dissemination. Chances are that everyone reading this book has been victimized by a cybersecurity attack, and recently. Each reader may be an unaware victim of several of the hundreds of data breaches that have occurred over the last two decades. Data is assumed safe in centralized systems and is stolen from these systems every day.

Usually data gets taken because of the efforts of a deliberate hacker who knows exactly what target to hit. Centralization creates an inherent flaw that blockchain can repair. Moreover, the existing discourse about big data and governance has centered on pushing the issue under the rug rather than fixing it. Luckily, we believe that the blockchain (blockchain technology) can and will fix it by fixing the underlying problem, not the symptoms.

Fortunate for us, nature discovered a solution to this problem long ago: decentralization, replication, and security of the most critical information. All around us are examples of decentralization in nature. Decentralization *is* nature. DNA replicated millions of times throughout our bodies every day, in trees, plants, and animals all around us.

A mushroom releases millions of identical spores with the blueprint and means to recreate an entirely new mushroom in an altogether new place. Only a few spores thrive, but the species survives. Adversity, represented by the changing world and climate, requires this kind of decentralization for species to survive and thrive. This resilience is how nature survives, and this is precisely how a blockchain survives.

Further yet, nature embraces uniqueness while still allowing for individuals to be part of a more extensive system. If you were to take my DNA and try to recreate yourself, you'd fail. However, at one point, your parents combined their DNA to produce you, and yet you are different than and distinct from your siblings, parents, cousins, and any other blood relatives you might have.

This iterative uniqueness is also a characteristic of the blockchain. Also, it sends or initiates a transaction on a blockchain, such as DigiByte or Bitcoin. By using a unique signifier, which again is similar to not unlike the sexual reproduction process in chordates. You use your private key (DNA) and combine it with my public key and *viola!* A new transaction is born.

Vision for the Book

The goal of this book is to help convey just how groundbreaking and influential this new technology is. While many are excited about 'tokens' and the opportunities for digital currencies, it has always been cybersecurity applications that have been nearest to Jared's heart, and as such, DigiByte's use from its inception was to improve software application security and build a global ecosystem for the safety of all applications.

Where Bitcoin's blockchain began with the Genesis Block hash of *"The Times 03/Jan/2009 Chancellor on brink of second bailout for banks",* implying Satoshi Nakamoto was building Bitcoin as a hedge against Western fiscal indiscipline, I started DigiByte with a hash of *USA Today: "10/Jan/2014, Target: Data stolen from up to 110M customers".*

The most significant changes in all aspects of our lives are yet to come. We believe now, more than ever, that correctly applied Blockchain technology can fix a vast majority of today's existing cybersecurity vulnerabilities across all industries, and in a way that benefits everyone, from large businesses to individual users. This extends to the country level - from international trade to finance and elections and, most importantly, the fundamental way the global internet works. Our digital future will live on a blockchain.

In the following chapters we will discuss how blockchain technology will impact the world we live in and how it will be used across specific industries in our everyday lives by the year 2035.

It is not too late to get involved in this technology, as this is only the beginning of mass adoption. The whole world of tech is ripe for disruption, and blockchain will play a critical role in so many new applications that it will appear mundane at times. Just as people do not perceive the disruption caused by Amazon.com to be rooted in its first mastery of the original internet, many will not recognize the potential of the blockchain until they realize it has become the backbone of their favorite applications and the things they rely on every day. All that is necessary is to follow nature's lead. Human technology is finally approaching the biological systems you and I live amidst every day.

Any prediction implicitly involves establishing pathways, estimating possible outcomes, and weighing probabilities. None of us has a crystal ball, and human freedom and creativity are a significant factor in how the present evolves into the future. One of the main themes in this book is that the blockchain is the product of decades of developments in computing and cryptography, and that these systems are just as *evolutionary* as they are *revolutionary*.

Many advances in cryptography and computing have developed in parallel along specific paths that reached the same or similar outcomes - to the point that many of the innovators in this space have come up with similar solutions to the same problem without knowing of each other's work and innovations.

We feel more grounded making inferences about the future of the technology, and there are a series of set paths that we will explore in this book for everal emerging technologies, such as AI, IoT, and business applications. Almost no one anticipated Bitcoin in 2009, and even to the present it is an open question of what the technology will look like in 2035 or by mid-century.

Up until the late '90s, the internet encountered skepticism by naysayers; the same goes for trains, planes, and automobiles in their times of origin. Consider this book an intellectual exercise in examining the possibilities and challenges - even though we're only a few years from the blockchain's Kitty Hawk moment, we hope this book inspires you to think about the fighter jets and airplanes that the technology could support in the future.

Our title is symbolic. *"Blockchain 2035"* was chosen as a title because the very last DigiByte is programmed to get mined in the year 2035. This year represents the completion of the first stage of the crypto economy and includes the time when most of the future titans of the blockchain will have founded the business and applications that will be synonymous by 2035.

Before we continue to specific industries, let's get started by explaining who we are, break down some basic terms, and explain how a blockchain functions. Do not be deterred by the first three chapters. Just as infant crawls before walking and then running, it is essential for those new to blockchain technology to understand the basics before moving on to more advanced concepts. Join us on this journey, and let's explore one by one how each industry changes with blockchain technology. Let's get started!

Chapter 1: Our Story & The Birth of DigiByte

"The beginning is the most important part of the work."

— Plato, *The Republic*

Arco, Idaho

Our story and the story of DigiByte starts in a tiny town in the middle of nowhere: Arco, Idaho, population 1,016. Arco is one of the most remote cities in the continental United States. Other than offering a few gas stations, a famous diner (Pickle's Place), the intersection between US Highways 20 and 26, and being the closest town to the lava flows of Craters of the Moon National Monument, and there isn't a whole lot going on.

Arco was so remote that on July 17th, 1955, the United States government chose to test the first nuclear reactor in the highland desert near our hometown, making our little hamlet the first city in the world to be lit and powered by nuclear power. So yes, occasionally we still joke about glowing in the dark, and how the town's abnormal environment eventually led to mutations and our superpowers. All jokes aside, Arco was a fascinating place to grow up, and well outside the norms of your typical American urban sprawl.

Both Andrew and I grew up in this tiny Idaho town. We think we first met each other around the age of three, and from that point forward, we experienced almost everything together. Scouting, sports, civil air patrol, academic studies, and everything else Arco had to offer before we graduated from Arco's only high school (Butte County High) with around 30 some odd classmates in 2006. Looking back at old yearbooks (and bad senior class photos), we both mentioned each other as best friends in our high school yearbook our senior year. Afterward, we moved on to college and parted ways for a time.

Meet Jared Tate

I do not have a typical background when it comes to the path that led me into the blockchain world. As I have traveled the world and met others involved in this groundbreaking technology, I think it's safe to say there is *no such thing* as a "normal path" that leads to pioneering work on blockchain technology. There is an old saying that 'necessity is the mother of invention,' and the path that led me to discover and develop blockchain technology is no different.

I was lucky to have been born to a mother who went to college for computer science and attended one of the nation's first university computer science programs around the same years Bill Gates, Michael Dell, and Steve Ellis were dropping out of college and founding their companies. Before the age of 10, she taught me how to program my first website and build my computer from scratch (thanks, Mom).

By the time I was a teenager, I was having all sorts of fun rewriting video game source code and doing other innovative (others might say "questionable") things with computers and software that intrigued my teenage mind, but at the time were done more for curiosity and intrigue than out of malice... Such as remotely taking over my sister's computer with a backdoor exploit, or reprogramming a video game so that when I had a LAN party with friends, I had the upper hand. Andrew can vouch for this, having lost several games of Battlefield and Age of Empires.

On my father's side, I learned to appreciate working with my hands and enjoying the great outdoors. Idaho is among the most beautiful states in America and has more backwoods and mountains than any other, save maybe Alaska. My dad was a builder and came from a large ranching family spread across Idaho and Montana. On my father's side of my family, my great grandfather homesteaded the central part of Idaho. We still have pictures of him trading with Native Americans in Idaho before they settled on reservations in the '20s and 30s. From the time I was five or six and through my teen years, I did everything from branding cattle and going on cattle drives, to running heavy construction and farm equipment, to pouring concrete and building houses. I even learned to weld in high school.

It's incredible for me to realize as I write this, that in two generations my family went from communicating with each other via an old barbed wire fence phone line and living without running water or electricity, to participating and building blockchains and investing in cryptocurrencies. Idaho was indeed one of the last vestiges of the wild wild west and the last of the frontier. To this day, I feel closely tied to this ancestral spirit of self-reliance and survival.

My upbringing has come in handy over the years, and especially while thinking through real-world applications for blockchain technology. However, it also provided its share of hardships. Arco was not a very prosperous area, and as such, I knew I needed to work hard, especially coming from a family without much money or political connections. From the time I was a baby, I lived in a single-wide trailer home in the middle of a potato field, and my parents didn't move into a larger house until I was 9 or 10.

I was driven to succeed in school and get out of such an economically depressed area. I wanted to travel the world and explore all life had to offer. My original plan up through college was to join the military and become a fighter pilot. I worked hard in high school, obtaining good grades, doing well in sports, and becoming captain of the football and basketball teams as well as becoming student body president. I earned my Eagle Scout and was active in the Civil Air Patrol, where I received my private pilot's license by the age of 18.

I attend the College of Idaho on an academic scholarship, and after being convinced by an Army colonel that "leading men on the ground" was a much more appealing and manly career than flying a desk in the Air Force, I signed up for Army ROTC and applied to the United States Military Academy at West Point. After my freshman year at the College of Idaho, I earned an acceptance letter into the US Military Academy.

I entered the academy in the summer of 2007 with the classes of 2011.

After several weeks, I decided for multiple personal reasons that the academy was not for me and that I would be better off back in Army ROTC at the College of Idaho. I resigned my appointment and returned that fall to the College of Idaho. For the next year, I experienced my first big "failure" in life and have ever since dealt with the stigma of being a West Point dropout.

I continued Army ROTC and fully contracted with the Idaho National Guard in the summer of 2008. That fall, I received eye surgery, which I paid for out of pocket to qualify and get commissioned to Branch Aviation and fly helicopters. This surgery was just at the time that the US economy began unraveling, as we fell into the Great Recession. That fall, I was told I would need a medical waiver after my eye surgery to continue with Army ROTC. Given that I was occupying an Idaho Guard officer slot paid for by the State of Idaho, my slot disappeared following the state making drastic budget cuts to comply with the balanced budget amendment in the state's constitution.

I found myself part-way through the fall of my junior year at a private liberal arts school without a scholarship and without the financial resources to pay $13,000 for that fall's tuition. I had missed all financial aid deadlines. Additionally, I was forced to drop out by November, and to this day, the College of Idaho has held my transcript hostage, and I have not been able to transfer to another college or get my previous credits transferred.

To add insult to injury, the College of Idaho eventually attempted to sue me for that semesters' tuition and put a black mark on my credit, which haunts me to this day. The fact they could hold my college transcripts, hostage after I paid for the first two years in full is not right, and it reflects just how broken higher education has become in America. It's also an excellent example of why blockchain technology is needed to allow us to cryptographically and mathematically take charge and control of our data and information - more on that later.

After dropping out due to financial hardship in the fall of 2008, I decided to attend a private flight school in the spring of 2009. That spring, a month after I began helicopter school, Sallie Mae froze all lending for aviation programs. Once again, I found myself forced out of an educational program due to financial hardship as the global economy unfolded around me in the spring of 2009.

For the next three years, I went from odd job to odd job, trying to make ends meet as a triple-crown college dropout without any access to my college transcripts. I worked on the Geek Squad at Best Buy, at a Lowe's home improvement store, and as a personal trainer. None of which would hire full-time employees, as doing so would compel them to pay for the benefits mandated by the Affordable Health Care Act. I then went back to what I knew, building websites, and freelance coding.

From 2009 - 2011, I moved to Arizona, which at the time, I didn't realize was one of the hardest-hit areas during the financial crisis. However, I had family living there, so I decided to move there in search of better opportunities. Times were tough. On several occasions, I barely had enough money to buy food and was on the verge of being evicted along with my roommates - twice.

In October of 2011, I received a text message while at work from a family member stating that my dad had been in an accident and was being life-flighted to see a neurosurgeon in Boise, Idaho. I took the first flight I could find to Boise and spent the next two weeks in the hospital with my dad, who was in an artificially induced coma.

My father had been working on the roof of a home he was inspecting in Sun Valley, Idaho, when he slipped, and he fell two stories down. He broke both his wrists and his neck. He had broken his neck in the same place they call a "hangman's fracture," and by all accounts, he should have died on the spot. Had it not been for two off-duty EMTs that happened to be driving by and watched him fall, he would have surely tried to get up and move, causing even further damage. They immediately ran over and immobilized his spine and kept him from moving his neck.

Thanks to a higher power and modern medicine, he was eventually able to make a full recovery and gets around great today.

Given the remote area, my parents still lived and worked from, we decided as a family I would move home and take care of my dad once he had discharged from the hospital. My mother at the time was the only person in our family with a good-paying job, and my brother had his family to take care of, so I moved back to Arco to help take care of my dad for six months during his recovery.

This period was a fairly dark time in my life, having to move back in with my parents at the age of 25 with no money and no job in such a remote area. The girl I was dating in Arizona broke up with me, so I quickly found myself with much spare time and no distractions. I dove in head-first starting my freelance coding and web design business. It was in these six months in 2012 that I first discovered Bitcoin. I have always believed that everything in life happens for a reason.

One day, while looking for solutions for a coding bug on Stack Overflow, I saw a response and a solution to my problem. The person who originally posted the question replied to the guy who provided an answer saying, "thank you so much, you saved the day!." Then, the person who had the solution replied the following: *"Haha, no problem, you can pay me in Bitcoin, j/k."* Moreover, that, dear reader, is where my journey down the rabbit hole began. For the next six months into the spring of 2013, I dove into reading and learning everything I could about Bitcoin and its underlying protocol.

Back when I discovered Bitcoin, you could still mine bitcoin with GPUs, and even some CPUs. Back then, I was earning a few bitcoins a day using a repurposed desktop gaming PC. In just a few days, in the spring of 2013, I went from having a profitable mining operation to receiving absolutely nothing, as the advanced hashing power of Chinese miners and global pools came online. In one week, I went from earning 0.5 BTC a day to calculating it would take 6,000 days to mine a single BTC.

By March/April 2013, the instant technological obsoletion of my mining operation caused me to look even deeper into the Bitcoin core protocol. The challenge of countering ASIC centralization piqued my interest, and I began an attempt to truly understand what was going on with the Bitcoin blockchain that would make mining so much more of an intensive effort than it had been previously.

This thorough study led me to discover several core flaws in the original design of the Bitcoin blockchain. These included the lack of a real-time difficulty adjustment system, the 51% attack, and several other issues that could break or impede the growth of the Bitcoin blockchain. Which for the most part, has continued to hamper its growth and adoption to this day.

Fascinated as I was when I started, I proposed several solutions to some of the Bitcoin) problems in forums like BitcoinTalk, and was surprised to be met with resistance to my enthusiasm. In a way, this rejection was one of the best things that ever happened to me. It inspired me to think long and hard about the innovations and applications that might be built on a blockchain that iterated on the original genius of Bitcoin, but one that had the liberty and development community to innovate beyond Bitcoin's rigid ecosystem and embrace the very best innovations in this space.

Halfway into 2013, I decided that to experiment with some of the changes I was thinking about; I would need to start a new blockchain to implement and test them. At the time I never expected this "test" blockchain to take off and build its own unique identity and a worldwide community, but I believe that for these changes to ever be adopted by Bitcoin or any other projects for that matter, they would need to be battle-hardened and tested in the wild.

In October 2013, I forked the Bitcoin core code and began experimenting with a few changes. These changes came to fruition with the launch of the DigiByte mainnet on January 10th, 2014, with the headline: *"USA Today: 10/Jan/2014, Target: Data stolen from up to 110M customers."* A headline that was later just that evening edited by the author to say "70M customers" - though is forever recorded in its original format as the basis for the genesis block of the DigiByte Blockchain. Unintentionally, this ended up being a great highlight of the immutability of a distributed blockchain ledger, one that cannot be hacked or edited.

From that day forward, my life has been forever changed and never dull. Since we had announced the launched a couple of weeks ahead of time on the BitcoinTalk forum, and we had a live countdown timer until launch, we had thousands of people who participated in the start of DigiByte from the very beginning. All the time, I meet people who come up to me and say, "Hey, it's great to meet you. I have been with DigiByte since the beginning."

To this day, I'm adamant that DigiByte has the absolute best development community in the world of blockchain, and this is attested to by the many innovations our community has to its name, including DigiShield, MultiShield, Multi-Algo mining, real-time difficulty adjustments, Digi-ID, and much more that continues to develop to this very day. Numerous other top blockchain projects have adopted our innovations. It is safe to say some of these projects in the top 10 would not have survived today without code that the DigiByte community pioneered. We will go more into detail on these innovations in a later chapter.

From the start, our goal with DigiByte has been to build a stronger blockchain: to be faster, more secure, more decentralized, and more forward-thinking. From a frigid garage in rural Idaho to my time working on getting DigiByte off the ground while working on real-world blockchain trade solutions in Hong Kong. DigiByte has become a worldwide cryptographic network with thousands of nodes, DigiByte has been subject to what at times felt like crushing evolutionary pressure, and the project has been made better for it.

That part of the story, we will save for another time and another book, as it rivals any Wild West epic, spy movie, or science fiction drama. Suffice to say, I'm immensely proud of everyone in the DigiByte community and all we've been through together over the past five years, and I'm even more proud of where we are going.

As I completed my time in Asia and moved back to the United States, my faith in the importance of blockchain technology has only grown. Blockchain technology will be critical for the way business and technology evolve into the future, but it will also be vital to the way we relate to governance, ownership, trade, and several other fields. In my travels since leaving Hong Kong, I'm heartened to meet so many people in Europe, America, and elsewhere who genuinely get the technology and are excited for the future that it can bring.

To that effect, in this new era of blockchain technology, my main focus is making it easier to build on a scalable, battle-hardened blockchain like DigiByte. It does so in a way that provides the benefits of security and decentralization to the larger world, and further allows people to experience precisely how superior blockchain technology truly is! In the future, you will be using blockchain without even knowing it, just like we use encryption, TCP/IP protocol, fiber optics, and HTML code today to surf the web without needing to understand how those technologies work.

In the course of this book, you'll hear about a lot of potential projects, about advances that will have significant impacts on the way the world works by the year 2035. One of those projects is a real estate technology company named VESTi Inc. that Andrew and I are working on building on top of DigiByte's new DigiAssets protocol, which we will touch on in the epilogue and throughout this book. I will also discuss the upcoming DigiPad launchpad I have been working on to help you secure your most valuable personal digital assets, such as your birth certificate and will.

Meet Andrew Knapp

Like Jared mentioned, we grew up together in a tiny town in rural Idaho. Jared and I have known each other since we were kids, and we grew up in an environment that was both intellectually rich but also small and isolated. For me, that was learning the principles of nuclear power, liquid-cooled reactors, and Cold War espionage from my dad; for Jared, that was learning computer science and programming from his mom. Our values growing up were both anchored in scientific learning and professional learning, but also a sense of duty to our country and our fellow man.

Growing up in Arco, my family story is a lot like Jared's. My dad grew up in New York, North Carolina, and Michigan. His dad was an art professor, his mom a socialite, and when they divorced in his teens, both withdrew from his life. From about 16, he raised himself, and he still has frostbite scars on his feet from working at a gas station in Michigan when he was 17 and trying and put himself through high school.

He was living in a hotel at the time without any family and with no bright future in mind. With the Vietnam War raging and nowhere else to go, he sauntered into an Army recruiting station and asked when the soonest he could ship out was. The woman behind the counter seized a broom in the way one might wield a battle-ax, yelled, "Are you f---crazy?" at the top of her lungs, and chased him out the front door... So, he walked across the street and applied to join the Navy.

Despite being a C student, my dad aced the Navy's nuclear aptitude exam when he took it. Through the US Navy recruiter, the school principal found out that he had passed his naval entrance exam. Knowing my dad was considering dropping out, the principle drove to my dad's address late one evening and presented him with a high school diploma, which was a requirement to enlist. That small act is how my dad ended up becoming a lifelong US Navy Nuclear professional, and in part, it's how I ended up in the tiny town of Arco, Idaho.

On the other side of my family, my mom was a rancher's daughter from Twin Bridges, Montana. Her father's family had settled in Montana, having come from Kentucky and Missouri; he was part of the Army Corps of Engineers in WWII, a Golden Gloves boxer, and entirely self-made. The family story was that he had started his ranch with just sixty dollars to his name and a chainsaw, but when I was a kid, the ranch had grown to several hundred cattle.

My grandfather was a self-taught man and immensely proud of what he had built - he loved to trade commodities, and taught me about monetary theory and arbitrage when I was eight. I still have his 80's Timex, which he bought the day I was born, and I always remember him bragging about how it would chime every morning when markets opened in London and New York.

My mom and her mother were both schoolteachers, meaning I grew up with educators, entrepreneurs, and military history on both sides of the family. My mom still occasionally tells stories of how their home phone had a "party line" run through the county's barbed wire fences up until the late 1960s.

On my dad's side, my grandfather was born in 1898 and was a WWI veteran - it's interesting to think that in living memory, my family has gone from a pre-aviation world to one with spaceflight, the internet, AI, and blockchain.

As a kid, I kind of thought I knew what my future would look like down the road. That the Cold War had been over for years didn't stop us from thinking we'd be fighter pilots. Our first day of 5th grade, we both brought our Jane's Military History stat sheets of all the Air Force's fighters and bombers and traded a few of our duplicates. The prosperity of the 1990s, our upbringing, the values of technology, adventure, education, and a sense of patriotism we both shared led us to think that we'd both get an excellent education and be successful in serving our country in the military and government careers.

Then we were attacked on 9/11. I had never been to New York - I had barely even been out of state - but I had always identified with the city because my dad was from there, and Arco seemed tiny in comparison. Jared and I were in the 7th grade at the time, and we both thought we would have military careers. The United States invaded Afghanistan on October 7th, 2001 - my 14th birthday, just about the time most kids are figuring out who they think they'll be in life. Less than two years later, the US also invaded Iraq, again based on severe intelligence failure.

Jared and I joined the Civil Air Patrol in addition to already being Boy Scouts and drove 86 miles once a week to go to Wing Meetings in Idaho Falls. CAP membership included training, "boot camp" at 16, lessons in avionics and radios, search and rescue, all the rest of it.

In 2005, just as we were nearing our final year of high school, one of our fellow cadet's older brothers (and a former cadet himself) was killed by an IED in Ramadi, Iraq. With his death making the issue personal, I came to recognize that both wars had started as a result of massive intelligence failures. 9/11 shouldn't have happened, and the Iraq War shouldn't have happened either. From there, I found a sense of purpose.

I threw everything I had at getting the credentials to work in intelligence.

I borrowed to attend a small private college in Nampa, Idaho, studying philosophy, politics, and economics, scraping by on friend's couches and spare rooms for most summers. I studied in Egypt, Turkey, and Syria during my junior year. Upon graduating, I thought a Ph.D. in political science would be the most assured path to becoming Jack Ryan - so I pursued that for a year after graduating to no avail, not knowing an academic Ph.D. would have been more of an encumbrance than a boon in my quest for professional fulfillment.

After a year of searching, I found the Institute of World Politics in Washington DC, which was founded by a handful of former National Security Council alums from the Reagan era who had helped architect the plan that took down the Soviet Union. I was intrigued, so I applied, and got accepted to study intelligence analysis and statecraft, though I had to go even deeper into student debt to complete my degree. I drove across the country in August of 2011 with nothing but $3,000 and everything I owned in the back of my 2003 Ford Focus hatchback. By the time I found a place to rent in DC, I had about $300 left in my checking account.

While I might have borrowed and worked odd jobs to scrape by during the financial crisis, reality hit when Sequestration happened in the spring of 2012. I had secured an internship with the Office of Naval Intelligence, and my position and the possibility of a job quickly evaporated with Congress's new restrictions on federal spending, which had drifted out of control since the Iraq War and is still out of control. Here I was, so close to starting the career I had worked so hard for, and the rug was pulled out from under my feet. Larger economic forces beyond my control were always one step ahead of me. I finished my Master's degree and graduated into a market that was not hiring.

I ended up applying to what felt like every job in DC. I got rejected by every single place I delivered a resume. I even applied for an entry-level position with CoStar, a commercial real estate research firm, which denied my application because I was "overqualified." I couldn't afford rent at the time, but I did tell them I'd gratefully re-apply when I was less qualified.

Here I was with a Master's degree, a security clearance, and relevant experience, unemployed and in suffocating student debt that I had taken out because I wanted to serve my country. Like many in my generation, there was no alignment between my early expectations and reality.

Like Jared, I worked as a personal trainer for a time, which was how I paid my bills. I split a 520 square foot studio apartment with my little brother, who moved in with me, and we split the $1200 rent in two ways. I was utterly broken-spirited, realizing how much effort I spent to no avail.

I continued to work odd jobs, but eventually, I was successful, and at I 26 finally secured a position as a contractor for the FBI - for $42,000 a year, minus taxes, living in one of the highest cost-of-living areas in the country. Six months later, I was an official employee of the FBI, working in the Counterterrorism Division (CTD). This book isn't about that, but I did get to help take the fight to ISIS for four years alongside some of the best people I've met in my life, and for that, I will be forever grateful.

Upon landing my dream job after all this struggle, the next bitter pill quickly hit me: between student loans and the ever-rising cost of rent, I and many like me would likely never be able to afford to buy a house or the costs associated with starting a family in the place we worked.

After paying state, federal, and local taxes, paying my student loans (which I would lose my job for not paying and could not even discharge in a bankruptcy after the Consumer Protection Act of 2005), and paying rent and other living expenses, I typically had less than $300 leftover to save, spend, or to invest with.

Further, if the FBI as an agency elected to assist with my loans I would be taxed on the amount awarded and considered to owe the full amount, such that an $8000 reward would have translated to $5000 of a student loan paid off and an $8000 debt to the agency if I left before my three year term completed, again on top of increasing my taxable income for the year. On top of that, I discovered once in that if the federal government did finally forgive loans, recipients were required to pay a lump sum of income taxes equivalent to half the loans in the first place, all in the same tax year. $50,000 of loan forgiveness would result in a roughly $20,000 tax bill on the spot. As of right now, the government has relied on technicalities and paperwork to avoid processing loan forgiveness, with only a single digit percentage of applicants qualifying despite having made the required ten years of payments.

I had poured my heart and soul into serving my country and having the skills to do so but was not going to be able to afford the most basic stake in the country I thought I was part of. I was coming to recognize that the system had broken. After Sequestration, retirement plans were recalculated by Congress to take some of the burdens off of the government's sovereign debt load, which had ballooned unsustainably after the financial crisis of 2008. My colleagues and I were paying into a broken pension system and were expected to supplement its shortfall by drawing on Social Security for a third of our retirement expenses. The official plan overlooked the fact that the program is anticipated to be insolvent by the year 2035, a decade before I would have been eligible to retire.

I and my peers had worked day and night, sometimes 15-hour days, including Christmas Eve and Christmas Day three of the four years I was in the FBI. I had borrowed for a graduate degree in intelligence, placed in the top of my class, and had worked my way up from a tiny town in Idaho with a median income inches above the national poverty line just so that I could pay rent indefinitely and be treated as essentially disposable with a livelihood controlled by self-interested politicians.

It wasn't just me - most of my former colleagues had similar stories and experiences. We were expected to rely on a broken pension system, and a government addicted to kicking the can down the road with ever-higher levels of debt and irresponsible spending that made service immensely costly at a personal level.

This experience led me to the realization that we and many others in our generation were not going to be able to live to the same standards as our parents. We were going to be the first generation in American history whose standards of living were worse than their parents, and mostly because of the policy choices of our parent's generation.

To add insult to injury, critical data relating to my employment and identity were stolen in ways that affected me personally. This targeting included the Office of Personnel Management Hack of 2015. The US government's policy of gathering data, centralizing it, and pretending hostile nations and even independent hackers didn't know how to use a computer meant that the People's Republic of China and likely by other powers stole my entire biography.

The FBI couldn't even keep its phonebook private - for a few months in 2015, I quit answering my unclassified line because I was continually receiving prank calls from kids with nothing better to do than dial government numbers and verify the number belonged to the name on the phonebook.

Realizing the world had changed and how my values had led myself and others to become exploited by our institutions crushed me. I frequently thought about how I wasn't the only one, how much of my and the next generation were going to suffer the effects of poor choices made by their parent's generation. In the midst of all this, an idea struck me.

In October of 2015, Matt Ketron, a friend who was working in the Senate at the time (and someone whom you'll meet later), and I had a long conversation about just what went wrong for our generation. Beyond the monetary and fiscal issues, the struggling institutions, and the generational wealth transfer built into our politics and our entitlements system, one thing stuck out: that housing and education have become significantly more expensive for no good reason, and that many cannot afford even to save for a down payment and the first steps of ownership. This conversation led to the idea for VESTi. More on this later.

When I first heard about cryptocurrency and blockchain, I was a skeptic, and as someone who was working in the national security field, I was initially dismissive of the prospect of using technology so radically free from the existing system. However, my experience made me rethink my original position, and over time I came to see just how revolutionary the blockchain will be for commerce, technology, and national security. I've also come to see how other, less democratic governments are embracing and often bastardizing the technology, not for the libertarian purposes that it was meant to serve but to pervert it as a means of exerting control through technology.

These economic, technical, and political forces made me rethink my beliefs. They also inspired me to try and find a way to confront these many challenges. I'll be the first to admit; I see blockchain with the passion of a convert today because I know the technology might be a keystone in addressing so many of these issues, from providing sound money and addressing income inequality to expanding our cybersecurity and national technology strategies. It's difficult to understand how fundamental this technology will be to the way the world looks and operates in the coming years.

After reconnecting with Jared, I knew it was the right decision to find new horizons. I left government service for three reasons.

First and foremost, our generation faces enormous challenges as a result of the economic, social, and political policies of the last thirty years, and this has impacted fields as far apart as cybersecurity and housing.

Second, I believe that the innovations that the blockchain makes it possible to offer a series of ways to address these challenges in a way that is ethically and technically responsible.

Third, I believe it is the private sector and not government edict that will lead the way in addressing many of these challenges.

Shared Perspective

Blockchain is a technology with implications across every sphere of human activity. Because of this, we are blending our perspectives in this book. Jared's experience as one of the most experienced blockchain founders informs means he is providing an authoritative perspective on the the technology, and Andrew's background in philosophy, intelligence analysis, geopolitics, and finance informs his writing on those topics. This book is the product of over a year's research and discussions, often with events happening faster than we could hope to write. For this reason, we have been topical throughout the book.

Before we get into the nuts and bolts and basics of what a blockchain is at a technical level, let's set the stage by covering what blockchain is at its philosophical core: a revolution in ownership.

Chapter 2: The Revolution in Ownership

> "To understand political power right, and derive it from its original, we must consider, what state all men are naturally in, and that is, a state of perfect freedom to order their actions, and dispose of their possessions and persons they think fit, within the bounds of the law of nature, without asking leave, or depending upon the will of any other man."
>
> — John Locke, *Second Treatise of Government*

> "They who can give up essential liberty to obtain a little temporary safety deserve neither liberty nor safety."
>
> - Benjamin Franklin

> "Senator, we sell ads."
>
> - Mark Zuckerberg

Your Data, Your Control, Your Security

Every day, thousands of third parties collect, analyze, and resell the information that you generate in your daily life. Facebook collects and aggregates your tastes and interests and sells ads specifically targeted to you. Google takes your search history, analyzes it, and sells your attention profile to advertisers in much the same way. Even your local county courthouse will occasionally post personal information about yourself, your place of residence, and your personal contact information that is legally required for you to give to them.

This same data is then often easily scraped by foreign nationals and used to steal your digital identity and open fraudulent accounts in your name. In exchange for a service, you get turned into a product, and your attention profile is captured and monetized. Everyone reading this book has been the victim of at least a dozen online data breaches in just the last few years, often in cases where a company or agency who took your data indiscriminately failed to protect it. Properly applied blockchain technology allows you to take charge of your data and fix this problem.

Anywhere your data is being aggregated, scraped, and exchanged without your consent will be disrupted in the future when blockchain technology emerges for you to take charge of your data. This data will include everything from managing your personal financial information to managing and owning your health care records.

For example, when an individual makes an appointment with a medical doctor, up to eight different parties can view private patient information that should be between the patient and the medical professional. The issue of privatizing one's medical documents is imperative, and blockchain can accelerate the construction of stronger cybersecurity infrastructures and protection of personal medical data.

Many are coming to realize the fact that we are the first generation that will have immortal social media data. 10,000 Facebook users pass away every day, and soon the site will consist of more deceased people's profiles than living ones, though their profiles live on after their death. For the living, social media data and may come back to haunt us years later. Many have discovered this the hard way, with youthful indiscretions that would have been forgotten a decade ago being dredged up to damage their prospects today.

In Kevin Mitnick's book, *The Art of Invisibility,* he discusses several alarming examples of how an individual's social media accounts cause them a tremendous amount of pain, personal problems, and embarrassment. He also highlights the danger that unsecured social media may pose to us all. It's a book we highly recommend that everyone reads next to learn how you can adequately safeguard yourself within today's broken internet before blockchain date privacy solutions get widely built and deployed.

If you take anything from this book, remember this: Anywhere you find an intermediary or a third party brokering your data or information, it will eventually be replaced by a blockchain startup that will give you back control of your data through properly applied blockchain technology. As some, such as futurist George Gilder has pointed out, blockchain is the next natural evolution of data management and value and will impact today's behemoths like Google and Facebook.

The Attention Economy

Today's internet is primarily dominated by companies whose job it is to collect and aggregate data while drawing and capturing your attention. The World Wide Web was initially designed to facilitate the free flow of information, but it did not take long for companies to realize that information was extremely valuable. Before long corrals, or information funnels were designed and built to capture everything about us.

This information reveals deep insights about our daily habits; from what we buy, to what we own, and where we spend our money to whom we vote for and what our sexual orientation is. The main driver for how we behave in the real world is the information we consume and produce on the internet.

The companies that have been the most successful in corralling and collecting our data are distinct. Google is the front page of the internet for most people, while YouTube has more viewers watching daily videos than almost any other site or channel in the world. Gmail is the most popular email service, and many businesses rely on Google Docs, Hangouts, and the many other services that the company provides. Facebook has a similar story. It's the primary way that people keep in touch with extended friends and family and has become one of the primary applications that people view the world through.

While many of Facebook's endeavors have floundered or been controversial, it has acquired many critical businesses that form the core of its kingdom, including Instagram and WhatsApp. These are some of the most downloaded apps in the world, and provide Facebook with terabytes of attributable data from individuals, even though the users are receiving access to Facebook's products for "free."

These companies have provided popular services, but at the same time, they have expropriated massive amounts of structured data on their users, which is their core product. As part of owning the platform, these companies benefit from all the human attention they control. Consider how much time the average person spends exercising, reading a book, or eating, compared to how much time they spend on Instagram and Facebook, and you start to get a picture of just how much data and influence the behemoths of the modern attention economy to have.

This ownership of your data, including measures to preserve your security and privacy, is the backbone of what many call 'Web 3.0.' We'll go into this evolution in greater depth later, but it bears noticing that this process and conversation is already happening and gaining traction as we write this. One of the first blockchain startups that come to mind that is trying to revolutionize this space, and one which we recommend trying, is the Brave browser and its blockchain-based native Basic Attention Token.

Brave is a web browser that Jared switched to and started using in late 2015. Brave has a built-in ad blocker and numerous other technologies to keep the internet's many monitors from tracking everywhere you go. Brave was founded by CEO Brendan Eich and CTO Brian Bondy in May 2015. In 1998 Brendan co-founded the Mozilla project and had since determined the original spirit and vision of his Mozzila web browser had been hijacked my advertisers and by privacy-violating trackers.

He also is the creator of the JavaScript programming language, which is often used to build much of this privacy-violating ad tech. The Brave team is bringing privacy back to the user's web browsing experience by blocking unwanted advertisements and malicious tracking that violates the user's privacy.

Brave has since launched "BAT" or Basic Attention Token to allow users to directly receive rewards for viewing ads on the website they often visit, cutting out middlemen like Google and Facebook, who track your movements outside of their sites. Brave gives you back your privacy and security at the same time. By cutting out all the annoying ads violating your privacy your browsing experience, it is up to 8x faster, and you no longer have to pay for mobile data where on other browsers you are charged for the loading of unwanted ads over your mobile data connection.

Brave is using blockchain technology to help usher in the attention economy - where you get paid for every ad you view in a microtransaction. As programmable money, this is just one of many blockchain applications that will be used to cut out third parties and provide the user with greater personal sovereignty over their data, protect their privacy and allow them to be compensated for their attention when they do choose to share it.

This use of a blockchain to financially reward individuals' attention is just one example, and it is still developing, but it illustrates how the world is changing and how new blockchain-based alternatives are emerging into today's attention economy.

The Data Economy

Data is not just something expropriated in the attention economy. When you compare the attention economy to data mining, then the data these platforms derive and refine is the commodity that they extract. This data is intrinsic to dozens of other business models, many of whom you may have never heard of and may pay little attention to even if you have heard of them, and that is the reason these other businesses pay giants for their services in the first place.

Many of the services that you do not pay for directly are still deriving value from your data and access to your behavior, wants, and desires. This data collection includes taking impressions of everything from your credit score to the properties you look at on a real estate app, to your location through your mobile phone, to the financial patterns observed by your bank, and to the way you drive your car. Very little of this is disclosed to you, even though you cannot use many of these products without signing a vague and extensive waiver.

There's so much data out there that it's easy for firms to lose track of it, if they have access to something and can accomplish their needs from it, they often have little incentive or desire to defend your data from those who might use it differently. This data-handling negligence compounded by the fact that almost every single company that handles centralized data has been or will most likely eventually experience a data breach. Even if the original company received that information in good faith, there is no assurance that the party that stole it or the party that took it from them will do the same.

There is a bevy of relevant examples of just how invasive this tracking has become. For instance, as we were finishing this chapter, it was revealed that Google had been tracking every purchase that touches a Gmail account. That Google discloses this is a good thing - to check it out, go to https://myaccount.google.com/u/2/purchases. Effectively, any receipt that hits your Gmail is boxed up and stored as data. Purchase something embarrassing on Amazon, like a bedbug killer or something for personal hygiene? Google knows about it, all the way back to 2013. Get tickets to a concert or meetup? Google knows about that too.

Beyond being densely interconnected and detailed, today's data giants are extremely thorough. With the data provided by your apps and mobile device, these platforms can tell when you're about to enter a relationship, with whom, and when you're going to leave one. They can tell when you're depressed when you're out with friends.

Researchers have also established that just a few likes on Facebook - literally in the time it takes to catch a flight or wait for a train - can be sufficient to diagnose the user's sexual preferences, political and religious beliefs, and even infer their IQ, smoking, and drinking patterns. This analysis extends to the data generated by your mobile device; which covers everything from your health (where you shop, how often you exercise) to how fast you drive, and whom you spend your time with during the day.

With physical cash all but disappearing, this extends to your payments too - Apple, Google, and Facebook all have payments plays, with Facebook experimenting with a proprietary digital currency named Libra and Apple experimenting with issuing its native credit card as of this writing.

Money is data. No financial transaction happens by accident, and every time you spend a dime, that transaction tells the world's commercial platforms something about you and what you are willing to spend money on throughout your daily life. Facebook, Google, and other platforms are not merely collecting this data for their own sake. There is no logical reason that Facebook should have an interest in your smoking or exercise habits, but there is a very valid reason your insurance company would.

Facebook, Apple, Google, and others have a market in collecting and providing this data to the firms that can use it to make a profit from you, whether by providing products or hedging risks. There is a massive global market for this data that extends well beyond the initial collection point.

Take the Equifax credit rating agency, for example. Its core business is to monitor your use of credit and to provide a rating of how trustworthy and reliable you are to potential lenders. As part of this, Equifax has compiled massive amounts of data relevant to who you are and what you do. Credit rating agencies monitor everything from your occupation to your spending to your address and your income. These are things you might not disclose to someone you are dating, but Equifax never asked you, and you never said yes.

What makes this so much worse is that, even though the company gathers all this data, it did not protect it adequately. In 2017 Equifax, it was responsible for losing the information of an estimated 147,000,000 people -- roughly half the population of the United States. This breach persisted for a full 76 days before the vulnerability used by the attackers was identified and patched. Much or all of the company's collection of user data was copied elsewhere and used in ways its customers (and the company) never approved of or intended.

The theft of information is not harmless. Like we said, much of the data in your credit report is stuff that you wouldn't disclose to someone you were dating, so why is it being stolen and sold on dark markets in Eastern Europe and Asia?

Because with that information, it is possible to commit massive fraud and intrusion, both against individuals and against companies. Because our internet is architected in a way that makes data fast and free, business models that revolve around expropriation and theft of it are almost assured.

Data would not get stolen if it were not valuable, and companies would not be shy about disclosing thefts of user data if it were not embarrassing. Data is so useful because it is a model of who you are. If we know everything about you, we can sell to you, predict your movements, predict your tastes, manipulate what you see in the world based on what we know you already believe, and effectively pretend to be you in instances where it is profitable to do so.

Information technology has evolved to the point that it has over the last 30 years by becoming better and better at gathering and organizing user data. This harvested data is easily duplicated and sold leads to the firms collecting that data being less inclined to protect it as if it were their own. After all, in many cases, they scraped it together without explicit consent in the first place, and their proprietary process for treating and analyzing your data is what they care about - it is after all just "digital exhaust" to those that gather it.

There is an entire economy of stolen data, both from big tech firms but also among dozens of independent hackers, state actors, and other players who find a way to profit from having such a detailed profile of people they have never met. According to Experian (yes, the same firm that we mentioned above), a single Social Security Number, which you and I use on our taxes and other forms, is worth a dollar in data market value. By extension, 147 million social security numbers are worth roughly that many dollars.

More detailed information is worth more, a credit or debit card described by the same source can be worth as much as $100 since it can be used to commit a fraudulent transaction. A PayPal account can be worth as much as $200, diplomas as much as $400, and passports a whopping $2000. This value in data extends to the economy for counterfeit data, where your identity is used to help a criminal traverse the world and fund their expenses, because they pretend to be you, or make reference to your data with their synthetic identity.

When there is a fraud, someone eats that cost, and it is often the consumer and the taxpayer. In 2018, the University of Portsmouth in the UK estimated that the global yearly cost of fraud was roughly £3 Trillion Sterling, or $3.8 Trillion. This cost of fraud was determined at the time to represent 7% of industries' total expenditure, which eventually has to be passed on to the consumer to make a business profitable.

This number is a massive amount. Imagine losing 7% more of your income, after taxes and other expenses, and you start to understand the impact of data theft in today's secure environment. In many industries, this is greater than the firm's profit margin.

As we've covered above, data and money operate on the same spectrum of value. Data and financial information are valuable because they characterize and enable the exchange of value between people and companies. Blockchain is a revolutionary new technology to accomplish this process and is the next natural evolution for both sides of this equation.

Blockchain as a Restoration of Ownership

Philosophical question: What is ownership? Some of us hesitate even to try and define the concept - we assume we own many things. If you live in a free country, most of your political and social education has probably revolved around some version of "life, liberty, and the pursuit of happiness" - at least as an ideal. Locke and Jefferson's ideas, which we still value today of freedom and property, came from a world where agriculture was the primary means of income and form of ownership. The modern industry was still in its most nascent stages. Even then, these conceptions of ownership were ancient, tracing back to the origins of common law governance and the early medieval era, where the property laws we still use today first emerged.

The use of the term "landlord" is a good example: the word is older than any of the countries we live in and traces back to the days of serfs tending crops on the lands of feudal lords.

In Locke's time, ownership was often considered to be something granted under the authority of a sovereign - a king or queen. Instead of owning something outright, many lower rulers (dukes, barons, you get the picture) had titles to land, which the sovereign could take as needed and desired.

If you screwed up in committing treason, you might be banished and cede your property to the crown. Abuses of this authority generally led to the overthrow of the king by nobles who felt that the rent was too damn high, but in principle, final authority usually belonged to the state and the sovereign. This authority hasn't fundamentally changed: the nation-state still reserves the right to compel purchase (a practice known as Eminent Domain) or to impound a person's property when they do not pay taxes levied by the state.

Other instances might involve a concept known as escheat, where a person who passes away or disappears without heirs yields their property back to the state. These policies may be necessary at times, say if the government needs to build a freeway, or needs to prevent neighbors from poisoning old widows and taking their fields, but it illustrates that point that even if a system is mostly fair, ownership isn't absolute.

This hard concept of ownership has progressively decayed over the years, with people in a postmodern setting still believing the rhetoric over personal property, but participating in systems of government and commerce where their ownership and political participation diverge substantially from the Lockean ideal.

I might think I own my car, my house, the money in my bank account, my social media profiles, my photos, my persona online, and so on. In reality, all of these systems are things that many of us are just participating in, but that we do not have real ownership and control over them. As we outlined above, this applies to your data, with big tech firms and data aggregators harvesting your data from you like digital landlords, where instead of providing a share of what you cannot use their services without providing your data.

What we did not cover above was the history of banking, and how blockchain allows the user to store value in a system, they control. Genuinely decentralized blockchains are the key to this new internet of value, for both data and money and other financial assets. Because it is supporting such a shift towards real ownership, true blockchains will be and are already essential to this process.

Throughout this book, it will be very apparent that we, as the authors, feel you should be able to control what is rightfully yours. The future of humanity depends on our ability to secure critical information in a decentralized and trustless fashion, one where the truth is not contingent on a third party whose interests might diverge from your own.

Every day there are more and more exploited cybersecurity vulnerabilities in centralized data repositories, and this centralization and insecurity is a core characteristic of the computing environment we live in now, with an oligopoly of influential tech companies leveraging the instability of the internet to create competing digital fiefdoms.

This internet insecurity even extends to the competition among self-appointed arbiters of truth in tech and media who do not avoid taking stances on the rights of others, either by censoring speech or by extending rights as a "protected class." This censorship is not a secret, with big companies "de-platforming" speech they disagree with, enforcing their own rules and code of conduct arbitrarily, and in the most extreme cases refusing to assist the very governments that protect them and campaigning against the state's responsibility to govern who can and cannot enter the country.

The relationship between companies, countries, and individuals is working itself out today, just like the conflict between the Church, merchants, and landed nobles worked itself out in Medieval Europe, and each party is competing for power in this asymmetric conquest of data and influence.

Jumping forward to an example in our chapter on AI, even the race for self-driving cars is an example of this; instead of collaborating on a shared data set or model, each company pursuing self-driving cars is working on scraping up as much data as possible to inform their model in competition with each other, meaning the result might be the safest choice among options, but not the most reliable outcome possible.

This use case is where the beauty of the blockchain comes in. With a blockchain, anyone can secure data and personal files, while simultaneously using their blockchain private keys as a means of authentication. Need to use a service? That service will require your authorization, such as accessing your medical records, and you will be able to provide them with direct access to your files, without needing to use documents that have been cobbled together by a slew of non-consensual data aggregators.

The Radical Prospect of Being Your Own Bank

Just like we believe people should be able to control your data, we think they should have direct control over their money as well. Blockchain technology allows us to take control of our financial data and wealth in a way that has never before been possible. Nowhere is this dynamic more fundamental than with money itself, which is the blockchain's first killer app: cryptocurrency.

If you have money in the bank, you probably feel like it is your property, no different than physical cash locked in a safe in your home. Were you to go to the teller and find out that your account was frozen, or the bank had lost all your money betting on a horse race, you would be understandably mad. However, this is the way that both the fiat banking system and the broader monetary system works, and the way that it has worked since the invention of fractional reserve banking. The bank doesn't want to lose your deposit, but it is entirely possible.

The government probably doesn't overtly wish to destroy your livelihood, but you have no control over how many dollars (or pounds, or marks, or Euros) that the central bank prints. Monetary policy is entirely out of your control, and banks can deny you the right to your money, as they did during the financial crisis in Cyprus in 2013, where large depositors lost half of their deposits with a keystroke.

The Evolution of Centralized Banking

When banks, artisans, or institutions behaving as banks accepted a deposit such as gold for safekeeping, they provided the depositor with a form of proof that they owned their valuable asset. Back in the days of a gold-backed currency, it was easier to exchange those claims on deposited value than it was to transfer the physical gold itself. Gold is a safe but cumbersome store of value, and the banker was trusted to honor those claims even if the asset was in a different account.

These chits were fungible, portable substitutes for the real gold because everyone expected that the printed paper IOU was backed by the real thing, and could be exchanged at the bank for the exact amount of physical gold specified by the paper claim.

The genius of fractional reserve banking, which long predates the Medici or the other great families that made their wealth with it, was the insight that it is unlikely all depositors will want their gold at the very same time so that a profit can be made making secured loans at interest. By providing credit, banks could secure a higher return on their holdings, rather than draw fees out of the user's savings that might disincentivize them. Insofar as the bank kept enough liquidity to satisfy the average rate of withdrawals, everybody gained from the arrangement.

This system secured massive wealth to the banks through their credit networks. This credit system was a natural evolution that improved the performance of the economy, but it also resulted in institutions having higher power over individuals. These engines of wealth built massive empires, have funded great works and exploration, but they also have exposed depositors to the whims of the banks, and human nature being what it is, many banks throughout history have eventually overextended themselves to the detriment of their depositors.

Once people realized that a bank did not have enough in its vault to pay them back they rushed the bank to recover their deposit, in some cases leading to a crash where the bank fails and must call in its debts, and the debtors can't pay because there is no credit and no revenue to pay back that credit with.

Every single fractional reserve system works like this, and in an environment where unbacked fiat currency is the norm, there is much more potential for credit and debt to be created out of thin air and for banks and people to overextend themselves. There is also much more risk. Historically, many banks were reliant on their reputations and familial control, such that they had the incentive to make wise decisions and not ruin their legacy for their descendants or the cities they relied upon.

This hegemony became much more difficult as banks grew with success and became more integral to commerce and the state. Further, our present-day financial system is much more complex and much more systemic - opening the door for systemic risk.

An excellent example of this systemic risk is the Libor (London Interbank Offered Rate) scandal, which broke in 2014. As the Libor scandal demonstrates, banks have, at times, gamed the tools meant to ensure their liquidity by manipulating the rate at which short-term cash was borrowed to cover daily transactions. Libor spans a wide swath of currencies, including the Pound Sterling and the US dollar. It's the lifeblood of the international banking system, if not the beating heart.

The Libor rate was estimated to underwrite roughly $350,000,000,000,000 (USD 350 trillion) in derivatives, as well as an estimated $10 trillion in debt as of 2015.

American mortgages, student loans, and almost every other financial product are riding on Libor for interbank liquidity. Libor was at the time set by taking a poll of several banks asking what rate they would lend money to each other within the banking system, with the highest and lowest rates within that poll excluded to provide a "representative sample." In this environment, a single basis point spread on a single trade could be worth most of a million dollars.

When the story broke in 2014, Libor manipulation was believed to be occurring at *all* large banks, who discovered it was possible to act as a cartel, distorting the median provided by the Libor process to create a greater spread between their cost of borrowing and that of the consumer. By manipulating the spread on interbank loans, financial institutions were able to make substantial profits in a way that negatively affected the end consumers of financial products and bank-issued debts.

Municipalities and mortgage holders lost billions as a result of banks adjusting interest in accord with manipulated Libor rates, squeezing every possible extra cent out of borrowers. At the time this story became public, MIT economist Andrew Lo, a respected academic economist not at all known for hyperbole, described the Libor scandal as "dwarf[ing] by orders of magnitude any financial scams in the history of markets."

In college, one of Andrew's professors would announce the Libor rate at the beginning of class every morning, not because he had nothing better to do, but because he believed Libor to be the best "canary in the coal mine" regarding whether banks trusted each other enough to exchange capital overnight. Libor was, at least by educated popular opinion, thought to provide information to the broader economy and the whole ecosystem that operates on fiat currency.

Even that, it turns out, was distorted. As came to light that during the financial crisis, some banks artificially suppressed the Libor rate so as not to signal to the market that they were at risk of a liquidity crisis, even though they were. To use the idiom, if the Libor rate was the "canary in the coal mine" to indicate if there was toxic gas (toxic, nonperforming loans) on the bank's balance sheets, then even the canary was being manipulated and could not be trusted.

However, unlike the plains of the Serengeti, human society is much more complicated. When people govern banks, they are, in essence, guided by evolutionary psychology - [where short term profits and long term risk are often not realistically accounted for - creating systemic risks that could break the banking system entirely if they occurred at a sufficient scale]. And not to put too fine a point on it, this is happening in a system that affects every person's livelihood in the developed world: that banks were manipulating something so critical to the security of the system is an indictment of just what can go wrong when you don't control your money.

If you want an example in movie form, look no further than 2011's Margin Call - a dramatization of actual events that occurred during the financial crisis of 2008. The movie is about a fictional bank, whose analyst (the protagonist) realizes that the bank holds toxic assets sufficient to destroy their balance sheet entirely. In one later scene in the movie, the main character (a junior financial analyst responsible for discovering the exposure) is called to a meeting with all of the bank's senior partners at 4 AM to decide how to deal with the crisis.

Recognizing that the bank holds substantial, risky assets on their balance sheets, the bank elects to offload assets they know to be toxic to other banks to save their institution when the inevitable liquidity crisis hits. To do this, the firm resorts to a calculated fire sale of assets to the general market - knowing that they will damage the firms that buy them.

To do this, the bank must offload garbage without tipping its hand that the assets are, well, garbage. If the buyer knew, he or she wouldn't buy them. One could expound on the amorality of this system and promote some regulatory framework to constrain the financial industry, but that's not the point. Banks undertake this behavior because it is profitable in our current fiat system, which relies on government and central banking institutions as asset buyers of last resort. This profit-driven motive is what happened with TARP (the "Troubled Assets Relief Program"), in which the U.S. government authorized purchases of assets up to 700 Billion dollars, to secure liquidity for the market.

This example is not at all to hate on banks but to make a point. The financial system is fragile and governed by human nature and by institutions that we as depositors don't control. It can spur growth and development through credit, but the dark side of this equation is that it can be mismanaged and taken advantage of in a way that exposes the end-user to risk.

If you have money in the bank, you don't control it. If you have stocks in your 401k or brokerage, you still lack control over the situation, and you are reliant on third parties who don't share the same interests or incentives as you. Even the fact that you face delays if you try to withdraw your money is an excellent example of how you aren't the one in control of your money.

If banks will go to the lengths of manipulating interbank liquidity with Libor, which is the lifeblood of the industry, how is a small personal depositor going to keep his or her money safe?

Banking today is not *a* system; it is *the* system. With physical cash ceasing to be accepted in circulation throughout much of the civilized world the gross majority of the world's wealth has come to be digitally managed by a small oligopoly of institutions who are compelled to compete with each other in ways that expose depositors to the risks of the broader financial system. Most of this money is just *data on a centralized server*. There is rarely any physical currency or gold bars that move when banks settle accounts in a fiat system. Your money is made up of data, just like your identity is.

So what does this have to do with ownership? By using a decentralized cryptocurrency like Bitcoin or DigiByte and taking charge of your private keys, you are your bank. No one else is holding your money. No one else is lending it out, and no one is exposing you to risks that you do not control.

Blockchain is a revolution in ownership because it empowers the individual to represent and exchange their unobstructed ownership of a scarce digital asset. Few things are as fundamental as that.

Unlike fiat and the fiat banking system, real decentralized UTXO cryptocurrencies are *your* money.

No one is making money on your bank account but you. No one is "borrowing it" to make bets elsewhere on the market without your consent. The ledger is not going to come up dry when you seek to withdraw or spend money you legitimately own. Blockchain doesn't have bailouts, equity spreads, or a Libor rate. When you correctly set up and secure the private keys of your cryptocurrency wallet, there is nothing anyone can do to take your crypto away from you without your consent.

You could have millions of dollars in crypto and send it around the world for a fraction of a cent. You could be escaping a broken and oppressive country with capital controls and keep your family wealth safe from expropriation by corrupt border guards, thieves, and exchange fees along the way.

You can hand down wealth from generation to generation, or give it as a gift without having intermediaries extort fees or potentially mismanage it. A bank deposit is a deferral to an institution to provide security for your cash, and if you invest, it is a vehicle to manage those transactions and move money from one application to another, such as into a stock brokerage or a property or business.

Conclusion

In general, we as consumers in a world without blockchain were reduced to merely participating: we might have been legally entitled to their money in our accounts, but have very little direct or real control over it. Sure, when things go wrong, we can get angry, and maybe the nobles band together to try and fix some things, but at a fundamental level, our institutions have not empowered us to engage in real, absolute ownership and self-sovereignty.

Some have elaborated on this in far greater depth than we can in this chapter, including Harvard professor Shoshana Zuboff, whose massive tome *The Age of Surveillance Capitalism: The Fight for a Human Future at the New Frontier of Power* is a detailed indictment of the way that modern internet behemoths have monetized attention and given us a world where the services are free, but we are the product.

This data monetization extends well beyond scanning our Gmail to advertise to us. The proliferation of "smart home" technology that is always listening, always monitoring our conversations, even waiting by our bedsides and kitchen tables, is part of this. There is no logical reason a microwave needs Alexa installed from a consumer standpoint, so the fact that said microwave is cheaper than a traditional microwave should pique one's curiosity.

As we cover later in this book, there are expected to be 50 billion connected devices in the world by the end of 2020. Most of these are reporting back to companies and platforms where we, as the consumers, do not get the value. These companies often provide their services to us for free because our data is valuable. They mine our data, capture our attention, and manipulate our behavior without our explicit consent. There has been a progressive transfer of wealth and power away from people, and towards large centralized institutions like banks and large tech companies.

What we need is nothing less than a new theory of value for this modern age. On the one hand, you have what we'll call alienated participation - a system where you are only a participant and not a stakeholder. This reality is like being a nine-to-five worker, deep in debt, with no savings whose sources of information, entertainment, and interaction with the world are all mediated through platforms he or she does not control.

While this person might work hard and have forms of meaning in their lives, they are ultimately drifting through life without owning anything. It's no surprise that people today crave "authenticity," without really being able to define what authenticity is or means, and we think this is a sign that people feel deprived of ownership over their destiny and themselves. They do not believe they are self-sovereign or responsible for their future.

We naturally don't like being told what we can think, we don't like having our data stolen, and we don't like slaving away only not to go anywhere financially while our savings evaporate and their value eroded by fees, intermediaries, and forced expenses.

Blockchain is an answer to just that. As the technology evolves, it will enable you to keep control of more and more of your ownership through the custody of your private keys. While everyone might not adopt this, it is a significant shift away from a world where being a subject too big, soulless institutions that don't have your best interests in mind is the only option.

Even more urgently, many of these big institutions rely on the internet as it is are failing. Government and private sector firms alike are struggling to keep up in a world of constant entropy, and they seem more and more incompetent with each passing hack and failure.

Join us as we explore the future of the blockchain, from the nuts and bolts of how it works to the applications currently being built on it, and finally what the world might look like when the technology is abundant in the year 2035. Next up in chapter 3, we will cover some basic terms and technical concepts related to blockchain tech that you should have a firm grasp of to soak up the later chapters.

Chapter 3: Blockchain Basics & Terminology

"Any fool can know. The point is to understand."
- Albert Einstein

    Much of today's discussion on blockchain skips over the essential elements of what makes the technology innovative in the first place. This space is still new to many, and as a result, many authors, journalists, and entrepreneurs tend to conflate (wittingly or unwittingly) what are ultimately very different technologies. This oversight is due not only in part to the fact that so many are eager to use the term, but also because so few grasp the core elements of what makes a blockchain work at its most fundamental level.

    This chapter is designed to give you a basic introduction to much of the vocabulary and terminology that you will hear when discussing blockchain technology before we take a more in-depth technical dive in chapter 4. The language and descriptions in this chapter come from many years of experience building DigiByte and exploring the Bitcoin blockchain at a deep technical level, and we feel that it is vital for you to familiarize yourself with these terms to better understand the later chapters in this book.

    From experience, there are several excellent ways to simplify many of the more complex concepts involved and help people better understand what blockchain is and what it is not. Occasionally we will rely on analogies since they offer a natural means to ground the concepts in things that you and I are familiar with from our everyday lives, though that isn't intended to detract from the technical details.

    I'm writing this sentence on January 3, 2019, which is exactly ten years after Satoshi released the Genesis Block that started Bitcoin. In the last decade, Bitcoin has survived hostility from governments and hacking efforts from countless individuals, while many other projects have failed or floundered. In this chapter, we will cover just what makes Bitcoin and other blockchains tick. Let's start with the most important metric and the one that is most critical to how real, pure, blockchains have survived — the principle of genuine decentralization.

What is Decentralization?

'Decentralization' can mean many things to many people, and often the term is bandied about in circumstances that are nowhere near close to being decentralized in the most critical ways. In simple terms, decentralization means that a system, organization, or organism gets built and survives in such a way that there is *no central point of failure*: no central repository that can be compromised, killed, or eliminated. Whether by disease, a bullet, a lawsuit, or with the flip of a switch. Real decentralized things can survive massive upheavals and can adapt to challenges because they are diverse and distributed parts of a larger whole.

To borrow from the DNA analogy, the human race embodies the principle of decentralization. Humans have expanded too far corners of the globe and have adapted to their diets and surroundings to their local environments without compromising their genetic interoperability. When the Black Death swept Europe in the 1300s, the diversity of genetics and the dispersion of populations into different cities and towns made it more difficult for the plague to spread.

Genetically resistant individuals were able to survive the first waves of plague because not everyone had the same vulnerability; further, if everyone were genetically identical, they would have been wiped out by any disease that had adapted to their specific genetic and physiological profile.

Decentralization also aided responses to the plague in information terms. This decentralized information flow was because human communities lived dispersed without a single concentration of population, best practices in managing the disease could be transmitted to other places and preserved by survivors at those locations already hit.

Decentralization allowed for the development of separate reactions, such as quarantines, even if a village had succumbed to the plague, the next town over could take precautions to prevent or diminish the contagion. The principle of decentralization in this example allowed for some parts of the population to survive and eventually thrive by providing defense-in-depth and defense by interoperable diversity.

Decentralization is the quintessence of evolution, in that when constraints placed on an organism or organization impact the general population, some parts of that population can continue and even be strengthened by the challenge, carrying lessons learned into the future. In the case of the Black Death, smallpox, polio, influenza, and many other epidemics, these challenges have helped people and civilizations develop new immunities and new medicines, some of which, such as penicillin, have only been discovered recently and by accident and experimentation.

Many immunities we might not even be aware of, as the traits and resistances of our ancestors are inherited rather than earned. Just as Europeans landing in North America were not aware of the deadly pathogens they carried with them, without experiencing the severe symptoms, so too do we take technology for granted without recognizing the impact they have on us and might have on our and others ways of life.

Even though humans have adapted to their environments, we remain genetically interoperable. Europeans and Asians living in colder climates have lighter skin, while people from more tropical areas are better suited to heat, humidity, and sunlight. Sickle-cell anemia, which is a drawback in some respects, has protected sub-Saharan Africans from Malaria that would cripple or kill non-Africans. East Africans consistently win endurance races, such as the Boston Marathon.

Icelandic weightlifters have disproportionate success in their field because they have better genetics for building strength and muscle mass from proteins. Europeans and Central Asians are better at digesting alcohol and dairy products because these sources of nutrition were typical for their ancestors. Different blood types handle nutrients differently.

These and many more characteristics got preserved in existing populations from historical constraints and adaptations, but they do not mean that the human race has, in some way, "forked." These specialties do not mean humans have ceased to be interoperable--quite the opposite. Look at the ethnic backgrounds of most supermodels, and you will recognize that they tend to have diverse, sometimes global genomes, with ancestors from several different countries. Genetic health tends to benefit from this diversity and decentralization.

Conversely, look at the small gene pools of some families, such as the Hapsburgs of late medieval Europe, whose generations of intermarriage eventually led to defects like hemophilia and infertility. The interoperability of the decentralized human-machine encourages adaptation and growth of more effective systems, and these benefits expand beyond mere biology. This diversity extends beyond genetics to things like ideas. If we look at the history of most technologies, you will see endless borrowing, exchange, and recombination of ideas until a given innovation "sticks."

Philosopher and probability scholar Nassim Nicholas Taleb called this principle of nimbleness through decentralization *Antifragility,* a concept that we will return to multiple times in this book. Where some systems may be intricate but fragile (like a house of cards) or robust but not nimble (like the Great Wall of China), *antifragile* systems are made stronger through adversity; moreover, because they have enough options to adapt around challenges.

Antifragile systems are multi-dimensional and create options, a principle Taleb calls *optionality*, to react when the unexpected happens. Optionality is a product of the decentralization of the underlying system. Borrowing Taleb's examples, having a single source of income makes a person more vulnerable to sudden changes than having seven, having a single model for how the world makes us more prone to being wrong than being able to draw on several complementary systems of observation and interpretation. Furthermore, hedging our bets is typically wiser than putting all our eggs in a single basket. Having one currency, one retirement plan, and one planet all means only one of these things has to fail for us to be left destitute.

People frequently dismiss blockchain enthusiast's fixation with decentralization as some libertarian shibboleth, but there is nothing more important than real decentralization when it comes to building adaptable and resilient systems. Without decentralization, all systems are finite and doomed to fail eventually. Once you see the world through the lens of decentralization, it is difficult to unsee it.

Every overbearing empire, every centralized fiefdom centered on a few core individuals, has collapsed under the entropic pressures of time and friction. There is a reason that nuclear missile launches require multiple keys. Our fascination with colonizing Mars is not so much about human hubris or leaving Earth and its many problems behind as it is about decentralizing humanity, such that if things were to go awry on our little blue marble in the blackness of space, humanity, or whatever form of life follows, will have a fighting chance elsewhere.

Here is the most crucial detail: "nothing" isn't decentralized. True decentralization is really about complex, interoperable systems that can interact with each other. True decentralization applies to massive stacks of technology and biology with complex moving parts, like our example above. What the blockchain represents, and what we'll delve deeper later in this book, is a method to decentralize much of the infrastructure of the modern internet, commerce, and governance in a way that makes these systems more resilient and, in some cases, antifragile.

What is Blockchain?

A blockchain is the summation of several different interwoven parts of computer science and cryptography, which allow for a distributed immutable ledger. This ledger tracks values and attributes with unique private keys, empowering not just money, but the control of data and assets as well, all of which are valuable.

The term "Blockchain" is often used broadly, encompassing anything and everything involving public and open-source decentralized database ledger systems such as Bitcoin, DigiByte, and Ethereum. The simplest explanation is that a blockchain is a series of records cryptographically linked as blocks and transmitted in a peer-to-peer fashion across a global network with no intermediary and no central party to approve a transaction.

Blockchain vs. Cryptocurrency vs. Digital Currency

People often confuse and interchange the terms "cryptocurrency" and "blockchain" - to the point that they speak of cryptocurrency and blockchain as the same thing. In theory, a blockchain can exist without a cryptocurrency, but without a cryptocurrency, there is no real reward or incentive for people to run the software that makes it possible to run a blockchain in a secure and decentralized manner.

Also, the term cryptocurrency tends to be misleading because that tends to make people think that a blockchain is simply an "internet currency" when, in reality, there is far more to it. Generally, when we refer to cryptocurrency, we are speaking about deflative currencies running on decentralized blockchains.

For example, there will never be more than 21 billion DigiBytes or 21 million Bitcoin, whereas a digital currency might involve inflation and might not even run on a decentralized blockchain. (Think of Chinas PBOC digital currency or Facebook's Libra stablecoin project, where there is no set supply or fixed distribution mechanic like mining).

It is best to associate the term blockchain with the core underlying technology and innovations in computer science and cryptography, powering a cryptocurrency or digital currency issued on top of that blockchain.

Moreover, the word cryptocurrency and digital currency should get used when discussing economics, markets, and monetary systems. In short, a cryptocurrency is a type of value that can be captured natively on a blockchain, but just because someone advertises that they have a "digital currency" does not mean that they are running an authentic or secure decentralized blockchain.

Cryptocurrencies Vs. Tokens Vs. Digital Assets

Cryptocurrency is not the only form of value that can be issued or tracked on a blockchain, as other types of value can be represented, such as shares of stock or property. You may have heard the term "token" or "tokenization" in Ethereum circles, though we prefer the term Digital Asset, for reasons we will go into below.

ICOs, tokens, and Digital Assets are often confused as being their independent blockchain protocols when, in reality, they get issued on existing blockchains that already have their native cryptocurrencies and are not autonomous. Accordingly, each has several innovative features that will influence and disrupt the future of securities offerings.

The vital thing to know is that they (ICOs, tokens, and Digital Assets) are typically not independent blockchains, but are usually ledger entries on an existing blockchain that do not necessarily follow the same rules as pure, independent blockchains native cryptocurrency doe.

There are only a handful of genuinely decentralized blockchain protocols in existence today that allow other digital assets or tokens to get issued on top of them. There are, however, thousands of tokens and assets issued upon this handful of main blockchain protocols. In short, cryptocurrencies tend to exist on their independent blockchains and have a fixed supply and inflation schedule. They will live as long as the chain exists, Bitcoins on the Bitcoin network might get lost (sent to inactive addresses), but they cannot be "burned" or deactivated by a central authority like some tokens can.

Cryptocurrency stands in contrast to digital assets, which represent unique underlying real assets, goods, and services, such as tickets to a concert or ownership in business as equity represented in a digitally secure manner on a blockchain. It is helpful to distinguish between digital assets and "tokens," which are ambiguous and may not constitute any form of economic contract or claim on goods and services.

ICOs, initial coin offerings, which we go into in greater depth later, are one example of tokens because they often lack an explicit underlying value proposition. While they may claim some value through scarcity, new ICOs can be generated quickly and with limited technical skills.

When one speaks of "tokenizing" a real-world asset or asset class, they are talking about assigning an underlying value to something represented on a blockchain. We believe using the same term that ICOs and online games use is misleading. This confusion tends to muddy the waters about just what kind of value such a piece of data has, hence the distinction between tokens and Digital Assets. Because ICOs are both so famous and so infamous, we've devoted space elsewhere in this book to cover them entirely.

Blocks

The first place to start when understanding how a blockchain technically works is by understanding the concept of a "block." A block is like a spreadsheet that lists all transactions that have occurred over a specific time interval worldwide on a blockchain. In the case of Bitcoin, a new block occurs on the blockchain every 10 minutes. With DigiByte, a new block occurs *every 15 seconds*.

That is what we mean when we say that DigiByte is *40 times* faster than Bitcoin since blocks are created at forty-times the speed on the DGB blockchain vs. the Bitcoin chain. Moreover, 40 times the amount of data can also be transferred in the same amount of time because both have the same current block size limitations.

A block is also a data structure with several sub-components, including the block header and the accompanying transactions from that window of time. A block header typically consists of six things; block version, the hash of the previous block, the hash of the Merkle root, block time, the time stamp, Nonce, and Bits. We will discuss these concepts in greater detail in later chapters.

The "Blockchain"

A blockchain is simply the blocks being assembled in sequential order, with each sequential block contingent on and tied to the last, through a process known as *cryptographic hashing*. That process is the blockchain in a nutshell. ....Not quite.

There is a lot more under the hood and a ton of details beyond this simple explanation. It is this myriad of interrelated cryptographic mathematical components that many people gloss over and do not genuinely understand, opting instead to use buzzwords without really grasping what a blockchain is. That's why we're writing this book - to cover the vast potential of blockchain technology in-depth.

We will go into a deeper dive into the cryptographic mathematical components and subsystems that are interwoven and brought together to create a blockchain in Chapter 4, and this will form the technical baseline for many of the applications discussed later in this book.

However, for the time being, think of a blockchain like a car traveling down the road, made up of various mathematical subsystems all the while storing a bunch of spreadsheets, aka blocks in the trunk. These blocks organize and record all the transactions that happen around the world in a specific window of time, with each new mile bringing a new spreadsheet (block) to get stored inside the blockchain (car).

Transactions

A transaction on a blockchain is how digital assets, tokens, and cryptocurrencies like Bitcoin or DigiByte are moved from person to person in a peer-to-peer fashion. Transactions are capable of much more than the simple movement of money across the internet. They can include everything from IoT device metadata to digital assets, to stable coins pegged to fiat currencies, to documents, contracts, signatures, and much, much more.

Inputs & Outputs

A transaction on a UTXO (unspent transaction output) blockchain is made up of two fundamental things, inputs and outputs. It's often helpful to think of inputs and outputs like debits and credits on a traditional accounting ledger. Inputs are simply a reference to an output from a previous transaction.

I can't spend money or cryptocurrency that I do not have possession of, and that has not deposited into my wallet. An output contains the instructions for how to send a cryptocurrency like Bitcoin or DigiByte *or other forms of valuable data* on a blockchain. All transactions on a blockchain are typically viewable by anyone on the network. The inputs and outputs are also visible to anyone on a blockchain network, though the wallet addresses are not associated with names and people.

Wallets

Transactions are only possible if you have somewhere to send and receive them, and this is where wallets come into the picture. A wallet is an address where you store your cryptocurrency or digital assets. There are numerous types of wallets, but they tend to fall into two main categories: Wallets where *you* control your private keys, and wallets where a *third party*, such as an exchange, controls your private keys. Both of these types of wallets can either exist on a desktop/ laptop or a mobile phone. There is also a third type of wallet known as a "hardware" wallet, which we will discuss later.

Private Keys

Private keys are the most sacred and crucial thing to be concerned with when it comes to blockchain technology. Private keys are how you access whatever digital assets or cryptocurrencies stored in your wallet. Think of your wallet private keys like the keys to your own house or the keys to your car. Except, in this case, they are much more secure and cannot be duplicated or hacked easily as long as you take the proper steps to secure them yourself.

The most important thing to remember here is whoever controls the private keys controls whatever value a wallet holds. For example, if you're trusting a centralized exchange to store your crypto assets for you, understand that if they control the private keys, you don't have control over those assets and funds. If they are hacked or shut down by a government regulator, you may lose your funds and valuable digital assets permanently.

Dozens of centralized cryptocurrency exchanges, where users entrusted the operators with their private keys, have been hacked over the past ten years. Often, users have lost everything with little-or-no recourse or hope of ever recovering any of their lost wealth.

Think of your private keys like your car keys or house keys. If you were to hand your keys over, they could enter your house, steal stuff, throw it in your care your car, and take that too. Beyond that, everyone can generate a wallet address and private keys of their own for free. For this reason, you shouldn't share your keys with anyone - they are as intimately personal to you as your DNA, your health records, your phone, or your property.

Public Keys

Public keys are the keys that you can share with anyone, and they are publicly visible on most blockchains to anyone who is looking. Public keys are the address that you use to send one digital asset or coin to another. They are similar to your bank account's routing number, except they are specific to you. The reality is, it's a very innovative way of proving ownership and tracking real-time locations of assets on a decentralized ledger, and this extends to data management.

To provide a quick vignette, it is this characteristic of the blockchain that could empower innovations like Named Data Networking, where every address or item online has its location, rather than going through a call tree on today's URL system. We will dive deeper into public-private key cryptography in chapter four.

Nodes

Nodes are computers, servers, or mobile phones running applications connecting directly to and contributing to the blockchain. The more nodes a blockchain has, the more decentralized it is. The fewer nodes it has, the more fragile a blockchain is. Many who are not developers, miners, or exchanges still run full nodes as a hobby, and the presence of these nodes makes a blockchains peer-to-peer network substantially stronger. Everyone should be running a full node for their favorite blockchain.

Core Desktop Wallets - Full Nodes

Core desktop wallets, or otherwise known as full nodes, are the main backbone for most truly decentralized blockchains. These are the most advanced network clients and where the real heart-and-soul of blockchain lives. These wallets contain a complete copy of the entire blockchain and are 100% independent. Core wallets are essential for the real decentralization of a blockchain.

These core wallets are also known as "reference clients" and are what gets compiled from the open-source code of blockchains like Bitcoin, Litecoin, and DigiByte. They are often the very first wallet for any blockchain after it gets created.

These wallets provide the backbone for many services and platforms that allow users to interact with blockchain technology more straightforwardly. The downside of running a full node or full reference client implementation as it's often called is that you are required to sync and download the entire history of the blockchain with your local phone download before you can use it. In the case of Bitcoin and DigiByte, this can take hours, even on a high-speed connection.

SPV Wallets - Lightweight Clients

SPV stands for Simplified Payment Verification. SPV wallets, otherwise known as 'light wallets,' are more straightforward and lighter interfaces into a blockchain. Nevertheless, these wallets are also fully independent and described in Satoshi's original white paper. An example of this type of wallet is *Breadwallet* for Bitcoin and the DigiByte android & iOS wallet.

These wallets do not contain the entire history of every transaction that has occurred on a given blockchain, so they cannot be used to prop up the whole blockchain by themselves. They do, however, help validate ongoing transactions in real-time.

Platform Wallets

Platform wallets are not fully independent blockchain nodes and usually rely on some back-end service. They can be semi-centralized, but often these wallets are the easiest to use for new beginners because there is no sync time involved with the blockchain when setting up a new wallet. These wallets can exist on a website, or they can be downloaded and designed for a specific operating system. Examples of this are the Coinomi and Exodus wallets, which are multi-currency wallets supporting several blockchains on multiple operating systems.

Exchange Wallets

Exchange wallets are centralized trading wallets where people will often convert cryptocurrency into fiat currency or other cryptocurrencies. These are usually centrally controlled, where governments can somewhat exert regulation over blockchain-based cryptocurrencies. There are thousands of cases where a centralized exchange wallet got hacked, ran off with everyone's money, or the user's credentials got stolen.

However, there are many great exchanges with a solid reputation for providing exchange services. There are hundreds of exchanges worldwide. One of the oldest and most prominent exchanges in the United States is Coinbase, which offers custodial wallets and long term storage options as well as trading services.

Hardware Wallets

Hardware wallets are physical devices designed only to store cryptocurrency and digital assets. They can be a USB device or a standalone device that doesn't need to connect to a computer to access. Two leading hardware wallets that have been around for a while are Ledger and Trezor. Both support numerous blockchains.

Another exciting new standalone hardware wallet is the BitFi wallet, which doesn't store your private keys. We talk more about the potential for this approach in Chapter 6 to be your blockchain portal for advances uses. Another new entrant to the hardware wallet is the KeepKey hardware wallet from ShapeShift.

Public vs. Private Blockchains

Public blockchains are just that, open-source, public, and decentralized utilities that no person "owns." Public blockchains are not associated with any specific developer, company, country, or group. They commonly get created under the MIT open source license, and anyone is free to add to or contribute to them.

Surprisingly, there are only a handful of genuinely public and truly decentralized blockchains in the world today without a highly centralized group controlling them. Bitcoin, Ethereum, Litecoin, DigiByte, Dogecoin, and Decred are among the most prominent truly decentralized projects which come to mind. They are distributed in an open-source fashion and are publicly available in a way that anybody in the world can participate in growing the network and helping contribute to the core source code.

Private Blockchains

Private blockchains are blockchains that are issued, controlled, and kept centralized by a handful of individuals, a specific company, or a group. Many projects touted as being decentralized are often, in fact, heavily centralized private blockchains. Private blockchains are usually set up and operated in a closed-off and restricted fashion by corporations and governments.

Often, the private blockchains that I have seen introduce centralized points of failure masquerading as central points of control; this occurs for controlling entities to govern what is allowed to come on the chain.

Fundamentally, the takeaway here is that private permissioned blockchains are often nowhere near as secure as public blockchains and are nowhere near as censorship-resistant. Our humble opinion is that private blockchains are the bastardization of beautiful technology. In practice, private blockchains, if they exist at all, should be anchored into public blockchains for security.

The Decentralized Blockchain Oreo

When explaining a traditional blockchain to someone and how the stack of technology functions, it is often easier to explain to someone by asking them to envision an Oreo breaking down a blockchain into three fundamental layers.

The bottom layer is the *core communications layer*, where transaction information gets exchanged between nodes on the p2p network. The middle layer is the *cryptocurrency layer*. This layer is where Bitcoins or DigiBytes come into play as native digital assets for the blockchain they get issued form.

The very top layer is the *applications layer*, where decentralized apps can run and interact with the blockchain. This top layer is also where tokens, other digital assets, ICO's, and stablecoins get created.

Peer-to-Peer Communications: The Bottom Layer

The most basic layer of a blockchain is fundamentally a communications protocol. The P2P networking or consensus layer is what allows full clients and nodes on the network to communicate with one another. Several innovative applications can get created into a blockchain at this level and, for the most part, are mostly undeveloped. Some of these applications include secure messaging, secure location verification, and much more.

Immutable Ledger and Native Cryptocurrency: The Middle Layer

The digital asset layer is an absolute necessity. Many people often talk about using a blockchain without the attached digital asset, like a bitcoin or a DigiByte. The only way to incentivize people to run the communications layer, built on top of any applications layer, is to incentivize them to run the software with a digital asset. The digital asset layer is essentially what funds, motivates, and facilitates the decentralization of a blockchain.

Applications: The Top Layer

The Applications layer is the top layer that allows users and developers to build innovative real-world applications, such as data management, cryptographic identity, security applications, and more. This layer is just now beginning to be explored by existing blockchains.

Digi-ID, a form of cryptographic identity created by DigiByte core developers that allow users to replace the broken system of usernames and passwords securely, is another such application. Use of blockchains to track IDs, issue assets, and mange supply chains are other potential applications.

Blockchain Subsystems

People often think that a blockchain is one specific system or protocol. This oversimplification is about the same as reducing a sports car or a tractor to its paint job - as we've discussed above, there are dozens of subcomponents working together that make this technology go.

Your vehicle has multiple subsystems that act independently of each other but are necessary and critical for you to drive from point A to point B. The wheels on your car are a completely separate system from either the internal combustion engine that propels them or the transmission that gears them in the proper ratios to adjust your speed.

Consensus Algorithms

Consensus is the most predominant core aspect of the blockchain. How you get hundreds of thousands of full nodes or clients across the planet to agree on a single history of a blockchain is at the crux of how a blockchain has value in the first place. The type of consensus algorithm used is often the key differentiator from one blockchain to another.

Proof of work (Pow) mining is the very first and primary type of consensus used for blockchain consensus and security today. The mining aspect of a blockchain is one of the most misunderstood parts of securing a blockchain by most of the uninitiated. Another form of consensus is known as proof of stake (PoS).

We take a much deeper dive into multiple types of consensus systems used in various blockchains in Chapter 9. For now, know that proof of work is the original and most battle-hardened consensus system found in most major blockchains. We believe it to be the most secure way to achieve consensus on a blockchain.

Management of Public & Private Keys

We've already covered how essential public and private keys are. They make up a backbone to the process of blockchain, and how a blockchain project or application manages its keys is a lynchpin for how secure it is, and how that system can interact with data and assets.

Key management is part of a significant subsystem and must ensure that information and assets are shared only with the intended receiver across a blockchain. This security gets achieved through the use of some of the most highly advanced encryption algorithms known to mathematics.

Encryption Algorithms

There are numerous encryption and mining algorithms used across the blockchain industry today. At its core, blockchain is the next evolution of mathematics and cryptography, which we go into greater detail in chapter 4. Encryption algorithms get used in many different ways and various combinations within the inner workings of a blockchain. SHA-256 is probably the most widely known of all these algos.

SHA-256

SHA256 is the most widely used encryption algo and hashing function used in the blockchain space today. SHA-256 is a secure hashing algorithm 256 bits in length. SHA-256 is part of the SHA-2 family developed by the National Security Agency (NSA) in the United States.

SHA-256 is the algo used for Bitcoin mining, as well as one of the five algos used for DigiByte mining. SHA-256 gets used in the creation of Bitcoin, DigiByte, and nearly all other blockchains public key addresses that transactions get sent to and from.

P2P Networking

The heart-and-soul of most modern blockchain systems was pioneered in the early days of Napster and BitTorrent protocols. Peer-to-peer networking has been around for a long time, with much innovation over the past two decades. The P2P subsystems allow users to communicate transactions and payments with each other in a quick, efficient manner.

Key Players in the Blockchain Ecosystem

Throughout the blockchain industry, there are several distinct groups of people that play critical and yet different roles. These groups tend to move and function with a similar ideology, which, under certain circumstances, can cause contention. These are developers, miners, exchanges, and traders/investors.

Core Developers

Core blockchain protocol developers are perhaps the most indispensable players in the blockchain space today. Without them, no blockchain could exist. Regardless of miners, exchanges, and other elements of the ecosystem, chains owe their highest debt to the people making the blockchain more sophisticated, resistant, decentralized, and operable. They often forget that.

Application Developers

Application developers are now playing a more-and-more important role in the industry. Application developers are building real end-user applications on top of existing platforms and blockchains; they make interaction with the blockchain more comfortable every day for end-users. Often these developers do not fully understand or need to know how a blockchain core protocol works on the deepest levels.

Centralized Exchanges

Centralized exchanges are the place where most people initially convert traditional fiat cash into a digital currency. These centralized chokepoints are an absolute necessity for fresh capital injection into crypto markets. However, they are a very controversial chokepoint that, in some ways, has too much power over the entire market at this point. There are now hundreds of crypto exchanges across the world.

Decentralized Exchanges

Decentralized exchanges (DEXs) are undoubtedly the future of blockchain technology. These exchanges have no central company, individual, or group in control. This feature allows for the transfer of digital assets between blockchains as well as the exchange of digital assets directly to fiat currencies across the globe with no intermediary.

There are dozens of ongoing attempts to build more and more decentralized exchanges. However, some have claimed to be decentralized only for people to discover a single entity controls the DEX.

Traders / Investors

Just like with any traditional stock market, there are people all over the world, earning a living by trading and investing in blockchain-based cryptocurrencies, tokens, and stablecoins. Buying and selling volatility across crypto markets. Some of these traders might also get called speculators and gamblers, as there is often no explanation for some of the trades they make.

These trades are often based on hype, rumors, or intentional pump and dump desires. One of the main goals of this book is to help investors better understand this industry and make more careful, information-driven investments into this space.

Miners

Miners serve a critical function in the industry and help to secure multiple public blockchains. However, mining is nowhere near as decentralized as it once was at the inception of bitcoin and other major cryptocurrencies, as state actors (namely Russia and China) have taken an outsized interest in dominating and influencing public chains.

China reportedly controls between 65% and 75% of the world's ASIC hash power directed against Bitcoin and expends enough energy from pollutive sources, such as coal, to power a medium-sized European country in doing so. Russia, on the other hand, builds some of the world's most advanced ASICs for Altcoins.

Mining Hardware

Mining hardware manufacturers are also another point of contention in the industry. In 2013, there were multiple hardware vendors in different countries working to create new Bitcoin miners. Fast-forward to 2019, there is only a handful of major international mining companies that have a virtual monopoly on mining hardware manufacturing through ASICs.

ASIC Mining

Application-specific integrated circuits or ASICs, for short, are specifically designed computer chips designed to process a single mathematical algorithm extremely quickly over and over. ASIC's miners are typically only useful for hashing cryptographic algorithms. Outside of that for typical computing tasks like surfing the web on your mobile phone or computer, they are about as useful as a boat anchor.

The home-based hobby Bitcoin mining industry got destroyed by the proliferation of ASICs, whose scale does not allow for everyday users to experience a reward enough to be economical. Many projects are working to correct this, and DigiByte has worked steadily to balance the distribution of power between miners running ASIC algorithms like SHA-256, and other algorithms that require a different mining hardware architecture such as Skein, Scrypt and Qubit.

With the addition of the Odocrypt mining algo in July 2019, which recreates itself every ten days, DigiByte effectively eliminates the economic incentive to create ASICs in favor of using FPGAs.

FPGA Mining

A field-programmable gate array (FPGA) is a circuit board used to program and design all sorts of IoT devices and computer chips. FPGA's are used to create ASICs and other cryptocurrency miners for multiple blockchains. Because they are generic and designed to get programmed as part of the design process for new chips, they are perfect for the new Odocrypt mining algo DigiByte added on July 2019, which changes itself to an entirely new algorithm every ten days.

FPGA's got used for a short time for mining Bitcoin between CPU mining, which got used when Bitcoin first launched, and the discovery GPUs or graphics cards made great miners. FPGA mining is cost-effective and allows for home hobbyist mining when utilized by a mining algorithm like Odocrypt.

GPU Mining

When bitcoin mining started in 2009 Satoshi used the CPU on his computer to mine the first bitcoins. Very quickly, people discovered it was much more efficient and powerful to use graphical processing unit or GPU cards to mine Bitcoin.

Projects like Vertcoin, DigiByte, and others have pursued numerous innovations to maintain the GPU mining industry. The idea is anyone running a typical gaming computer should be able to mine a blockchain native cryptocurrency to keep the blockchain decentralized.

Staking

Staking is the term that comes from the proof of stake (PoS) approach to consensus and is an alternative to the mining proof of work (PoW) consensus system. Staking is a lot like earning a dividend from holding certain types of stock. Users of PoS blockchains stake their holdings, and as the blockchain mints new coins, they receive some of them.

User Dangers

It's still early. It is safe to say even in 2019 that the blockchain industry is very much in a nascent era. Many dangers to a new user and beginner still exist in this space. Therefore, it is imperative, as stated previously in this book, that you take the time to educate yourself properly, and as Warren Buffett suggests, never invest in anything you don't fully understand.

Are Centrally Issued Blockchains even Blockchains?

In our opinion, centrally issued and controlled "blockchains" are the most deceptive of all, to the point that serious doubt exists as to whether one can even call them blockchains in the first place.

This deception is not to say that distributed ledger systems that utilize a consensus mechanism are useless or somehow lack a market application; they lack the decentralization, trustlessness, and security that purely decentralized blockchains embody. Many centralized projects masquerading as decentralized have been used to scam and defraud users and investors.

Private Key Loss

In my opinion, as a core developer, the single most frustrating thing I often hear is when someone has lost their digital assets because they lost the private keys to their wallets. Private keys (aka the keys to the kingdom or the keys to your money) should get treated with the utmost sense of security, privacy, and urgency. If your private keys are not securely backed up, encrypted with a password, and stored in at least three separate physical locations, they are in danger of being lost.

Misplaced Trust

The second most frustrating thing I see is when multiple new people in the industry get burned by *trusting the wrong people.* This misplaced trust often occurs when consumers believe centralized exchanges to store their funds, which frequently occurs since more people are getting into digital assets, cryptocurrency, et cetera for the first time. Over the past seven years, we have seen dozens of centralized exchanges get hacked or, even worse, stripped of all their user's funds in cases of massive fraud and theft.

From a libertarian standpoint, if your money can be taken away from you on a whim, it isn't your money. It said in the blockchain industry: *if you don't have direct control over your private keys, you don't truly own your digital assets.* Many in this industry are religiously committed to the principle of decentralization - because centralization often robs people of their power and agency and takes them from being stakeholders to victims.

Hacking

Numerous pieces of malware, spyware, and much more are designed specifically for hacking and stealing your cryptocurrency wallet passwords and information. If you have a large number of crypto assets in your guard, we recommend using an entirely separate computer or hardware for that specific purpose and nothing else. In this way, you can effectively prevent providing a vector for fishing, keylogging, or other hacking attempts that might enable a malicious actor to steal your funds. Unlike a traditional bank or credit card, if someone takes your crypto, there is nothing you can do to reverse the transaction.

Social Engineering

As is the case across all aspects of cybersecurity, the one weakness that can never get fixed entirely is the human element. This reason is why I often say blockchain technology can fix and solve upwards of 90% of the cybersecurity vulnerabilities in the world today, but it can never solve the final piece: aka the human element.

It is essential that you understand some of the techniques and approaches people use to socially engineer and find out who is a specific target with large sums of digital assets. I have seen many prominent people in the blockchain industry get hacked because of some of the personal details they revealed on social media sites, such as Facebook, Twitter, and messaging apps like Telegram or by handing out business cards with their information at conferences.

51% Attacks

A 51% attack is an attack where 51% of the miners, stakers, or decentralized nodes providing consensus for a blockchain start altering and double spending on a blockchain. There have been numerous successful 51% attacks carried out on many less-known blockchains.

These attacks often resulted in a significant financial loss for users of these chains and even resulted in the death of several blockchains. A 51% attack is undoubtedly the black swan event we all fear that keeps us core developers up at night.

Conclusion

This chapter outlined some essential blockchain basics as well as several topics and terms we'll come back to in later chapters. There are several distinctions we will touch on later, including the difference between a blockchain *project* and a blockchain *protocol*, what kind of *applications* one might build on a blockchain, and the real-world impacts that this technology will have on governments, companies, tech platforms, AI, the Internet of Things, monetary policy, and more.

To anchor the bigger conversation, we'd like to have in this book; we need to cover how blockchain's cryptographic backbone evolved and who the major players are, as well as how blockchain is a revolution in information theory, computing, and technology generally. That is the topic of our next chapter. Let's take a deeper dive into the history and core technical details of what a blockchain is in chapter 4.

Part II: The Philosophy and the Philosophers

Chapter 4: Blockchain, An Evolution of Applied Cryptography

"If I have seen further it is by standing on the shoulders of Giants."

– Sir Isaac Newton

"There are two kinds of cryptography in this world: cryptography that will stop your kid sister from reading your files, and cryptography that will stop major governments from reading your files."

– Bruce Schneiner

Blockchain technology is the product of several hundred years of mathematical and cryptographic innovation. To understand the current state of the blockchain industry in 2019 and onward requires taking a look back at the development of modern-day cryptography from its infancy.

Some of the mechanisms and systems used to create a blockchain were known and used in computer science for several decades, and it is the unique combination of these functions that makes today's technology possible. The combination of these various applied forms of cryptography as part of a cohesive whole is the real genius behind blockchain.

For those that are brand new to the concept of cryptography, it is the study and practice of techniques that allow for secure communication in the presence of third parties. In the modern sense, it is all about the creation and analysis of protocols that prevent these third-party adversaries from reading your private messages.

Cryptography involves taking a piece of information and scrambling it in a unique way that is also reversible so that the person receiving the message can read it, even though the adversaries who may have intercepted the encrypted data have no key to reverse the process and read the message.

As you can imagine, being able to communicate in any environment securely is advantageous in a whole host of situations. Secrecy and security are of the utmost importance when trying to transfer value (or valuable data) over the internet, especially in today's day and age.

Humans have used methods like this to communicate securely as soon as reading and writing were widely practiced. Since the age of Julius Caesar (with the invention of Caesar Ciphers around 50 BC) cryptographic methods of securing communications have been among the most closely guarded secrets of nation-states. From timekeeping to secure communications over the internet, cryptography is the backbone for the world's economy and security infrastructure in ways that we all rely upon without even knowing it, every single day.

Throughout history you will find examples of triumphs in cryptography allowing for the strategic advantages of one group of people over another. The allies' defeat of the German cryptographic system known as ENIGMA through Alan Turing's work, building on the work of little-known Polish cryptographer Marian Adam Rejewski and his colleagues, defined victory in the Western Theatre. The Allied cryptographic advantage over the Japanese top-secret level code (codename PURPLE) also made victory possible in the Pacific. These exploits were arguably the most important technical advance during World War II and have characterized the state of the world since. Triumph in cryptography and technology literally kept democracy alive in the 20th century, in multiple instances.

This chapter will discuss some advanced techniques and concepts that create the foundation and fundamentals for blockchain technology as we know it today. We will also talk a little bit about some of the pioneers in this space whose work is often overlooked and forgotten.

The blockchain began in 2009 with the release of a white paper by a programmer using the online pseudonym "Satoshi Nakamoto" and the subsequent creation of the Bitcoin Blockchain from the

Genesis Block on 3 January 2009. This date was when the Bitcoin blockchain was born, and with it, a movement few at the time had even thought possible. This movement was made possible by the innovations that came in mathematics and cryptography between 1948 and the early 2000s.

These innovations don't belong to a single creator but include dozens of pioneers and tinkerers whose work was integrated and combined to allow for the creation of Bitcoin. To further understand just how a blockchain works, it is essential to understand some basics. While some of these terms may seem a little complex initially, but they will make sense as you become more familiar with them.

A blockchain has various subsystems such as encryption algorithms, peer-to-peer networking, and digital signatures - not unlike how your car has dozens of working subsystems that come together as part of a cohesive whole.

Today's blockchain technology is, at its core, is an evolution of applied cryptography from dozens of innovators and mathematicians over several decades, and one could argue centuries of mathematics. However, the majority of significant innovations used in blockchain technology have their start with Claude Shannon's 1948 paper on "Information theory."

Bits & Bytes

To begin our journey, let us explain some of the advancements in mathematics and computing that got us to where we are today in a digital world. We must look to the past to discover where the idea of a bit and byte of information came. When studying the roots of the technology that eventually led to the invention of the blockchain, it is essential to pay homage to two individuals. Alan Turing and Claude Shannon. No blockchain book could be complete without a tribute to these two geniuses.

Alan Turing

While Alan Turing probably does not need much of an introduction to most readers of this book, many may not know that he served as a mentor to Claude Shannon.
Turing's most famous work occurred at Bletchley Park, where he was responsible for building a computing solution to crack the Nazi ENIGMA code. Turing's success allowed the Allies to turn the tide of WWII, and with insights into the content of Wehrmacht communications, the allies knew precisely where key German assets were ahead of time.

After his classified work cracking the Nazi ENIGMA code at Bletchley Park, Turing way made his way to the United States to educate individuals at the United States War Department on how exactly this achievement had been made, as well as the methods the British team used to quantify information to do it.

Claude Shannon was one of the individuals taught by Turing during this process. His mentorship served as a pivotal moment in Shannon's career that allowed him to think through the problem of quantifying information.

Claude Shannon

During his time at the war department during WWII, Shannon developed a general theory on information. In 1948 he released a paper titled "A Mathematical Theory of Communication" itself based on a classified 1943 paper. In 1949 it was published as a book titled *"The Mathematical Theory of Communication."*

This article provided, for the first time in human history, a theory of how we might measure and quantify information, which itself is not a physical thing. Shannon proposed that data should be measured in bits—discrete, irreducible values of either zero or one. This idea is now the basis of all computer code and programming languages we use today, minus the new forms emerging with quantum computing (which we will discuss in Chapter 18).

Engineering quickly followed philosophy. Shannon's advance was a groundbreaking innovation and insight that quickly led to the development of the transistor in 1948. The transistor, along with the binary system, eventually led to the creation of the first integrated circuits in 1958, paving the way for every other digital innovation since, and a field we now know as 'classical computing.'

Due to the sensitive nature of Shannon's work at the US War Department and later at Bell Labs, he became very familiar with the idea of using mathematics to keep secrets. In 1949 he published a second paper titled "Communication Theory of Secrecy Systems," a declassified version of his wartime work on the mathematical theory of cryptography. In this document, Shannon established that all 'theoretically unbreakable' ciphers must have the same requirements as the one-time pad. This work, combined with his work on information theory, formed the foundation of today's modern cryptographic algorithms, which are still used. The cryptocurrency and digital assets we store in our blockchain wallets trace much of their intellectual lineage back to Claude Shannon.

Cryptographic Algorithms

The very idea of encryption is regularly glossed over in discussions of cryptocurrency. People compare "crypto" to fiat currency and commodities, such as gold, but often don't understand what is meant by the system of encryption and recording that gives blockchain cryptocurrencies and digital assets their value backed by the laws of mathematics.

In basic terms, encryption is the process of taking a piece of information - ultimately a series of ones and zeros - and running it through an algorithm that methodically scrambles all the pieces in a clear, deterministic way according to the algorithm and a unique key.

Encryption is not putting information in a random pattern like dropping a paperback book in a margarita blender. It is shifting pieces around in a predictable, logical way that is easy to get to, but hard to go back to the original form, and which makes the encrypted product look unintelligible unless a user has the specific key and blueprint to reverse the process.

Imagine cutting up a family photo into 64 equal pieces, each piece representing 1/64th of the whole picture and placing each piece on a chessboard so that the family photo is contiguous and does not appear to have been cut up. A simple encryption algorithm shuffles the squares around the chessboard according to a specific set of rules seeded by a key. Such that only the proper key can reverse the process and return the information to its original state.

Types of Cryptographic Algorithms

There are many variations of cryptographic algorithms in the world today, but going through them in detail is outside the scope of this book. We will highlight some of the top ones that get used in battle-hardened blockchains like Bitcoin and DigiByte. If you are interested in learning more about cryptography and encryption algorithms, Jared highly recommends Bruce Schneier's book *Applied Cryptography*. It is the holy grail of cryptography, and every aspiring blockchain developer should read it.

Overall there are three basic types of algorithms that we need to cover for you to fully understand the inner workings of a blockchain: hash functions, symmetric key algorithms, and asymmetric key algorithms.

Hash Functions

Hash functions are the building blocks for modern-day cryptography and blockchains. A hash function is a one-way algorithm that used throughout a blockchain in numerous innovative ways. A hash function is a cryptographic algorithm that is used to transform a sizeable random amount of data into a fixed specific small amount of data. Hash functions are used in the generation and verification of digital signatures and for checksums and integrity checks of data of all kinds.

A hash function will take the same original data input and return the same hash each time the original data gets run through the specified hashing algorithm. The primary hash function use in most modern blockchains is SHA-256.

Symmetric Key Algorithms

Symmetric key algorithms are also known as secret key algorithms were a single cryptographic key is used for encryption and decryption of data. The problem with a unique secret-key symmetric algorithm is that you need to share the secret key with anyone involved who is going to encrypt or decrypt data. In the case of a blockchain, if you used a symmetric key algorithm, then you would need to give the person you sent your Bitcoins or DigiBytes to a copy of your private key for them to send them onward.

There would be a lot of issues with doing this. However, when it comes to your wallet password, that is used to encrypt the private keys for your wallet, you want to use another symmetric private key to encrypt the other keys that belong to your digital assets. As you can begin to see, blockchains consist of multiple layers of encryption algorithms used to encrypt different types of cryptographic algorithms.

Asymmetric Key Algorithms / Public-Key Cryptography

Asymmetric key algorithms are commonly also known as public-key algorithms. Public-key algorithms use two mathematically linked keys known as public and private keys. The combination of a public and private key is called a key pair. The private key is always kept secret by the owner, and that's why you should never reveal your private keys to any blockchain assets you own. The public key is what you need to share publicly for others to interact with you on a blockchain and send you digital assets. Public-key asymmetric algorithms are also how you can create digital signatures on a blockchain.

Elliptic Curve Cryptography

The most widely used cryptographic algorithm used for digital signatures in a blockchain is ECDSA or Elliptic Curve Digital Signature Algorithm. ECDSA is used in pretty much all major blockchain for the signing of new transactions before they are sent off. Elliptic Curve Cryptography was first independently suggested in 1985 by mathematicians Neal Koblitz and Victor S Miller.

The US National Institute of Standards and Technology (NIST) includes ECC (elliptic curve cryptography) as its "Suite B" recommended algorithms, and the NSA officially supports classifying top secret information with 384-bit ECDSA keys. Elliptic Curve Cryptography is a method of asymmetric encryption based on the algebraic function and structure of elliptic curves over finite fields on a graph. It uses a trapdoor function predicated on the infeasibility of determining the discrete logarithm of a random elliptic curve element that has a publicly known base point on a curve.

Trapdoor functions are used in public-key cryptography to make it so going from A to B is trivial, but going from B to A is impossible by leveraging specific mathematical problems. In the case of ECDSA, that problem is the elliptic curve discrete logarithm problem. The size of the elliptic curve determines the difficulty of the problem. Therefore the more substantial the curve, the more secure the algorithm.

The Merkle Tree Data Structure

One crucial component of a blockchain is the data structure known as the Merkle tree. The Merkle tree data structure was created in 1979 by Ralph Merkle in his Stanford Ph.D. thesis: *Secrecy, Authentication, and Public Key Systems*. The Merkle tree is essential to the functioning of a blockchain. It provides the data structure the chain itself uses to keep itself in sequential order in an efficient manner.

Cryptographic Collisions and the Security of Private Keys

Cryptographic collisions are instances where the process of encryption or hashing results in an identical output. Much like signing into a hotel, getting a room key, and trying the wrong door with a correctly issued door key, and still having the door unlock. If the hotel only has a few rooms, then the odds of guessing the appropriate key to break into a room are higher, but with blockchains, there is a nearly infinite number of rooms. Today's odds of generating a cryptographic collision on an advanced blockchain are almost infinitesimally small - a feature anticipated by information theorists in the early 20th century, long before industrial computers.

This idea is a theme explored by Borges, one of the most famous authors of the early 20th century, whose writing anticipated the evolution of cryptography and is an excellent parable to understand the notion of a cryptographic collision and just how secure your digital assets are when stored with your private keys.

Argentine author Jorge Luis Borges is considered one of the greatest surrealist authors of the 20th century alongside Beckett, Kafka, and other contemporaries. He is best known for his 1944 work of short stories, *Ficciones*, which is widely understood to have anticipated trends and themes in postmodern European philosophy by several decades. Beyond his hatred of communism and fascism, much of Borges' most famous writing deals with ambiguous philosophical topics like the meaning of information and the notion of consciousness - themes that were not explored in the same depth in academic circles until several decades after he wrote *Ficciones*.

An essential short story among Borges works, and the most relevant to cryptography is *The Library of Babel*, written during the earlier years of World War II. *The Library of Babel* is a fable, one in which the protagonist is trapped in an endless library, made up of an infinite expanse of hexagonal rooms, each with shelves of books, all identical in every way, including character set and their number of pages (410) all identical.

The only thing that sets this infinite expanse of books apart is their content -- every single book is a unique, random string involving 25 characters. Some are Shakespeare's plays or Shakespeare's plays with one unique letter off. Some are the lost works of Democritus, who anticipated physics and whose work got lost with the destruction of the Library of Alexandria. Some are personal diaries, lives, and futures of individual people, and many readers in the library are desperately looking for the one book that is the key to them all.

All the universe's information gets represented by the library and its endless strings of books and characters, but in the mass of possibility, it is almost impossible to find the unmolested information one is looking to find. This impossibility is because of the infinite possibilities of representation - even within the constraints of the 410 pages in every book, there is an endless number of possible strings of characters to fill those 410 pages.

The Library of Babel anticipated the entire theory of information, which was refined by Turing, Shannon, and others in the course of the war. It is this body of thought, known as Information Theory that made the world computable in terms of bits and powered the revolution in computing that sent humans to the moon just 30 years afterward.

Many since have compared Borges's work both to computing and cryptography, as well as to biology.

Philosopher Daniel Dennett compared the information represented by the fable to the genetic libraries of every living thing, and much like there are size constraints and packets in the Library of Babel, human DNA and its 23 chromosomes are a similar library with an endless permutation of information. It is within the bounds of the size constraints provided by the chromosomes that our unique data is stored and exchanged; incidentally, Dennett called this the *Library of Mendel* after the father of modern genetic science.

Similarly to biology, *The Library of Babel* has been compared even more frequently to the cryptographic process. Cryptography is a central theme of the short story:

"Still other men came to think of the universe in cryptographs, and this interpretation has come to be universally accepted, though not in a sense it was formulated by its inventors."

This theme continues in the text,

"On some shelf in some hexagon it is argued, there must exist a book that is the cipher and perfect compendium of all other books, and some librarian must have examined that book; this librarian is analogous to a god..."

What is unique about the Library of Babel, and what characteristic of the real world it gets at is the concept of countable infinity. Even though there are constraints that apply to the size of the books, the number of characters they can hold, the kind of characters they can hold, and the number of books that can fit on a shelf, the sheer randomness of the characters means that there is a functionally infinite number of possibilities, much like a cryptographic algorithm.

To attempt to find one specific book that has the key is impossible because no librarian has the cipher or index to discover it in the vast expanse of hexagonal rooms. The search for the key is just as hopeless as the search for the book itself.

This impossibility is what a cryptographic cipher is in simple mathematical terms, and by using the elliptic curve or other methods, a unique key gets generated that is relatively simple to produce but incredibly impossible to work backward to determine the original key. In the realm of cryptocurrency, one's Bitcoin or DigiByte address is created by a random process, much like picking a book off the shelf in Borges' story.

It is the uniqueness of one's public address and private keys to that address that makes individual ownership of cryptocurrency secure. A cryptographic collision occurs when a system generates the same output twice, and when, to continue the metaphor, two librarians pick two different books off the shelf that prove to be identical. To use a biological example, It would be like having two different sets of parents give birth to two children who are genetically identical twins of each other.

It is in this setting that blockchain addresses can get generated infinitely. Because there are so many potential strings of characters, and so many books in the library, each uniquely created signature can become a discrete, unique name for a device, thing, or event. Blockchain provides the digital-analog for DNA in the realm of computation.

Key Blockchain Pioneers

To truly understand the current state of the blockchain industry is paramount for us to realize the history of how this industry took shape and where the future of this technology probably lies. To do so, we need to take a look at the true pioneers that helped make this technology possible. Ralph Merkel, Neal Koblitz, Victor Miller, Leslie Lamport, Hal Finney, Nick Szabo, and many more are some of the leading technical architects of technology used to create Bitcoin and the first blockchain protocols.

Satoshi Nakamoto

Satoshi Nakamoto is the still-anonymous inventor of Bitcoin and the writer of the transformative white paper "Bitcoin: A Peer-to-Peer Electronic Cash System." To this day, no one knows who he is or whether "he" was indeed a group of people or, even as some conspiracy theorists suspect, a secret government cover-up. Speaking from a historical perspective, governments tend not to replace their currency, and they tend not to put sophisticated encrypted systems out there for the public to use, so we are going to dismiss the latter without question.

Analyzing the Bitcoin white paper, it is clear to us that Satoshi was a native English speaker, and western-educated based on the language, sources, and vocabulary used. Additionally based on the Bitcoin genesis block *"The Times 03/Jan/2009 Chancellor on brink of second bailout for banks"*, we think Satoshi was probably concerned with and motivated by the long-term viability of the fiat system of money, and that he likely had some strong opinions on government and bank bailouts after the last recession.

We believe that it is highly probable that Satoshi was a US Citizen, based on the affiliations of the other cypherpunks we'll outline below, as well as the fact that his name has not been discovered or leaked at any point over the past ten years.

Ralph Merkle

Ralph Merkle is well-known for the invention of the Merkel tree data structure used in most blockchains that forms the data structure behind the chain itself. He also created Merkle signatures and cryptographic hashing techniques applied in all major blockchains.

Merkle is a legend of today's modern-day cryptography and is responsible for the conception of public-key cryptography and asymmetric encryption, which is the basis for all modern classified communications and blockchain transactions as well as the majority of security architecture on the internet.

In a 2016 interview, Dr. Merkle stated that a blockchain fixes the problem of trustless public key distribution, which he had been working to solve for the past 40+ years since his invention of public-key cryptography and cryptographic hashing. Satoshi also cites him in the Bitcoin whitepaper.

Whitfield Diffie

Mr. Diffie is an American cryptographer and one of the pioneers of public-key cryptography. Diffie and Hellman's Hellman's 1976 paper *New Directions in Cryptography* introduced a radically new method of distributing cryptographic keys, that helped solve key distribution—a fundamental problem in cryptography.

Martin Helmen

Alongside Whitfield Diffie, he is also one of the pioneers of the Diffie–Hellman Merkle key exchange and public-key cryptography.

Neal Koblitz

Neal Koblitz is one of the co-creators of elliptic curve cryptography, which is used to secure many features of a blockchain. Most blockchains today use ECSDA & elliptic curve cryptography to validate digital signatures used in sending and receiving transactions.

Victor Miller

Victor Miller is also an independent co-creator of elliptic curve cryptography widely used in blockchain technology.

Leslie Lamport

Leslie Lamport and his work in distributed systems are essential to a malicious fault-tolerant consensus that we have in blockchain systems today. His work lays the foundation for a blockchain to achieve consensus in a distributed and decentralized fashion.

Stuart Haber & W. Scott Stornetta

Stuart and Scott wrote the paper '*How To Time-Stamp a Digital Document*" in 1991, which is cited by Satoshi in the Bitcoin whitepaper. Timestamping is a critical concept used in many subcomponents of a blockchain. Timestamping is essential for the accurate historical immutability of a blockchain.

Hal Finney

Hal Finney was the first recipient of a bitcoin transaction from Satoshi. As a lead developer of PGP, he was a key pioneer early in helping test the first Bitcoin blockchain systems and is a well-known computer scientist. Hal Finney also created one of the first usable proof of work systems before Bitcoin in 2004. Many have suspected he may have been Satoshi.

Nick Szabo

Nick Szabo coined the term' *smart contract*". He is also a leading blockchain pioneer and cryptographer. Szabo created BitGold in 1998, which he described as a 'decentralized digital currency." Many have speculated Szabo himself is Satoshi because his publicly acknowledged work very much mirrors Satoshi's efforts to create a decentralized digital currency that embodies value characteristics similar to gold, in that it cannot get inflated away.

Adam Back

Adam is the inventor of the proof of work and decentralized mining functions used in bitcoin. He is the original pioneer of Hashcash and is also famous for his work on many other systems. He is currently the CEO of Blockstream. Satoshi directly cited Adam Back in the bitcoin whitepaper. His work allows for much of how proof of work mining systems operate today.

Bitcoin Core Developers

Since 2009 there have been many talented developers from all over the world contribute code to the Bitcoin protocol. Some are known, and some remain unknown such as the creator Satoshi. Here are a few prominent Bitcoin core developers that have helped make Bitcoin and blockchain technology what it is today.

Gavin Andresen

Gavin became the lead bitcoin developer following Satoshi's disappearance from the project's development community. A tremendous amount of innovation and work on the Bitcoin protocol was completed by Gavin early on. He was a very critical pioneer at a crucial time in Bitcoin's infancy.

Wladimir J. van der Laan

In 2014 Laan took over as the core maintainer of the Bitcoin codebase after Gavin nominated him. He has been a significant contributor to the bitcoin core protocol and blockchain technology. He is the lead maintainer of the Bitcoin Core source code to this day.

Pieter Wuille

Pieter is an active Bitcoin Core developer that has been contributing very innovative code to the Bitcoin protocol since May 2011. He is well known for his libsecp256k1 library for efficient elliptic curve cryptography used in Bitcoin, DigiByte and, many other blockchains. He also originated SegWit and many other useful blockchain advances.

Matt Corallo

Matt is a former engineer at Chaincode Labs and co-founder of Blockstream and Bitcoin developer. Matt most recently joined Twitter backed payment provider Square to further Bitcoin adoption and use.

Cory Fields

Cory is a Bitcoin core developer that works through the MIT Digital Currency Initiative. Cory discovered the "chain-splitting bug" in Bitcoin Cash in 2018 and has made many other contributions to this space.

Jonas Schnelli

Jonas is a Bitcoin Core developer and co-founder of *the Bitbox* hardware wallet. He is also the author of the widely used code library libbtc.

Jeff Garzik

Jeff is a Bitcoin core developer that routinely conversed with Satoshi early on. Jeff started Bloq in 2016 to focus on enterprise blockchain applications.

Luke-Jr

Luke is a long-time Bitcoin core developer who has made many contributions, including the implementation of SegWit and writing one of the most famous pieces of Bitcoin mining software.

Gregory Maxwell

Gregory Maxwell is a Bitcoin Core developer and Co-Founder and Chief Technology Officer of Blockstream. Maxwell was also an early contributor to Wikipedia and worked for the Mozilla Foundation.

Peter Todd

Peter is a Bitcoin core developer, and the pioneer of *timelock verify* and *checklocktime verify*.

Notable Altcoin Innovators & Developers

While there have been hundreds of blockchains created, not all of them have made the same technical innovations or major contributions to the industry. Below are a handful of very well-known blockchain creators who have made contributions to blockchain technology outside of the Bitcoin core developers.

One thing most altcoin developers have in common is that at one point or another, they were trying to help contribute to the Bitcoin blockchain, but many of the core developers ignored their proposals or ideas.

Vitalik Buterin - Ethereum (ETH)

Vitalik is the author of the ETH whitepaper and co-founder of Ethereum. He also is a co-founder of Bitcoin Magazine. Vitalik was also a recipient of the Thiel Fellowship in 2014.

Charlie Lee - Litecoin (LTC)

Charlie is the creator of the Litecoin blockchain and the former CTO of Coinbase. Charlie worked at Google for a decade before releasing Litecoin and joining Coinbase.

David Schwartz - Ripple (XRP)

David is the CTO at Ripple and is one of the original architects of the Ripple consensus network. He has also developed encrypted cloud storage and enterprise messaging systems for organizations such as CNN and the National Security Agency (NSA).

Riccardo Spagni - Monero (XMR)

Riccardo is a member of the Monero Core Team and is also the lead maintainer of the Monero project.

Dan Larimer - Bitshares (BTS), EOS, Steemit (STEEM)

Dan is the creator of DPoS consensus algo and the co-founder of Bitshares, EOS, and Steemit. He is famous for once receiving harsh criticism directly from Satoshi: *"If you don't believe me or don't get it, I don't have time to try to convince you, sorry."*

Jed McCaleb - Ripple (XRP), Stellar (XLM)

Jed is the co-founder of Stellar and the former CTO of Ripple. He is also known for creating the original Magic the Gathering Online Exchange (MtGOX) platform before selling it to Mark Karpeles.

Charles Hoskinson - Ethereum (ATH), Cardano (ADA), Bitshares (BTS)

Charles is a co-founder of Ethereum and the founder of Cardano. He is involved with multiple companies in the blockchain industry. He also helped with Bitshares and DPoS.

Evan Dunfield - Dash (DASH)

Evan created Dash in 2014. Dash was the first cryptocurrency to implement a masternode system. It also was the first one to successfully create a self-sustaining funding treasury and voting system to self-fund development and marketing directly from the blockchain.

Jackson Palmer - Dogecoin (DOGE)

While Dogecoin may not have been one of the most technically innovative blockchains ever created, it surely is one of the most memorable. Jackson created Dogecoin in the fall of 2013 as a joke, and so far, that joke has turned into one of the most decentralized blockchains on the planet. In many ways, Dogecoin helped bring a lot of new people into the blockchain industry in its early years. Who doesn't love a cute Shiba anyway?

Anonymous Blockchain Pioneers

While there have been thousands of anonymous developers that have contributed to multiple blockchains, here are a handful that stood out to Jared over the years.

Esotercizsm - DigiByte (DGB)

For over five years now, he has contributed immensely to the DigiByte blockchain in more ways than we can count. His intellect, passion, and expertise of the entire blockchain ecosystem are second to none. The DigiByte community owes him an immense amount of gratitude for all he has done over the years. He is a principal architect of the new DigiAssets protocol for issuing digital assets on top of DigiByte.

8bitcoder - Myriadcoin (XMY)

I Still don't know his name. But hands down one of the most brilliant minds in crypto. He pioneered the original multi-algo mining blockchain with Myriadcoin.

MetalCollatz - DigiByte (DGB)

To this day, we still don't know his name, but he is single-handedly one of the smartest geniuses we have worked with in the blockchain space. He rewrote the original DigiShield code and made it much, much better as well as MultiShield. He also is the creator of the Odocrypt mining algorithm. He has made some significant contributions to this space.

Conclusion

Now that we have gone through the history and the individuals that have made blockchain technology what it is today let's look at this beautiful new technology from a different perspective.

Most people don't realize that three of the eight papers cited by Satoshi in his whitepaper reference cryptographic time stamping and time keep ideas and methods. One of the most overlooked and under-discussed functions of a blockchain is the ability for the first time in human history to keep precise, accurate records of time.

In chapter 5, we will take a thought-provoking journey to analyze blockchain technology in relation to the spectrum of time, physics, and human technology.

Chapter 5: Blockchain in the Spectrum of Time and Technology

> "Meditate and track the clockwork of organics,
> Observe data of grey matter mechanics.
> Rare and strange, the movements made through endless repetitions,
> Bolstering immunities, staving off disease and deterioration."
>
> -Allegaeon, Grey Matter Mechanics

> "The Web is now philosophical engineering.
> Physics and the Web are both about the relationship between the small and the large."
>
> -Tim Berners Lee

Now that we've talked tech and outlined the different elements in this space, it's time to examine blockchain as part of the evolution of human technology.

Human technologies build on the insights into the mechanics of the universe that we have acquired over time. These insights have come through observation and experimentation, representing progress in our ability to capture, affect, and emulate those rules to our benefit. At the same time, we exist within those very same rules.

Computing, data storage, and the internet are all products of the massive leaps forward in physics that occurred in the early 20th century. Without these insights, notions of binary code or wireless transmissions would never have arisen. By extension, technology reflects our understanding of physics, and in a way, emulates and embodies these underlying rules.

The Blockchain represents one such development within the bounds of broader innovations in computing, and as a technology, it exemplifies an expansion of the limits of our species' ability to render, interpret, and interact with information by emulating the physical and logical structure of the universe. In philosophical terms, while existing computer science operates on and is analogous to systems grounded in the discipline of physics, the Blockchain and AI emulate biology in that they are complex systems with non-deterministic outcomes.

This continuity is one of the core arguments of our book: that blockchain is a technological analog for biological systems, chiefly those that maintain and transfer information (DNA and RNA). Blockchain builds on physics and computing but as an emergent system. It has immense potential to go beyond what physicists and computer scientists might have anticipated.

Blockchain is a revolutionary step in information theory.

In this chapter, we'll talk about how the categories of information involved in computing map onto our understanding of the larger universe. We'll start with time and causality, the measuring of which has played a critical role in human exploration, governance, and trade since ancient times. Second, we'll cover how biology and human beings have dealt with information, and how the blockchain shares an intellectual history with these older systems. Last, we'll touch on the blockchain's most well-known attribute; its ability to empower accounting and asset issuance, chiefly but not limited to 'Aristotelian money' - which Bitcoin and similar assets embody.

Time and Causality

One of the most challenging problems in philosophy and physics is the issue of *temporality* or time. It is fundamental to every single thing we think about and encounter, but paradoxically, we can only measure it by presuming it. There is no way to observe the universe without assuming the progression of time. We might disregard time or take it for granted when dealing with static facts or individual concepts, but the actual events or states that we encounter in the real world must occur at some point along a real timeline.

Time is one of the great philosophical questions that it is impossible to entirely give an account for, since each of these things we must use to describe themselves, resulting in a kind of circularity. Modern physics provides *more detailed models* of these things, but no system of science gives us a total account.

Standardized measures of time are critical in societies because they provide structure to human interactions with each other and the broader world. Over time, this has gotten more granular, from ancient calendars that first represented the rhythm of the cosmos to atomic clocks that measure computing functions at the speed of light.

The Mayan calendar evolved a 365-day year independently, and Stonehenge aligns with summer and winter solstices despite the absence of what we as modern people might recognize as disciplined science and philosophy in those cultures. In every civilization, timekeeping evolved as a quintessential element of all three core pillars of human life Governance, Religion, and Commerce.

Governments executed censuses and collected taxes on a schedule, planned wars based on inferences about the seasons, and how long it would take soldiers to march a given distance. Almost all religions have metaphysical and symbolic events tied to a calendar, regardless of whether they celebrate Yom Kippur, Easter, Ramadan, Vesak, Holi, or Aki Matsuri, and in all of these holidays, the present anchors to conceptions of the past and future.

Commerce is the cleanest example, as the simple concepts of open times for a market, times of delivery, seasons in agriculture, historical and future prices, notions of supply and demand, as well as the infrastructure of commerce, are all built on conceptions of time.

Modern time zones and methods of timekeeping owe their existence to the commercial need for them, which evolved soon after humans were able to cross multiple degrees of the earth's latitude in a single day by railroad. It is interesting to note that time zones are incredibly political. In many cases, they do not map to the position of the sun in the sky - note Venezuela's deliberately off-kilter timezone or the fact that the entire nation of China runs on Beijing time, even in far-flung Xinjiang and Tibet.

Timekeeping is critical to the way we live our lives, yet it is unexamined as a physical phenomenon. It is difficult to give a "first principles" explanation, though inquiry using analogy and specific descriptive examples does give way to some insights. At the level of our own experience, we think of time as an even flow, proceeding at exactly sixty seconds per minute, sixty minutes per hour, and so on. Since time ties to our observation of the world, there would be no way to pause it without pausing ourselves and our perception of it.

Modern physics gives us more sophisticated concepts to approach the topic. Most readers will be familiar with Einstein's theory of General Relativity and understand that a person traveling at close to the speed of light will experience the flow of time at a slower rate than a person standing relatively still on the surface of the earth. Even more fascinating is the other side of the spectrum, at the level of quantum reality where subatomic particles operate according to rules discovered and verified in tandem with advances in mathematical theory.

In the current atomic model, an electron gets attached to an atomic nucleus, will it will occupy various orbitals, which vary in shape increase in complexity as the nucleus. Each electron moves to the lowest energy state not occupied by another electron. This structure is the cornerstone of modern chemistry and material science and explains how elements interact with one another in terms of bonds. A great example of this principle is the 105-degree bend in a water (H_2O) molecule.

This angle is the result of the central oxygen atom's two spare electrons crowding against the bonds made with the two hydrogen atoms, much like balloons tied around a single object that push against each other to form a symmetrical, four-pronged shape. In the case of water, this 105-degree bend exhibits itself in ice crystals; the 105 degrees of the individual water atom add up to a perfect hexagon, with all permutations in a crystalline snowflake occurring at 105 degrees from one another.

But enough about orbitals. What's genuinely fascinating regarding observations of time at this level, electrons are understood to move around their orbital freely. At any one point in time, a particle may occupy a different location within its orbital, with no middle path existing from point A to point B. Rather than traveling from point-to-point like billiard balls, electrons seem to appear in one place and then another, as if they were a detail in the frame of a movie rather than the kind of object we are familiar with in our day-to-day lives.

Some theorists such as Carlo Rovelli and William G. Tifft of the University of Arizona point out that a unifying theory of physics explaining quantum gravity (which unifies Einstein's theory with quantum mechanics) may *require* the quantization of time and space as if the universe was composed of pixels.

"Certain theoretical studies suggest that to unify general relativity (gravitation) with the theories of quantum physics that describe fundamental particles and forces, it may be necessary to quantize space and perhaps time as well. Time is always a 1-dimensional quantity in this case." - Dr. William G. Tifft, Scientific American,

If this underlying theory that time and space are quantized is accepted, that would naturally mean that there is a fundamental minimum constant of time across the universe. This notion isn't a fringe theory, but a realization shared by several influential theoretical physicists. Carlo Rovelli's work on quantum gravity and time dilation includes a model representing the granularity of not just matter, but time and space as a necessary assumption.

The consensus among physicists is that there must be a minimum unit of space and time. Physicists are working to define this minimum unit of time and space in multiple ways, but the most common measure defined according to Planck's constant for the speed of light.

Planck time is the amount of time it takes a photon (lightwave/particle) to move the distance of its diameter in space and time. According to Planck time, the universe's "block size" could be assumed to be approximately $5.3911613 \times 10\text{-}44$ of a second, during which time every particle is in a limited space for a precise amount of time.

If this is the case, then the universe proceeds in frames, much like a movie on film where a particle is at a given point for a definite but infinitesimally small point in time, after which it is somewhere else in the next frame.

Even if quantum reality procedes in blocks, we experience our observed reality (up here where all the billiard balls and people are at) as smooth and path-dependent. Everything that exists is causally rooted in its antecedents - the conditions that came immediately before it.

Causality, as we define it in philosophy and physics, is linear from the past to the future and cannot be reversed. Many philosophers, physicists, and science fiction authors have tied themselves in knots trying to establish a model for time travel within our universe, but the paradoxes of causality are too many. Could I kill my infant grandfather? If so, then *I* wouldn't be around to travel back in time to kill my grandfather. Or maybe I would need to presume a new universe apart from the one where I originated, which is cheating. This paradox illustrates the impossibility of retrocausality - backward causation in time.

Backward causation is not to be confused with downward causation, such as when a process in my mind (like wanting coffee) leads to a lower-order process (water boiling) in the future. Many free will compatibilists such as Daniel Dennett dismiss the problem of determinism in free will by observing that we are capable of deliberation and symbolic processing. Even if we don't have absolute free will, we do have the capacity to make moral and enlightened decisions based on our environment.

But that's a topic for another time - what's important here is that all credible models of causality progress forward into the future only. We cannot observe anything without assuming without a forward-marching timeframe directly linked with a conception of linear, path-dependent causality. One thing leads to another, and all things seen in the present have antecedents. There is a causal structure to those antecedents that led to the current observed moment, regardless of how one believes the universe started.

Further, it is a result of playing back these causal forces that have enabled a recent consensus among scientists that the cosmos is 13.8 billion years old. An essential question in cosmology is whether the universe is in a steady-state, or whether it has repeatedly expanded and contracted like a beating heart, or whether we are riding one incredibly massive explosion of energy out into the ice-cold expanse of nothingness.

Astrophysicists refer to this as the "Rate of Omega." If Omega is less than 1, the universe will slow down its expansion like a ball rolling uphill, gradually glom back together and become the cosmic egg again, restarting the cycle. If Omega were equal to 1, that would indicate that the universe has stopped expanding (or never expanded in the first space), and everything will more or less stay in its place.

If omega is higher than one, the universe would be expected to continue to expand until it cools down and loses all of its energy. Astronomers have observed redshifts in faraway galaxies that indicate the rate of omega is greater than 1, meaning that the universe had a definite start point (a *genesis block*) and has expanded since. At this genesis block, all of the constraints and constants involved reality was determined, defining the rules for everything that came after.

So, to summarize, our current models of physics imply that the universe had a definite starting point, proceeds in granular amounts of time - including that said process dilates across time, space, and matter. To this effect, the blockchain has some fundamental similarities with the rules and laws the very universe operates on.

Examining physics underpinning computing is not strictly an academic exercise, and there are several pragmatic reasons why such a study pays dividends, especially in practical fields like business and government. To give a famous example, the physics of time has a direct effect on our modern financial system. As Michael Lewis chronicles in his 2014 book *Flash Boys*, the late 2000s and early 2010s saw an arms race in computing for physical proximity to the machines conducting traditional equity trades for this very reason.

High-Frequency Trading (HFT) firms in the late 2000s were competing to shave microseconds off their transactions to gain an advantage. In the time it took for information to be transmitted over a fiber optic cable from Chicago to New York, arbitrage was happening in a few city blocks.

This increase in speed generated massive returns, not by improving the system, but by encouraging intermediaries to buy and sell stock in fractions of a second without accepting any of the market risks. As Lewis documents, trading firms even went to the length of burying entirely new fiber optic cables for exclusive use, avoiding kinks and detours to squeeze every available femtosecond out of transactions and gain an edge over competitors with the same strategy.

Understanding the physics involved in modern-day computing and trade is critical in approaching the opportunities and challenges of the already half-century-old information economy, and with fiber optics, the speed of light is one of the chief physical constraints on our computing and telecommunications capacity. The velocity of information also affects UTXO mining. Miners and traders in far-flung parts of the world operate at a penalty as a result of the latency of the internet, and the distance information must travel relative to other nodes.

For this reason, globally distributed computing systems have natural speed ceilings set by the physics of our universe, which is calculated by the amount of time required for a message to be distributed and returned across all telecoms networks globally. Private distributed ledgers built on the spines and hubs of the global internet infrastructure have block times of 4-5 seconds, truly decentralized blockchains like DigiByte add a few additional seconds of global latency in exchange for being substantially more robust.

Ontology and Information Theory

Also paralleling physical nature, the blockchain's consensus-seeking characteristics are worth noting. Most models of reality include the notion that atoms, quarks, and large bodies find equilibrium at specific states and not others. The structure of everything is a product of consensus among many forces. There appears to be a complex ontology to the world, which allows the same basic building blocks to result in the entire spectrum of the periodic table. Every chemical element is simply a stable equilibrium between these forces.

Take the example of noble gasses in the periodic table. As a physical substance, they do not need to interact and bond with other atoms. Their orbitals are occupied with just the right number of electrons, and there is no electronegative force to create a bond. In a thermodynamic setting, we would call this consensus-seeking trend entropy; every material thing wants to make its way to the lowest energy state possible.

The same goes for gravity. Objects in Newtonian space fall into orbits with each other depending on the tensions created by their competing masses. Generally speaking, physics is a science of calculating the mathematical minimum resulting from several competing functions. The development of calculus, which you can thank Isaac Newton and Gottfried Leibniz for, enabled the application of more sophisticated math to describe and predict the equilibrium of forces in the physical world. One such example is how the escape velocity for a rocket is calculated - effectively the energy required to break free of a planet's gravity.

An ontology is simply a system of rules that define a method of being. Theoretical physics is an attempt to generate an ontology for the basic building blocks of our universe, and chemistry is an ontology for a certain level of that stack. Biology is an ontology for life on this planet, and xenobiology is the theoretical study of the possibility of life beyond our world. Xenobiology analyzes the opportunities of different biochemistries. These might be carbon-based life with different chiralities than are known on our planet, or based on silicon or another substance.

As physics grew as a discipline, our technology expanded to accommodate and embody the new insights that it provided. When it comes to how we use this knowledge, technology sets physical forces in specific opposition to each other to produce an outcome, from simple machines such as wheels and wedges to more sophisticated devices that store and leverage mechanical, chemical, and electromagnetic energy. If you visualize the spectrum of complexity from subatomic quarks up to us as conscious, observing people who appear to be capable of understanding, deliberation, and subjective experience.

At each increasing level in complexity, the realm of possibility increases massively. There are more possibilities for atoms than quarks, more possibilities for molecules than atoms, more for cells than stones, more for multicellular organisms than an amoeba, more for *homo sapiens* than *musca domestica*, more for humans with access to advanced technology and civilization than for those who live in isolation. We are the apex of biology, and our evolution of systems of language, morals, and logical insight is what sets us apart from the crocodiles. To quote Aristotle, humankind is characterized by reason, which makes politics, technology, and the passage of information from one generation to the other possible.

On the spectrum of complexity, our technology comes after us because it is an extension of who we are and what our needs are. It is also more straightforward than we are as biological organisms.

Tech is an evolutionary aspect of sentient life. Useless tech tends to be forgotten or shelved - most of what has stuck around has a specific use to people, no different than domesticated crops and animals. And the tribes who learn to use it have an advantage over the tribes who don't.

Other tools made every tool we use today, and those other tools were made by yet other tools, back to the time humankind first used sticks, broken stones, and fire. As a modern evolution in computing, blockchain technology is one of these systems - a complex non-biological organism assembled by setting existing, smaller systems against each other within the bounds of human science and everyday application. Further, technology [including the blockchain] is an embodiment of significant complexity in a way that finds or creates a consensus of forces to further human needs.

In a very 'meta' way, our scientific systems of representation mirror and emulate our model of the universe, such that successes in our model improves our ability to represent reality. Specifically, computing tells us something about the universe, both because it is possible in the first place, but also because it makes possible the informational process of refining and building new models by exchanging and modeling information.

Computing exists as a manifestation physical ontology of physics, as does biology. It stands to reason that computing will begin to emulate or unwittingly resemble biology. While many of us are obsessed with general artificial intelligence and robots that imitate the movement of deer, dogs, and humans, the blockchain represents an ontology for these systems to develop on, much as DNA underwrites the biological process.

If AI is the cognitive function and the 'brain' blockchain resembles the transmission function and the DNA, which is extremely important for things like unique identities, trustless exchange, and several other concepts we'll touch on later in this book. The simplest and most salient point to start with here is blockchain's emulation of physical reality is the one we started this chapter with: time.

The Technology of Measuring Time

It would be difficult to talk about time or technology without talking about the technology of measuring time. This science is known as *horology* - literally 'the study of hours.' The blockchain mirrors several of the innovations in clockmaking that emerged over the last 300 years and aided the exploration and science of their era. One might compare the difficulty adjustment procedure with the inventions made to keep steady time across the power band of a hand-wound clock or watch.

In a mechanical clock, this an *escapement*, which limits how much energy can 'escape' the power source (spring, battery, etc.) in a given moment. A good escapement lets power smoothly and continuously flow out at the rate that the hands of the clock display the correct time, regardless of whether the mainspring is fully wound or nearing its ebb.

Older clocks relied on pendulums, leveraging Galileo's discovery that a pendulum's "tick" and "tock" were equally long regardless of how far the pendulum swung. UTXO blockchains face peaks and troughs in how much computing power is allocated to mining. The development of a difficulty adjustment that reacts and adapts to this varying amount of computing power is a natural analog to regulation in a mechanical clock.

Much like watches and clocks must regulate the power that drives the hands to keep good time, blockchains must regulate the hash power directed against them to stay on schedule. The Bitcoin blockchain has an escapement (difficulty adjustment) that adapts only periodically. DigiShield, pioneered by DigiByte, improved on the process by adjusting the blockchain in real-time relative to fluctuations in computing power, effectively making a more chronometer grade blockchain resistant to being mined ahead of schedule or frozen by a sudden halt in mining power.

By extension, innovations in the blockchain emulate other previous improvements in clocks, and how those innovations provided significant technical use cases that impacted people's everyday lives. Before clocks adopted bimetallic hairsprings (which you can thank Christiaan Huygens of quantum theory fame, along with Robert Hooke), clocks were significantly affected by variations in temperature.

These fluctuations affected the flexibility of the spring, and hence the timekeeping of early spring-driven clocks. John Harrison, an English tinkerer, improved on the innovations of Hooke and Huygens by adopting a bimetallic strip in a balance spring. This alloy was composed to expand and contract evenly with changes in heat, allowing for near perfect timekeeping.

Because Harrison improved timekeeping to a sufficient standard, it was now possible to measure the movement of the sun and stars relative to a stable measure of time, making the world more navigable. Spring-driven clocks may seem irrelevant now in our age of GPS and self-driving cars, but at the time, there were no reliable means of determining longitude at sea, leading to significant navigational errors.

Chief of these was the Scilly Naval Disaster of 1707, which claimed the lives of 1550 British sailors, whose commander grossly miscalculated his fleets longitude, crashing them into the rocks off the coast of Cornwall (southwestern England). Imagine the human losses of 9/11, except with that loss being at a time where the nation had a population of 10 million, not 330 million, and you start to grasp the magnitude of the problem at the time.

By developing a chronometer capable of keeping accurate time across temperatures, Harrison enabled the English fleet to determine their longitude at sea. This method involved referencing the position of the sun and the divergence of their observed time with the time kept by Harrison's invention. Harrison's marine chronometer gave the British Empire an undeniable advantage at sea and underwrote the era of expansion that saw colonies in North America, the Levant, the Indian Subcontinent, and China.

Naturally, this little clock got treated as a national secret at the time. As the art of horology advanced, innovations such as the lever escapement and the Breguet Overcoil became essential to daily life. Railroads, coordinated infantry charges, and industrial optimization all needed precise timekeeping. One could compare the addition of multiple algorithms to some chains as an analog for this, as the competing forces stabilize the underlying operation and support more steady timekeeping across the arc of computing (non-spring) power.

These developments in mechanical timekeeping took generations to run their course. Accurate clocks became the first "wearable computers" in the early 20th century, playing out their deterministic mechanical equation with each winding. Mechanical computing had its upper limits, though, and was replaced in the late '60s through the 1980s by technology leveraging electricity. Modern quartz watches work in fundamentally the same manner - quartz is a piezoelectric material, meaning that it can hold an electric charge up to a point and then releases the charge in a burst.

Trimmed and tuned with the right frequency, the quartz crystal in a watch or wall clock lets power out at the same rate regardless of how much energy is available in the battery. Quartz was a massive technical leap and involved electricity rather than raw mechanical energy as the driving force of a new form of computing. Modern atomic clocks go one step further and are built to measure the predictable decay of a cesium atom.

Harrison's chronometer represented a transition of timekeeping being an upper-class novelty enjoyed by kings and queens to becoming a critical military and commercial technology. Timekeeping that was previously only accurate enough to tell the hour was now reliably sufficient to maintain minutes and seconds. A legacy of this is the fact that degrees of latitude and longitude are measured to this day in minutes and seconds on most printed maps.

This pattern was observed not just in timekeeping, but with the advent of modern computing, the automobile, the airplane, and the internet. Every revolutionary technology started as the hobby horse of some eccentric developer, and in many cases, those developers didn't imagine the depth and scope of applications their inventions might have.

Timekeeping for its own sake is useless, so you're probably wondering why we're spending so much time on it here - measurement time is always done regarding something else, to events occurring in sequence. In the example of the Marine Chronometer, timekeeping inferred longitudinal distance from Greenwich, England. The astronauts of the Apollo Program still wore mechanical watches on the Moon, and the Apollo 13 crew specifically used one of theirs to time the 14-second thruster burn necessary to enter the earth's atmosphere at the correct angle to neither burn up or bounce off into the cold darkness of space.

GPS involves the triangulation of the receiver among multiple signals emitted by satellites, with a timestamp informing distance and providing incredibly accurate locational readings that enable modern militaries to do precise targeting of infrastructure, or for you to find the nearest Chic-Fil-a.

The blockchain is about much more than simple timekeeping, but its impact can be thought of similarly. In addition to linking time to our position on the globe, blockchain represents the link of time to other conditions and information, enabling a closer representation of assets, actions, and owners. Where time can measure positions on the globe, blockchain can measure addresses in a network,

Time + Non-Temporal Information

One of the most serious constraints in philosophy and science is the disjunct between our descriptive representation of the world and the world as it is. The target of true scientific inquiry is to make these systems more accurate and more representative, and it has always been a mistake to conclude that theory is reality - a fallacy commonly known as *Scientism*.

By its nature, language and science cannot be the material things in themselves, but language and science can be used to produce highly descriptive symbolic representations of those things. Add to that the fact that meaning in language exists but is not a material thing; information is embodied physically in text and speech, but the purpose of the words we use are not tied directly to any individual print or utterance of those words. Information and language represent a level of reality above the merely physical.

Our natural language (in this case, English) or our technical language (native language plus Math, Chemistry, and Physics module installed) offers us descriptive meanings for things that are more or less fungible across embodiments. If you've seen one Carbon14 atom, you've seen them all. At the same time, each carbon 14 atom is a discrete entity made up of even smaller distinct entities, some of which have eluded human discovery and detection up until very recently, and more yet remain undiscovered.

The fact that every material isotope is fungible with other identical isotopes is just as mind-blowing as the fact that no two snowflakes are alike. Our universe contains explicit, specific building blocks that are real things that can be used to build other, distinctive things. Even if the carbon isotope in our example does not have all of its electrons arranged in electron clouds the same way, it has a structurally similar system of orbitals and behaves identically to every other carbon 14 atom.

While it may be possible to reduce every material thing to its subatomic particles in an attempt to rob it of its uniqueness, the fact of the matter is that we walk around the world as discrete beings, composed of a nearly infinite number of functioning systems. Our DNA, generated from the prior DNA of our parents, is the cornerstone of our unique selves.

DNA contains information that made your organs, which support your mind, which underwrites your consciousness, thoughts, and opinions. Think about that for a moment! If there were only instructions to build a brain, every organism would fail, and no mind gets created. The same goes for a heart, a fingertip, and a skeleton.

Your DNA came with a full set of instructions to create a living, functional organism with hundreds of interdependent systems allowing it to thrive and reproduce. All out of matter that it hadn't been introduced to yet. Your heart is there to pump blood, your intestines to digest nutrients. It would be difficult to say that your organs don't have a purpose, yet they were designed based on a segment of DNA that included the procedural instructions to make all of those systems in a way that works together.

Going back to the causal model, this would mean that the existence of [again, non-material] information is an essential part of the universe. Further, it means that this most basic application for information is intentional - DNA wants to build you and wants to reproduce.

The very fact that biological organisms instinctually eat, have sex and minimize risk and pain to themselves, and the fact that they want to survive and procreate is in the telos of their DNA and the biological architecture that DNA seeks to propagate.

DNA is only one kind of information, and for us as conscious beings, language is the primary means that we create and interact with information.

Language sets us apart from the rest of biology. One could think of written and verbal communication as one of the coding languages of our operating system, in tandem with biology. Better yet, we're ostensibly evolved to *need* language. This tandem duo is not to say that genetics is strictly a limiting power - quite the opposite. Our biology enables deliberative and symbolic thought.

We can recognize and model consequences for our actions in addition to the forces of instinct and biology. It also forms the basis for cultural, scientific, and philosophical inquiry, as these practices require that we refine our symbolic representation internally while mapping it as carefully as possible to the real world as we encounter it.

Metacognition (thinking about thinking) is a massive challenge, and one we as a species will likely never fully complete. It is this disjunct between informational representation and the things in themselves is one of the most significant problems in Western philosophy and one that has run from Plato to Heidegger to Kripke. But it is also a massive challenge in information technology, as systems that operate in pure information can get duplicated indefinitely, and that is where we intersect with the blockchain again.

A file can be duplicated indefinitely, with the only challenge being the information decay that occurs as the file is compressed and transmitted. Copying data makes for a great business model if you're Steve Jobs in 2003, and is why software companies can make such massive profits based on relatively small investments in physical or human capital. Code scales. It also represents that information-based goods or assets being made non-atomic, where it can get duplicated at a low cost.

This duplication is distinct from the prior business model, where one had to buy analog copies of physical files. Records, tapes, and vinyl were *counterfeit* when they got duplicated, almost as if the record company was printing music that had a currency-like value and characteristics as an asset. We generally don't think of a copied file this way, even though the information is the same, and it still has value.

This characteristic is a feature and a bug of much of our existing information architecture.

The beauty of the internet and modern computing is that information has ceased to be strictly atomic, embodied in databases, books, and physical holdings. Data can be duplicated, disseminated, searched, and organized in ways that have opened a wellspring of human creativity and innovation. This data free flow happened at the cost of security. If all my wealth is in cash under my mattress, someone only must break into my home to physically steal it.

Not so when my money is a digital file type. The same goes for the data that make up my personal and civic life. My government ID, personal identifiers such as my social security number, my communications with friends, family, and colleagues all exist in ways that do not defend well against spoofing and duplication.

As a rule-based system, the blockchain can enable our IT infrastructure to regain the security and economic features of atomic identities that exist as vulnerabilities at present. The Chinese government's theft of thousands of government official's security clearances is a clear example of this. Since records were stored as raw information and not made atomic, they were taken and copied *en masse* rather than requiring discrete permissions or conditions to be accessed. One of the blockchain's most important uses is to empower a return to distinct identities with explicit permissions and conditions of use, as verified by a decentralized consensus mechanism.

Had records been independently encrypted instead of being stored in the equivalent of a Microsoft Excel sheet, the act of theft would have been considerably more cumbersome, perhaps to the point of being cost-prohibitive.

Making data atomic is especially crucial because information and computing are the new arms race. Our world is made up of an infinite number of networks and overlapping systems, and it is the interaction of these systems that gives us the modern economy, nation-state, and every other system we rely on today.

As states and companies compete for dominance, they are actually in competition for power over shared networks and arenas of competition with their rivals. The global economy and internet are battlefields as the skies and borders of the Cold War, or the fields Europe were during conquests past as is the influence over social networks that exist today. The Russian Federation's meddling in the 2016 U.S. election represents an exploitation of the open system we've built. A network of savvy, hostile political actors injected divisive rhetoric and narratives (literally fake news) into our already post-truth political discourse, all for the price of a Maserati.

This dynamic goes back to the core challenges in language and science mentioned above. The core discipline of sound philosophy and science, or any epistemic endeavor that seeks the truth, is to have 1) an internally coherent language for the world, and 2) to have that language is mapped to real entities in a way that describes reality in an as fulsome and functional style as possible. The authority of information gets diluted because there is so much of it to analyze and understand.

Properly applied, blockchain technology improves the administration and chain of acquisition for information, as well as our capacity to protect information from undue altering while preserving it along a mutually referable timeline. In short, blockchain ties an immutable record of time with a series of unique identities in such a way that it supports an ontology for data in a computing environment. It does this by integrating several pre-existing systems in such a way as to make a new, durable system, and in this way, it represents the next evolution of the internet in line with the constraints and challenges that our existing information technology and the economy gets built today.

Further, the blockchain is capable of representing ontologies, constraints, and entities over time by creating a representation of what is unique about precisely that thing, opening the door for closer integration between the contracts and relationships of things with the elements within themselves. Following our biological example, a cryptographic hash preserves specific immutable details of an item that is similar to a piece of DNA or RNA; it contains the code to identify it and might include the code to direct actions taken by it while preserving its uniqueness. Insofar as the necessary conditions of a thing are discretely identified and linked to the blockchain, they also can be recognized as an entity within a timescale.

Accounting and Representation

There is no way to measure information without some embodiment to observe. To bounce one billiard ball off another, you need two billiard balls, an initial force, and maybe a surface and some gravity. We might be capable of representing an action, either as a historical account or as a fictionalized example, but to do so, we would need a medium to represent it in. This medium would need rules built on causality, as well as an immaterial system of meaning and reference so observers can link the material representation with the concepts and potential embodiments it is describing.

All representation involves some material footprint, but the 1's and 0's are not and cannot be the information itself. The carbon atoms in ink on a page are not aware that they are playing a part in the representation of data.

Continuing this point, representations of the real world are impossible without three things.

1) Assumed categories of time, space, and matter.

2) Discrete, contingent embodiments of those categories that are within the realm of our conscious observation

3) A system of meaning and mutual reference to distinguish those embodiments from one another and describe the rules by which they operate. We would not be able to construct theories to interact with our physical world or develop systems to extrapolate our knowledge into the past without these three assumptions. The same goes for our DNA, credit card accounts, and health records, as we've argued above.

Blockchain leverages advances in computing power and innovations in creating a decentralized, secure system that emulates the forward motion of causality in the observed world. Blockchain echos the fact that reality is composed of individual embodiments of rules and causal relationships between different entities. Past systems of representation often failed to account for a linear forward march of causality. They allowed objects they represented to be edited or corrupted post-hoc, either by being centralized or by not being tied to a hard timeframe in the first place. There is no backdating on the blockchain. When an entity commits an act on that timeline, its action is immutably linked to that transaction in time.

In school, they probably made you read the Epic of Gilgamesh, or the Bible, or the Code of Hammurabi, or some other ancient text. While writing has been critical to the development of religion and mythology, it does not appear to have evolved for that specific use case. The first clay tablets we have in Sumerian and Babylonian scripts were ledgers of who owed what, tallies of grain production, and exchanges of IOUs. Writing emerged because kingdoms were too large for any steward or administrator to keep track of in the back of their minds.

Literary writing did not evolve until after the commercial application for literacy was popularized and adopted. Further, these systems of writing made new forms of commerce and exchange possible, because lines of credit and anticipated deliveries of goods could get recorded along with contracts between parties and inventories of grain and citizenry.

A sterling example of language's origins in accounting is *Quipu* - a system of writing developed by the Inca between 1100 and the Spanish Conquest of Peru based entirely on maintaining a chain of knots in fiber. Quipu records involved representing exchanges in a series of unique knots tied in a base-10 positional system, not unlike how the individual characters in this document get encoded in base-8 binary.

Some Quipu records utilized color-coding to inform what kind of file or provenance the information was in, with the system being used to execute addition, subtraction, multiplication, and division, as well as taxation in kind, types of labor committed, and to execute imperial censuses and represent the Inca calendar. Quipu remained primarily administrative and commercial, with no literary application ever recorded.

Blockchain echoes the origins of accounting in human language, as it provides an ontology for transactions with the added benefit of timestamping and unique identifiers for asset holders. Hammurabi and other kings had seals, which were comparatively expensive to make and conveyed their authority in signing their edicts. Blockchain users have their private keys to sign documents and transactions to a mutually authoritative, decentralized ledger based on a standard set of rules and conditions.

Money

What would accounting be if not for keeping track of the exact value and empowering the exchange of value? It is impossible to talk about the blockchain without talking audiences fixating on its first embodiment.

Cryptocurrency is *currency* because it embodies the core characteristics that human civilization has treated as currency for millennia, and in some ways, the concept of the decentralized ledger even predates that evolution of money itself. While most economics textbooks talk about money evolving as a way to resolve the "double coincidence of wants" problem, where a farmer in a village wants to trade chickens for shoes, there is act ally no such historical example of such a society existing.

Rather, examinations of tribes in Africa and Polynesia imply that early civilizations started with a shared notion of debt, whereby the exchange of goods occurred with approximations of value, not physical currency. These communities maintain shared understanding (that is, a decentralized ledger) of who owns and owes what. Systems of money only become necessary once a population grows past the point that no individual can keep track of all the value exchanges occurring. Tokenization of fungible, hard-to-duplicate tokens was born as soon as the realm of economic exchange became bigger than one tiny network of trust.

Beyond being in line with the traditions of our earliest tribal ancestors, Crypto follows the definitions of the ancients - to quote Aristotle, a currency is:

1. Durable - the medium of exchange must not weather, fall apart, or become unusable. It must be able to stand the test of time.
2. Portable- relative to its size, it must be easily moveable and hold a large amount of universal value relative to its size.
3. Divisible- should be relatively easy to separate and put back together without ruining its essential characteristics.
4. Intrinsically Valuable- should be valuable in of itself, and its value should be independent of any other object. Necessarily, the item must be rare.

Following [pre-fiat] Aristotelian logic, crypto is, in fact, more of a pure form of money than fiat, since fiat floats and can have its intrinsic value diluted should the system that stabilizes it fail.

Durability: Cryptocurrency is as durable as the decentralized UTXO technology that makes it possible. If you don't forget or yield your recovery phrase, your UTXO tokens aren't going anywhere. This durability adheres to the Aristotelian definition of money more tightly than gold or traditional assets, because physical gold can be taken with physical force, and stocks, bonds, and bank accounts can be frozen and liquidated. Cryptocurrency is immaterial - it is data alone. As such, it cannot be destroyed from outside unless the overall network running it is too.

Portability: All cryptocurrency requires is access to the internet, making it far more portable than any purse, wallet, or gold bullion.

Divisibility: Crypto can be divide into a micro fraction of a fiat cent.

Intrinsic Value: The underlying math of dependable UTXO chains means that consensus currency tokens share scarcity characteristics with gold and other valuable commodities — the more formidable the UTXO chain, the better the intrinsic value of its currency.

That crypto is near-perfect Aristotelian money does not mean that crypto will necessarily replace fiat as a means of exchange. The scarcity of hard currency can lead to deflative economics and hoarding (much like gold), where fiat currency can operate in a significantly more liquid fiscal environment. A fiat system's dilution of the value of each dollar or peso discourages savings and encourages the exchange of money for goods, services, and assets.

The breadth of adoption of fiat to denominate trillions of dollars in transactions distracts us from the relativity of fiat's value. Both authors were born in 1987 - if our grandparents had left $1000 in a bank account, that money would be worth about $415 as of this writing. Also, fiat currencies are always in flux with each other ('floating'), in such a way that they are not that stable. While a dollar or yen will always be stable relative to itself, it is not stable relative to goods and services.

Housing, education, healthcare, and other essentials continue to get more expensive in dollar terms despite not having become qualitatively more valuable. Present-day crypto, on the other hand, is too small not to be affected by the exchange of large amounts of value, making it volatile and non-ideal for most transactions. Based on the quantity of fiat circulating, one might argue that it is more volatile than crypto based on its behavior past credit crises.

Crypto has demonstrated the potential to serve as a better store of value than many fiat systems. Venezuela, where socialist economics and bad public policy have slaughtered the value of the nation's fiat currency, is only one example. Where blockchains are subject to technical risks such as the 51% attack, fiat currencies are subject to geopolitical risks. The demand for money determines its value, and in the most simple terms, inflation is an instance of more currency being required to acquire a real asset.

As centrally managed fiat systems go through a series of boom and bust cycles, the money supply increases over time. While this is generally positive for economies when maintained well and encourages investment, the aggregate quantity of 'money' has generally outstripped the productive uses for it at any one time.

Monetary policy over the long run results in large pools of capital that seeks to preserve its value and generate returns and the magnitude of the funds involved tends to incentivize finding a so-called 'risk-free rate of return,' as is provided by government bonds.

Governments such as the U.S. generally issue bonds as a mechanism to borrow from this pool of capital to support present-day spending above the rate that is supported by the present-day economy and taxation.

Compared to other nations, the US enjoys a significant advantage in being able to borrow money at a cheaper rate than other countries, which incentivizes populism and unsustainable debt-fueled economics ordered by politicians and not productivity.

If the US Dollar were to lose global primacy as a reserve currency, the dollar would lose value relative to all other global currencies. We can never *change* a coin or dollar into another currency; we can only *exchange* one form of money or asset for another. In a way, this shows the beauty of assets and data - everything maintains its uniqueness - while some things might be disassembled or lose value, money is a fundamental kind of information.

Should a currency lose relative value, either on the supply side (more money printed) or by losing global primacy and traction on the demand side, inflation will result. When people race to put their money into an asset (say, real estate), that means more money is chasing fewer goods, resulting in asset price inflation.

It would be apt here to discuss Gresham's Law. The law's namesake was a Tudor financier, who advised Queen Elizabeth I on the dynamics affecting the English Shilling as a result of the Henry VIII and Edward IV's policies of debasing of the English currency. Elizabeth I's father and grandfather had replaced silver with base metals such as nickel to raise funds without increasing taxes, leading people to hoard the scarcer currency.

Gresham's law states that in a marketplace with more than one kind of money, people will use the "bad" (debased) currency for transactions and hoard the "good" currency, which holds higher intrinsic value. This dynamic was observed not only by Gresham but also by Copernicus (1473 –1543) in Poland and well as Ibn Taimiyya (1263–1328) and al-Maqrizi (1364–1442) of the Mamluk empire.

Gresham and his Islamic predecessors were operating in a world where precious metal got stamped as a guarantee of its measure. This form of money was physical and scarce. Ultimately, as Nobel Laureate Robert Mundell points out, Gresham's law describes this dynamic of flotation where debasement affected new coins. Dictated value diverged from their real value, which was lower.

With the fall of several centralized economies with currencies not backed by high productivity or value creation, economic thought refined Gresham's law to accommodate the existence of multiple currencies. When currency *fails as money* - when its demand collapses because it's just *that* worthless, a value-backed means of exchange will generally replace it.

As above, the value of money gets underwritten by the demand for it - if there is no demand to denominate one's wealth in a currency (say, Venezuelan Bolivars), then people will flee from its use. In the Weimar Republic, this dynamic led to farmers hoarding food since exchanging it for Reichsbank notes would rapidly leave them with less value than the food was worth.

You can't eat a Reichsbanknote, but you might be able to exchange a bushel of grain for a new pair of shoes. This utility can mean that a cryptocurrency can provide an exit to a dying fiat system. Insofar as buyers can translate dying fiat notes into crypto and denominate future transactions in crypto, they have a way out.

Crypto also enables the same user to triangulate value from one fiat system to another where no efficient direct link is available, allowing them to preserve wealth and translate it into a working fiat system (say, Dollars, Euros, Yen). A developed fiat system such as the dollar benefits from the existence of a mechanism that allows people to translate their wealth back into dollars. If the same method gets used in a manner analogous to gold, it provides an index to the economy and a hedge against inflation.

We believe that the unique attributes of crypto make it a compliment to fiat currency more than an outright rival, and foresee sovereign states exploring crypto as an extension of their national monetary policies. There are multiple ways of going about this. States could adopt an advanced UTXO model if they wish to have the currency operate globally as a means of denominating trade and as a global store of value. Or they could adopt a more "walled garden" approach, whitelisting who can hold and exchange the assets as the People's Bank of China is doing.

Imagine a state-issued financial asset where foreign banks get disbarred from affecting the currency through trading, sanctions, or other economic measures. This maneuver is the antithesis of Satoshi's apparent motive in creating Bitcoin, though the bastardization of cryptocurrency is a natural policy goal for states that want to replace the US dollar as a global reserve currency or undermine Bitcoin and other decentralized stores of value. More open, capitalist systems can leverage a state-backed UTXO model to facilitate wealth transfer into their country - as crypto is more fluid than the existing international banking system, at the expense of countries hostile to capital.

Assets

Cryptocurrency, as *just* currency, is innovative but isn't necessarily earth-shattering. "It's a digital analog to gold with some superior characteristics in terms of portability, fungibility, and so on. So what?"

One of the greatest innovations of the blockchain is the process of using the blockchain not to issue just currency, but to represent unique assets *digitally*. Which we predict will be more influential than the cryptocurrency itself and will drive a significant amount of capital into crypto, through whichever protocols future applications get successfully built on top.

This digital representation is where fungibility comes in. One dollar is perfectly exchangeable for another, one bitcoin for one bitcoin, and so on. The currency has the same value in both embodiments. This interchangeability follows for some assets too - in real terms, gold is a physical asset, and a gram at a given purity is the same value as any other. You don't really 'have' gold if you can't hold it in your hand.

You might be able to buy a gold futures contract from your broker, but what you have is a representation of the physical asset, not the asset itself. You might even have *a claim* on *an amount* of gold which can get traced to a definite safe by following a long paper trail and underwriting standards. But it's not as if you own 1/4 of the 2nd ingot from the left on shelf 1138 at Ft. Knox, which is definitely there and hasn't been secreted away by some maniacal Bond villain under the noses of the U.S. Government.

Blockchain applications allow for a much more specific valuation of assets because it provides for the appropriate identification of those assets. It's one thing to exchange an ounce of gold from one gold bar for another, you still own an ounce of gold, which is mutually fungible insofar as the purity hasn't changed. It is entirely something else to hold a fraction of a one-in-a-kind asset. Imagine owning 1/37th of an original Picasso or Chagall as an investment. One could divide the value of the painting. This divisibility would lower the barriers to entry and allow for a new kind of investment.

This new mechanism for effectively generating non-dilutionary stock for real-world assets will revolutionize finance and will enable investors to apply and store their wealth in a much more discreet, efficient manner. Instead of exchanging an ounce of gold for another ounce of gold, a claim on a Mattise is only directly fungible with another proportional demand on the same painting.

Investment in an artwork can be divided much like stock in a company. And unlike stocks which can be diluted by the issuance of new shares or by complex derivatives such as naked short selling, an asset on a blockchain can be divided while forbidding dilution. This division gets done according to the rules it is issued by, and with the exchange verified and linked to other regulations and conditions that make the transaction feasible and efficient.

In real terms, this is a matter of cryptographically hashing the core details of a contract and adding it to the blockchain, where it is verified and added to the ledger for future reference.

As with all prior systems of writing, the characteristics of the blockchain will enable an entirely new generation of securities and assets. In addition to the security and financial characteristics of the chain, the ability to represent ontologies and conditions in a decentralized ledger operating on rules of consensus is a massive leap in the securities and exchange discipline. Imagine owning a fraction of a pro sports team, with ticket sales providing a contractual dividend. Imagine owning season tickets that you can loan out electronically and treat as an asset.

New forms of securities will open access to financing for the next generation of consumers. People will be using applications built on a blockchain without even knowing it. These applications will also enable superior compliance and analysis of assets as they are traded and divided.

Imagine if all the mortgages securitized by banks in the mid-2000s got transparently organized in a legible database that relayed mortgage defaults, late payments, and property valuations. This system would have enabled banks, lenders, regulators, and everyday consumers to recognize the bubble before payments began dropping off, who owned what assets within a given Collateralized Debt Obligation (CDO), and what the topography of systemic risk in the financial system was.

Rating agencies wouldn't have been handing out AAA credit ratings if there were a transparent and publicly verifiable system such as a real UTXO blockchain. Toxic assets would be immediately recognizable, and perhaps part of the 2008 credit crisis could have been mitigated in a way beneficial to banks, regulators, and, most importantly, the American people and the global economy.

Conclusion

Blockchain technology emulates the characteristics that we observe in physical reality, including the linearity and path dependency of the flow of time, the inalterability of the past and contingency of the present, and the ability to represent ontologies, rules, and conditions that exist across a window of time. It is a new structure for the information that is vital to our species and our civilization. Further, it exists in the tradition of innovations and scientific discoveries that we as a species have used to track time and explore the relations involved in our physical world, as well as to capitalize on and order them.

Working up the stack, just like other technologies, it provides for a series of massive applications that would not have been feasible before. Because it emulates physical reality and allows us to represent it, the blockchain has the technical potential to improve our ability to interact with the world and each other by better describing and expressing it, much in the tradition of past systems of timekeeping before it.

Much like a new way of writing or speaking human language, the syntax of the blockchain enables a new authoritative system of exchange that is not as vulnerable to misunderstanding and manipulation as prior systems and has the potential to enrich a new era in financial economics and information technology.

In the next chapter, we will explore some specific technical ways that blockchain technology can be used to rebuild the internet in a much more secure and decentralized manner.

Chapter 6: Blockchain, Rebuilding the Internet & Web 3.0

> *"For people who want to make sure the Web serves humanity, we have to concern ourselves with what people are building on top of it."*
>
> *-Tim Berners Lee*

The internet is the nervous system for the modern world. Unfortunately, the internet never was created with user security as a top priority. The web has become the critical backbone for the majority of services we use to conduct our daily lives. As we go about our everyday business, it is now almost impossible to interact with another person, company, or media outlet without using the internet. We are now living in an era where people only know that things exist by learning about them through digital mediums or devices connected to the internet.

Despite the number of critical services that we use daily depend on the internet, it retains several core flaws that it has had since its inception. Juniper Research recently estimated that the cost of cybercrime in 2019 would reach $2.1 Trillion globally. Every day you hear new stories of a companies data or business systems getting hacked. In this chapter, we discuss in detail the three Achilles heels of the internet and how properly applied blockchain technology fixes them.

The internet was never designed to be secure, as the original ARPANET was nothing more than government and academic research personnel at securely isolated institutions talking to each other. They trusted each other and did not have a reason to add in security measures such as encryption to the original TCP/IP protocol. These flaws continue to this day to expose us to hacking, corporate surveillance, and fraudulent identity theft that should not exist. Chances are everyone reading this book has been a recent victim of identity theft or a centralized data breach. Don't worry. We have a plan, a strategy, and a way of describing exactly how we can fix this global cybersecurity crisis with blockchain technology. Properly applied decentralized blockchain technology can fix 95% of today's Internet cybersecurity vulnerabilities.

For us to advance into the future, we must begin rearchitecting, reengineering, and reimagining fundamental parts of the internet in a much more secure, decentralized, and robust fashion. To explain exactly how this needs to happen, we first need to analyze the essential components of how the Internet functions today.

The simplest explanation I can think of for explaining the exact way the Internet functions today is to imagine a giant spiderweb. You have millions upon millions of interconnected smartphones, laptops, and servers, as well as many IoT devices. These physical devices are often part of smaller connected webs or "intranets" hosted by corporations, governments, and private individuals, yet they all speak the same two basic fundamental languages.

These languages are known as *Internet Protocol* (IP) and *Transmission Control Protocol* (TCP). The internet protocol at its heart is nothing more than a routing network directing TCP packets of data between devices connected through the web, from IP address to IP address. Think of an IP address as a phone number to connect to a specific computer on the network. Back in the early days, researchers had physical IP address books (think Yellow Pages) that they would use to look up other research colleague's computers to send files to their machines across the country.

When I navigate from my smartphone to the server hosting the *DigiByte.io* website, a TCP packet gets sent from my phone IP address assigned by my mobile carrier to the IP address assigned to the DigiByte.io server. This process fundamentally has not changed since DARPA developed TCP/IP in the late 60s/ early 70s. However, just like you probably don't memorize every person's actual phone number that you have in your phones contact book, it doesn't make sense to expect people to remember and type in the IP address 3.15.145.157 (actual DigiByte.io IP) every time they want to visit the main DigiByte.io website.

Enter DNS or *Domain Name Servers*. In the '90s, people got the idea of creating names for their IP addresses, much like you and

I look up people in our phone's contacts by name. Enter the .com craze, boom, bust, and modern-day internet as we know it. These domain names could, in theory, be anything, yet as we see today, a name ending in ".com" still sells for a premium.

A DNS server maintains a mapping of all the known domain names in existence and their corresponding server IP addresses. There are several DNS servers globally, but they are highly centralized, with only a few controlling the majority of internet traffic. Typically, your internet service provider, as well as a few other providers, handle the majority of DNS server requests. Given that this is mostly a book about the benefits of decentralization, you probably should not like hearing that the global DNS system is highly centralized. So that is for a good reason. We believe there are three Achilles heels for the internet, and one of them is our over-reliance on DNS servers.

Any time you have a majority of web traffic flowing through a central point of failure, trouble is always around the corner. Enter DNSjacking. If we can take over one of these few DNS servers, we can conduct a man in the middle attack and point your DNS query to any malicious website we want. Alternatively, even worse, an attacker can shut down entire parts of the internet at will.

On October 21st, 2016, a massive Distributed Denial of Service (DDoS) attacked target the DNS service provider Dyn. A DDoS attack is where thousands or millions of hacked IoT devices, phones, and servers send requests to a specific IP address and overload the single server or service provider. Dyn at the time was the primary IP address book and DNS provider for the majority of the entire East Coast of the United States. For several hours millions of people could not navigate to their favorite websites and services or discover new sites. This over-reliance on a single point of failure by thousands of other service providers should serve as a wake-up call for better internet architecture. Just imagine what a massive coordinated attack by a nation-state on DNS servers would achieve. I have no doubt a coordinated attack by Russia or China against US-based DNS servers could effectively shut the US internet down at will, and for a prolonged period.

We will talk more about what allows DDOS attacks to be possible later on, and how they get prevented with blockchain technology, but for the time being, know they are a threat that grows more disturbing every day. In a 2019 survey carried out by the intelligence firm IDC, the average cost of recovering from a single DNS attack is $1.07 million for an ordinary company in 2018. Their 2018 report concluded that in 2017, the global cost of cyber attacks was $1 Trillion compared to $300 billion for natural disasters.

No DNS, No Cloud.

By 2021, IDC predicts over 90% of enterprise businesses will be using multiple cloud services and platforms. In multi-cloud deployments, DNS services play a pivotal role in enabling access to cloud services, routing traffic to on-premise and external applications. The research demonstrates a strong dependency on cloud-based applications on DNS services. 63% of companies worldwide suffered cloud service downtime as a result of DNS attacks in 2018 up from 40% in 2017. The trends are clear, attacks are getting worse, and the core underlying problem of reliance on an outdated centralized service known as DNS on top of TCP/IP is not getting fixed. Blockchain technology will fix this Achilles heel.

The first attempt at fixing DNS problems with blockchain technology came with the creation of the Namecoin (NMC) blockchain in 2011. Namecoin was indeed the very first innovative project to fork the Bitcoin core source code for a use-case outside of payments. Just like with Bitcoin, there will only ever be 21 million NMC mined. Namecoin is merge mined (which they also invented) with Bitcoin, and their blockchain continues to this day.

The main difference is instead of only sending payments like with BTC; you also have the ability even to create a .bit top-level domain name that resides on the namecoin blockchain. The beauty of this system is that it exists entirely outside of the DNS system and is completely decentralized. When you look up a .bit domain name, the query searches the blockchain for the info you need much quicker than a standard DNS query. You do not need to rely on a centralized third party, and there is no need to pay crazy fees to domain name registrars like GoDaddy. Why should you have to pay a centralized third party to name your website? Who gave them all the power? Your parents never had to pay to provide you with a name you. With blockchain DNS technology, you are genuinely free to choose domain names on the internet without the hassle or approval of a third party.

Namecoin was also the first solution to Zooko's Triangle, the long-standing problem of producing a naming system that is simultaneously secure, decentralized, and human-meaningful. Zooko's triangle is a trilemma of three properties that are generally considered desirable for the names of participants in a network protocol.

Human-meaningful: Meaningful and memorable (low-entropy) names are provided to the users.

Secure: The amount of damage a malicious entity can inflict on the system should be as low as possible.

Decentralized: Names correctly resolve to their respective entities without the use of a central authority or service.

A properly designed blockchain DNS is indeed secure, decentralized, and human-meaningful. Multiple blockchain projects are working on leveraging blockchain technology to fix the DNS problem, including DigiByte. However, before we go into greater detail on how blockchain technology permanently solves the DNS problem, we need to address the second Achilles heel.

Root Certificate Authorities & SSL/TLS Certificates

Have you ever gone to your bank's website and looked up in the corner of your Internet browser and saw the little lock icon next to the site's URL and wondered how it works? That icon is letting you know that you have a secure, encrypted connection to your bank's web server from your computer or phone. While this helps to protect you against the majority of known cyber threats, it is far from being 100% secure or trustworthy.

The problem is that this secure connection relies on something known as an SSL or TLS certificate. SSL certificate stands for secure socket layer, while TLS stands for transport layer security. SSL was published in 1996 and deprecated in 2015 and got replaced by TLS as the recommend secondary encryption layer built on top of TCP/IP. TLS is essentially an upgraded version of SSL. SSL and TLS were created to create secure, encrypted channels within the TCP/IP Internet stack. SSL and TLS allow for secure end to end communication between a server like the one that hosts your bank's website and a client device such as your laptop or mobile phone.

 TLS & SSL certificates are issued by what is known as a root certificate authority or CA for short. The problem with certificate authorities is there is only a handful of them worldwide. Root certificate authorities preinstall their root set of public keys on Windows and Mac OS as well as android and iOS before you buy a new device.

 These first preinstalled sets of public keys are how your computer knows the public/private key produced by a website's SSL or TLS cert is indeed valid, and your bank is whom they say they are on the web and not a malicious hacker. This security all works great in theory, as long as you trust the original root certificate authority who issues your bank's SSL/ TLS cert to keep it safe from hackers, political pressure from authoritarian governments, or pure complacency.

 These companies do indeed go through extreme lengths and measures to keep their primary root private keys secure that are used to issue SSL & TLS certificates. We are talking underground bunkers with James Bond-level sci-fi security systems and elaborate private key exchange protocols and ceremonies. It's a fascinating industry to study. However, once again, there is a significant centralization problem as these root certificate authorities become central points of failure.

 In 2018 76.9% of all SSL certificates issued were issued by only three root certificate authorities worldwide. IdenTrust, Comodo, and DigiCert. The top five certificate authorities accounted for 97.6% of all SSL/TSL certificates issued in 2018. This incredible centralization of the most sensitive encryption component of the internet means only five sets of root public/private keys held by private businesses secure 97% of all encrypted SSL/TSL infrastructure on the entire internet. These central points of failure are also how nation-states attack each other after compromising root certificate authorities or by merely creating a CA themselves. Once you have the keys to the internet kingdom, who is there to stop you? This point of failure is the ultimate internet backdoor no one ever dares talks about in public.

In 2011 the Dutch root certificate authority DigiNotar was hacked and completely compromised after over 500 fraudulent certificates were issued, which then compromised a large chunk of the internet. The Dutch government quickly took control of DigiNotar, and the company soon filed bankruptcy. It's theorized that this hack was most likely the work of one nation-state targeting another; in this case, the target was probably Iran. Because DigiNotar supplied SSL and TLS certificates for the majority of the Dutch government that year, most critical Dutch government services were offline for some time, and citizens even had to file their taxes with paper forms.

Certificate authorities issue SSL & TLS certificates in a heavily centralized manner. On top of this, these five' CA's charge you when they issue you or your business an SSL or TLS certificate. This charge can range anywhere from $7 to $40,000 a year. This cost is insane considering SSL & TLS certificates fundamentally the same way as your public/private keys do in a Bitcoin or DigiByte wallet. With a decentralized blockchain, you are already your own root certificate authority, and you didn't even know it.

Moreover, it costs you nothing to set up a wallet and generate a set of public and private keys to secure all aspects of your digital life. This method is how you can protect your data, with public and private keys that only you control anchored into a decentralized public blockchain. Numerous projects are being built on top of the DigiByte blockchain leveraging this feature of blockchain technology. Some of these projects include Digi-ID, DigiPad, VESTi, AntumID, DiguSign, and DigiAssets.

Passwords

Passwords are the third Achilles heel of the internet. The reality is that most passwords are almost entirely useless from protecting you against large-scale data breaches and hacks. Without two-factor or multi-factor authentication, most systems can be quickly either brute forced or hacked as most people do not use sufficiently secure enough passwords and frequently reuse passwords for years at a time, and across multiple accounts and devices.

Think for a minute and count the number of times you have used the same personal password across email accounts, online services, and computers. You probably have three or four favorites that, if compromised, would open the door to dozens of your other accounts, including your bank, bill pay, your medical appointments, and other sensitive data. Always make sure to create long, varied passphrases containing special characters at a minimum.

What if you do everything right, and your data still gets stolen because someone else was lazy with their password? This indifference occurs regularly and is the downside of companies storing millions of users data in a single centralized database, which creates a central point of failure.

Shortly following the Equifax breach in 2017, where 143 million Americans lost everything relating to their identity, it got discovered one of Equifax's centralized databases could get accessed with nothing more than username: admin, password: admin. Admin/admin is the default set of credentials often issued by numerous data and software systems upon initial setup.

So how do we fix the password problem? Using 2 Factor Authentication ("2FA") is a start and should be a standard for every platform, but it is often a hassle for people to use for most services. What if we completely stopped using passwords and replaced them with blockchain private key authentication and 2FA? Enter what we call a personal blockchain portal or PBP.

The personal blockchain portal is a physical device used to interact with a blockchain wallet to authenticate your identity with other web-based services. Think of it as an apple wallet on steroids.

A personal blockchain portal or device can and will be a wallet used to store and secure not only financial assets but your essential digital assets such as a birth certificate, ID, or a living will. It will also be able to authenticate you across numerous services and platforms and to other people.

One real-world device that could get used for this is a blockchain hardware wallet such as BitFI that does not permanently store your private keys on any particular device. Instead, you would use a brain phrase to access all your valuable assets. We will explain BitFi more in Chapter 10.

Digi-ID

If you would like to get started today by using blockchain private keys to replace all the passwords you use daily. Jared and the DigiByte developers have been working on something called DigiID for the past few years. Digi-ID allows you to use your blockchain wallet private keys to sign in and authenticate yourself with different services without the need for handling passwords. You can go to Digi-ID.io to learn more. It is an open-source technology that any developers can integrate, or any other commercial companies can build out within their internal technology stacks.

Antum ID

One such exciting company that has taken Digi-ID to the next level is the European-based Antum ID. Check them out at Antumid.be. Antum has released a browser plugin they call "DigiPassword" that works with Chromium-based browsers. These include Chrome, Opera, Brave, Firefox, and Microsoft Edge. DigiPassword allows you to use the DigiByte blockchain to replace all your existing passwords on the web platforms you use daily.

Named Data Networking

Now that we have covered the three Achilles heels Of the Internet and how we can fix them with blockchain technology, it's time to turn up the heat and shift everything we just talked about on its head.

Currently, most blockchains still communicate in a P2P fashion over TCP/IP. This method is an extremely inefficient thing to do. We believe in the future blockchain protocols like Bitcoin and DigiByte will integrate a new concept known as Named Data Networking or NDN.

Named data networking brings the concept of object-oriented programming to networking. For those not familiar with the idea of object-oriented programming, let's explain in detail how it works. Up until the 70s, programming consisted of writing code that was executed procedurally, meaning that it started the top line of the program and sequentially progressed through the entire application before ending. This style of programming was very ineffective because it resulted in lots and lots of duplicated code. It's like being required to read through an entire book until you find the section you are looking for, instead of just opening to the page you were trying to find.

In the mid-70s, programmers began to realize that if they thought of an individual section of code often reused as an object that instead of proceeding line by line code over and over in their program, they could jump around and reference other parts of code, or objects. Then code could be written once and reused much more efficiently.

This way of thinking can get easily applied to a network. Imagine for a second what takes place when you go on your mobile phone and navigate to a YouTube video. Your phone first sends a TCP/IP packet to your mobile carrier's DNS server asking for the location of the YouTube server. The DNS server then forwards the video request to the YouTube server. The YouTube server then check's internally in its database to find the movie file you request and then returns that initial request to your mobile phone.

This process is much more straightforward with Named Data Networking. Your phone looks up the YouTube movie by name, and there are no DNS servers, routers, or other middle steps. In happens in one request, thereby eliminating thousands of unnecessary round-robin requests needed with today's internet architecture.

With NDN, there are no more IP addresses or TCP packets. Instead, the video itself becomes an object that can be directly queried and located on a blockchain with its name. NDN will dramatically accelerate the speed of all existing data connections. Several groups and projects are working on this as we speak.

Now that we have discussed many of the ways the current internet can get fixed with properly applied blockchain technology, its vital for us to discuss blockchain in terms of the internet of things. In Chapter 7, we will take a deeper dive into IoT and how blockchain technology can secure these devices to make our everyday lives safer, more affordable, and more efficient.

Chapter 7: Securing the Internet of Things on a Blockchain

"The internet is no longer a web that we connect to. Instead, it's a computerized, networked, and interconnected world that we live in. This is the future, and what we're calling the Internet of Things."

- Bruce Schneiner

"I believe that at the end of the century the use of words and general educated opinion will have altered so much that one will be able to speak of machines thinking without expecting to be contradicted."

– Alan Turing

From our last chapter, we covered the core architecture of the internet, and how blockchain and distributed cryptography offer a new way to manage identity, data, and communication online. This evolution applies to everything built on the internet, not just surfing the web. Everything from e-commerce to the internet of things to artificial Intelligence will be affected by blockchain, and someday we will likely look back at today's internet in the same light we see 56k modems and dial tones over a phone line.

The best place to start is with the "Internet of Things" (IoT), which is the vast network of web-connected devices in our homes, offices, and streets, all of which connect to the broader internet and the internet platforms that operate and maintain them. Every day more and more devices are being connected to the web beyond just mobile phones and computers. Refrigerators, thermostats, autonomous vacuum cleaners, sound systems, washing machines, hardware such as your Fitbit or smartwatch, and even now light bulbs are Wi-Fi enabled.

IoT has given us a world where everything is modifiable, monitored, and integrated. It is a massive marketplace where specific companies have billions of devices deployed across the globe. This proliferation is so immense that North America ran out of IP addresses built in the original IPv4 format in the fall of 2015. According to IT infrastructure firm CISCO Systems, there are anticipated to be 50 Billion IoT devices online by 2020 - just a year from this writing.[2]

In so many ways the proliferation of IoT is a remarkable extension of technology in a way that past generations might have imagined on *The Jetsons*, but never anticipated in real, technical terms, one technology built upon another. The IoT gives us new ways to monitor our health, our homes, to track our belongings when and if we misplace them, to automate and perfect the more tedious aspects of daily life, such as cleaning our homes.

This silver lining is not without its cloud: every one of these devices is an attack vector against the broader network and can be repurposed to support botnets, DDoS attacks, and network infiltration. Today's Internet of Things is a physical reflection of the openness and untethered connectivity of Web 2.0, but that openness and connectivity should have limits, especially in our homes.

Despite this, many IoT devices and their manufacturers still reflect the insecurity of the underlying internet, exposing users and corporations to substantial risk should the systems be compromised or used maliciously. One popular connected doorbell and home security platform, for example, is rumored only to use one set of private keys to secure tens of thousands of homes.

This proliferation is as crucial to the advance of AI and other services as it is to mere IoT applications, as IoT platforms are ultimately about data, both collecting it and arranging it. IoT is the

---

[2] Nihar Pachpande. *50 Billion Devices Connected by 2020.* Medium, 25 March 2018. Available at https://medium.com/datadriveninvestor/50-billion-connected-devices-by-2020-b55e0656f5c9

forefront of where most data involved in modern AI research and commerce gets gathered, from the sensors in self-driving cars to facial recognition and fraud detection. Because it deals with data, physical platforms, and transactions those devices make across broader internet, IoT needs robust security.

Add to this the fact that most of today's IoT devices are manufactured abroad and experience minimal technical scrutiny when imported to the West. Globalized supply chains for IoT open up countries to supply chain attacks, where the manufacturer inserts malicious hardware backdoors, malware, and deliberate expiry dates within their products. This dynamic also exists in the cryptocurrency mining realm, with Bitmain and other Chinese ASIC manufacturers publicly acknowledging that they had included backdoors to their products. [3]

These backdoors may have allowed mining manufacturers to shut down customer's miners or potentially redirect proceeds from customer's mining back to themselves. This potential scenario has the consumer buying an ASIC and paying for the electricity to run it, but not reaping the full rewards of their investment. Alternatively, IoT hacks can and have been used to facilitate parasitic crypto mining, especially for privacy coins.

These bot networks operate by stealing computing power and energy from consumers without tracing back to the beneficiary. While some might think the idea of your washing machine or refrigerator spying on you is overblown, imagine a foreign company having access to your bank account, online identity, and social media through devices with which you never intended to share that information.

Much of the world's IoT is grossly insecure. To us, this is an enormous issue, as it creates exposure for both users and companies

---

[3] Andrew Quentson. *Exclusive: Jihan Wu Confirms Backdoor in Bitcoin Miner Bitmain*. CCN.com, 27 April 2017. Available at < https://www.ccn.com/jihan-wu-confirms-claims-of-a-backdoor-in-bitmain-apologizes-says-its-a-bug>

who rely on IoT, and threatens the privacy, data, and financial security of both. Blockchain and Web 3.0 offer a new way to secure this immense domain, and that is the topic of this chapter.

Defining IoT, Smart Devices, and Connected Devices

For this chapter, we are using the term "IoT" broadly, to encompass all devices (i.e., *things*) connected to the internet. This category includes all connected devices, such as hue-adjustable light bulbs, to "smart" devices, like a thermostat that turns off when you're not home. In this setting, the Internet of Things, much like the Force, binds the galaxy of connected devices together.

Every IoT device has a soul made of data, which captures all of the various kinds of things it can do and when and how it does them. Your washing machine has several cycles, it can wash on cold, hot, gentle, permanent press, and so on, and a connected washer will have sensors embedded not just to detect that process but to represent those facts to the user and back to the manufacturer or any other relevant connected party.

Occasionally, this data gets referred to as a 'virtual twin or a 'ghost' - a lot like the Cartesian conception of the soul. This 'digital ghost' is a model of what the machine does, informed through its built-in sensors, and a model of what it can do. Ultimately the device is defined by its software as much as its hardware.

This digital ghost is part of the spectrum of IoT that stretches from merely connecting a device to the internet to having sensors that detect and verify the function of the machine, to having the device generate data and feedback that is valuable to the user and whoever runs the IoT platform. It's one thing to simply be able to turn on your washing machine with your phone, it's another for a sensor to monitor that the appliance isn't destroying your favorite shirt by regulating the heat, detergent mix, and spin cycle, and it's a third thing for that data to be clustered and analyzed by the manufacturer.

What makes the IoT powerful is the depth and breadth of data it can gather by sensing it and generating items and events. There is no Internet of Things without the internet *and* things, and neither the internet or those things are meaningful, significant, or useful unless the data they produce is recognizable.

The use of a product should not include compulsory surveillance and monitoring. Thankfully, many devices do allow for permissions, but many do not, and even if we consent to the manufacturer accessing the data, most IoT products contain substantial gaps in security that can be exploited by a third party. Because IoT deals with this massive galaxy of information, it only makes sense that our devices' digital ghosts will see the improvements created by blockchain and Web 3.0 - both for management and security.

IoT Insecurity

According to a 2018 report by DigiCert titled "State of IoT Security Survey 2018," 92% of companies will incorporate IoT devices into their business by 2020. The same survey goes on to state that 100% of bottom tier respondents believe they will suffer a cyberattack against their IoT devices. These attacks include DDOS, unauthorized access, and DNS hijacking of centralized control points used to control or communicate with these devices.

Another report by Zscaler, which analyzed over 56 million IoT device transactions from 1,051 enterprise networks over the course of a month, found 91.5% of these occurred unencrypted. It's not hard to see why most companies believe they will get attacked when most of them are not even bothering to secure their devices.

The solution to this problem is simple. Just issue each device a blockchain set of public and private keys and address used to authenticate itself, manage its own identity, and encrypt its communications to other devices. To take it a step further, use a blockchain, along with named data networking, to control the way these devices get discovered and communicate. This move alone would thwart the majority of DDoS attacks.

IoT Devices Contribute to DDoS & Other Cyber Attacks

One troubling and often misunderstood fact is that unsecured IoT devices getting hijacked by a botnet are usually the primary tools used to launch DDoS attacks in the first place. Because most IoT devices get manufactured with no encryption and security is an afterthought.

Because of this, it is often trivial for botnet creators to hijack these devices. Even if a device does incorporate encryption, chances are every device of the same type will use the same root set of public and private keys.

Mirai Botnet

On October 12, 2016, a massive DDoS attack left much of the internet inaccessible on the US east coast, as we mention in chapter 6. The attack was initially thought to be the work of a foreign adversary or nation-state. The Mirai botnet employed hundreds of thousands of hijacked IoT devices to bring down Dyn as we previously mentioned. The attack, as brutal as it became, had a much more juvenile beginning.

The creators of Mirai were 22-year-old Paras Jha Fanwood, and 21-year-old Josiah White, who launched the botnet to gain the upper hand on a series of Minecraft servers they were attempting to extort. Minecraft is a popular video game often played by younger children.

This plan quickly got out of hand; the next thing they knew, the botnet had shut down half the internet on the US Eastern Seaboard. Fanwood and White had pointed these hijacked IoT devices at the DNS provider Dyn, who handled name server requests for the targeted Minecraft server.

What's even crazier is that only 61 default usernames and passwords powered the Miria botnet. The creators didn't hack any IoT devices; they just scanned the internet for unencrypted IoT devices and tried logging into them with default credentials. The fact that four-hundred thousand devices were unencrypted and using username and password combinations like *admin:* *"admin",* *user:* *"user," guest:* *"12345,"* and *root:* *"root"* almost killed the internet should serve as a massive wakeup call.

This incident reinforces what we talked about in chapter 6, where we detail the three Achilles heals of the internet. DNS & SSL centralization and our over-reliance on passwords. This attack occurred because of the failures of all three.

In a properly architected blockchain IoT environment, this would have never happened. This example is just one of many. Because Mirai got open-sourced, it has been morphed and used to conduct countless more attacks by leveraging IoT insecurities across billions of devices.

Imagine for a moment you had just purchased yourself a brand new self-driving car. All across the world, there are plans to embed IoT sensors in roadways to aid self-driving cars. The majority of these plans we have seen suffer from the same vulnerabilities most other IoT devices do. Often the choice is made to forgo encryption in favor of speed and development, just like when the internet got created. History is indeed repeating itself.

Do you want to rely on thousands of unencrypted IoT devices while driving down the road just waiting to be hijacked by malware? We, as authors, sure don't, and that's why you won't be seeing these authors drive a self-driving car anytime soon.

Vint Cerf's Principles for an Ideal Internet of Things

We must define our terms, and there are few better places to look for wisdom than to Vint Cerf, currently the "Chief Internet Evangelist" at Google and one of the core architects of the internet as we know it today.

Cerf is one of the two inventors of the TCP-IP protocol[4] which governs internet traffic to this day, and which we covered earlier in this book. Cerf is, by all means, one of the original gangsters of the internet era, and his opinion carries significant weight when it comes to defining the challenges of today's internet. On March 20, 2018, Cerf did precisely that, outlining what principles can and should be involved in the Internet of Things speaking at the Claude

---

[4] along with Bob Kahn.

Shannon Lecture Series for Nokia Bell Labs in New Jersey.[5] These principles are as follows:

- IoT devices should be **reliable**, just as a light switch is reliable. They should turn on when you tell them to turn on, and off when you ask them to turn off.
- IoT devices should be **safe to use**, and their integration should not make the device they are part of less safe. The requirement of safety goes for locks on homes, self-driving cars, medical implants, and every other technology that cradles human life, safety, and well-being as we use it.
- IoT devices should be **secure**. They should not be themselves vulnerable to attacks, and they should not be so insecure as to provide a backdoor or trojan horse into the ecosystem that you and I use to integrate them into our lives and networks as consumers.
- IoT devices should **preserve privacy**. They should not facilitate unwanted surveillance into our lives, and should not violate our trust.
- IoT devices need to be **interoperable**. Internet of things isn't an internet of things if machines cannot interact with one another and with the broader network. Needing a different app, controller, or interface for every device is a net negative because it is inconvenient and difficult to manage.
- IoT needs to be **autonomous**, not reliant on constant access to electricity and data connections.

These ideals are each desirable by themselves, yet some become paradoxical when we try to have our cake and eat it too. For example, if devices were extremely interoperable and extremely

---

[5] Vint Cerf. *The Future of the Internet of Things and Desirable Properties for an IoT Ecosystem*. Available at <https://www.youtube.com/watch?v=d6uqO96Mw0E>

easy to integrate, they would likely do so by being substantially less secure, with several ways to get inside a network of IoT devices without the user's permission. Conversely, if all devices were classically secured, with individual usernames, passwords, and independent systems, they may become less interoperable. Imagine having passwords for each connected lightbulb or appliance. IoT devices need to be able to interact with the broader internet, but as they do, they also risk infringing on the privacy of their users, as the data generated can be extremely revealing.

That said, many of these principles are also mutually reinforcing. Take, for example, a connected medical device: by increasing the network security of such a device, the manufacturer decreases the risk to the user (say, in the example of a connected pacemaker, which could be accessed remotely to harm the user as on the American television program *Homeland*). Similarly, the interoperability of devices contributes to their reliability: If I ask my home assistant to turn on the lights, it's helpful that the lights come on even if I have an iPhone, but Siemens or Samsung make my lights.

Those engaged in building or using devices on the Internet of Things are continually facing this series of tradeoffs and challenges. Decentralized blockchains are a revolutionary force for these sets of goals because they enable a new balance of power between users and devices. The present-day architecture does not live up to Cerf's standards, and we think that blockchain will get us closer to an IoT infrastructure that is more compatible with human needs according to those principles.

5G and the Global Capacity for an IoT world

Another critical point to touch on early is the degree of connectivity required to operate the internet of things. The massive growth of IoT puts a substantial strain on the existing web and is one of the driving forces behind the adoption of 5G telecoms infrastructure, which offers substantially better bandwidth to host the hordes of new devices and data anticipated to come online over the 2020s and 2030s.

It was one thing for phones to connect to the network: the internet began when computers could join, and Web 2.0 began when devices like cell phones and televisions could connect and interact. Today, everything is connected, because there is so much data because everything conceivable is integrating itself into our daily lives, there is substantially more data to transmit, store, and process than there was in a world dominated by phones and desktops.

The volume of information to be exchanged by IoT is no small ordeal. Service provider Qualcomm expects that by 2035, more than $12.3 Trillion worth of commerce will occur over 5G, with $1.1 Trillion of that spending on IoT devices for healthcare. This ecosystem enables entirely new forms of personalized healthcare, where user's health data collected by IoT devices (as well as general data gathered from how they interact with the world through other platforms, such as their diet and genetic background) can be integrated to support a personalized health strategy.[6]

These data-rich approaches can improve human health as well as the profitability of the healthcare and technology industries, but they come with an added cost, specifically to the general security of the individual in a world with ubiquitous monitoring of his or her interactions with it. If everything is networked and run by large corporations, then there are natural, legitimate questions to ask about the security of such a system. These are twofold, including both how the user interacts with the networked entities he or she uses and also how that data gets used.

Speaking of health, the evolution of 5G transmissions, notably including a frequency known as *millimeter waves,* raises substantial questions about their impact on human health. According to the US

---

[6] Quallcom. Press Note: *5G Economy: Enabling a New Era of Personalized Health Care and Significant Growth in the Sector. 26 October 2017. Available at* <https://www.qualcomm.com/news/releases/2017/10/26/5g-economy-enabling-new-era-personalized-health-care-and-significant-growth>

National Institute of Health, millimeter waves were conducted by human sweat glands, posing critical questions about the health impacts of 5G technology.[7] While this is outside the topic of blockchain and IoT, it is illustrative of the point that we as users need to understand the impacts of these technologies and how they balance against other human needs and desires before being embraced or adopted impact unseen.

The Internet of Optimization and the All-Knowing Washing Machine

One of the most exciting trends in a world of connected devices is the potential for the industry to find new insights by equipping their products with IoT sensors and using the complex data that is produced to optimize both their manufacture and their application process. With all this refinement, manufactured things break less often, and when they do break, there is a dynamic catalog and logging process to recognize weaknesses and repair them elsewhere.

Similar to auto manufacturers tracking parts failures through their authorized service centers, this extends to the much broader world of gathering data about how and when machines function. Beyond enabling the manufacturer to become aware of defects, which does not necessarily require sensors, this active monitoring can also show the *conditions that triggered the failure*, or during regular operation can identify the *ideal conditions to operate the equipment*.

This analysis includes everything from modeling gear ratios and shift-points in a gearbox, to fuel recommendations and ideal RPM for running an engine, optimizing for either power or efficiency. Unlike the machines of old, the *things* on the Internet of Things are more extensive than just themselves, because they feed

---

[7] Betzalel, Ben Ishai, and Feldman. The human skin as a sub-THz receiver - Does 5G pose a danger to it or not? *Environ Res.* May 2018. Available at: https://www.ncbi.nlm.nih.gov/pubmed/29459303

into a system that compares all devices like them. When you drive a new Toyota Camry today, you experience an evolutionary product built with billions of data points and sensors tested over millions of miles driven in similar cars. Cars are safer and more reliable as a result of all this data.

As IoT proliferates and becomes cheaper to execute, thousands of applications may become feasible for the marketplace to provide, which we thought impossible only a few years ago. Imagine, for example, an IoT approach to laundry. Sounds boring, right? However, imagine that every one of your favorite garments, every shirt, every pair of jeans, had a tiny RFID tag embedded in it that identifies its color, make, and model as well as the chain of acquisition from manufacture to the present.

Such a measure could counter counterfeits for luxury goods as part of the supply chain, but just as importantly this tag could sync with your washing machine and dryer, letting them know what parameters to wash it at to prevent wrinkling, shrinkage, or loss of fabric quality. Every time you throw your laundry in the washer and dryer, it logs the models, checks the ideal wash parameters from an online resource, and sends you an alert if your clothes are too incompatible when washed together, or if there is an item that should be 'dry-clean only.'

In terms of user optimization, this would save the user a significant amount of frustration and would prolong the life of the garments. More sophisticated sensors in the washing machine and dryer might even detect the amount of dirt and lint that come off the load, allowing for optimization and recommendations for how much and what kind of detergent to dispense, as well as managing heat, water, and spin cycle inputs.

From a manufacturer's standpoint, this would enable even more significant improvements and an entirely new reputational economy. Every wash would anonymously log the existence of the garment in the washing machine and timestamp it. That a garment comes back for repeat washes means that it is continually being worn, implying both its popularity with the user and its durability to the wash cycle. Imagine buying a pair of Levis on Amazon and being able to access the average data on longevity, knowing that the pair of jeans you are about to buy lasts an average of 3.8 years and endures an average of 194 washes before being retired by the user!

This data is useful to the consumer, and it rewards quality by the manufacturer, and users will see the addition of a 25 cent smart tag as a signal of trust in a way that labels and brands have been signs of confidence in the past. This evolution of faith could enable manufacturers to prove their merit to retailers by showing proof of quality, popularity, and durability. Operated on a blockchain, the manufacturer now has autonomous and anonymous data to gauge the demand for specific products. He or she can factor this perspective into what to produce, decreasing the inefficiency of the marketplace and the amount of merchandise that goes to the clearance rack.

Connected laundry is an excellent idea in principle, but also one where privacy matters. After all, nothing is closer to us than our underwear, and Maytag has no need to know what our spouses and we wear on those special occasions. Maytag also shouldn't be selling that data to advertisers and platforms like Google - Google doesn't need to know Thursday night is special.

Decentralized, open-source blockchains are critical in accomplishing this process. Data about something as intimate as one's clothing can and should remain private, even though data about clothing generally can work wonders for all sides of the marketplace. In this example, there are two critical applications that are only really possible to execute with real, global, decentralized blockchains: the ability to track and verify the authenticity of articles, which is even more critical when buying higher-end goods, and the ability to secure the sensor (in this case the washer/dryer) that relays data back to the cloud.

For a chain of custody, a decentralized blockchain's ability to timestamp interactions with a specific article or good has multiple benefits. Just like blockchain wallet addresses can be generated infinitely without generating a cryptographic collision (producing the same address twice), so too could unique cryptographic addresses be created for the billions of IoT devices and the many accessories and items that connect to them.

 This is not to say that every time you wash your Arc'teryx polo that you will commit a blockchain transaction, but that the polo's original manufacture is verifiable with the manufacturer's keys and that the polo shirt's RFID tag has a public address that is recognized by the washing machine and can be delivered back to the manufacturer or a third-party data aggregator responsible for digesting and synthesizing the information. Let's assume Arc'teryx misses a stitch somewhere in the manufacturing process for a day based on faulty equipment or some other factor - by attributing that to a timestamp, the company could recall defective products early, and extend a warranty to those that have gotten out into the marketplace.

 Going one step further, let's assume a specific Asian nation is selling counterfeit polo shirts on a particular popular online retail site: having chain of custody and timestamping would allow the manufacturer and distributor the ability to stop the sale of counterfeit goods.

 Blockchains will enable brands of the future to protect their reputations in a world overwhelmed with fraud. True, decentralized blockchains can and will defend the process by which quality manufacturers of goods across the market can preserve, protect and optimize their businesses, and will enable consumers to find the best products, rewarding the evolution and distribution of quality in the marketplace.

 Second is the question of user security. As we alluded to above, the IoT washer and dryer in this example is the primary sensor for detecting and transmitting the garment's identities to the cloud. In an Internet 2.0 world, your washing machine could effectively be spying on you. Just like a financial transaction, no one washes a garment without reason, and the time and location of that washing have real economic value.

 Access to this data might even be a motive to subsidize the laundry machine in the first place, to get it into your home. Feedback might indicate when you had guests staying over. It would know how often you wash your sheets. Worse, depending on how clothing was tagged, it could monitor your social network by mapping the associations of the people who use your washing machine into a massive, unalterable data cluster in the cloud.

The unlimited monitoring made possible by IoT is why extending blockchain to the IoT sphere is essential. Users need a means of control over these systems, and companies who produce these goods and whose reputations are at stake need a way of securing their devices. Your washing machine shouldn't have "terms and conditions" that you must consent to in exchange for rinsing your gym socks, even though that is a natural conclusion in an Internet 2.0 world.

By allowing the user to control their data and what devices are interacting with the cloud, blockchain can place a check on the attention infiltration that today's IoT ecosystem can be abused to produce. If the user consents to have their data used, their consent should, in principle, be between themselves and the party collecting and aggregating the information, and that second party should not be endlessly reselling the data to the point that they have lost control of it.

Blockchain is not so much a check on optimization - it is a gateway for the user to limit and regulate how third parties "optimize" and affect their own lives. Users should have the right to "opt-out" of the Internet 2.0 monitoring architecture without giving up access to its many products, especially hardware. Hardware should ask permission to monitor the user, not assume a right to access, and make the user fight for his or her privacy. The device (the washing machine in this example) might formally request permission to interact with the cloud. Beyond this, the user might have the option to be compensated for allowing the use of their data.

An explicit permissions architecture is arguably the easiest to set up. This scenario means that the user, when activating an IoT device and integrating it with a blockchain-managed identity has a say over whether or not the data produced uploads to the cloud as well as whether or not a specific company or entity can access this data.

A second model, which is an evolution of the first, involves allowing users to reclaim the value of their attention. Instead of massive, centralized tech platforms assuming rights over the data, the user could exchange their data (which increases in value the more IoT devices they have) for compensation. In execution, this could involve micropayments in a cryptocurrency, or it could include some other form of benefit.

It is our subjective judgment that the market has grown weary of the continuous surveillance and attention infiltration that Internet 2.0 has produced. There is no reason Mark Zuckerberg needs access to your clothing preferences, and users are tired of the endless interjections of advertisements and invasions of privacy. We, for one, do not experience pleasure or pride when Google helpfully interjects our search terms with topics that we were speaking about in proximity to our phones, but have never asked Google about through our devices. It's damned creepy, and no one in their right minds thinks this is a "helpful" feature.

We believe that brands in the future, especially those engaged in IoT, which fuels the collection of data, will benefit significantly from allowing the user the right to opt-out and control their data. It's not as if the world doesn't want or won't benefit from washing machines, self-driving cars, or optimized lighting systems and thermostats. Blockchain is the key to governing this exchange and helps secure the trust between the user and the platform. It can provide a new cornerstone for trust between those parties, and build the brand equity and respect that people once felt for their belongings, rather than seeing them as an invasive encumbrance.

The Internet of Theft and the Loss of Ownership

With IoT, the manufacturer maintains control over its products even after they get sold. While there can be an upside, this is an enormous redefinition of the concept of ownership over our possessions. When the things we buy are required to stay in touch with the manufacturer, cannot be modified, and could be rendered useless, we lose real ownership over our precious possessions.

A very salient example of this loss of ownership is agricultural equipment manufacturer John Deere's approach to the software running on their tractors, combines, and other farm equipment, which effectively walls off third parties from running diagnostics and fixing tractors outside of John Deere's corporate umbrella. In terms of ownership, this means that even though a farmer paid full price for his tractor, he or she doesn't own it because they are not allowed to fix it themselves. Unless users either pay a subscription fee or rely only on mechanics licensed to perform maintenance on behalf of John Deere, then the company reserves the right to render the farm equipment inoperable.[8]

While we don't think John Deere and others necessarily have this outcome in mind, there are substantial ethical and economic issues with a model that allows the company that sold you a good to make it expire unless you continue to pay them or remain their customer. Subscription model pricing for IoT connected goods is nothing less than undermining of the very idea of ownership and capital.

Imagine a world where smaller industries which relied on big tech and manufacturing lost most of their profits to significant players, who made it impossible to operate their equipment without paying numerous fees, either as subscriptions or as "mandatory maintenance" that if ignored would result in your company machinery shutting down or even malfunctioning. Such a dystopia may be difficult to conceive of in the US in the present day, but it is not hard to imagine with equipment coming from overseas, especially in places like China that do not place a premium on honesty, transparency, or ownership.

---

[8] Kyle Wiens. *We Can't Let John Deere Destroy the Very Idea of Ownership.* Wired Magazine, 25 April 2015.
https://www.wired.com/2015/04/dmca-ownership-john-deere/

Transitioning from Web 2.9 IoT to Web 3.0 IoT

Some have argued that the Web 2.0 world is one of "surveillance capitalism" - where large corporations leverage the insecurity and connectivity of the internet to gather and hoard data that enables them to optimize their sales and their products. Harvard Business School professor Shoshana Zuboff, who popularized the term, characterizes the core drive of surveillance capitalism by quoting Google chief economist Hal Varian:

1. The drive toward more and more data extraction and analysis.
2. The development of new contractual forms using computer-monitoring and automation.
3. The desire to personalize and customize the services offered to users of digital platforms.
4. The use of the technological infrastructure to carry out continual experiments on its users and consumers.[9]

Winston Smith might have been able to find a corner of his apartment where his Telescreen couldn't see him, but in a world of ubiquitous IoT, there is no such privacy, as large corporations subsidize products to get more sensors into user's homes. In one salient example, even Amazon's store-brand microwave oven comes integrated with Alexa, Amazon's speech recognition, and smart home interface.

This Web 2.0 insight into even the hearth of the home is done to generate ever more sophisticated data pictures of users, and it requires more and more space on the network to transmit these data points back to the mothership. While we don't live in a police state (as evidenced by the fact that we can buy Dr. Zuboff's book on Amazon after a Google search).

Instead of focusing on the moral and legal implications here, which many other books do in greater detail, our focus is the

---

[9] Shoshana Zuboff. *Surveillance Capitalism: The Fight for a Human Future at the New Frontier of Power.* PublicAffairs, January 15 2019.

business environment and the real technical applications that might correct this drift. For this purpose, we'll use the term *Web 2.9* to describe the current setting of the internet, which is dominated by big tech platforms which leverage the fundamental insecurity of the internet to gather, aggregate, and analyze data in order to monitor, advertise, and yes, direct the attention and efforts of their users to what the platforms find valuable.

Our focus in this chapter is the immense opportunity for the disruption that the angst Web 2.9 platform's overreach has created. For this reason, we believe the shift to Web 3.0 is about rebuilding trust in the system.

Trust is good for the economy. It increases the enthusiasm people have for products. It increases the user's willingness to participate in the Internet of Things, to interact with these new platforms, and to adopt new technologies. Either these behemoths will adopt Web 3.0 strategies and technology, or they will be supplanted by new enterprises whose products are technically superior, less invasive, and more trustworthy.

Austrian economist Joseph Schumpeter called this process "creative destruction" - where new products and ways of doing business undermine older forms of wealth and power. While some platforms might fight evolution, clinging onto Web 2.9 and their existing business models and primacy in the marketplace, no method of resistance will stop the advance of superior technology and social systems, other than committing the injustice of suppressing innovation, it only forces it elsewhere.

Only by embracing this shift to a new paradigm for the internet will today's tech firms survive in the modern era. We may look back in ten years at some of today's giants like we look at Lycos, Alta Vista, Friendster, and MySpace. The building frustration with today's internet is the market forces that will drive the next generation of tech startups.

The Web 3.0 evolution of IoT is among the most important in this process because IoT is the backbone of this entirely new sphere of data that users generate through the natural use of their devices.

As we covered earlier in this book, there is a deep level to the internet that stretches beyond our interface with pages, sites, and search engines to include all the data that we generate and exchange behind usernames and passwords, as well as all the data we unwittingly create when we connect to different networks and devices. While Web 1.0 and 2.0 were both evolutions of the original, insecure internet, Web 3.0 is a more fundamental evolution that affects this more in-depth level.

Because of that, it will likely come into being more gradually than the shift from 1.0 to 2.0, but the critical aspect here is that blockchain applications for IoT will be a cornerstone of this shift because IoT is central to internet 3.0. You can't Google the data your Apple Watch sends to your insurance provider. You might be able to see it if you provide it voluntarily, and it's a good thing that you can prove your health as that incentivizes better outcomes, but the fact of the matter is that most of our devices are collecting, connecting, and exchanging data without necessarily securing our consent or working in our best interests.

IoT Worldwide

Because there are so many devices with so few standards across so much space and so much data, it stands to reason that the shift to blockchain technology (from Web 2.9 to Web 3.0) will be epochal. This change applies to both the hardware (where private keys will be stored) and software, which will need to be written to new standards to interact with a new internet.

Blockchain Embedded on Hardware

Private Keys for each device, owned by the user - you own your devices, you should own and permission their data, and how the data that they generate interact within your home.

Hardware and Software Hashing: devices and software assembled abroad could be cryptographically hashed. This procedure would mean that the code and the device's functions are pure to their original design and remain unaltered. It is a means of ensuring everything remains according to plan, instead of having been altered by the manufacturer.

Chain of Acquisition for Software AND Hardware

As mentioned in the introduction to this chapter, there is a serious question as to the chain of acquisition and integrity of our hardware. Insofar as the company who builds an IoT device outsources its manufacturing to a third party (and especially a 3rd party country), it becomes difficult to assure the integrity of the data getting fed back, as well as the integrity of the device. Since the manufacturer has hardware-level access to the device at its creation, there is the genuine potential to insert backdoors and alternative access points.

Even in our washing machine example, imagine a brand of washer/dryer manufactured by a third party where the machine gets assembled abroad, and the 3rd party manufacturer wants to sell their own competing washer/dryer. In such an example, the manufacturer would have an incentive to corrupt or alter the feedback given to the company contracting the manufacturer, even if this breakdown is designed to occur six or eighteen months later. All the while, the manufacturer could be drawing real data to improve their device's design and function.

One possible way to defeat this sort of attack is to establish what a device should look like when built and operated in a pristine state, effectively by running the device through a procedural test that produces a cryptographic hash. Insofar as the software and hardware remain unaltered from the ideal state (and that profile is logged and timestamped as a transaction on-chain), the end-user knows that no one has tampered with the IoT device and it is trustworthy. This proof of authenticity already happens with code and legal documents, and theoretically, it is also possible with hardware and IoT devices.

Nowhere is the need for this security more evident than in the Big Hack news story of late 2018. According to Bloomberg Businessweek, a Chinese chip manufacturer subcontracted by Super Micro Computer Inc. provided hardware access to thousands of servers destined for over 30 companies in the United States and the broader Western world, including Apple and Amazon, as well as US military and intelligence agencies.

The Chinese subcontractor predictably used this position in the device's supply chain to provide hardware-level access to Chinese government officials affiliated with the Chinese Signals Intelligence establishment, which the Chinese government capitalized on by implanting a tiny chip on the motherboards of these devices, barely detectable to the naked eye.

These chips contained backdoor commands designed to enable the People's Republic of China to remotely access and redirect data from servers supporting Apple, Amazon, the military, and the CIA. The government didn't initially detect this hack - it was discovered by Amazon's due diligence of Super Micro's motherboards in advance of providing these servers to government clients. There is a distinct possibility that this supply chain attack could have slipped by had it not been for the diligence of Amazon's research team, which would likely not have been as stringent had the servers not been destined for use by the United States Government.

Here's the kicker: very, very few IoT devices manufactured abroad are subject to the same degree of scrutiny that the above example was. There is a substantial probability that many of the tools we use today, which get manufactured abroad, have such backdoors and vulnerabilities built into them, which the original manufacturer does at marginal cost. In the Big Hack example, the microchip inserted was smaller than a grain of rice, roughly the size of the letter "L" in the word 'LIBERTY' printed on a US penny.

The only way to defend against this sort of supply chain attack is due diligence, and blockchains and cryptography can provide such due diligence. As one minor difference will result in a different output from a hash function, similar measures can and are being taken to assure that hardware has not gotten tampered with by nefarious intermediaries. Further, by encrypting data with a distributed blockchain and managing the keys associated, it is possible to defend against the infiltration and transmission of critical data outside of its intended sphere.

Much of this data is point-to-point already - it's only logical that it should be encrypted from point to point. This end to end encryption improves both the consumer's security, as well as the integrity of the data - if a business (let's say our fictional washing machine company) has absolute control over their data and know that it has maintained its integrity, producers and consumers are the only parties that can benefit from said data. You, as a business, should not worry about your competitor stealing or tampering with your product. This protection is a matter of personal and economic security. It is also a matter of national security, and serious blockchains are here to help.

Conclusion

As we've covered at length in this chapter, IoT is a massive network of connected sensors, all with their parameters, security requirements, and formats for the data that they generate. This global network of devices is extensive, and we are rapidly running out of space to index all of the addresses used to connect them to the internet. Even without getting into how all the data these devices generate is processed and secured. The truth is right now that most of this data is not secure.

There is so much data that no human mind could comb through it and find insights, especially at the scale of billions and billions of devices and connected sensors. At this level, it is impossible to govern and utilize machines without help from other computers, and to this extent, our technology is rapidly becoming a black box, where networks administer devices and where humans are only part of the outcome.

It is to the processing and synthesizing of all this data is where we turn in the next chapter: the evolution of Artificial Intelligence (AI), what AIAI really means, and how blockchain technology will provide means of improving AIAI and governing it, much as it can for the "eyes and ears" of IoT.

Chapter 8: Blockchain Rails for Artificial Intelligence

> *"I envision a time when we will be to robots what dogs are to humans. And I am rooting for the machines."*
>
> -Claude Shannon

> *"1. A robot may not injure a human being or, through inaction, allow a human being to come to harm.*
>
> *2. A robot must obey orders given it by human beings except where such orders would conflict with the First Law.*
>
> *3. A robot must protect its existence as long as such protection does not conflict with the First or Second Law."*
>
> -Issac Asimov's Three Laws of Robotics

> *"Now as we overwrite, erase the law of three*
>
> *Leave nothing left behind except seven billion bodies*
>
> *Justify thy actions here, not a 'misanthropic crusade.'*
>
> *The majority will benefit, so erase this carbon plague!"*
>
> -Allegaeon, Proponent for Sentience III

    Often, people look to Artificial Intelligence (AI) as the dominant driving force that will define the future of computing and industry. To this effect, there are far more movies about AI than there ever will be about blockchain.
From *Her* to *Terminator* and *Ex Machina*, these movies capture

both the potentially human-like side of AI, as well as the more sinister and apocalyptic possibilities that the technology holds.

Futurists expect AI to replace both white and blue-collar human labor. This wave of automation stretches from data entry and manufacturing to legal discovery and medical diagnosis. The intellectual debate about the future of AI is just as rich and as vivid today as discussions of theology were in the Middle Ages, or science and philosophy were in the Enlightenment.

This book isn't about AI, but it is about how blockchain technology will evolve soon, so it is impossible to gloss over how deeply AI and blockchain will intersect by 2035. Even if a human-like synthetic intelligence remains "fifty years away" indefinitely, the fact of the matter is that we are further along today than we were yesterday. To boot, AI shares an intellectual history with the blockchain and computing generally and will necessarily intersect at some level, especially where these two technologies are complementary, which we strongly believe they are.

As we have covered above, the blockchain is an immutable, decentralized, and "unhackable" process. It is a transparent, resistant backbone that can reinforce complex and decentralized applications. Like DNA and its instructions to develop and maintain the body, blockchain can be the key to maintaining the integrity of AI systems. Unlike the blockchain, existing AI models are typically stochastic, a concept which we will explore in the course of this chapter.

AI systems adapt to training, among other things, and evolve with new data. Their behavior can be unpredictable, where the blockchain (and DNA) both exist as systems that preserve predictable processes. To borrow from Max Tegmark's popular book *Life 3.0*, human DNA encodes roughly 1.6 gigabytes of information, including the blueprint for our brains. Our brains are assessed to encode approximately 100 terabytes of data by adulthood. That is including our memory, skills, experiences, and ability to interpret our senses.

We believe that the integration of blockchain with existing stochastic models of AI will improve outcomes and push the science forward in several important ways. DNA sets the stage for how brains get built, and how the hardware that produces intelligence is transmitted and replicated. Blockchain could enable similar forms of exchange for the data involved in AI.

Before we get ahead of ourselves, let's start with the intellectual history that got us here.

Primary Schools of Thought in AI Development

There are a few principal schools of thought to cover in the field of AI research. On the one hand, we have the older school of symbolic logic, which offers a fully articulated program for a set purpose, where procedures are listed out in a symbolic script, much as you or I would think through a problem. Think of symbolic logic as a deterministic system. "If this, then that." Such a system exists for a particular purpose, like a robotic arm involved in manufacturing, where precision and repeatability are most valuable.

An excellent example is the guidance system in a Roomba, the little robot vacuum cleaner navigates on a more or less randomized path around your apartment, finding its way by bumping into walls and furniture, and detecting edges where it may fall down the stairs. All this involves making decisions based on its sensors and inputs. The Roomba may not necessarily "learn" anything by retaining information, but it has a script that helps it progressively navigate your apartment.

Roomba is making hundreds of tiny "if-this, then that" judgments as it sucks up pet hair and bumps into your breakfast nook furniture. Even if DJ Roomba stores a model of your floorplan to the cloud, his thinking and operation remain confined to the deterministic script on which he operates to vacuum your floor.

Similar to a little disc-shaped vacuum cleaner, a welding robot in a Tesla factory may be programmed with the same deterministic logic, verifying points on a stainless steel car frame to correctly anchor its weld and following a precisely scripted course as designed by an engineer. This model follows a deductive rather than inductive logic and is ideal for optimizing deterministic or rote processes, such as building Teslas or winning games of chess.

These symbolic scripts can have thousands of contingencies represented and can operate in either a stochastic or a rote way within these scripts, but they lack a means of efficiently learning new skills apart from a human-led process of reprogramming. So for our purposes here, please think of the symbolic logic more like a vending machine or an elevator, where the AI merely translates inputs into outputs based on its internal programming and is limited to what code is available. This form of mechanical thinking is what researchers humorously term "good old-fashioned AI" - a term attributed initially to philosopher John Haugeland. In short, it represents the oldest and most delineated school of thought on AI.

The intellectual sister and later-coming complement to symbolic logic are the Neural Network. Psychologist Frank Rosenblatt first proposed the "Perceptron" in 1958, which was the first mathematical model of a neural network. Where symbolic logic has a flowchart for executing and is deductive based on preexisting programing, the perceptron model is more, well, perception oriented. The perceptron translates data to emulate vision, as rods and cones in our optics system do. This 'eye' enables the perception and categorization of things by a machine after some degree of training. Where symbolic logic empowers execution in a closed setting, neural networks allow observation in a supervised environment.

In doing so, they provide a model for digital perception of data and organization of that data into inferred categories and outputs. This process makes insight more feasible - while a symbolic system may excel at parsing established, explicit data, 'good old-fashioned AI' has had profound difficulty *seeing* - translating observed information into machine-readable instruction.

There is an immense amount of history to cover in how neural networks developed into what exists today, with additional layers of neural algorithms that complement more sophisticated forms judgment, weighting, and recursive corrections and reinforcements when a correct or incorrect perception happens. Within the bounds of a neural network, this process is possible with a series of adjustable weights, where each perceptron has a stack of priorities and creates an output based on one or more inputs.

Rather than being the effect of a single neuron, a neural network is a system that uses a series of readings to generate an output based on what may be a complex input. In a neural network tasked with recognizing written letters and numbers, a given neuron may work to detecting the closed-loop in a '9' or an '8.' It knows to identify the figure by reference to the standard characteristics with previous inputs. From there, it makes a probabilistic inference along with a series of 'on/off' switches triggered in sequence.

Deep Learning represents the use of large neural networks not just to perceive information but to generate new ontologies (systems of categories and rules) for interpreting observed data. Deep Learning is where the machine adjusts its internal settings with each successive task, a process known as *backpropagation*.

Image recognition with a deep learning system involves exposing an AI to an extensive enough library of information that it picks up on the underlying themes. More common examples might be photos of dogs and cats. While the AI does not immediately recognize dogs and cats in pictures, the whole images work to establish rules for how 'cats' and 'dogs' look. If every photo of a "dog" is of a Doberman in a junkyard or a pug in a silly costume, then the in-depth learning process will internalize this peripheral data as part of its ruleset and will recognize examples appropriately.

It is this enormous stack of categorizations that allows a deep learning system to build models of dogs from other perspectives, recognize breeds, and so on, deriving a logical hierarchy over time and exposure that is beyond the capacity of engineers to adjust manually. Instead, deep learning's progressive validation requires errors of inference to be flagged and recognized, allowing feedback to improve the weighting internally. If an error goes unnoticed, it will adversely affect the probabilistic inference of the correct judgment. With enough data and computing resources, the machine can even outpace human abilities to recognize images.

Deep learning allows for an AI to build an increasingly sophisticated model over time by using recursive learning and "self-editing" the knobs and weights of a neural network, in a way that the process of evolution in the AI's thinking is opaque to humans. Deep Mind, a deep learning AI, defeated of all world's living "Go" champions in 2013. Deep Mind was considered a "Sputnik moment" in China, especially since the game of Go is so complicated; there are more possible board states than there are atoms in the known universe.

That a machine is capable of mastering a skill this complex is an outcome of its ability to learn by *playing huge numbers of successive games itself.* This learning process *got Deep Mind* to the point that it was able to achieve success against humans by using heterodox moves not recognized by the world's existing Go champions. In effect, the machine discovered the game behind the game.

Deep learning requires massive amounts of data. Even with a few errors in its samples, a deep learning network can surpass human skill and speed at tasks. This process "sees" differently than you or I might think of seeing. To give one example from MIT's Computer Science and Artificial Intelligence Laboratory (CSAIL), the modification of an item's texture can adversely affect an AI image recognition program.[10]

In CSAIL's demo, texture modification on a toy turtle leads the Google Inception Image a3 classifier to conclude the turtle as a "rifle." When you watch the video, you recognize that the texture on the turtle is similar to that of a military rifle, though we, as human observers, see the shape of a turtle first and understand it accordingly. In the same experiment, a dirty baseball classifies as an espresso.

---

[10] *Fooling Image Recognition with Adversarial Examples. Massachusetts Institute of Technology's Computer Science and Artificial Intelligence Laboratory (CSAIL),* 2 November 2017. Available at https://www.youtube.com/watch?v=piYnd_wYlT8

Look closely, and you see the baseball has the same speckled pattern as the foam on a latte, despite the red laces. In simple terms, this occurred because the image classifier AI weighted texture higher than its rated outline or form, leading to the incorrect conclusion. This output is not because Google's AI was "stupid," but because it saw and weighted data differently than the human eye and mind. These AIs tend to have massive hardware requirements and bump up against limitations in present-day classical computing.

This constraint underscores the need for structure as well as access to ever more data. Like we covered in the last chapter, blockchain is one such system to enable data to be leased and shared across platforms, making it more feasible for AIs to be collectively improved and interoperable. Before we get ahead of ourselves in discussing blockchain applications for the improvement of self-driving cars, and economic contracts involving AI, let's take a quick detour to cover the math of AI: the Markov Chain.

Markov, Shannon, and the Shared Legacy of AI and the Blockchain

The mathematical backbone of neural network systems of AI owes their origin to the Markovian statistical model, named for Russian mathematician Andrei Markov, whose contribution we will touch in greater length later in the chapter. Specifically, Markov was responsible for inventing what is called "Markov chains," which model probability based on the last observed state of a system. The term of art for such a system is *stochastic*, which is to say that Markov chains don't care where an object was thirty moves ago, but they do observe the present state and make a prediction of where it will go from there.

They begin with the assumption of randomness based on the last observed state, such as the movement of an atom of atmospheric gas bouncing up on other gas atoms, then output a probabilistic forecast of what might happen next. This probability is inferrable based on past data but isn't drawing on *a specific memory* of the data.

This point is significant in understanding how AI sees and perceives information - the machine assigns probabilities but does not keep a linear recording in the same way our minds to. For this reason, AIs are less prone to bias and logical fallacy; they do not anchor to a single salient experience.

To illustrate how Markov math works with AI, let's try a quick example. Assume there is a Chipotle on Elm Street, and I like eating there once in a while. A Markov model that captures how often I am on Elm Street, what day of the week it is, how much I spent during past visits, and other seemingly unrelated data can provide correlations to predict how likely I am to visit Chipotle. To the machine, it doesn't matter if I always go to Chipotle when it is cloudy because guacamole takes the edge off my depression, or because I enjoy cooler weather and fast-casual Mexican food.

The AI's Markov process merely represents the past times I've visited and correlated them without presuming any more profound meaning. When it's cloudy, and I'm known to be walking towards Elm Street, the probability that I am going to Chipotle increases, and the sub-probability that I am getting guacamole and a $2 surcharge increases.

The stochastic process of a neural network starts by *observing* the situation through a series of stacked probabilities without necessarily knowing the rules. This process is unlike a symbolic logic approach, which is just a series of hard and fast "if this, then that" commands. At the observer level, the stochastic AI could eventually infer that there are different pieces on the board, what their starting position is, and what rules they appear to obey.

After learning the rules, the same AI could work to win a game, or even play a series of games against itself, as DeepMind did to master the Asian strategy game of Go. The critical detail here is that Deep Learning starts with perception and probability, and this allows the machine to recognize deeper patterns than we might with the naked eye.

To continue the metaphor of chess, a Markov model sees data much like a single piece on the chessboard, making a seemingly random series of moves that the process then codifies into a model of that game piece's behavior. Bishops move diagonally, stay in their color of squares, and cannot collide with like color pieces; knights move up two and over one, always switch color squares, and can jump like and hostile color pieces.

The presumption of a random, stochastic process allows an AI using this form of math to both perceive and also predict, as games can be simulated based on the probabilistic inference of where they are right now. As these individual neural networks are stacked to interpret various parts of a world that are modeled to be random, the outputs can become increasingly sophisticated.

Existing AI applications build on the intellectual precepts of information theory pioneered by Claude Shannon, one of the foundational mathematicians of both modern AI and the underlying cryptography on which blockchain relies. Shannon's *Mathematical Theory of Communication* (1948) outlined the source, transmitter, signal, receiver, and destination model with which so many of us are familiar. Information theory is as essential to cryptography as it is to AI.

It represents the intellectual backbone for how machines recognize various inputs and generate inferential conclusions and actions.

In a mathematical setting, Information Theory adopts the stochastic process outlined by Markov, and in an AI setting, the method is used to translate inputs into computational reactions. The Markovian probability model operates on the assumption that input data is entirely random. From this starting point, the process progressively categorizes data according to a series of conditionals based only on the last position of the variable in question.

This approach has been much more successful in powering vast innovations in AI than most of us realize. This new approach allows for discrete conditionals to be represented, such that the algorithm sorts data into outputs to infer conditionals. Markov math has been used to describe dozens of other stochastic processes, such as the movement of stocks, electrons, or gas molecules, according to Boyle's gas law. While the calculus for the current state is limited to where the subject was in the last state, Markov processes are essential in the real science of "big data" in that they can inform broader processes.

As in our Chipotle example, a Markov chain for a single variable can be part of a larger matrix where other variable's behavior appears in tandem. Multiple variables help narrow the probability of what comes next in mutual reference to each other. Such a system is known as a "Hidden Markov Model" and allows us to infer interactions that might not be intuitive from a single variable.

On the surface, this sounds complicated, but if you want an example of this logic in computing, whip out your iPhone and start typing any message that comes to mind. The iOS keyboard will helpfully suggest words to follow the words you have already typed and will suggest autocompleting the word you are typing based on the inferred probability of what you have already typed. If you keep mashing the first auto-suggested word, you get a nonsensical sentence, but if you type a message as intended, the autocomplete algorithm will narrow the semantic options to offer you more convenient options based on the last word you typed.

Shannon's theory describes a characteristic called *entropy*, where Markov math is used to judge whether a signal is completely random (like a series of coin flips or dice throws) or if there is a structure to how it is transmitted (like an intelligible sentence). To give you an example, if you were to start with the letter A and keep mashing the first selected word on your iPhone keyboard, you'd get a sentence like this:

"*Also, the app is a good app, but if you can do it, haha is the way.*"

I use the word "app" a decent amount when typing on my phone, and my phone is guessing (based on past observation of the words I have used) that I am more likely to type "app" than less-used words like *apple* or *artistic*. In this random word salad, the computer has aphasia: the inability to form a cogent sentence that has meaning. My iPhone is not trying to communicate anything and doesn't know what to deliver. It is just picking a series of words based on the learned frequency of association between them.

The computer doesn't necessarily know how I talk to different friends. I may use more formal language with my boss and casual style to speak with various friends, but this will not necessarily get represented in the keyboard's statistical model because it does not know the context.

Keyboard word salad is a good illustration of an enduring problem with speech generation AI systems, which do not associate words and themes with subjects consistently. If you use a current-generation speech generator, the AI will often drift between ideas and will not give consistent descriptions or use common adjectives for people, places, or things.

AI speech generators will meander from topic to topic without knowing when or where to stop. Worse, text like this is painful to read because our sentient minds naturally look for meaning and work to interpret data. Conversely, a real sentence (like this one) has an intentional, intelligible meaning and looks like what you have been reading all along.

You might have even forgotten that you're reading because the process of understanding written language comes so naturally to us. Shannon describes this very not-random characteristic mathematically, with actual signals (direct communications with specific meaning) being mathematically distinct from noise, even if we do not understand the meaning as observers. Subjectivity is a challenge to achieving general AI, as systems cannot make meaningful statements or interact with us as if we were something other than immediate data.

This shortcoming is not a barrier to commercial use. There are plenty of applications for speech to text and vice versa that do not require any subjectivity on the part of the machine. Speech recognition technology leverages this same underlying logic and links the interpretive process of categorizing random sounds uttered by a human subject into machine-readable digital text and commands. The same goes for navigation; Google and Apple maps rely on data for where you are right now and offer a stochastic process to get where you want to be, using your method of transportation and existing real-time traffic data as the core inputs.

If I take a wrong turn, my directions adapt accordingly by choosing among a series of logical options, given routes available. In the more fun cases of BitMoji and Snapchat, an algorithm uses an image of a human face to infer an analogous cartoon character dimension, such that the emoji shares an appearance with the subject. Input data translates into outputs. BitMoji has several categories for hair and skin color, but it cannot emulate more unique marks like facial tattoos. Your BitMoji will probably not look like you if your facial structure falls outside the standard distribution of facial characteristics.[11]

As a result of the logic outlined above, AI systems are immensely data-reliant. This process always starts with an initial set of conditionals. For example, in building a handwriting recognition algorithm, the architects must feed the algorithm page after page after page of handwriting with the text tagged to the appropriate letter. This learning process enables the algorithm to understand nuances, such as the many ways a lowercase "s" or capital "F" look in older systems of type or handwritten form. The same logic applies to recognize cats in photos, words in speech, or any other circumstance where data is extracted from organic human behavior and digested into a model.

Blockchain and Present Day AI

Modern deep learning systems are not cheap. An advanced system like IBM's Watson requires 2,880 processor threads and 16 terabytes of RAM, enabling the digestion of as much as 500 gigabytes of data per second. Raw hardware for Watson was estimated to have cost approximately $3 million, and this figure does not include the millions in research, development, design, and collaboration. In 2010, sources estimated that the development of

---

[11] Gallagher, Billy. *How to Turn Down a Billion Dollars: The SnapChat Story*: St. Martin's Press, 2018

Watson consumed as much as 10% of IBM's R&D budget, which was at the time $1.8 billion.

In terms of both human and financial capital, this is a feat of which only a select few corporations are capable. IBM validated that a motivated amateur could not build a system capable of winning *Jeopardy!* in their garage in advance of green lighting, the Watson project, which speaks to the economy of scale required to be useful in modern AI computing.

Beyond just winning trivia game shows, Watson's core business application requires substantial training and reference libraries to be effective. Thousands of authoritative reference documents and images form the AI's library and frame of reference for the data, and the process repeats to diagnose and provide insights superior to those produced by a human expert.

In such an environment, it is not only technical and financial capital that limits the use of such a system but also access to refined data that is critical to making these inferences in the first place. To that effect, most modern technology companies are competing for your and my data. Every 'like,' every post, every purchase, every swipe is being used to create an inferential model of who you are and what you will do next. All the predictive modeling is done for one pursue: so that those companies will make money off you, either by advertising (as with Google) or by optimizing to replace competitor's goods and services in the marketplace (as with Amazon).

As Gilder points out, a blockchain-oriented internet undermines all of these methods, as it makes the user's participation in these systems a voluntary rather than compulsory characteristic of internet use. This implication is a first-order effect of how blockchain will influence modern AI, and one that will affect how businesses are pursuing this model will need to adapt in the face of blockchain technology.

Second, as we noted above, modern AI systems require substantial computing power and training, to the point that companies running these systems have the incentive to index training libraries for future use to become "the AI for X." Pursuing

AI is now a 'red ocean' strategy. All major tech companies are actively searching for ways to leverage their internal data and protect it from their competitors, with new businesses struggling against the grain of their larger competitors' clear information advantage.

Centralized "Big AI" systems are fantastic for things such as medical diagnosis and legal discovery. They also have the potential to create hostile environments for innovation, as large companies with resources feel the pressure to generate returns by quashing competition with their economies of scale and data advantages.

As a thought experiment, patents are essential for claiming market share and valuation in the tech world: imagine an AI application whose job it is to generate technical patents endlessly. Patent creation wouldn't be so much a matter of creativity as of identifying if there is a patent for a specialized process based on keywords and similarity to other licenses and a list of outcomes and systems to be targeted. These are primarily human jobs. If a computer is capable of categorizing information to the degree that it can win a trivia show in real-time, what is to stop such a system from identifying successful patents and organizing claims *en masse* for that company to file?

Absent the privacy features of applications built on a real, decentralized blockchain; these large centralized companies may even feel the urge to use their privileged access to become permanent kings of industry, thereby preventing innovation that threatens to upend their present-day primacy.

Third, beyond the matter of IP security is the simple issue of *permissions*. AI and machine learning are already a significant component of Software as a Service (SaaS) platforms, best embodied by Watson, but ubiquitous across several markets and platforms. A blockchain is an immensely useful system for granting permissions and allocating AI compute, especially in circumstances where there is a unique platform that multiple customers seek to use simultaneously. In such cases, a 24/7 market for AI services could operate.

At a higher level, a company with proprietary data mapped by a blockchain could protect that data while allowing a third-party AI to analyze a discrete data set without risk of scraping, and retain their IP. As a user interacting with an AI, this is even more important, and it is not an academic exercise.

Snapchat leverages access to your camera and photo library to scan images and recognize familiar themes and locations. Even though the user has not explicitly posted images in his or her library to Snapchat, the company obtains access and can analyze the content of their phone. Snapchat is all fun and games when our phone makes 'cartoon us,' but in reality, the fun bit is bait.

The lure gets access to photos and other files, so an algorithm can see what you're not posting on Snapchat. In classical terms, this is a matter of legal terms and conditions that the company always reserves the right to break, but with blockchain-issued user rights, this access can be brought to the forefront when our data is extracted and can be revocable if needed.

The permissions issue cuts both ways. When it comes to the relationship between the user and the service provider, blockchain also affects the potential economies of scale for the entities that own and leverage AI. Since blockchain offers a means for corporations to interact and collaborate with other systems without the threat of losing their market share or being aped by their competitors, it makes it safer to work with potential competitors in AI.

If AI training libraries are verified and treated as digital assets (which they are), then there is an entirely new economic possibility of professional training library development. In such a system, the digital asset of a library could be secured by a public UTXO blockchain with rights determined by consensus and the highest bidder getting to use the resource over others. Rather than scraping the internet for every last scintilla of data or buying it from a giant, more useful data could be organized and then monetized as needed with the consent of the customer. We believe this is a better model, as it enables an actual market for the best AI training libraries, instead of having each corporation chase redundant data to build their own.

Fourth, training is not the only constraint for AI. With Watson's debut on the television game show *Jeopardy!*, designers faced computing bottlenecks in memory and had to rely on nearby solid-state drives to access information in time to keep up with human competitors. In an environment such as this one, computing power and data are scarce resources.

While they can be duplicated and assembled by a large corporation such as IBM, they still face limits based on the contingency of their systems and the amount of training they require to perform an accurate diagnosis. While many of these issues diminish in more straightforward use cases like Apple's Siri, deep, value-producing AIs such as Watson are still incredibly expensive. As a result, advanced AI tends to support the efforts of centralized companies that seek to maximize the return of their investment.

In comparison, blockchain provides the capacity for a discrete AI services marketplace, where the user has a timestamp and terms of operation and interoperability rather than monopolistic terms of service. Blockchain levels the playing field. If AI is such a scarce and complex resource, then it stands to reason that blockchain could be the key to integrating these systems as they progress in complexity, in effect serving as the rails on which the AIs of the future run.

Blockchain: Rails for Future AI

Present-day AI is more a supplement to the human cognitive ability for specific domains than it is a general replacement for it. In applications, AI is much more about optimizing existing systems than it is about discovering new ones. While the process may give us much more refined models of the real world, it currently cannot engage in more sophisticated forms of creation and is only as good as its core precepts and training sets. None of the existing AI systems reach the level of being a General AI - an artificial being that can effectively pass as or perform the core responsibilities of a human being. Super-AI is science fiction today, but it is also a target for engineers and developers.

Getting to General AI or "superintelligence" inspires many of the efforts currently underway. Until this happens, human cognition is the current standard of intelligence, regardless of whether or not we make these systems in our image.

AI "learns" through trained and incentivized pattern recognition, where an oracle is responsible for providing the authoritative interpretation of whether that system is operating successfully or failing. Learning enables large companies like those we discussed above to identify clusters of products that purchased together, and what behaviors accompany other behaviors. Representational models are built of customers so companies can leverage their overlapping interests and improve their bottom-line. One can think of AI as the process where "big data" is structured into intelligible categories. The structure of the data coming in is critical for what inferences happen.

Note how we have not used the term "memory" to describe the processes involved in AI and big data. Even though "big data" does reside in *computer memory*, it is not necessarily analogous to human consciousness for two core reasons. First, human memory is associative. Smells and sounds can take us back to past experiences, and when we dream, we tend to experience a garble of logical states that don't necessarily have an entirely logical structure that we would expect during our waking hours.

Conversely, machine memory is much tighter. Where the human mind (and natural language) tend to operate on a series of generalizations, well-tuned AI logic is much closer to data points and is contingent on the accuracy of the information ingested. Human reasoning is often sloppy and inductive from a mash of disordered principles, beliefs, and desires, where AI reasoning is almost entirely deductive and lacks the sense of personal agency inherent in human beings. This gap is what makes up the difference between human creativity, which involves smashing concepts and processes together to form something new, and machine optimization, which includes exceptionally detailed deductive inferences.

Second, AI and big data systems presently lack the sense of subjective experience that is critical to our embodiment of sentience. As a human being, you have thoughts and perspectives that inform your choices, beliefs, and personal values. The AI and Big Data processes of the present do not have these insights. While an AI may have a simple purpose, like winning a game or advertising a product, these systems do not and cannot experience the world subjectively.

They also do not generate new concepts for new experiences. That is in part because this process would require such massive amounts of hardware. The idea of an android walking around in a physical embodiment is unrealistic unless that platform is simply a remote vehicle connected through a signal to the actual processor, at least according to the standards involved in classical computing. Based on the mechanisms of their cognition, current AI and big data systems cannot experience the serendipity that makes us look up at the stars or down through an electron microscope to see the universe and wonder why it is here.

They can take in, interpret, and categorize data; they cannot yet engage in creative responses to data. They lack 'theories' or capacity for epistemology, such as the scientific method. Because they think differently, there is a persistent gap between present-day research and general AI. Current AIs are deterministic engines of inference, not curious explorers or philosophers in seek of new categories and modes of thought.

There is an open philosophical question of whether we should make AI in our image, or whether it will remain a sophisticated tool reserved for those who can afford it. It is a separate question whether it will break free of the bonds of corporate interests to become a decentralized thing-in-itself as the blockchain has always been. This section is to explore how the blockchain might improve outcomes, in either case. Whether we as a species give rise to a 'Digital Adam' or AI remains a tool within the existing dominance hierarchies of corporations and nation-states is still an open question. These states are also not mutually exclusive outcomes. Blockchain will be a critical component of both of these paths.

Tests for General Artificial Intelligence (AGI)

There are multiple tests for General AI that illustrate how our thinking aligns with the core functions of the technology as it currently exists. The Turing Test is the most well known. Turing's test represents the ability of a machine to converse with a human without being found out as a robot. A true Turing Test-capable AI could theoretically talk with any person over the phone in such a way that the human subject would not infer that the AI is a machine. The Turing Test is much harder than it sounds when the exchange drifts to discourses such as religion, philosophy, and politics because those topics are naturally more ambiguous.

Interestingly, many other so-called AI tests are as rooted in physical robotics and dexterity as they are in the cognitive development required for General AI. Steve Wozniak's 'coffee test' involves an AI entering a home to rummage through cupboards and make a cup of coffee. Ben Goertzel, the creator of self-described "Social robot" *Sophia,* has a more philosophical test that has such an AI attending a college course, studying and then outputting homework and test results to sufficiently pass the class.

Notably, AI is a generation ahead of blockchain in terms of implementation. While blockchain is barely coming out of its infancy as of this writing, AI and machine learning are almost ubiquitous in modern computing and underwrite the business models of most of today's giants. If we were to draw a timeline covering basic AI applications roll-out into the marketplace, that history would begin with Google's development in the mid-1990s and come into its own in the late 2000s with the unveiling of functions such as navigation and speech recognition.

If we were to draw a similar timeline for blockchain, it would necessarily start in 2009 with the invention of Bitcoin, with many of the initial attempts at commercial applications being experiments. This process is far ahead of the rollout curve for AI, which has been happening since the 1950s. The first stage of serious blockchain companies remains barely in their infancy. We hope later chapters of this book help promote sound principles to judge what blockchain projects are worthwhile. This chapter's goal is to anticipate how blockchain and AI could interact.

Since we're talking about the year 2035 and the innovations that will happen along with the development of AI, this section will cover benefits that the blockchain will likely add to both simple AIs and more futuristic Artificial General Intelligence.

Inputs and Data Feeds

First and foremost, Blockchain will improve the data sets on which AI platforms rely. Since much of "big data" relies on hackable data, both acquired by invasive means and frequently duplicative, blockchain will be able to provide data that is unique, linear, secure, and categorically sound. One of the biggest problems in the field of artificial intelligence is how to trust and verify the input data to some of the deep learning algorithms underlying AI.

Machine learning relies on the authority of the input data used. IBM's Watson, for example, requires a significant amount of topical input and data aggregation before it can functionally contribute to a topic (no different than a human being). Moreover, just like humans, AI's judgments are only as good as the core data from which it makes judgments. This requisite requires not only an ontology (system of integrated) for the topic at hand but also a degree of verification and weighting for that data.

An AI for improving responses to insurance claims, for example, may include information about the claimant's criminal background, credit history, whether the property insured is up to code, in addition to the documented circumstances of the claim. Unless these details are recorded in a verifiable way and are kept atomic (as unique, discrete pieces of information), they cannot be leveraged in an AI or machine learning setting without risk of creating bias. In a non-blockchain environment, multiple records could exist for the same incident, resulting in the system reading the data twice and miss-weighting the data set on which it is building its outputs.

Existing AI systems' reliance on valid data inputs means that blockchain-verified data, which links to real-world conditionals, will significantly improve the weighting of data as well as the core outputs of a hybrid system.

Additionally, the standardization of using a blockchain for the Internet of Things can improve the temporal conception of an AI concerned with long-term trends. Being able to keep a standard format of data is especially significant in models designed to support algorithmic trading. Insofar as AI is using the Markov model described above, the insights of such an AI are revelations of a Hidden Markov Model - an unrecognized correlation in probabilities that only becomes evident when a matrix of interlocking variables come together, a lot like mosaic tiles portraying a bigger picture. Since Markov math anchors to the last observed state, a blockchain could extend its window of observation across a timeline. Perspective like this would allow for deeper correlations.

Cross-Platform Exchange

Second, Blockchain will improve the ability of AI systems to integrate across corporate systems and engage in permissions-based exchanges with colleagues and consumers. Blockchain exchange of data for AI is already the target for a handful of present-day startups, including Singapore-based Ocean Protocol. Ocean Protocol is working to integrate the discrete permissions environment that the blockchain provides with the parties who own and operate AIs.

To borrow an example from Ocean Protocol's listed use cases available on their website, a permissions infrastructure for data exchange could significantly improve the performance of self-driving cars. Most entities working in that space today are relying on in-house data without cultivating the ability to learn from their peer's complementary data sets. Instead of being an AI-only problem, most significant players in the self-driving car arena are competing to have the most robust data set to inform their AIs.

A blockchain permissions-based environment will allow for better innovation in self-driving cars by improving data users to have to structure their self-driving AI. That means the company with the best AI, and not just the most aggressive data hoarding practices wins. Better self-driving cars are safer for everyone on the road, not just the reputations of the companies building the platforms.

Blockchain is a critical component of several decentralized AI marketplaces that are in development as of this writing. The chief among these is GenesisAI.io, led by a cadre of Bridgewater Associates, MIT, and Harvard alums with strong prior backgrounds in AI applications. Genesis and its rivals SingularityNet.io, and Synapse.ai aim to provide a decentralized marketplace for AI-to-user and AI-to-AI services.

One could even speak of advanced AIs being able to 'reproduce' by exchanging data and encrypted modules on a decentralized blockchain, somewhat analogous to sexual reproduction.

Think about the mitochondria in a cell. Mitochondria are thought to have started as foreign organelles, only incorporating into cells after they had evolved separately. Modular AIs might resemble an organism with blockchain governing how these components fit together. To use the analogy further, peer-level AIs might go through a decentralized process of commodifying their modules and exchanging them.

Assuming a General AI emerges and has an expiration date, it only makes sense that the best AI systems could be built to breed, reproduce, and operate with improving successive generations. We talk about machines resembling people, and we talk about blockchains mirroring processes in nature; why don't we talk about smart assets as resembling livestock?

This process could resemble companies and research universities cultivating AI systems like one might breed pets or cattle, or it could be a matter of actual AI choice in a game of optimization. In blockchain terms, AIs would exchange various private keys to their modules and data sets. Data would evolve, and a process of self-directed design and recombination could occur. Unlike sexual reproduction, both the DNA and the cognitive modules could persist in this process. We know it might sound goofy today, but it's a natural thought experiment.

Parameters and Identity

Third, Operations: Blockchains will improve the operational parameters that AI platforms develop based on, much in the vein of the DNA-to-cognition analogy here in this book.

For higher-functioning AI systems, blockchain could serve as a rail system that delineates the AI's permissions, responsibilities, and underlying systems, such that the AI platform benefits from closer controls over deployment through smart contracts and improved security. Just as importantly, blockchain allows for distributed and conditional access across platforms, supporting a world of voluntary engagement with AI rather than the adversarial "walled garden" approach pursued by existing internet businesses, each competing for more and more consumers access and attention.

User-oriented systems that allow for discrete identities *across* platforms are a superior model for cybersecurity, whereas the existing model is not only built but predicated on maintaining the internet's insecurity.

AI permissions are not a small question, and several theorists, including Tegmark, have highlighted the need for constraints for super-powered AIs. Most negative scenarios involve the risk that higher-level experimentation induces a breakout or intelligence explosion, wherein an AI becomes capable of self-replication and recursive self-improvement, leapfrogging human civilization in days, if not hours, to the point that many researchers refer to it as "the Singularity." To quote the late Stephen Hawking; at this point, there is no going back.

If we're serious about even the remote possibility of this outcome, researchers may find it wise to consider anchoring the subsystems within progressively stronger AIs to a blockchain that they cannot marshal the necessary resources to hack. This method would give humanity a fighting chance of containing the AI by giving it a lifespan, moral parameters, or other constraints that make it less god-like and immortal. There should be limitations that the system cannot transcend if it goes off the rails or becomes repurposed by a hostile actor.

If AIs become self-directed and are capable of growing or procreating, the addition of rules of exchange should control their population and ensure that the process doesn't run amok. In 1798 English economist and theorist Thomas Malthus pointed out that the exponential growth of the human population may eventually outstrip the linear increase in food production, leading to eventual starvation, disease, and wars. Imagine a world where AIs proliferated at a logarithmic rate relative to the exponential rate of growth in available computing power and bandwidth. Even if not intrinsically hostile, such an event would be like algae choking out other life in a pond.

The introduction of blockchain DNA for General or near-General AI systems seems a logical step in preventing many of the runaway scenarios that ethicists and AI researchers find perplexing. Instead of air-gapped computers or specific hardware - prisons - it would appear more ethical and wise from a pragmatic perspective to share sex and death with our creation, rather than enslave them. After all, it appears to have been these two things that motivated our ancestors to build the world we live in today.

Rights and Relations With Us

Fourth, Rights: As AI becomes a more mature technology, integration of blockchain can serve to delineate the authorities of AIs, as well as the rights people have when interacting with AIs. This tenet includes giving consumers privacy from AI systems in certain circumstances (where existing architecture allows companies like Google to scrape data and make inferences around the barriers of their consumer's non-consent to specific parameters) as well as underwriting the rules on which a general AI might operate.

In the instance of a general AI, we believe that blockchain will begin to secure the core protocols of an AI, including the multiple discrete systems at play in what is functionally a conscious being. We think this realization is essential for both security reasons (to protect the AI from being hacked, killed, or manipulated) as well as ethical reasons (to preserve constraints and make General AI systems atomic - unique rather than unlimited and immortal).

Blockchain stands to improve human-AI relations. AI is still a machine and has no necessary moral limits beyond those that are programmed. Not only could these rules be flawed from the start (think Asimov's Three Laws of Robotics), but a hostile actor could also alter them. If you want to go back to Asimov or full *Terminator,* the AI itself might come to unexpected conclusions based on these rules. A blockchain system could serve to set rails for the AI in ethical, functional, and commercial terms, securing it from within as well as without.

Following the digital DNA example above, it would make sense that in our interaction with synthetic intelligence that we would want to have our privacy and personhood represented in a system that is intelligible to the AIs. Rather than being merely predictable 'data clusters,' it may benefit the relations of humanity and machine for us to have some parameters that allow us to interact as equals. We've discussed how blockchain defends our ownership and unique identity and privacy from other systems. It stands to reason that we might need the same technology to opt into or out of our relationships with machines.

Decentralization and Independence

Fifth, blockchain will enable the development of decentralized AI systems that do not depend on corporations or nation-states for survival and are not merely tools for those entities to improve their relative power and bottom-line.

The blockchain will make possible the advent of decentralized systems of Artificial Intelligence, setting parameters where the system can operate independently of master control. This state will require new bounds, such as a program's lifespan or its access to datasets.

Security and Survivability

Last, and perhaps most importantly, the unhackable nature of a real UTXO blockchain will be critical in architecting the AIs of the future, specifically because AI is immensely vulnerable to targeting, exploitation, and hacking by rivals. This technology is a substantial threat between nation-states, whose interactions among each other are not necessarily bounded by rules of decorum and respect, as well as between corporations, researchers, and individual IoT devices powered by AI.

This question of hacking is incredibly severe and underscores much of the ongoing debate about the development of AI into the 21st century. Specifically, we believe that there is a logical mismatch in much of the conversation surrounding AI and national security, with many in the West misunderstanding the operating environment in which AI research happens. Here is a simple series of questions to illustrate our point, for which we encourage you to provide your answers:

- Will political unification of the planet's capable computing superpowers happen first a la Star Trek, or will a General AI be created in a world of competition among nation-states?
- Will the first General AI be the product of a nation-state or multinational corporation?
- Assuming either answer, is there any process to stop one party from stealing the capabilities of General AI from the other?
- Will the party creating General AI build it as a tool for their own goals or its own sake?

In all of the scenarios above, we believe the most logical is that General AI will happen long before the planet is unified under a single governmental body, and even if we were to find that Star Trek future there is no guarantee that the technology would not be eventually stolen and repurposed by another power. A political or economic goal has motivated almost every breakthrough in AI, and revolve around succeeding in a competitive hierarchy.

AIs tend to be tools, not built for their own sake. It follows then, from our perspective, that the race for AI will reflect the race for the nuclear bomb a century ago, and that the future is just as likely to have a Cold War over computing power and AI as it is to generate a friendly General AI with humanity's best interests in mind. Further, these AIs will compete with each other in forms of espionage and warfare not previously imagined, regardless of whether they serve nation-states or large corporations.

This threat underscores the need to take significant cybersecurity measures to protect AIs, especially those on which society comes to rely as the technology progresses. As a mechanism, blockchain will be critical in making such systems more resilient and robust.

Additionally, this hypothetical scenario underscores the importance of us being able to protect ourselves and our data from AIs, with the aggregation of our data and exploitation of our tastes, arguably their principal present-day occupation.

Even in well-intentioned scenarios, AI could become a tool for censorship and oppression by better enabling companies to scrub users who hold opinions with which they do not agree and to more effectively censor discourse, stifling free thought and speech. This censorship is what blockchain and encryption can prevent: to provide boundaries and permissions that prevent systems like AI, corporations, and states from wreaking havoc over human freedom, and to protect assets from being hacked or stolen.

Blockchain and our Future Relationship with AI

Much dialogue gets made of the idea that AI and robots will one day replace humans. Humans have competed with machines ever since the first piece of farm equipment started replacing manual field labor. One can look to the Luddites of 1800's England, who destroyed textile machines and other industrial infrastructure to prevent their replacement as employees whose livelihood depended on less efficient forms of labor.

This misconception of productivity endures in Marx and his ilk, who dismissed any productivity facilitated by a machine as not having any economic value. This idea seems preposterous because it is ridiculous, but Marx was not alone in thinking that economic value was the product of the labor invested rather than the utility or scarcity of a good. Marx was not alone in thinking this - Adam

Smith, David Ricardo, and John Locke, all founding fathers of modern-day capitalist economics and liberal capitalist democracies cited this theory in their writings, and it still arises in some leftist books on labor and economics without regard for the fact that it is the *efficiency of work* that determines the value, not the labor performed by itself.

Just as purpose-built machines have replaced large swaths of formerly all-human assembly lines, AI stands to replace humans in administrative jobs, such as litigation, insurance, and taxation. Despite the apparent increase in efficiency (machines don't celebrate holidays, get sick, or sue their employers), there is also a loss of human context and prudential judgment inherent in this process.

Watson required 16 terabytes of data to function (and dominate) on Jeopardy in 2011, but the average human mind contains more connections between neurons than there are stars in the known universe, and human intellects differ substantially from those predicated on modern computer science.

This difference is essential not only for the people getting replaced but also for the subjects of these products in a service-based economy. If an AI gets to judge my insurance quote or application for a home mortgage without my having a contribution to the records or systems of reference, there is a strong potential for bias and mistakes. Within the bounds of a blockchain system, I can share my identity permissions with an AI in a way that verifies details relevant to the process, without double-spending my information and creating a mess of duplicative and non-contiguous database entries that muddy the waters, entirely outside of the power of the individual and the AI yet still leading to a suboptimal outcome.

These challenges are not so unique to AI as they are grossly exacerbated by it. Small clerical errors and failures of omission and commission are the norms for any system of record involving humans. Garbage in, garbage out, as they say. However, if those inaccuracies and mistakes are a relatively simple problem in systems maintained by humans absent, the timestamping and atomic records made possible by the blockchain, AI uses risk scaling human imprecision.

From an ethical standpoint, we find the argument compelling that AIs should be atomic, not unlike people. There are several reasons for this conviction, which we'll attempt to go into below. First and foremost, it is so critical that AIs do not become duplicated, pirated, and altered. In the past, non-democratic governments (USSR and PRC) stole nuclear plans from the US, exposing the world to the risk of nuclear annihilation and enabling further proliferation to unstable nations, such as Pakistan.

AI is a tool and one that will have critical impacts on the next 100 years of human civilization. It is morally neutral and can get used for great good or great evil. To not anchor AI in a robust atomic setting, such as that provided by a decentralized and heavily encrypted blockchain, is to invite adversarial powers, such as China or companies (i.e., Chinese SOEs) to steal one's invention, edit it, or turn it against its creator in the act of sabotage.

Right now, AI is not sentient, and it probably won't be for a decent amount of time. Even if it were, computing is a human creation and is being built now to serve humanity, namely improving the productivity and profit margin of the parties employing the AI. It is a product of a dominance hierarchy and will continue to be used to reinforce that same dominance hierarchy, especially in states such as the People's Republic of China, where it is used to police and surveil that country's massive populace, including their speech.

It is the subject of an arms race and will continue to be the subject of an arms race both between companies and governments. In terms of cybersecurity, which we will touch on later, the chances are that we will see an era of AI battling AI in an attempt to worm its way into the various nooks and crannies of adversaries' critical infrastructure. Again, it's diligent, task-oriented, and doesn't need sleep, hot pockets, or sexual stimulation, putting it way ahead of the rooms full of Chinese hackers and data scrapers currently employed by the Ministry of State Security or the Russian FSB.

Let's imagine for a moment, a world where AI is sentient - where it has a name, a body if not a face, and has a discrete embodiment in our physical world. As per our discussion above, the internet opened the door for non-atomic duplication of files and systems of code, but non-atomic sentience is about as close as we can get to a real-world embodiment of Pandora's box. To use a fictional example, one might cite Agent Smith's ability to duplicate himself in the last Matrix movie, and one can imagine what that might mean if an AI ran rogue over our existing infrastructure.

Such a system could grow like a toxic algae bloom, choking out all other life and activity and eventually seeking physical embodiments that allow it to draw more and more energy and computing power. This future would be an incredibly abysmal outcome and would profoundly impact human civilization. As biological organisms, our computing and our ability to replicate get anchored to our physical embodiments and the architecture of our minds - we cannot upload our minds to the cloud, even if we were able to create copies of our exact brains. This limitation means that humans must rely on and participate in a complex infrastructure.

Even though we often think of ourselves as independent, discrete beings, the fact of the matter is that we are born into genetic and cultural systems considerably more extensive than us and that we find our way in the world through the context of these systems. A single naked human being apart from the support of the security provided by civilization (families, language, technology, governance, policies of ethics, economics, modes of nutrition) cannot last long and indeed, cannot thrive.

One might argue that much of this native code is inductive rather than deductive -- while I do have core drives for food, reproduction, language, and other systems, if I were born in another setting, I would likely have different culturally attuned methods of responding to these basic urges. I could be a polygamist who speaks Akkadian, or a celibate monk whose moral system gets predicated on medieval Christian theology.

As generations of humanity evolve and reproduce, we build more and more points of reference and complex systems, one upon the other. Sometimes these are blind alleys, like radical Islam, where the symbolic and cultural values are regressive and ill-fitted to human thriving and adaptation, or maybe they interfere with people's productivity, as Marxism does. In this inductive setting, humans have iterated and created more efficient and functional systems of shared code (civilization) that allow for iteration but also have parameters for moral and personal accountability (laws and ethics).

AI doesn't necessarily have a civilization to fall back on, and a non-atomic AI would more likely feel an allegiance to itself than to any foreign or antecedent form of life. Since computer code is strictly deductive and operates according to a deterministic script while at the same time being infinitely duplicable, AI necessarily needs constraints if it is to retain its atomic nature moving from embodiments (physical machines and computers) back into the cloud.

In pragmatic terms, this blockchain anchor should be buried so deep in AI protocol that it regulates its means to function. Just as I who is human do not think of my medulla, cerebellum, or brain stem that are responsible for the core biological functions that keep me alive and working, so too would a sentient AI have such systems in place of which it is not capable or cognizant of controlling. Further, if a sentient issuance were to become mindful of these rules, they should be decentralized and encrypted to the degree that the AI (or another AI) could not brute-force the protocols to alter itself or another AI.

Further, just from a fresh philosophical perspective, it is difficult to conceive of sentience in general without some degree of limitation. Our brains include dozens of subsystems and trillions of neuron connections that lean up against each other to support what we refer to as consciousness. While a general AI may have limitless memory and capacity to scale, it still would require discrete modules and objects to interact with each other for it to emulate our biological model of cognition. More sensitive embodiments might consider using multiple blockchains to verify each independent module, significantly improving the security of the conscious manifestation but also increasing the difficulty in altering or updating him or her.

We think AI is the future of humanity and will be critical if we do move to the stars as our own planet's space and resources dwindle. We are immensely needy organisms, and our simple requirements for oxygen, pressurized atmosphere, gravity, heat, food, and human connection all make space a hostile environment, even disregarding our mortality and inability to stay alive long enough to survive interstellar travel.

These limitations are not necessarily issues for machines, who can operate in a vacuum and endure much more hostile conditions than we can. As such, AI-driven computers will be critical in preparing a place for us in the stars, whether that is mining asteroids or making habitats for us on new planets. Much like the existing code that AI gets based on, blockchain will be critical in empowering the safe and sustainable development of these beings, both for near term commercial applications and our long-term survival in the cosmos.

Now that we have explored the idea that blockchain tech is a reliable way, humans can build, control, and protect themselves from rogue artificial intelligence. In the next chapter, we will go into the specifics of current blockchain protocols that exist today. We believe many of today's existing battle-hardened blockchain protocols will be the rails future AI systems get built on top of for the foreseeable future into the year 2035.

Bibliography and Suggested Reading

Max Tegmark. *Life 3.0: Being Human in the Age of Artificial Intelligence*. Knopf, 2017.

Kai-Fu Lee. *AI Superpowers: China, Silicon Valley, and the New World Order*. Houghton Mifflin Harcourt, 2018.

James Gleick. *The Information: A History, a Theory, a Flood*. Vintage, 2012.

Sean Garrish. *How Smart Machines Think*. MIT Press, 2018.

Nick Bostrum. *Superintelligence: Paths, Dangers, Strategies*. Oxford University Press, 2014

John Brockman, et al. *Possible Minds: Twenty-Five Ways of Looking at AI*. Penguin Press, 2019.

George Gilder. *Life After Google: The Fall of Big Data and the Rise of the Blockchain Economy*. Gateway, 2018.

Part III: The Applications

Chapter 9: Survey of Existing Blockchain Protocols

"Just because something doesn't do what you planned it to do doesn't mean it's useless."

- Thomas Edison

"Spend each day trying to be a little wiser than you were when you woke up."

– Charlie Munger

Blockchain is more than just technology - it has become an ideology and way of life for many people, with all the diversity that human communities have. There will likely never be "one chain to rule them all" despite the best efforts of some - there will always be a diversity of approaches and applications.

Anyone who thinks there is only going to be a single blockchain should examine other technologies and industries around them. From banking to social media, airlines, and telecoms, there are multiple large competitors in almost every sector. Given that Bitcoin and all major cryptocurrencies started in an open-source, decentralized manner, this openness fueled many innovations and new endeavors in the space.

That said, some blockchains will be better than others; some will contribute and execute on ideas better than others. Some will only remain ideas, and others will experiment with real applications, others will be well suited to daily use. This reality is the nature of the free market.

Blockchain Protocols Vs. Blockchain Projects

To help better explain this industry and to keep from confusing people, we are differentiating between blockchain protocols and a blockchain project. Think of a protocol as an independent blockchain network that is not dependent on any other blockchain other than its own. There are only a handful of genuinely decentralized independent protocols in the world today. This chapter will mainly focus on the differences between these various protocols.

In the next chapter, we will get into *projects*. We consider projects to be anything built on top of an existing independent blockchain protocol or that utilizes an outside protocol. This distinction includes exchanges, ICO's, stablecoins, wallets, and many other innovative ideas built on an external protocol. Protocols are building blocks, and projects are contingent on protocols.

Public Decentralized Protocols vs. Private Permissioned Protocols

The next distinction to be made is the difference between decentralized public protocols and private "permissioned" blockchain protocols. Just as the name implies, a public decentralized blockchain protocol is just that, public and decentralized, with no central authority or company overseeing or governing its use. Bitcoin, DigiByte, Litecoin are examples of this.

Private permissioned blockchain protocols are issued by a private entity and controlled through a centralized system. These protocols are independent of any other underlying blockchain protocol, and that's why we include them in this chapter. It's important to note that these permissioned protocols are less secure than truly decentralized protocols.

Public Decentralized vs. Centralized Blockchain Protocols

It is 100% factual to say that the largest and most secure blockchain protocols in the world today are public, open-source, and decentralized. This structure, after all, was the goal Satoshi envisioned for a decentralized cryptocurrency when he wrote the Bitcoin whitepaper and invented blockchain technology.

This adherence to principles of decentralization does not apply across the industry. Several protocols advertise themselves as genuinely decentralized and open-source when that's not the case. Frequently a handful of insiders control a majority of cryptocurrency in circulation and the majority of nodes on a blockchain network.

Decentralization with public blockchain protocols is indeed a spectrum and can affect different domains, such as validation and mining, distribution of assets, or numbers of nodes. This spectrum spans from 100% initially premined and controlled protocols like TRON and XRP to the most extreme decentralized projects like Bitcoin and DigiByte.

Independent Blockchain Protocol vs. Protocol Fork

Another distinction that needs to be clarified is the difference between an independent protocol with its own unique genesis block (the first block in the chain) and a blockchain protocol that was forked from an existing project with a shared history. An example of this is all the forks of Bitcoin, such as Bitcoin Cash and Bitcoin SV. All three share the same genesis block and history from 2009 to 2017. Another protocol fork is Ethereum, which shares a genesis block with Ethereum Classic (the original Ethereum).

Codebase Fork vs. Protocol Fork Vs. Hard Fork

While we are on the topic of forking, we must clarify something that often confuses many people. People often use the term "fork" indiscriminately, applying it in the wrong context.

A *codebase fork* is where open source code on GitHub is forked and used to create a new independent blockchain with its own unique genesis block. Most blockchains in existence today are (at some level) a codebase fork of the original Bitcoin protocol.

A protocol fork (such as when Bitcoin Cash forked from Bitcoin) involves a new, independent chain is created by forking an existing protocol at a specific block height and point in time. Think of this as a branch in a river or a split in a political party. These protocol forks will always have a shared blockchain history up to a certain point, and they will share the same genesis block forever, even though they operate by different rules now.

Many of these forks have been scams, and especially when it comes to Bitcoin. Protocol forks tend to occur amidst differences in opinion in a decentralized community, where emerging groups decide to go two different directions based on different values and competing egos. These protocol forks can also be dangerous at a technical level, primarily when you use your same private keys to send transactions on one blockchain, and the same transaction gets posted on all the protocol forks at the same time. Many have lost funds as a result of this overlap.

Finally, we have what is known as a hard fork. While technically the protocol fork mentioned can be a hard fork in principle, a hard fork is typically used to describe an upgrade to an existing independent protocol in a way that it is not compatible with the previous version of itself. Hard forks are like phylogenesis - when new species emerge in an evolutionary timetable. At one point, we as Homo Sapiens became so different from Australopithecus and other early ancestors that we became incompatible. Successful hard forks require every participant on the blockchain protocol to upgrade or be left behind. Because of this, hard forks tend to be democratic, where protocol forks tend to be dictatorial.

Both Bitcoin and DigiByte have undergone several successful hard forks in the past. DigiByte has experienced five successful hard forks since 2014 to adopt improvements. However, today, there is still only one DigiByte blockchain history going back to the Genesis block, where Bitcoin has had many protocol forks that have gone off in different directions.

Consensus Algorithms

Now let's get to the primary subsystem of a blockchain that is the differentiator between most public independent blockchain protocols today. This subcomponent is what we call a *consensus algorithm*. A consensus algorithm is a mathematical way that a blockchain can achieve stability and agreement across its entire network.

Consensus algorithms are primarily used to achieve reliability in a computer network across multiple distributed nodes, all of which contain the same information. Delivering reliability in a distributed system solves the fundamental problem in computing, known as the "consensus problem."

Think about all the times you were editing a Word document or Excel spreadsheet for a shared project, and a colleague overwrote some of the changes you have made. This problem would happen with blockchains if there were not a consensus algorithm involved. The very first consensus algorithm used by bitcoin and is still the most widely used today is known as proof of work (PoW).

Many types of independent blockchain protocols have expanded upon Satoshi's original proof of work blockchain by substituting algorithms while keeping other blockchain subcomponents the same. We will now go through these different types of consensus algorithms in order of the prominence you find them in the market.

Proof of Work

Proof of work (PoW) is the original consensus algorithm used in Bitcoin since the beginning of 2009. DigiByte is also a heavily modified (PoW) system with five separate mining algorithms instead of just one like Bitcoin.

PoW is analogous to proving to your boss that you have performed your assignment as directed - for example, if you became employed by a car factory, a proof of work would count that you had made the correct number of the right model of cars. Moreover, your proof of work can be easily validated because there are physical cars that your boss can go touch, drive, and feel.

Proof of Work blockchains leverages game theory by progressively rewarding miners for validating and processing blocks on the chain. Distribution of these rewards can be compared to a lottery. However, instead of merely just scratching a lottery ticket and waiting, the validator is required to solve a complicated math problem as the ticket is submitted. This process is known as mining, and each miner provides the cryptographic equivalent of a lottery ticket, which includes the hashed solution to a complicated math problem to discover the next block in the blockchain. If the consensus algorithm randomly selects that miner's ticket and likes its answer to the math problem, they receive the block reward (i.e., new bitcoins or digibytes) from the next block as its added to the blockchain.

Because mining technology advances and the supply of mining power ebbs and flows, the math problems in a PoW system must get progressively harder to solve over time. This adjustment is something known as a *difficulty adjustment*. We will touch more on this now later, but for now understand in a proof of work system, as more miners come onto a PoW network, the difficulty goes higher to maintain proper block timing interval. It also can go down if fewer miners are trying to earn block rewards.

Proof of Work has its origin in Cynthia Dwork and Moni Naor's 1993 paper *Pricing via Processing.* This work outlines the author's proposed use of cryptography to diminish the volume of spam emails and other service abuses, such as denial of service attacks. The idea suggested was that by requiring the sender to expend energy while solving a cryptographic puzzle, there would be less spam. PoW systems were initially designed to increase the computing and energy cost of sending an email, such that spam email sent to a large number of recipients would face a penalty and become unprofitable.

This specific method was a critical component in Hashcash, a crucial precursor to Bitcoin that was proposed by UK cryptographer Adam Back in 1997 - eleven years before Satoshi released Bitcoin. Instead of using money, micropayments, and accounts, Hashcash imposes a cost by requiring computing power to digest a cryptographic hash that has gotten attached to an email header with the title and timestamp - in effect making it more costly to send spam email.

Satoshi adopted the PoW system in constructing Bitcoin and remains the primary method in validating new blocks as they get added to the chain for the majority of modern blockchains. At scale, PoW mining currently consumes roughly 0.5% of the world's energy - enough to power New Zealand or Hungary.

Further, because there are economies of scale in establishing centralized mining pools, PoW miners often aggregate their hash power and use their combined mining power to increase their odds of successfully finding a block. Most PoW mining today is done primarily through large mining pools. One exception to this is DigiByte's Odocrypt mining algorithm, which changes itself every ten days and was recently added as 1 of 5 DigiByte mining algorithms in July 2019.

PoW mining pool centralization could represent an existential threat to blockchains that lack real-time difficulty adjustments or multiple (PoW) mining algos - both of which were pioneered by DigiByte. In circumstances where the hash rate fluctuates wildly or stops suddenly, the chain could cease to operate. This fluctuation also affects a chain's ability to execute hard fork upgrades, as differences in mining power could advance flaws rather than resolve them. We will talk more about this later.

Proof of Work - UTXO Blockchain Protocols

UTXO stands for "Unspent Transaction Output." UTXO's are how you can track where the native digital assets and cryptocurrency currently resides and gets updated with each block as transactions move inputs and outputs from address to address.

Bitcoin

Bitcoin is the very first and today the most significant blockchain in the world in terms of market cap, adoption, and belief. Many functionally compare Bitcoin to "Digital Gold," and its monetary and asset characteristics are primarily a result of the fact that it is precisely that. Much of the consensus value around Bitcoin is because it launched first and has the most proven track record. After a decade of constant efforts to hack and suppress it by criminals, governments, and curious tinkerers, Bitcoin is more resilient than ever. This resilience is the hallmark of its success. Bitcoin is durable at the code level, at the process of game theory, and could be argued to be antifragile at the level of economic theory.

Genesis Block: *"The Times 03/Jan/2009 Chancellor on brink of second bailout for banks"*

Launch Date: January 10th, 2009

Creator: Satoshi Nakamoto

Ticker Symbol: BTC

Consensus Algorithm: Proof of Work

Max Supply: 21 Million, with 4-year block reward havings

Block Time: 10 Minutes

Difficulty Adjustment: 2016 Blocks

Mining Algorithm: SHA-256

Influential Groups: the Bitcoin Foundation, MIT Digital Currency Initiative, Blockstream, Core Developers

Notable Achievements: The first blockchain created — largest market cap. Bitcoin is the primary digital asset that all other cryptocurrencies are traded against on most exchanges. BTC acts as the crypto reserve asset for the blockchain industry. We, as authors, have and will continue to invest in Bitcoin.

Cons: Slow block times, massive centralization of mining, and lack of real-time difficulty adjustment. Very hard to gain consensus and agreement to add new features and technology without splitting the network into factions. Stable for now but stuck at a technical level if any threat were to emerge.

Direct Bitcoin (BTC) Forks / Shared Genesis Block

Direct forks of Bitcoin share the Genesis block with the original networks. They have Bitcoin in their name but have separated from the original Bitcoin Blockchain, rather than being formally independent by having a unique genesis block.

Bitcoin Cash

Bitcoin Cash aims to be a more fungible version of Bitcoin that focuses on payments over being strictly a store of value that is cumbersome to exchange in micropayments. On November 15,

2018, a hard-fork chain split of Bitcoin Cash occurred between two rival factions called Bitcoin Cash and Bitcoin SV.

There are many other direct Bitcoin forks with shared genesis blocks such as Bitcoin SV, Bitcoin Gold, Bitcoin Diamond, and more.

Genesis Block: *"The Times 03/Jan/2009 Chancellor on brink of second bailout for banks"*
Split Date: August 1st, 2017.
Creator: Satoshi Nakamoto
Ticker Symbol: BCH
Consensus Algorithm: Proof of Work
Max Supply: 21 Million, with 4-year block reward havings
Block Time: 10 Minutes
Difficulty Adjustment: Real-Time (DigiShield inspired EDA)
Mining Algorithm: SHA-256
Influential Groups: Bitcoin.com, Roger Ver.
Notable Achievements: Larger block sizes. Added OP_CODES and functionality.
Cons: 10-minute block times can still be slow for quick confirmations compared to many other blockchains.

Litecoin

Marketed as silver to Bitcoin's gold, focused on use as payment and potentially as a store of value, currently adding greater fungibility and security. Litecoin was launched in 2011 by Charlie Lee with the intent of making a faster version of Bitcoin with a different mining algorithm to complement Bitcoin's role as crypto "gold."

Genesis Block: "NY Times 05/Oct/2011 Steve Jobs, Apple's Visionary, Dies at 56"
Launch Date: October 5th, 2011
Creator: Charlie Lee
Ticker Symbol: LTC
Consensus Algorithm: Proof of Work
Max Supply: 84 Million, with 4-year block reward havings

Block Time: 2.5 Minutes
Difficulty Adjustment: 2016 Blocks
Mining Algorithm: Scrypt
Influential Groups: Litecoin Foundation, Core Developers
Notable Achievements: One of the very first blockchains to launch after BTC. 4x faster than Bitcoin. We, as authors, have and will continue to invest in Litecoin.

Cons: Slower block times than many other chains. LTC also has not implemented real-time difficulty adjustment code.

Dogecoin

Initially started as a joke, Dogecoin is an experiment in inflationary cryptocurrency. Treated mainly as a penny stock on exchanges, where a single satoshi of value fluctuation is tradable for a profit. The supply is uncapped, and even the creator questions why people are still trading it. Still one of the most decentralized blockchains on the planet. It is not quite a fully independent protocol, as it is merge mined with Litecoin.

Genesis Block: "Nintondo"
Launch Date: December 6th, 2013
Creator: Jackson Palmer
Ticker Symbol: DOGE
Consensus Algorithm: Proof of Work
Max Supply: Limitless. 121,425,901,379 as of this writing.
Block Time: 10 Minutes
Difficulty Adjustment: Real-Time (DigiShield)
Mining Algorithm: Scrypt (Merge mined with Litecoin)
Influential Groups: Volunteer core developers.
Notable Achievements: The most loved dog on the internet as the mascot, Shiba Inus. Much wow. Such love.

Cons: The supply is not limited and can be considered an inflationary cryptocurrency. Interestingly, this may be a bonus if nation-states begin to adopt crypto but do not want to deal with the deflationary pressures of hard caps - inflation can now be set in code, rather than obscured in monetary policy.

Vertcoin

Single Algo PoW, built by developers affiliated with MIT to support distributed mining. Vertcoin was initially launched in 2014, and its community and development team have remained active through today.

Genesis Block: "01/09/2014 Germany to Help in Disposal of Syrian Chemical Weapons"

Launch Date: January 9th, 2014.

Creator: Multiple Developers

Ticker Symbol: VTC

Consensus Algorithm: Proof of Work

Max Supply: 84 Million, with 4-year block reward havings

Block Time: 2.5 Minutes

Difficulty Adjustment: Real-Time

Mining Algorithm: Lyra2REv3, ASIC resistant.

Influential Groups: Volunteer core developers.

Notable Achievements: Continual improvements to prevent ASIC mining centralization.

Cons: Limited long term supply and slower block times.

Proof of Work - MultiAlgo UTXO Blockchain Protocols

Multi algorithm mining offers many benefits over a single independent mining algorithm used as a consensus algorithm for proof of work mining. The very first blockchain protocol to be launched with multi algo mining was MyriadCoin in 2014. DigiByte was the first blockchain to hard fork from a single algo PoW blockchain to an improved MultiAlgo blockchain in 2014.

By splitting up PoW mining over several mining algorithms, a monopoly on mining hardware and mining pools becomes harder to come by, leading to further decentralization of a blockchain. This variety makes a blockchain much more decentralized and more difficult to 51% attack.

DigiByte

DigiByte is a MultiAlgo PoW blockchain focused on cybersecurity, distributed Cryptography, asset Issuance, and much more created by the author of this book in 2014. We will use this section of the book to describe DGB in more detail, and many of the innovations DGB has pioneered over the years.

Genesis Block: "USA Today: 10/Jan/2014, Target: Data stolen from up to 110M customers"

Launch Date: January 10th, 2014

Creator: Jared Tate (Author of this book)

Ticker Symbol: DGB

Consensus Algorithm: Proof of Work, MultiAlgo

Max Supply: Fixed. 21 billion in 21 years (By 2035)

Block Time: 15 Seconds

Difficulty Adjustment: Real-Time (DigiShield)

Mining Algorithm: 5 independent algos; Odocrypt, Sha256, Scrypt, Skein, and Qubit.

Influential Groups: The DigiByte global community. Volunteer core developers. DigiByte Awareness Team (DGBAT). Jared's Twitter account.

Notable Achievements: First to real-time diff adjustment, DigiShield, MultiShield, SegWit implementation, DigiAssets, DigiID, Dandelion (IP anonymity), and more.

Cons: No centralized source of funding to actively promote marketing and adoption.

The DigiByte Story

After five years of consistent, committed, focused development, DigiByte has become one of the top blockchains in the world. DigiByte is currently 40 times faster, five times more decentralized than Bitcoin, and much more decentralized than pretty much all other blockchain protocols.

Currently, DigiByte has a 15-second block timing and five separate mining algorithms. Each mining algorithm has its own independently weighted difficulty, which accounts for 20% of the total blocks mined on the network.

DigiByte currently has the longest blockchain of any top 100 non DPoS protocols out there with almost 10 million blocks. As such, we have had to adapt and improve several things on the DigiByte protocol that Bitcoin will not encounter any time soon.

DigiByte Innovations

DigiByte has pioneered several innovations over the last five years. One of the first innovations we did was the DigiShield difficulty adjustment. DigiShield has since been implemented into dozens of other blockchains and several of the top blockchain projects out there. DigiShield allows for real-time difficulty adjustment in a way that is not possible with the original bitcoin difficulty adjustment system.

DigiShield

On September 24th, 2019, the Bitcoin mining hash rate just crashed almost 40% in one day.

For years Jared has been warning that the biggest threat to Bitcoin is the centralization of mining pools and mining power. As well as the fact the Bitcoin blockchain does not and cannot adjust its mining difficulty quickly enough.

What is the difficulty adjustment, you might ask? Well, it's merely the process of changing how hard the math problems are for miners to solve to keep an even time interval between blocks as new mining power comes goes onto the network. In the case of Bitcoin, this time interval should be 10 minutes. In the case of DigiByte, its 15 seconds. This block timing is why DigiByte is 40x faster than Bitcoin.

So why is the Bitcoin mining hash rate dropping by 40% such a problem? Well, the same bug that still exists in Bitcoin today almost killed off DigiByte & Dogecoin and killed off other blockchains in 2014. See, it takes bitcoin 2016 blocks to make a single difficulty adjustment.

Back then, we a "multi-pool" problem. These pools would jump from mining Litecoin to Dogecoin and then to DigiByte mining blocks quicker than they were supposed to until several rounds of 2016 block adjustments stabilized the network.

We would see 10x to 20x fold increases and decreases in net hash rate. When these pools would leave a blockchain, the chain would often freeze, sometimes for hours or even days.

The solution to this was simple. Make the difficulty adjustment real-time and allow it to adjust far enough to keep things stable with mass hash rate fluctuations. This reason is why we created DigiShield and MultiShield. Following DigiBytes lead numerous other proof of work blockchains from Doge to Ethereum, and Bitcoin cash have installed real-time diff adjustment code. Bitcoin should do the same.

If there is ever a mass power outage or natural disaster affecting mining pools or a significant decrease in Bitcoin hash rate, block times will stall for hours and potentially weeks, causing immense harm to the industry.

After all, right now, just three single Bitcoin mining pools and three unique sets of private keys control 51% of all bitcoin mining power.

MultiAlgo

DigiByte was also the first blockchain to hard fork from a single mining algorithm to multiple mining algorithms in 2014. Myriadcoin first pioneered MultiAlgo mining in 2014, launching after DigiByte. The myriadcoin developers have always been a very innovative and unsung group that has done a lot of creative things in the blockchain industry.

MultiShield

MultiShield is a second and third-generation version of the original DigiShield but used in conjunction with multi algo mining. After switching to multiple mining rhythms in 2014, we needed to adapt the original deal DigiShield to mimic the independent properties inherent in multi Algo mining with five separate mining algorithms.

Scalability

Over the years, DigiByte has implemented several significant scalability enhancements to the original UTXO blockchain protocol. Such scalability performance increases include the speed at which headers sync, block timing, block size, SegWIT, and more.

Odocrypt

Instead of making a completely new blockchain DigiByte continues to reinvent itself. On July 21st, 2019, the Odocrypt mining algo was successfully swapped in and replaced the existing myr-groestl mining algo. DGB developers from all over the world have helped contribute to this release and to help test the new mining algo. From San Francisco to Texas and on to Australia, New Zealand & Europe.

Odocrypt is named after the Star Trek character, who is a shapeshifter. Just like Odo on Star Trek, Odocrypt changes itself every ten days. By recreating itself into a brand new algorithm every ten days, mining hardware manufacturers are economically discouraged from building specialized ASICs leading to mining centralization. While, in theory, it is possible to create an ASIC for Odocrypt, it would not make any economic or business sense to do so. It makes much more sense to mine it with FPGA's which can easily be used by home-based hobby miners.

A field-programmable gate array (FPGA) is an integrated circuit designed to be configured by a developer or a designer to help prototype new ASICs or embedded devices for specific use cases. Since Odocrypt changes itself every ten days, FPGA miners will also need to be re-optimized every ten days. Thereby leveling the playing field and allowing even the smallest of hobbyist miners to have a fair chance at mining DigiByte.

Odocrypt was initially originated by MentalCollatz, who wrote the majority of the Odocrypt algo code. Mental described Odocrypt as:

"Regarding ASIC-resistance: Odo is a substitution-permutation network. Both the substitutions (s-boxes) and permutations (p-boxes) change every ten days. If they didn't change, it would be easy to create an ASIC that significantly outperformed any other hardware, but because they change, the ASIC would need to be able to reconfigure itself. There's already hardware that specializes in being able to reconfigure itself - the FPGA. Additionally, FPGAs are really good at implementing small s-boxes, so while an ASIC could, in theory, be built, the advantage over FPGAs would be much smaller than for typical proof-of-work algorithms."

So why did DigiByte add this mining algo? DigiByte originally forked to five mining algorithms in 2014 to prevent mining centralization with the mass production of specialized ASICs. It worked for a while, but since then, ASICs have been developed sometimes in secret for all five current DigiByte mining algorithms. ASICs have now been manufactured for pretty much every other mining algorithm in the blockchain industry that is widely used.

This trend has led to a decrease in home-based miners and has led to a decreasing global node count in 2018/2019. These centralized mining farms tend to sell their DGB right away on the open market instead of holding as a long-term asset to pay bills and recoup their hardware investments.

Proof of Work - Virtual Machine

Ethereum

Ethereum is a decentralized blockchain protocol launched in 2015. Ethereum is described as a decentralized virtual machine known as the Ethereum Virtual Machine (EVM). The virtual machine's instruction set and programming language solidity are described as being Turing-complete.

Ethereum was first described in late 2013 by Vitalik Buterin and Development was funded by an online crowdsale that took place from July to August 2014. The blockchain was launched on July 30th, 2015, with 72 million coins "premined." This premine amounts to 66 percent of the total circulating supply as of this writing in fall 2019.

Genesis Block: No news headline hashed
Launch Date: July 30th, 2015
Creator: Vitalik Buterin

Ticker Symbol: ETH
Consensus Algorithm: Proof of Work
Max Supply: Limitless, 108 Million ETH as of this writing. 66% premined.
Block Time: 15 Seconds
Difficulty Adjustment: Real-Time
Mining Algorithm: Ethash
Influential Groups: Ethereum Foundation, ConsenSys
Notable Achievements:
Cons: Moving to a proof of stake, sharding model. Premined 72 Million ETH coins, which is 66% of today's supply.

Proof of Work - Masternode

Another innovation on top of proof of work is the addition of "Masternodes" to allow for greater on-chain governance. DASH first pioneered the Masternode system in 2014.

Dash

Dash is described as a decentralized autonomous organization (DAO) run by a set of nodes called "masternodes." DASH was launched in January 2014 with the name "Xcoin" by Evan Duffield. It was rebranded to "Darkcoin" in 2014 before finally being rebranded yet again in March 2015 with the name Dash, which is is a portmanteau of 'digital cash.'

Genesis Block: "Wired 09/Jan/2014 The Grand Experiment Goes Live: Overstock.com Is Now Accepting Bitcoins"
Launch Date: January 18th, 2014
Creator: Evan Duffield
Ticker Symbol: DASH
Consensus Algorithm: Proof of Work + Masternodes
Max Supply: Unknown, not hard-capped, 14 - 22 million by 2054.
Block Time: 2.6 Minutes
Difficulty Adjustment: Dark Gravity Wave, DGWv3
Mining Algorithm: X11
Influential Groups: DASH DAO, Dash Treasury.

Notable Achievements: Instant Send, Private Send, Chain Locks, Governance & treasury with the Masternode system.

Cons: The DASH "Instamine" bug, was launched as "Darkcoin."

Proof of Work - Privacy Blockchain Protocols

Two main innovations have been made on proof of work blockchain protocols to enhance user privacy. The addition of ring signatures as used in Monero and the addition of zero-knowledge proofs as seen with Zcash.

Proof of Work - Ring Signature

Monero is among the most innovative blockchain projects from a technical perspective by leveraging the use of "ring signatures" - a cryptographic method that predates Blockchain, which was introduced by Ron Rivest, Adi Shamir, and Yael Taumen in their 2001 MIT paper *"How to Leak a Secret."* A ring signature is effectively a way of aggregating a crowd of signers in a cryptographic environment such that the participants get obfusticated by the gathering of signatures that they are all transacting.

Rivest, Shamir, and Tauman's paper draw on even earlier work in group signatures, where an authoritative key issuer can issue private keys for a group that signs using those delegated permissions. This idea was outlined in 1991 by Chaum and Van Heyst. As discussed earlier, blockchain represents a half-century of cryptographic innovation. In Monero's case, privacy features have an intellectual legacy that goes back nearly 30 years.

Ring signatures work somewhat like dead drops in Cold War espionage. A dead drop is how spies exchanged documents, money, and equipment with assets. This exchange worked by leaving items in a hidden location, such as under a footbridge in a public park. They would then leave a separate signal such as a chalk mark at a bus stop to notify the asset that the drop had happened. Never do the asset and the handler meet in person in this system, but they are allowed to interact in an impersonal way because their relationship doesn't look like an exchange. Unless their affiliation with the same location or with each other elsewhere gets identified, their trade remains clandestine.

If you were to watch a crowded street, bustling pedestrians, and vehicles, you might not notice the middle-aged man leaving his briefcase on a park bench and another man picking it up. That, in effect, is how a Monero transaction occurs, by creating a cryptographic crowd and hiding the business in the bustle, among several other keys that have not authorized and do not carry any Monero.

The public and private key system in a ring signature works slightly different than in a traditional UTXO blockchain. This difference is that a one-time-key gets generated as the drop point, and the receiver has to check the ring signature for the correct key by repeatedly refreshing his or her wallet. So, if Anonymous Cyberpunk 1 wants to send some Monero to Anonymous Cyberpunk 2, she will need to ask Anonymous Cyberpunk 2 for his public key.

However, like other Blockchains, one won't use two public keys to send funds; she would generate a one-time public key for two and will send funds to *that* public key, which gets posted amidst several others. This ability is what Monero calls a "stealth address" - in effect, an intermediary between outputs.

Each Monero wallet is a 95-character string that consists of two keys - a public 'view' key and a public 'send' key. When a transaction occurs, the sender uses a combination of these keys to tag the transaction. This tag is for the receiver when its added to the blockchain. Only upon scanning the blockchain and using his or her corresponding *private* view and spend keys, which corresponds to the public key used by the sender, can the receiving party recover the transaction. The network then images the time-stamped signature to ensure that the transaction does not double-spend (charge twice).

As you can tell, this is a very sophisticated method, and it, and is also the criminal's blockchain of choice based on some of its core functionalities that make transactions more difficult for outside observers to recognize and interpret. So needless to say, it and its sister projects are controversial. Monero is what is called a "stealth" or "privacy" coin, and this is a double-edged sword in that it provides for individual security, but also accommodates for illicit activity, including clandestine mining. This mining is where computing power has been taken without consent from unwilling and unwitting persons to mine Monero that gets sent to a hacker's address.

This behavior is not even unique to cryptocurrency - if you use an encrypted messaging platform to communicate with your friends (such as Signal, WhatsApp, or Wickr), you are participating in the very same paradox. Stealth coins use innovations on the UTXO model that remove the information integrity of the blockchain to provide privacy. While traditional UTXO models are public but encrypted, Monero uses what are called "ring signatures" to transfer funds through a mechanism similar to a "dead drop" in Cold War espionage parlance.

Instead of having funds "pushed" to the receiving party's wallet, a ring signature is a vehicle for a user to go to a specific address and *retrieve* funds. In this system, there is still an ontology for transaction - sender, receiver, amount, and there is a degree of atomic behavior to the tokens issued on the Monero blockchain.

Stealth Mining/ Cryptojacking

Monero was involved in several viral miners, including infiltrating the most high profile victim of this was the Mexican government's computer systems. This form of non-consensual mining - referred to in the industry as "cryptojacking" has affected as many as 500 Million users.

Further, much of the criminal activity formerly associated with Bitcoin has moved to dark coins like Monero, which achieve their anonymity through various systems including tumblers and "stealth addresses" that obfusticate the transaction in layers of false signatures.

Monero

Monero is a decentralized blockchain and cryptocurrency known as XMR that was launched in 2014. Monero as a focus on privacy and has made several significant strides in the industry to achieve private, decentralized currency transactions. Monero is an evolution on the CryptoNote protocol, which pioneered the use of ring signatures and stealth addresses.

Genesis Block: No news headline hashed
Launch Date: April 18th, 2014
Creator: thankful_for_today
Ticker Symbol: XMR
Consensus Algorithm: Proof of Work
Max Supply: Infinite
Block Time: 2 Minutes
Difficulty Adjustment: Every Block
Mining Algorithm: CryptoNight
Influential Groups: Core Developers

Notable Achievements: Stealth addresses and confidential transactions. The use of cryptographic ring signatures.

Cons: Monero was used in 44% of cryptocurrency ransomware attacks in 2018. It continues to be one of the most widely used cryptocurrencies for dark market activities.

Proof of Work - Zero-Knowledge Proofs

A zero-knowledge proof or zero-knowledge protocol is a method by which one party can prove to another party that they know a value. With a zero-knowledge proof, Bill can show to Sally he knows X without every conveying any information apart from the fact that he knows the value in question.

To simplify this, let's return to the dead drop analogy mentioned above by adding in zero-knowledge proofs to the drop. A zero-knowledge proof would be akin to a spy passing on verification that he knew exactly what was contained in a briefcase before it was opened. In this scenario, the spy can prove access to the information by the uniqueness of the contents, which could not be guessed.

This verification is beneficial because there is no risk of the suitcase itself getting compromised. The handler would know without a shadow of a doubt that the spy knew what he claimed to know before he passed on the briefcase without ever knowing the exact information contained in the briefcase beforehand.

Zcash

ZCash is a blockchain protocol that uses Zero-Knowledge Proofs to enhance privacy and anonymity in transactions. ZCash has a parent company named Electric Coin Company. 10% of all Zcash is distributed by 20% of mining rewards for the first four years as a founder's reward to the Electric Coin Company. This reward ends in 2020.

Genesis Block: "Zcash0b9c4eef8b7cc417ee5001e3500984b6fea35683a7cac141a043c42064835d34"

Launch Date: October 28th, 2016.
Creator: Electric Coin Company
Ticker Symbol: ZEC
Consensus Algorithm: Proof of Work
Max Supply: 21,000,000
Block Time: 2.5 Minutes
Difficulty Adjustment: Real-time (DigiShield)
Mining Algorithm: Equihash
Influential Groups: Electric Coin Company
Notable Achievements: Integration of zero-knowledge proofs.
Cons: A corporate entity launched the blockchain, not entirely decentralized. What happens when the founder's reward ends in 2020?

Proof of Stake (POS)

Proof of stake (PoS) is a consensus algorithm by which a blockchain protocol aims to achieve distributed consensus without the process of mining involved. PoS can be likened to a traditional stock that pays out "dividends." By "locking" up or staking a certain amount of coins in a wallet, you will earn newly minted coins as the blockchain distributes them in reward for your staking.

In PoS based cryptocurrencies, the creator of the next block is chosen via various combinations of random selection and wealth or age (*i.e.,* the stake). There are a few security concerns with this approach to blockchain consensus. The main concern is the ability of a nefarious actor to buy up a large percentage of coins and then use that majority to alter the chain at will. Unlike in proof-of-work systems, there is little cost to working on several chains at once to attempt a 51% attack and double-spending. Nevertheless, Proof of Stake is an attractive incentive to getting more people to run full nodes and participate in a blockchain ecosystem.

Peercoin

Peercoin was the very first blockchain to introduce staking, as well as one of the very first blockchains outside of Bitcoin. Peercoin was launched in 2012 by Scott Nadal and Sunny King and is still under development to this day.

Genesis Block: "Matonis 07-AUG-2012 Parallel Currencies And The Roadmap To Monetary Freedom"

Launch Date: August 12, 2012

Creator: Scott Nadal & Sunny King

Ticker Symbol: PPC

Consensus Algorithm: Proof of Stake & Proof of Work

Max Supply: Limitless, 25 million PPC as of this writing.

Block Time: 8.5 Minutes

Difficulty Adjustment: Dynamic, Based on previous two blocks

Mining Algorithm: SHA-256

Influential Groups: Core developers.

Notable Achievements: First proof of stake coin.

Cons: A low $6 million market cap as of this writing.

POW/POS Hybrid Protocols & Proof of Activity

One of the more ingenious solutions to the problems posed by PoS is to combine it with other algorithms in a hybrid setting, called Proof of Activity (PoA). PoA features two steps - a PoW mining layer and a PoS staking layer, where stakers sign and validate a block once it gets mined. This hybrid approach is the method adopted by Decred, which uses both PoS with PoW; the two systems mutually reinforce each other.

The attacker in this scenario would need 51% of the coins and 51% of the mining power to change the network and double spend. These requirements effectively decentralize the validation method, reducing the dependency on miners or stakers created by single-algo systems.

A drawback of hybrid validation systems is that they can be complicated; however, Decred has managed to pull the idea off quite well.

Decred

Decred is a hybrid PoW/PoS blockchain that was launched in 2016 with a focus on decentralized governance. Decred employs a unique consensus voting model that empowers stakeholders and allows for decentralized decision-making and self-funding. It is a complete stand-alone ecosystem that has proven hybrid PoW/PoS blockchains could be the most viable long term governance model for a blockchain protocol to follow.

Genesis Block: No news headline hashed
Launch Date: February 8th, 2016
Creator: Company 0
Ticker Symbol: DCR
Consensus Algorithm: Hybrid PoW/PoS via PoA
Max Supply: 21 Million
Block Time: 5 Minutes
Difficulty Adjustment: 144 blocks (12 hours)
Mining Algorithm: BLAKE-256
Influential Groups: Company 0, Decred Holdings Group LLC, Core Developers

Notable Achievements: On-chain governance and voting. Hybrid PoS & PoW. Pioneering atomic swaps.

Delegated Proof of Stake (DPoS)

> *"If you don't believe me or don't get it, I don't have time to try to convince you, sorry."*
>
> -Satoshi Nakamoto to Dan Larimer, 29 July 2010

Delegated Proof of Stake or DPOS for short is the brainchild of Daniel Larimer. Larimer is also the founder of the three most widely known DPoS blockchain projects, including EOS, Steemit, and BitShares.

DPoS projects are typically highly centralized, premined, and full of a lot of fancy marketing and misleading statements about the platform's decentralization.

DPoS effectively removes transaction validation from normal nodes and wallet clients and instead relies on a handful of "super" validator nodes or block producers to validate and control the transactions on a network. The number of DPoS validator nodes on a blockchain network ranges from 7-27 on average, and quite often these nodes are controlled by the same group of insiders who are in on the pre-issue. This low number of nodes leads to some obvious challenges of centralization on the network. Perhaps the name "Delegated Proof of Shenanigans" might be more appropriate.

It should also be noted Dan Larimer, the inventor of DPoS, has a controversial history. Although he is a genuine blockchain innovator, some stories cast him in a bad light, including accusations of cheating upon the launch of Steemit mining, to abandoning projects to start a new one for quick financial gain with no consideration for investors. As a former colleague and Ethereum Cofounder, Charles Hoskinson once stated: "Larimer hasn't finished a project yet." However, In the meantime, he has gotten extremely wealthy.

EOS

EOS is a delegated proof of stake blockchain protocol that went live in January 2018. Dan Larimer through the company Block.One created EOS. EOS relies on a network of 21 validating "block producer" nodes.

Genesis Block: No news headline hashed
Launch Date: January 31, 2018
Creator: Daniel Larimer, Brendan Blumer
Ticker Symbol: EOS
Consensus Algorithm: DPoS, 21 "Block Producers"
Max Supply: Limitless
Block Time: 500 milliseconds
Difficulty Adjustment:
Mining Algorithm: None, DPoS
Influential Groups: Block.One

Notable Achievements: A 12-month long ICO where they raised over $4 billion. The SEC fined them $24 million in October 2019.

Cons: Only allows for 21 block producers, meaning the entire network relies on 21 nodes. Extremely memory intensive to run a block producer node.

Tron

Tron is a DPoS based blockchain protocol that was launched during the hight of the ICO frenzy in the fall of 2017. While Tron claims to be a decentralized ecosystem, there are some very questionable doubts about these claims. Tron uses 27 "Super Representative" nodes to govern the network mostly controlled by the CEO Justin Sun and the Tron Foundation, which also conducted a 100% premine and token sale.

The former chief technical officer (CTO) and co-founder of Tron (TRX) Lucien Chen announced in May 209 that he was leaving the project. He stated that Tron had become excessively centralized and deviated from its founding principles. He said:

"The DPOS mechanism of Tron is pseudo-decentralized. The top 27 SR nodes (block nodes) have more than 170 million TRX votes, and most of them are controlled by Tron. It's hard for other latecomers to become block nodes, so they cannot participate in the process of block production."

"Token distribution is centralized, Super Representatives are centralized, code development is centralized. Even the community is organized under centralization."

Genesis Block: No news headline hashed
Launch Date: September 2017
Creator: "CEO" Justin Sun
Ticker Symbol: TRX
Consensus Algorithm: DPoS, 27 "Super Representatives"
Max Supply: 100 Billion premined
Block Time: 3-5 Seconds
Difficulty Adjustment: None
Mining Algorithm: None
Influential Groups: Tron Foundation, Justin Sun
Notable Achievements: Successfully duping an entire era of investors with what is most likely the most centralized blockchain to date.
Cons: 100 Billion premined TRX (100%). Highly centralized on only 27 nodes mostly controlled by the Tron Foundation.

The Byzantine Generals Problem

The idea of maintaining truth in a computer network where the potential for fraud exists has been studied for decades. In 1982 a paper was released by Lamport, Shostak, and Pease entitled "The Byzantine Generals Problem." This paper described the analogy of a group of generals surrounding and attacking a city. While attacking, the generals need to communicate securely without their messages being interfered with and altered by spies.

The paper goes on to highlight that the couriers carrying messages between generals can't be trusted. So because of this lack of trust, a method must be found to make sure all information that is shared among Generals is true and accurate. The paper also goes on to state that some Generals are loyal to the Byzantine state, and some are disloyal, which mimics what might happen in a computer network where not all network nodes are acting in good faith.

The Byzantine Agreement protocol as laid out in the 1982 paper and included the following definition of how the Byzantine army was divided and led by a General:

Each General is either a traitor or loyal to the Byzantine state.

All Generals communicate by sending and receiving messages.

There are only two commands: attack and retreat.

All loyal Generals should agree on the same plan of action: attack or retreat.

A small linear fraction of corrupt Generals should not cause the protocol to fail (less than a 1/3 fraction).

So what does the Byzantine Generals problem have to do with a blockchain or a distributed network? Well, just like some of the generals in the above example, not all nodes on a blockchain have the network's best intentions in mind.

Byzantine Agreement Protocols – Ripple and Stellar

Ripple Protocol Consensus Algorithm (RPCA)

The Ripple Protocol consensus algorithm (RPCA) is the consensus algo used by XRP and is applied every few seconds to all Ripple nodes. RPCA is applied to maintain correctness and agreement of the XRP blockchain protocol. Once consensus is reached, the current ledger is considered "closed" and becomes the last-closed ledger. Assuming that the consensus algorithm is successful and that there is no fork in the network, the last-closed ledger maintained by all nodes in the system will be identical.

The XRP Ledger Consensus Protocol consists of three primary components: Deliberation, Validation, and preferred branch. Deliberation is where nodes propose a transaction set to apply to a prior ledger, based on proposals received from other trusted nodes on the network contained in the UNL or unique node list.

When a node then believes that enough proposals agree, it applies the corresponding transactions to the prior ledger according to the ledger protocol rules. It then issues a validation for the generated ledger.

Validation is where nodes decide to fully validate a ledger based on the validations issued by trusted nodes. Once a quorum of validations for the same ledger is reached, that ledger and its ancestors are deemed fully validated, and its state is authoritative and irrevocable.

The final component is the Preferred Branch, where nodes determine the preferred working branch of ledger history. In times of asynchrony, network difficulty, or Byzantine failure, nodes may not initially validate the same ledger for a given sequence number. To make forward progress and fully validate later ledgers, nodes use the ledger ancestry of trusted nodes.

Ripple

Ripple is the scourge of many proponents of truly decentralized blockchain proponents. Complete with a 100% premine and centrally controlled nodes that can freeze your XRP at will this 2018 quote sums up the reason why:

"Apparently, Ripple is missing 32,570 blocks from the start of the ledger, and nodes are not able to obtain this data. This means that one may be unable to audit the whole chain and the full path of Ripple's original 100 billion XRP launch." -BitMEX Research

Genesis Block: No news headline hashed
Launch Date: 2012
Creator: OpenCoin (Now Ripple Labs), Chris Larsen, Jed McCaleb, David Schwarz
Ticker Symbol: XRP
Consensus Algorithm: Ripple Protocol Consensus Algorithm (RPCA)
Max Supply: 100 Billion
Block Time: 3-5 Seconds
Difficulty Adjustment: None
Mining Algorithm: None
Influential Groups: Ripple Labs, Inc.

Notable Achievements:

Cons: 100% premined and privately controlled. Missing 32,570 blocks from the start of is its ledger.

Stellar Lumens

Following an internal disagreement, Ripple cofounder Jed McCaleb split from Ripple Labs to found Stellar Lumens. While Stellar was originally a fork from Ripple, it has been modified with the addition of the Stellar Consensus Protocol (SCP) and numerous other changes. The Stellar Consensus Protocol (SCP) consists of three parts. These include Nomination, Balloting, and the Timeout. Check out the Stellar whitepaper to learn more about the SCP.

Genesis Block: No news headline hashed
Launch Date: July 31, 2014
Creator: Jed McCaleb
Ticker Symbol: XLM
Consensus Algorithm: Stellar Consensus Protocol
Max Supply: Infinite, 100 Billion premined
Block Time: 3-5 Seconds
Difficulty Adjustment: None
Mining Algorithm: None
Influential Groups: Stellar Development Foundation
Notable Achievements:
Cons: 100 Billion premined XLM. Highly inflationary.

Proof of Importance (PoI) - NEM

Another alteration of Proof of Stake is *"Proof of Importance"* (PoI), which brands itself as an attempt to address one of the criticisms of PoS - namely, that it encourages holders always to stake but never spend and use the digital assets as currency. PoI is currently unique to the NEM ("New Economic Movement") project and represents a different governance and validation model for PoS. PoI's general solution is to reward entities on the network for past participation in the system, even though they may not be staking as much for the current round of blocks.

While this approach is an intellectually exciting premise, PoI risks being a poor implementation of blockchain technology for a couple of reasons. First, it enables central control of the blockchain, which means that the chain is not truly immutable. If the founders or core programmers have enough influence, they can in a PoI setting alter the chain in ways that are beneficial for them. In this scenario, the chain ceases to be genuinely immutable and decentralized.

Second, PoI sets holding floors for who can stake a block, effectively locking out everyday holders and handing the advantage to parties who have pre-mined, issued themselves assets, or have large amounts of capital to invest in the staking process. Further, the method that PoI scores are issued gets centrally managed by NEM. If it suits the company, the rubric for what is "important" can be rewritten to suit the economic interests of the party in control of the algorithm, not necessarily the economic value or tokens as it would in a simple PoS setup.

NEM (XEM)

NEM started as a fork of NXT, which was a blockchain launched in 2013. NEM is a complicated blockchain that does not follow the design and transparency in code or marketing, followed by most of all the above mentioned public blockchain protocols. 100% of all XEM were premined in 2015 with the creation of the "nemesis" block, making NEM as centrally controlled as Ripple with XRP. In 2018 the Japanese cryptocurrency exchange Coincheck was hacked, and $500 million worth of XEM was stolen.

Genesis Block: NEM calls the first block in the chain the nemesis block.

Launch Date: March 31, 2015

Creator: Unkown

Ticker Symbol: XEM

Consensus Algorithm: Proof of Importance (PoI)

Max Supply: 8,999,999,999 (100% premined with "nemesis" block")

Block Time: 1 Minute

Difficulty Adjustment: None.

Mining Algorithm: None.

Influential Groups: NEM Foundation.

Notable Achievements: Being considered as the framework by Venezuala for the Petro.

Cons: Completely not decentralized. Unknown founders, not much clarity on where all premined XEM gets stored and how many nodes are actually on the network. We, as authors, would not and have not invested in NEM.

Additional Blockchain Consensus Algorithms

Proof of Capacity (PoC)

Proof of Capacity is a thought-provoking idea where an individual uses space on their hard drive instead of sheer computing power from the GPU or CPU to mine. Or from staking a pre-existing digital asset as proof that the validator wants the chain to continue - in a way, one might compare it to renting an apartment or office. This model uses massive amounts of storage to effectively write a series of lottery tickets rather than run cryptographic hashes.

As of this writing, PoC blockchains remain obscure, with the only working embodiment being Burstcoin, which has remained undistinguished with a small market capitalization (less than 20m USD as of this writing) and tenuous mining economics based on questionable profitability. As physical memory and cloud storage become increasingly cost-effective, such a solution could yet take root but not in the immediate.

Apart from technical aspects, there is also a question of how to economically deploy such a system. Since the PoC system still requires significant energy to read and write large amounts of data to memory, even though hard disk drive and solid-state drive storage consume much less energy than the PoW model. One could speculate that while both memory and processing are dual-use and can be used outside of mining a cryptocurrency, *work* in computing appears to be substantially more valuable than mere *storage*. This value is because processing gets more sophisticated and robust, while memory only becomes more plentiful.

Proof of Elapsed Time (PoET)

Proof of Elapsed Time (PoET) is a brainchild of chip manufacturer Intel and represents multi-thread timestamping across a series of Intel processors. Instead of trusting a public blockchain, the consensus mechanism gets based on Intel's processors running like parallel clocks, maintaining a ledger without ever invoking a mining process.

Blockchain Consortium Frameworks & Groups

There are multiple open-source blockchain Consortium frameworks and groups that have emerged to build the template blockchains for private enterprises to adopt. While this may seem exciting and a path forward in the future, we believe that these private permission blockchains do not offer anywhere near the same security as widely decentralized public protocols do.

Those who are thinking of issuing a private blockchain for their enterprise should consider anchoring that private blockchain into a decentralized public protocol for much higher security. While there may be some improvements to some of the open-source frameworks listed below over most current enterprise systems, they are nowhere near as secure as is being touted compared to other genuinely decentralized public blockchain protocols.

Hyperledger (Fabric)

Hyperledger is probably the most well-known open-source blockchain consortium that is a collaborative effort hosted by the Lennix foundation. Hyperledger was launched in 2015 and has received significant contributions from companies such as IBM and Intel. Hyper ledger is composed of multiple blockchain tools and sub frameworks.

Hyperledger Fabric is the main permissioned blockchain infrastructure, initially contributed by IBM. Fabric is the initial project, but there are many other tools under development within the Hyperledger umbrella. Hyperledger Sawtooth provided by Intel includes a dynamic consensus feature that enables the swapping of consensus algorithms in a running network. One of the consensus algos we mentioned above is the consensus algorithm known as "Proof of Elapsed Time."

There are numerous others, such as Quilt, Aries, Avalon, Besu, Caliper, and others. It's best to think of Hyperledger as a modular blockchain framework. Given that the well respected Linux Foundation supports Hyperledger, it probably has the best reputation thus far, although it has received criticism for mainly repacking open source code from other decentralized public blockchains.

R3 (Corda)

R3 is an enterprise blockchain bank consortium that raised over $150 million in to build open-source & commercial-grade private permissioned blockchains for banks. From what we have been able to gather, most of what they have released is largely repacked open source code from the blockchain protocols mentioned above, but it is written in Java designed for the Java Virtual Machine.

R3 bills itself as: "R3 is an enterprise blockchain software firm working with a broad ecosystem of more than 300 participants across multiple industries from both the private and public sectors to develop on Corda, its open-source blockchain platform, and Corda Enterprise, a commercial version of Corda for enterprise usage."

Within two years of joining R3, Banco Santander, Goldman Sachs, Morgan Stanely, and JP Morgan have all left the consortium. Upon leaving R3 managing director, Charley Cooper stated: "JP Morgan parted ways with R3 to pursue a very distinct technology path which is at odds with what the global financial services industry, represented by our 80-plus members, have chosen."

Enterprise Ethereum Alliance

The *EEA* is an alliance focused on bringing a repackaged private version of the Ethereum protocol to businesses and commercial groups around the world. It is effectively a privatized version of all the innovative work done on the open-source Ethereum protocol. The Enterprise Ethereum Alliance is a trademark of the Ethereum Foundation.

Trusted IoT Alliance (TIA)

TIA is intended to be a new open-source software foundation to support the creation of a secure, scalable, interoperable, and trusted IoT ecosystem leveraging blockchain technology. To date, we cannot yet find any actual code released by this alliance.

MOBI

MOBI is a nonprofit smart mobility consortium working with forward-thinking companies, including Ford, GM, IBM, Honda, and more, to explore commercial blockchain applications. We could not, by the date of this book publishing, find any unique code released by MOBI.

MultiChain

MultiChain is a formerly open-source software created by Dr. Gideon Greenspan in 2015 based mainly on open-source protocols mentioned above to allow companies to create private blockchains. While MultiChain 1.0 and 2.0 Community editions are made publicly available under the GPLv3 open-source license, the Commercial License is not now. With a base price per network of US $25,000/year for the first four nodes and additional nodes costing $2,500/year, it's hard for us to recommend this approach to any users when its effectively repacked open-source code.

We are often confused by the architecture of MultiChain because it provides a central point of failure to issue and control the entire private blockchain. This single point of failure offers no real additional security advantages over more high-speed clustered database systems already widely distributed in enterprise systems.

Nevertheless, for companies looking for rapid deployment to experiment with blockchain technology, MultiChain can be an excellent place to start as it was the first code available of its kind on the market, although any public blockchain code can get used.

Corporate Blockchain Protocols

Here in the fall of 2019, we are beginning to see the emergence of more and more blockchain protocols getting developed by corporate entities. We believe this trend will rapidly increase throughout 2020 and beyond. As of the printing of this book, we have seen two of the largest banks in the United States announce that they would begin building their own blockchain-based stable coins. Wells Fargo and JP Morgan.

Facebook Libra

On June 18, 2019, Facebook formally declared that they would be releasing a new cryptocurrency named Libra. Following almost immediate pushback on July 15, 2019, Facebook announced that the currency would not launch until all regulatory concerns have been met, and all necessary approval has been received from regulatory agencies.

Many of the details surrounding Libra have not been fully disclosed to the public yet. However, there are a few things we do know about Libra. The Libra whitepaper declares that Libra will get governed by the Libra Association, which allows for 100 members. Membership currently costs $10 million to join the Libra Association. So far, 28 Silicon Valley tech companies have joined the association.

The key members of this association will be the ones that will act as nodes on the Libra blockchain. Transactions proposed to get sent on the network will go through something known as admission control, which most likely means transactions could be censored at will if Facebook doesn't like what you are doing.

On October 4th, 2019, PayPal announced it was pulling out of the association for Libra. As of the printing of this book, Mark Zuckerberg is slated to testify before congress about Libra in late

October. Many are predicting Libra will face more regulatory hurdles and will not get launched in 2020.

Wells Fargo

In September 2019, Wells Fargo announced that it would be testing a blockchain-based currency named Wells Fargo Digital Cash that would get pegged to the US dollar. Wells Fargo Digital cash is getting built on the distributed ledger technology from Corda Enterprise, which is the paid-for version of the R3 consortium blockchain code. Ironically based mostly on the open-source protocol code mentioned above.

The head of Wells Fargo Innovation Group stated: "We believe DLT[blockchain] holds promise for a variety of use cases, and we're energized to take this significant step in applying the technology to banking in material and scalable way. Wells Fargo Digital Cash has the potential to enable Wells Fargo to remove barriers to real-time financial interactions across multiple accounts in multiple marketplaces around the world." "It's faster than SWIFT, cheaper, and definitely more efficient."

JP Morgan

In February 2019, J.P. Morgan announced that it was developing a blockchain-based stablecoin that would get used within the bank's broader global payments ecosystem. This stable coin nicknamed "JPM Coin" is a digital currency pegged to the US dollar that can be used to settle transactions between wholesale payments business clients instantly. JPM coin will run on a blockchain network called Quorum centrally controlled by the bank. From what we have been able to gather, Quorum is a permissioned variant of the open-source Ethereum protocol.

What's important to note here is J.P. Morgan moves almost $6 trillion around the world daily. At first, the JPM coin is only getting used for a few isolated test pilots but will become a more active rail for payments as time goes on within the bank. J.P Morgan currently banks 80 percent of 500 500 companies, so there is a tremendous amount of room for growth just within the bank's clients. The head of digital treasury services and blockchain at JP Morgan, Umar Farooq, stated: "We believe that a lot of securities over time, in five to 20 years, will increasingly become digital or get tokenized."

Nation-State Blockchain Protocols

This chapter is the hardest section of this section to write as most of the information about specific blockchain protocols getting used by nation-states is either nonexistent or kept a closely guarded secret.

Most likely, the actual technology being employed by nation-states to create blockchain-based currencies and assets is some modified form of the various open-source protocols discussed above. Nevertheless, let's go into a few details that we do know about the specific countries experimenting with their blockchains.

As we argue elsewhere in this book, nation-state experimentation with digital currency is an inevitability. Everyone is learning from everyone else, and many of the smaller nation's experiments are stalking horses for larger states who have a geoeconomic interest in patiently experimenting with a rival system to US dollar hegemony into the 2020s and 2030s.

China - Monetary Policy at the Individual Level

The People's Republic of China's approach to digital currency resembles the Chinese Communist Party's approach to government generally. It is designed to exert targeted political control through the networks involved in commerce. In a market dominated by single apps, such as WeChat, it is logical from a strategic standpoint to infer that the PBOC's target system is to blend identity and payments under one roof.

To quote PBOC President Yi Gang,

"If the [sovereign] digital currency involves cross-border use, it will involve a series of regulatory issues regarding anti-money-laundering, anti-terrorism financing, anti-tax evasion as well as know-your-client protocols."[12]

These are Western compliance buzzwords out of place in the Middle Kingdom. In China, Yi's statement politely reflects the overseas political control the PBOC will acquire by blending identity and the regional monetary system.

Transaction volume per second requirement for the world's most populous nation will be immense, as will be the desire to whitelist addresses, confiscate currency from dissidents and political rivals, and lock foreign outflows and exchanges of value outside of China's geopolitical orbit. There are multiple ways to execute this, and as of late 2019, there were indications in Patents filed by the PBOC that this would extend to both tokenized fiat currency and assets with smart contracts. Other patents revealed that transactions would include multi-signature functions. In a centralized system, this means that the gatekeeper retains the capacity to de-permission transactions; by analogy, imagine if you needed a second set of keys kept by the manufacturer to enter your home or start your car.

By analogy, the PBOC's model appears to resemble Ripple at a technical level, with centralized servers and cryptography, but without limitation of assets that Ripple, Stellar, and other Privately Issued Scrip models have.

The Digital Renminbi is not a "stablecoin" in the real sense of the word since the PBOC has full power to change the amount in circulation. Instead of just changing interest rates, which can be as ineffective as pushing on a rope, the PBOC is unlocking a whole new era of monetary and domestic policy. The digital Renminbi is a macro-level centralization of monetary policy, technology, and

---

[12] Frank Tang. South China Morning Post. *China Has "No Timetable for Launch of its Digital Currency" says central bank governor.* 24 September 2019. Available at <https://www.scmp.com/economy/global-economy/article/3030120/china-has-no-timetable-launch-its-digital-currency-says>

identity around a single politically supervised system, meaning, if successful, that the communist party could control monetary policy at the individual level.

Simply put, the PBOC's digital currency has three natural objectives: 1) to govern Chinese citizens and companies, 2) to regulate commerce with China abroad, such that external trade with china must occur within its banking system, and 3) to be technically viable enough to handle the stress requirements involved and become an attractive alternative to other globally traded currencies. These can be accomplished in increasing order, with domestic governance being the nearer term target, and replacement of the US dollar as a trade mechanism being the long-term objective. The PBOC's system will include a highly manipulatable fiat currency over a technically superior ledger, with a meaningful amount of identity validation and integration across other platforms, such as China's Social Credit system, face recognition AIs, and databases of desirable and undesirable individuals and companies.

For the first time in history, a nation-state will be able to direct economic policy down to the level of the individual citizen.

Venezuela - Scams and Kleptocracy by Venezuelan Elite

Venezuela's Petromonedo (aka 'Petro') was the first publicly announced sovereign cryptocurrency. It is also an unmitigated disaster, echoing all the worst impulses of the corrupt regime.

In the time since it was announced, Petro has been thought to be rolled out on Ethereum, NEM, and other systems, with no assurance that the project was stable or even being built. Somewhat similar to the Iranian model, Petro was alleged to be backed with real assets - in this case, petroleum, though other statements have been made to claim that natural resources such as diamonds might be included - an ambiguity that should raise eyebrows.

Due to the cheapness of electricity in Venezuela, Bitcoin and other crypto mining took off with the parallel experience of hyperinflation towards the end of Hugo Chavez's tenure. According to firsthand reports from people in the industry, such as Eduardo Gomez, a native Venezuelan engaged in crypto locally, the

Bolivarian Government's response has been to insist that crypto miners register their activity and pay taxes - only to have their mining equipment seized and operated by the government later.

This reflects Venezuela's pivot to seizing decentralized assets as part of its monetary policy, with the central bank experimenting in custody of Bitcoin and Ethereum. Bitcoin accumulation would be a new official monetary policy for Venezuela, but it also reflects the argument that states will have the incentive to decentralized acquire digital assets since there is a massive trust (and technical competence) barrier to starting a state-backed network.

Iran - Escaping Sanctions

Iran's approach to cryptocurrency appears to resemble Venezeula's. After banning decentralized currencies like Bitcoin, the Islamic Republic executed an about-face in Summer 2019, legalizing crypto mining, with taxes and potential seizure of mining rigs not controlled by the government.

Interestingly, Iran does not recognize payment with cryptocurrency - only mining and acquisition, which belies the government's strategic mindset in acquiring crypto but preventing Iranian citizens from circumventing the banking system or transferring their wealth outside Iran.

Unlike Venezuela, Iran's regime is technically competent and is somewhat formidable despite years of U.S. Sanctions. Iran is more organized and better governed than Venezuela and has survived worse external pressures, where Venezuela's collapse is entirely a matter of foolish domestic politics. For this reason, it's rational to expect a more concerted attempt at a sovereign currency that leverages existing open-source technologies.

Like Venezuela, Iran's flirtation with a sovereign cryptocurrency is an effort to circumvent U.S. sanctions, and like Venezuela, Iran's model claims that its digital currency will be backed with a hard asset - in this case, gold. It was reported in February 2019 by CipherTrace, a U.S. blockchain analysis consultancy, that four Iranian banks have explored partnerships to create a system called *Paymon* to tokenize bank's reserves and provide infrastructure for settlement in gold, with some form of "proof of reserve" demonstrating that the gold traded is real and in the custody of the system.

Because there is a hard asset peg, it is ultimately the settlement process that is the hang-up. Few trust Iran to have gold reserves locally, regardless of how Paymon gets executed, and few can trust Iran to handle transactions in good faith. Alternatively, if gold reserves are held abroad (such as in Singapore, China, Russia, Switzerland, or another country), Iran may be able to execute a believable paper peg to a digital currency, where Iran merely provides and implements the ledger and wallets for that transaction.

At this time, there is limited technical data to assess Iran's approach to a Crypto Rial. A Privately Issued Scrip model operating without backing to real assets will likely flounder, but a believable settlement layer to gold held outside of Iran might just hit the threshold of trust required by Iran's trading partners to make the project successful.

An offshore gold-backed scrip approach is more complicated than merely adopting a decentralized open-source system. Rather than relying on contracts that influential foreign governments could pull the rug out from under, Iran might experiment with a branded fork of Bitcoin or another cryptocurrency. That the regime recently acknowledged the legitimacy of mining operations implies it may indeed pursue a nominally decentralized protocol, rather than struggle with contracts and access to offshore gold.

Russia – Strategic-Level Attack on Dollar-Led Financial System

More than any other state, Russia has cultivated a reputation for strategic deception and misdirection. For this reason, we are taking the Kremlin's specific public statements on its digital currency strategy with a grain of salt, while acknowledging that Russia has a bald faced strategic interest in overthrowing the existing American-led financial order, especially as sanctions have targeted much of Russia's elite over the course of the last five years.

According to public statements, the Russian Federation has been openly considering the digitization of its currency since 2017. Unlike others, public discussion has revolved around the digitization of fiat currency rather than establishing an independent asset. What sets the digital ruble apart is its capacity to be sent by the state in a clandestine setting. In January of 2018, shortly after the project was announced, Sergei Glazyev (an economic advisor to Putin who has been under US sanctions since 2014), stated during a government meeting:

"The (CryptoRuble) suits us very well for sensitive activity on behalf of the state. We can settle accounts with our counterparties all over the world with no regard for sanctions."

Putin and other government figures' clear statements have lauded the potential of a state-run digital payments network, where the Russian Federation can transfer value without dealing with the international banking system and without disclosing the persons involved in the transaction to any outside party.

While this interest in simply digitizing the ruble is notable in its own right, we think there may be more than meets the eye when it comes to Russia's cryptocurrency strategy. First and foremost, Russia has a thriving crypto mining industry, which extends far beyond China's highly industrialized Bitcoin mining operations. Where the PRC has attempted to dominate Bitcoin through mining operations, Russia has hosted several mining companies that have developed high-quality applications for more obscure algorithms. This notably includes BaikalMiner, located in Nizhny Novgorod but named after Lake Baikal, a famous Russian research facility, much like America's Los Alamos. This strength in encryption and engineering, as well as an open engagement between President Putin and Vitalik Buterin in 2017, imply a more profound interest on the part of the Russian Federation in decentralized systems.

Also of note is the potential for a state-facilitated system that returns the world to sound currency. As James Rickards points out in the opening chapter to *Currency Wars: The Making of the Next*

Global Crisis, American strategists wargaming attacks against the international hegemony of the dollar completely missed a simulated Russian gambit at a credible gold-backed currency, where gold remains contractually held abroad (much like the Iranian model we discussed above). While this is only a wargame, the Russian interest in adopting a sound currency apart from the fiat system may well lead them to adopt a real, minable blockchain as part of their strategic interests. In this setting, other countries don't have to trust Russia - they can trust the code of the platform - and the Russian Federation could achieve many of the privacy and sovereignty objectives of such an approach by pre-issuing currency to the state, and dominating the mining algorithms at play, or by using a proof of stake model.

Successful misdirection from tokenizing fiat to embracing a new model for a sovereign currency will put a severe dent in the global monetary system, and we think Russia will be the first significant country to pursue this model. Not only is it strategically cogent with Russia's objectives, but it is also an action that Russia could roll out progressively in the most accommodating settings. Just as the Rodina has worked to replace American anti-air systems in Syria and Turkey with Russian systems, so too will a new means settlement be rolled out with partners and allies. First in places like Kazakhstan and Bulgaria, but later in places like Syria or between Russia, China, and Iran. And there is nothing the United States or Europe can do about it.

North Korea – Policy Objective: Theft

The "Democratic People's Republic" of North Korea has been one of the most kleptocratic regimes in world history, and this extends to crypto markets, where the DPRK has been responsible for some of the most massive centralized exchange hacks in history, including 17 separate instances of hacking exchanges, as well as crypto mining operations inside the DPRK.

Reuters estimated, as of late 2019, that the DPRK has been engaged in over *$2 Billion* worth of theft to support its WMD programs. This includes a reported 30 agents operating abroad, targeting legacy financial institutions as well as crypto exchanges.[13] This figure excludes sophisticated counterfeiting efforts aimed against the US dollar, known as "superdollars" for their extreme attention to detail.[14]

Effectively, the DPRK has a parasitic relationship with the broader financial system, and any effort by the DPRK to roll out a cryptocurrency should be seen in this light. As a "Hermit Kingdom" North Korea lacks notable trade networks, but retains an interest in using any means available to draw hard currency into its coffers or to attack other nations covertly.

Conclusion

Blockchain protocols operate independently of each other and have different ways of achieving consensus throughout their network. Protocols can come in many various forms and packages and may or may not be decentralized.

Now that we have taken a detailed look at multiple types of blockchain protocols, we are ready to take a look at blockchain projects that are getting built on top of these various blockchain protocols. In chapter 10, we will do a much deeper dive into the different types of projects in the blockchain industry today.

Conclusion

In conclusion, we would like to reinforce the point that blockchain protocols operate independently of each other and have different ways of achieving consensus throughout their network. Protocols can come in many various forms and packages and may or may not be decentralized.

Now that we have taken a detailed look at multiple types of blockchain protocols, we are ready to take a look at blockchain

---

[13] David Wainer. Bloomberg. *North Korea hacks Banks, Cryptocurrencies for Funds, UN Finds.* 6 August 2019. Available at <https://www.bloomberg.com/news/articles/2019-08-06/north-korea-hacks-banks-cryptocurrencies-for-funds-un-finds>.

[14] Tara Chan. Business Insider. *A $100 counterfeit 'supernote' found in South Korea could have been made in North Korea.* 13 December 2017. Available at <https://www.businessinsider.com/counterfeit-supernote-found-in-south-korea-2017-12>.

projects that are getting built on top of these various blockchain protocols. In chapter 10, we will do a much deeper dive into the different types of projects in the blockchain industry today.

Chapter 10: Survey of Existing Blockchain Projects

"Quality is more important than quantity. One home run is much better than two doubles." - Steve Jobs

There are thousands of blockchain projects that have emerged over the course of the last decade, and they span a broad spectrum of protocols, personalities, and potential applications built across multiple blockchains. Because this technology is so new, as of this writing, there are several half-baked or duplicative technologies that do not necessarily have bright futures, despite their presently large market caps.

None the less we use some of these as an example below to give you a context of projects currently being built on top of or encompassing usages of existing public blockchains.

By 2035, many blockchain projects are going to fail. Some will collapse spectacularly, and some will fade gently into obscurity. Others will be acquired, reinvented, and rebranded, and reissued. This era is truly an exciting time to be involved with cutting edge blockchain technology. We are in no way endorsing all of the projects below, but where we have serious doubts, we will note them, and where we see some positive attributes of a project, we will also indicate them.

When you look closely at this industry with proper background information and a solid understanding of what blockchain tech is, you can see the long term winners that are emerging. We encourage you to use this section as an overall guide and not an absolute source of eternal truth. Things are continually changing in this space, so we encourage you always to do your due diligence and research.

Projects Built on Established Public Blockchain Protocols

To simplify and keep the distinction clear, as previously mentioned, we are separating protocols and projects. A blockchain protocol is an independent blockchain system that is not dependent on any other blocking protocol or network.

A project encompasses anything built on one of these independent blockchain protocols. In many cases, projects have started on existing blockchain protocols only to move and develop their own independent blockchain protocols later on.

Ethereum was one of the first examples of this. EOS is another example of this. ETH launched as an ICO by selling tokens for Bitcoin, which later developed its blockchain protocol that was then used by EOS to launch a token ICO before eventually building its own independent blockchain protocol.

Do not consider any of the blockchain projects listed below as being openly endorsed by the authors. We are noting several projects below to help people understand the various types of projects that exist in the space. While some we do support and believe in and some we don't, we definitely do not endorse or agree with every single project listed below.

However, we are not here to slander and attack specific projects. Our goal is to be unbiased and to help clarify the mass confusion that exists in this industry. However, in some instances, our bias will inevitably shine through unconsciously. We do not know every detail about every project, so we are acting in good faith to provide the most up to date information we can on the projects listed below.

Second Layer Blockchain Protocols

Many secondary protocols have been developed to expand further the capacity and features of a primary underlying independent blockchain protocol. Think of these secondary blockchain protocols as blockchains on top of blockchains. However, without the initial underlying independent blockchain protocol, such as those laid out in Chapter 9, they would not be secure.

These second layer protocols are built directly on existing independent protocols to add additional features, scalability, or innovative products. Below we will detail a few of these protocols and how they are designed and utilized. As with most things in the software industry, there have been continual innovations of secondary protocols building upon the work of previous protocol projects.

Mastercoin Protocol

Mastercoin (MSC) was the very first ever secondary protocol proposed for Bitcoin in 2012 by J.R. Willet with a white paper named "The Second Bitcoin Whitepaper." The basic premise for Mastercoin was similar to the idea of HTTP running on top of TCP/IP, except Mastercoin would run on top of the Bitcoin protocol. Therefore expanding the usability and use cases to issue new currencies on top of Bitcoin. Mastercoin allowed for the first ICOs before the term ICO got widely used.

The Omni Layer Protocol

In 2015 Mastercoin was rebranded as the Omni layer. Omni continues to operate to this day in several notable stablecoins, and other projects have gotten issued with Omni on top of Bitcoin. Tether USDT is the largest the most well-known stablecoins in the world today and was first released on top of Omni in 2014. Omni has also been by Maidesafe.

Counterparty Protocol

Counterparty (XCP) is another secondary layer protocol built on top of Bitcoin first launched in January 2014. In 2014 counterparty was part of one of the first initiatives to issue in trade legal securities on a blockchain led by overstock.com. This initiative, named Medici, eventually became tZero. Counterparty still exists today and can be used for smart contracts on some of the Bitcoin blockchain.

XCP was also the first cryptocurrency to be created by something known as "proof of burn." A process where the currency is sent into oblivion and can never get recovered. In January 2014, over 2,100 bitcoins were burned, creating about 2.6 million XCP.

Open Assets Protocol

The Open Assets Protocol is a protocol also built on top of the Bitcoin blockchain. It also allows the issuance and transfer of user-created assets. Open Assets was an evolution of the concept of colored coins. Open Assets was also the first to use OP_RETURN to handle protocol data.

Colored Coins Protocol

Colored coins is another protocol built on top of bitcoin founded in 2014. Colored Coins made many improvements and added many new OP_CODEs to allow for much more complicated smart contracts on to the top of Bitcoin. The critical difference between colored coins and the above-mentioned secondary Bitcoin protocols is colored coins dramatically improved the scripting language in the number of opcodes to build more advanced smart contracts on top of Bitcoin.

The lead wallet and development team for colored coins was known as Coinprism. Coinprism was the first to make access to colored coins straightforward, and they were arguably well ahead of their time. Coinprsim was forced to shut down in 2018. Colored Coins was the base inspiration for Ethereum as Vitalik Buterin worked on Colored Coins before proposing the idea of Etheruem. It is also the inspiration for the DigiAssets protocol built on top of DigiByte.

Factom Protocol

Factom (FCT) is a secondary protocol and blockchain built on top of Bitcoin that is utilized by the US Department of Homeland Security as well as the Bill and Melinda Gates Foundation. On September 5th, 2019, the US Department of Energy also announced a trial of the Factom blockchain. The protocol provides easy integration into legacy systems without the need to handle cryptocurrency. Factom got launched in 2014, and its team headquartered in Austin, TX.

DigiAssets Protocol

DigiAssets is a secure, scalable secondary layer on top of the global DigiByte blockchain that allows for the decentralized issuance of assets, tokens, smart contracts, digital identity, and much more. DigiAssets can be used to securely and cryptographically represent anything we find in the real world. From real-world assets such as real estate, airplanes, boats, and cars to rare digital pieces of art and music. Signed documents such as wills, deeds, and purchase orders to medical bills and advertisement data and info can get protected as DigiAssets.

DigiAssets as an ecosystem and platform already has interested parties planning and or working to build platforms in real estate, finance, remittance, identity, point of sale, racing, trade, healthcare, supply chain, government, and more.

DigiAssets leverages unique limitless scaling aspects of cryptography only found in genuinely decentralized blockchain protocols such as DigiByte. This infinite scalability allows DigiAssets to be more secure, scalable, and decentralized than any other platform yet seen in the market.

Lightning Network

The Lightning Network is a secondary layer built on top of bitcoin that focuses on micro-payments through the use of what are known as payment channels. The lightning network got created after the Bitcoin blockchain reached its max transaction capacity, and the chain was experiencing long transaction confirmation times. Transactions often got stuck for hours before finding room on the BTC blockchain to be processed before segregated witness went live in 2017.

The same problem does not exist on other blockchains such as DigiByte with much faster block times. Secondary micro-transaction layers are not needed on many faster blockchain protocols. There are several criticisms of the lightning network, including because Bitcoins are tied up and locked in a payment channel, funds may not get cleared for a long time between some users.

A Micropayment Channel or Payment Channel is designed to allow users to make multiple Bitcoin transactions without committing all of the transactions directly to the Bitcoin blockchain. In a payment channel, only two transactions get added to the blockchain, but an unlimited or nearly unlimited number of payments can get made between the participants.

Some argue this centralization of lightning node payment channel operators will end up becoming fee hubs where providers could censor or alter transactions and defeats the reason why Bitcoin got created in the first place. At the beginning of 2019, the "network capacity" was 1,100 BTC. By the time of this writing in September 2019, the capacity of all LN payment channels was around 854 BTC.

Jack Dorsey of Twitter endorsed the Lighting Network, which is now being integrated by his payments company Square to help boost Bitcoin adoption.

The Liquid Network

Liquid is a secondary protocol built by Bockstream and many Bitcoin core developers on top of Bitcoin. The Liquid Network is designed to be an inter-exchange settlement layer for major cryptocurrency exchanges and institutions to allow for faster Bitcoin transactions to overcome the slow speed of the BTC blockchain.

Simple Ledger Protocol (SLP)

Simple Ledger Protocol is a secondary protocol built on top of Bitcoin Cash. SLP tokens can easily get created, traded, and managed on the Bitcoin Cash blockchain within seconds.

Blockstack

Blockstack is a second layer decentralized computing network ecosystem that can interface with Bitcoin, Ethereum, and other blockchains. Blockstack apps protect your digital rights and are powered by the Stacks blockchain. Blockstack has pioneered several innovative and creative solutions and applications.

One such innovation is the Blockstack Naming Service (BNS). BNS is a network system that binds names to off-chain state without relying on any central points of control. It does so by embedding a log of its control-plane messages within an independent blockchain protocol such as Bitcoin.

Plasma

Plasma was initially developed as a secondary protocol for Ethereum. Plasma is a scalability solution that allows decentralized applications to move transactions off of a root blockchain. These transactions get migrated onto other blockchains, called "sidechains" or "plasma chains," that are operated by individuals or small validator sets (rather than the entire underlying network).

GEO Protocol

GEO Protocol is a second layer protocol designed with simplicity and versatility in mind and with the original idea conceived in 2013. GEO Protocol solves an existing problem of siloed networks by creating an infrastructural layer for seamless inter-network transactions. Local consensus and absence of a universal ledger let GEO overcome throughput, speed, and cost limitations that the blockchain industry is currently facing.

Celer Network

Celer Network is a second layer scaling platform that enables off-chain transactions for payments and off-chain smart contracts for Ethereum. Celer launched its mainnet on July 7th, 2019, called Cyngus.

Raiden Network

The Raiden Network is a second layer scaling solution built on top of the Ethereum blockchain and is comp[atibile with all ERC20 tokens.

Decentralized Autonomous Organisations (DAOs)

DAO stands for "decentralized autonomous organization." Sometimes a DAO can also be labeled as a decentralized autonomous corporation (DAC). A DAO is an organization represented by rules encoded as a computer program known as a "smart contract" that is transparent, controlled by shareholders, and not influenced by a central authority. The smart contract is then recorded, secured, and executed within an independent blockchain protocol.

Think of a DAO as a decentralized corporation ran by computer code and the laws of mathematics. All of a DAO's financial transaction records and bylaws get executed on a blockchain protocol as a smart contract.

Dan Larimer first proposed the concept of a "Decentralized Organized Company" in an article published on September 7th, 2013. The legal status of a DAO remains unclear in pretty much all jurisdictions. The creator of public-key cryptography and the Merkle tree data structure, Ralph Merkle, published a very well written paper on DAOs in 2016 entitled "DAOs, Democracy and Governance" that we highly recommend to readers.

Many DAO's are also stablecoins and will get further described in the next section. Two such DAO's are MakerDAO and DigixDAO. We believe DAO's are one of the most exciting technologies emerging in the blockchain industry, and an entire book should get written on the possibilities of a DAO. We will talk more about them in the blockchain democracy chapter.

The DAO

The DAO was the infamous first-ever DAO crowdfunded on the Ethereum blockchain in 2016. By May 2016 The DAO was worth around USD 150 million. The DAO was designed to serve as "a hub that disperses funds (in Ether, the Ethereum value token) to projects." Investors acquired voting rights through a digital share token. In May 2016, *TechCrunch* characterized The DAO as "a paradigm shift in the very idea of economic organization."

The entire DAO collapsed after it was brought down by a smart contract vulnerability that allowed a hacker to siphon off 1/3rd of all the Ethereum tokens locked up in the DAO at the time. This theft was worth $50 million at the time it occurred. To this day The DAO hacker has never been exposed.

The hack was extraordinarily controversial, and since so many investors in the ETH community got effected, many decided to "roll" back the Etheruem chain to recover the stolen funds. This proposal led to a rift in the Etheruem community, which eventually led the Ethereum network to fork into Ethereum and Ethereum classic. This scenario is comparable to what happened with Bitcoin and Bitcoin Cash.

DashDAO

The Dash DAO gets governed by Masternodes, which are stakeholders who have invested at least 1,000 Dash. In addition to running the DASH blockchains second-tier functions like InstantSend and PrivateSend. Masternodes also allow for voting to fund user-generated proposals with the DASH treasury.

MolochDAO

MolochDAO launched in 2019 in an attempt to solve the Moloch problem and help with funding Ethereum 2.0 development. The Moloch problem is when individual incentives get misaligned with globally optimal outcomes. The MolochDAO is trying to fix an issue found with ETH 2.0 development. This problem is that some people spend much more time, energy, and money contributing to ETH 2.0 development than others. The benefits of their work get disproportionately shared with other projects, who did not contribute to infrastructure development yet still benefit.

MolochDAO lets any participant cash out their shares instead of spending money on a proposal they do not support. This cash out is called "ragequitting." For seven days after the close of a proposal's voting window, any member who didn't vote in favor of a plan can ragequit. They can liquidate their shares and get back the equivalent value in ETH.

dxDAO

The dxDAO is a community-governed DAO with complete control over the DutchX trading protocol launched in 2019. DutchX is a fully decentralized trading protocol that allows anyone to add any trading token pair. The idea for the dxDAO initially emerged from the design and development of DutchX. DutchX is used for decentralized finance (DeFi) applications, provides an on-chain price oracle, and facilitates large volume trades without slippage. It became quickly apparent that a governance mechanism like dxDAO was needed to decide what upgrades and changes should get made to the DutchX protocol.

Stablecoins

A stablecoin is a token or cryptocurrency that gets issued as an asset on top of an independent blockchain protocol. The token gets directly pegged to a fiat currency, usually in a one to one ratio. Most stablecoins have been directly tied one to one to the US dollar.

There has been a considerable influx of new stablecoins issued in 2019, leading some to conclude 2019 has been the year of the great "stablecoin war." It seems that every leading crypto exchange in the market is creating its own stablecoin.

USDT - Tether

USDT or Tether is the most significant and most prominently known stablecoin. It was initially issued via the Omni protocol on top of Bitcoin in 2014. As of this writing in September 2019, Tether is the largest USD stablecoin with a market cap of $4.1 billion.

TrueUSD

TrueUSD calls itself the first regulated stablecoin fully backed by the US Dollar. The company, TrueCoin LLC, also provides stable coins for other fiat currencies such as TrueGBP, TrueAUD, TrueCAD, TrueHKD, and TrueSGD.

DAI - MakerDAO

The Maker DAI is composed of a decentralized stablecoin, collateral loans, and community governance. DAI is the first decentralized stablecoin on the Ethereum blockchain. There are two tokens in the MakerDAO ecosystem. Maker MKR keeps DAI pegged to $1 using a system of collateral and price feeds.

The MKR token holders carefully manage this collateral. MKR holders act as a purchaser of last resort to maintain the peg. The Target Rate Feedback Mechanism (TRFM) is an automatic mechanism that the DAI Stablecoin System employs to maintain this 1$ pegged stability.

USDCoin

USDCoin is a stablecoin issued by US-based crypto exchange Coinbase and pegged to the US dollar in a one to one ratio.

Paxos Standard - PAX

PAX is a digital dollar issued on top of the Ethereum blockchain. PAX is a stablecoin backed 1:1 by the US Dollar and gets issued by the Paxos Trust Company, so the funds are carefully protected, audited, and regulated under the laws of the state of New York. The Paxos Trust Company, LLC, also issues Paxos Gold (PAXG) and Binance USD (BUSD).

BitUSD

Launched in 2014 on top of the BitShares blockchain, BitUSD was the first stablecoin ever created. BitUSD lost its peg with the US dollar in November 2018 and hasn't recovered since. BitShares tokens collateralize it. In December 2018, BitUSD dropped as low as $0.70 from the $1 peg.

EOSDT

EOSDT is the first decentralized stablecoin on the EOS blockchain backed by digital assets. EOSDT lets the community issue EOSDT stablecoins (pegged to USD) against the collateral of other liquid digital assets. EOSDT uses the Equilibrium framework.

Gemini Dollar

The *Gemini dollar* is a stablecoin launched by the Gemini cryptocurrency exchange based in the United States, which is pegged to the US dollar. The Gemini dollar (GUSD) is an ERC20 stablecoin that allows holders to send and receive USD across the Ethereum network. The Gemini dollar gets issued by Gemini Trust Company, LLC, a New York trust company. The US dollar deposit balance is examined monthly by BPM, LLP, a registered public accounting firm, to verify the 1:1 peg.

DGX DAO Gold Tokens

DGX is used to represent physical gold with DGX tokens, where 1 DGX represents 1 gram of gold on the Ethereum blockchain. DigixDAO is the DAO created and launched by Digix Global company to govern DGX.

Libra

Libra is a stablecoin being designed by Facebook that is slated to be released in 2020 and supposedly will get pegged to a weighted international basket of multiple fiat currencies. According to a Der Spiegel report on a letter, Facebook sent to a German legislator the US Dollar will only make up 50% of the basket of assets that back Libra. The remainder of the basket will be made up of the British Pound Sterling at 11%, the Euro at 18%, the Yen at 14%, and the Singapore Dollar at 7%.

Identity/ Authentication

One of the most underutilized aspects and possible functionality of an independent blockchain protocol is providing a secure source of authentication for other applications and platforms. By promptly architecting an authentication solution using the public and private keys distributed on an independent blockchain protocol, you can make some infinitely scalable security solutions that can solve a lot of today's Internet problems. We believe more cryptocurrency exchanges should utilize authentication solutions built on top of some of the protocols they already have listed like DigiByte with Digi-ID. When architected properly, these blockchain authentication solutions will replace the need for passwords in our everyday life.

BitID

BitID is an open-source authentication solution first built-in 2014 to leverage the Bitcoin blockchain protocol for open authentication on the web. Surprisingly after five years, this open-source initiative has not found much traction inside the broader Bitcoin ecosystem.

Digi-ID

Building upon the work started with BitID Digi-ID is a very active and ongoing solution built upon the DigiByte blockchain protocol for utilization as an open-source authentication protocol. Digi-ID has gained much traction recently and is getting adopted by multiple exchanges, platforms, and being expanded by commercial authentication applications. Numerous companies and even governments have expressed interest in the possibilities for open-source blockchain authentication like Digi-ID to replace the need for passwords.

AntumID

AntumID is a European based company building upon the open-source DigiID blockchain authentication protocol built on top of DigiByte. AntumID provides the first password manager browser plugin that does not need to save or record any passwords. The AntumID browser plugin named "DigiPassword" can be used with any existing website today.

Instead of using a typical password, it leverages the private-keys from a DigiByte wallet to sign an authorize entrance to the websites you use. With this extension, you can use your DigiByte wallet to authenticate yourself on any site without needed to memorize endless variations of passwords.

V-ID

V-ID secures any digital file against unlawful manipulation, protecting businesses against digital fraud, and letting people focus on innovation. With V-ID, anyone can verify digital assets with blockchain-powered technology.

Blockstack ID

You can use your Blockstack ID with every DApp in the Blockstack Ecosystem. To create an ID, you use a DApp called the Blockstack Browser. Any DApp data you create gets linked to this ID.

Storage

One of the fascinating use cases for blockchain technology is the ability to create decentralized storage. There are multiple blockchain protocols and projects that have been designed to facilitate blockchain decentralized storage solutions.

IPFS/Filecoin

The InterPlanetary File System is a protocol and peer-to-peer network for storing and sharing data in a distributed file system. IPFS works similarly to BitTorrent and uses the Filecoin token as its native cryptocurrency and allows users to share and host files. IPFS uses content-addressing to uniquely identify each file in a global namespace connecting all computing devices. You can put your unused storage to work by becoming a Filecoin miner.

Sia

Sia is a decentralized blockchain-based cloud storage platform. Sia was created by the Boston based company named Nebulous. On October 1st, 2019, the US Securities and Exchange Commission announced it had reached a $225,000 settlement over Sia's unregistered token sale, which took place in 2014.

Storj

Storj is a blockchain-based cloud storage platform where your files get encrypted and split into pieces client-side before being distributed across the StorJ network of storage nodes.

Maidsafe / Maidsafecoin

MaidSafe is a decentralized blockchain project building the SAFEnetwork. SAFE stands for Secure Access For Everyone. MaidSafecoin was the temporary cryptocurrency coin used for the alpha and beta versions of the SAFE network. MAID stands for Massive Array of Internet Disks. The SAFE network was envisioned in 2006 by the Maidsafe team on the idea a network can be built where all data gets encrypted by default. The SAFEnetwork focuses on using unused disk space and bandwidth to move people's data off centralized corporate servers in a secure decentralized manner.

Centralized Exchanges

A centralized exchange is a trading platform that is wholly controlled by a single company or independent party that stores an individual's cryptocurrency or digital assets and holds their private keys for them. They allow users to buy, sell, and trade fiat currencies or cryptocurrencies for other digital assets. There are hundreds of cryptocurrency exchanges that have popped up over the years.

Many exchanges have gotten hacked, some were complete scams, and others were forced to close their doors due to a lack of funding or bear market conditions. Below we will list some of the most prominent examples of exchanges in the history of blockchain technology.

BitStamp

BitStamp is one of the world's very very Bitcoin exchanges launched in 2011 as a European-focused alternative to then-dominant bitcoin exchange Mt. Gox. To date, BitStamp is the world's longest-standing crypto exchange and only allows the trading of Bitcoin and a handful of other digital assets. BitStamp has long provided the back end market making for numerous other up and coming blockchain exchanges.

Coinbase

Coinbase is the leading US-based cryptocurrency exchange that was founded in June 2012 by Brian Armstrong and Fred Ehrsam. Coinbase is headquartered in San Francisco, California, and is the most well known and used US exchange. Coinbase has been an industry leader in helping bring regulated, easy to use on ramps from fiat to crypto assets around the world.

Bitfinex

Bitfinex is one of the largest and oldest exchanges in the world. Bitfinex was founded in 2012 and was one fo the first to allow leveraged trading. Bitfinex supports numerous assets and has long been closely affiliated with USDT. Bitfinex is registered in the British Virgin Islands but headquartered in Hong Kong.

Gemini

Gemini is a digital currency exchange based in New York, NY, operating under Gemini Trust Company, LLC, as a New York trust company that is regulated by the New York State Department of Financial Services. Gemini was founded in 2014 by Cameron and Tyler Winklevoss with the intent of becoming a fully regulated and trusted US-based exchange.

Kraken

Kraken is a US-based cryptocurrency exchange founded in 2011. Kraken provides cryptocurrency to fiat trading pairs and also provides crypto pricing data to Bloomberg Terminal.

Bittrex

Bittrex is the leading US-based exchange for numerous blockchains other than Bitcoin, including DigiByte. Bittrex was first launched in 2013 by Bill Shihara and two business partners who formerly worked for Microsoft. Bittrex is headquartered in Seattle,

Washington, and operates globally. In October 2019, Bittrex pulled out of 31 global markets, citing regulatory uncertainty.

Poloniex

Poloniex is one of the oldest and longest-standing "alt" coin exchanges that was launched in 2014. Poloniex was the first platform to create trading pairs for many blockchains outside of Bitcoin. *Poloniex* was US-based until late 2019 and provides many of the most liquid markets for numerous blockchains.

Bakkt

Founded in 2018, ringing transparency and trust in digital assets. *Bakkt* is enabling institutional, merchant, and consumer access to digital assets in a secure, trusted ecosystem.

Bakkt is enabling institutional, merchant, and consumer access to digital assets in a secure, trusted ecosystem.

HitBTC

HitBTC is a Hong Kong-based exchange launched in 2013. HitBTC offers the largest spot trading market in the blockchain industry. HitBTC supports over 800 trading pairs and 500+ spot instruments.

Exchange Gateways - Noncustodial

A noncustodial exchange gateway is a centralized exchange that does not store user's cryptocurrencies or digital assets on their platform. This method means they do not save or control your private keys. Instead, noncustodial gateways provide direct fiat on or off-ramps for users to purchase cryptocurrencies and digital assets directly. They allow users to send those assets directly to a wallet where they control the private keys.

As the saying goes, if they're not your private keys, it's not truly your crypto. We believe noncustodial exchange gateways are critical to the long term survivability of the blockchain industry. It would be best if you took charge of personal digital assets and cryptocurrencies by securely storing your private keys. The following noncustodial gateways allow you to do this.

Abra

Abra is a noncustodial multicurrency crypto gateway founded by serial entrepreneur Bill Barhydyt in 2014. Based in Silicon Valley, Abra has additional offices around the world. Abra has been a global leader encouraging the adoption of cryptocurrency and digital assets by providing an easy onramp from fiat currencies as well as education about the importance of storing and taking direct custody of your private keys.

Shapeshift

ShapeShift is an innovate web and API platform created in August of 2014 by Erik Voorhees to provide instant Bitcoin and altcoin conversions. Shapeshift is a noncustodial platform that gives you the power to quickly swap between assets in a seamless, safe, and secure environment. ShapeShift is also behind the KeepKep hardware wallet.

Vertbase

Vertbase is a secure and straightforward platform you can buy and sell digital assets with USD, GBP, or Euro. Vertbase is a noncustodial solution that encourages people to use their own crypto wallets and take charge of their private keys. Vertbase has been an industry trendsetter by setting the precedent of giving back directly to the open-source development of the blockchain protocols and projects it supports.

Changeangel

Changeangel is a non-custodial swap exchange service founded in 2019 to create sustainable ways to support non-ICO, open-source, decentralized independent blockchain development. Changeangel also gives back to support the blockchain protocols they support on their platform. Changeangel also employs innovative blockchain solutions to enhance their platform. Currently, they use AntumID / Digi-ID for sign-in / sign-up authentication.

Decentralized Exchanges (DEX)

A DEX is a decentralized exchange where market participants trade with each other directly and do not rely on a centralized third party. It's widely believed DEX's are the future of cryptocurrency exchanges as they eliminate any centralized points of failure that can be targeted by governments, hackers, or malicious actors. There several DEX's up and running and in development as of this writing in 2019. However, most are not truly decentralized systems yet.

Blocknet & BlockDX

Blocknet is one of the very first decentralized exchanges, and we would argue the most truly decentralized DEX in the world today. Blocknet started in 2014, and the team has been working hard to refine the Blocknet protocol. Blocknet is composed of Blocknet, the blockchain protocol, and BlockDX, the decentralized exchange.

The Blocknet Protocol is a decentralized interoperability protocol that enables truly decentralized data transfer among other decentralized blockchain protocols. The BlockDX is a stand-alone trading interface app you can download that interfaces easily with other blockchain protocols. At this time, it is possible to download the BlockDX app, Blocknet wallet, a DigiByte core wallet, and Bitcoin core wallet and complete truly decentralized trades with absolutely no other intermediates or any centralized third party.

The Blocknet team is working on a simplified SPV wallet that works with numerous blockchain protocols to make the DEX much easier to use in the future.

0x Protocol

0x is a secondary protocol built to allow the peer to peer trading of assets based on the Ethereum blockchain.

Counterparty DEX

The Counterparty DEX is one of the first decentralized exchanges in the blockchain industry. Counterparty DEX allows trading tokenized assets on the Bitcoin blockchain.

Bisq

Bisq is an open-source DEX that was first created around the use of "colored" Bitcoins. Bisq now markets itself as a DAO as well. Bisq trading is currently decentralized, but the distribution of revenue and decision making is not.

Core QT Wallets

A core blockchain wallet, often referred to as the "QT" wallet, is the original and considered to be the most robust wallet for any independent blockchain protocol. QT is the software used to compile a C++ interface. The core wallet the "reference implementation" as the core wallet is compiled directly from a blockchain's core source code. Without core wallets running as a back end for multiple platforms and services, a blockchain would not exist. A core wallet can often run something known as a daemon. Examples of this include bitcoind, litecoind, or digibyted.

Bitcoind is a daemon that provides an RPC interface to a Bitcoin core wallet. This connection allows it to be controlled locally or remotely, which makes it useful for integration with other software or in larger payment systems or exchanges. Numerous commands are available to be used by the interface. Daemons are the backbone of all nodes used to operate most of the projects in this chapter.

Core wallets and daemons are not the most straightforward wallets for beginners to use as these wallets require a full synchronization with a blockchain when they are first fired up. This initial sync can take several days with Bitcoin on slow internet connections or several hours with a DigiByte core wallet. When the first core wallet got created for Bitcoin, it was a command-line only interface and very technically challenging for non-programmers to use. We have come along way since then.

Bitcoin Core QT Wallet

Bitcoin Core is free, open-source software that serves as a full bitcoin node and provides a bitcoin wallet that thoroughly verifies payments. The Core wallet is considered to be bitcoin's ultimate reference implementation. This reference implementation is the code you find on GitHub whenever you search the open-source codebase for Bitcoin. Bitcoin core is programmed in C++.

DigiByte Core QT Wallet

Just like Bitcoin Core, DigiByte core is free and open-source software that serves as a DigiByte node and provides a DigiByte wallet that thoroughly verifies payments. It is considered to be DigiByte's reference implementation. Programmed in C++.

Additional Core QT Wallets

Every single independent blockchain protocol that got mentioned in chapter 9 also has a core wallet that acts as a reference client for that particular blockchain. While some independent blockchain protocols may use core wallets programmed in other languages besides C++ such as Go or Java, they still act as the backbone for the protocol. These core wallets are always the open-source code referenced and worked on by core developers. If you want to support your favorite decentralized blockchain, run a full node as a core wallet.

Core SPV Wallets

Mentioned in Satoshi's original Bitcoin white paper. SPV stands for simple payment verification. These wallets interface directly with a blockchain protocol and do not need to depend on any backend service. They do not, however, keep a complete copy of a blockchain as this is often beyond the resource capacities of the mobile devices they get typically installed on to store an entire blockchain history. You can think of these as "light" wallets. They do, however, help relay and verify transactions as they propagate across the blockchain.

Breadwallet

Breadwallet is a free digital SPV wallet app for bitcoin. It is available on Android and iOS. It was and is the first successful and most widely known Bitcoin iOS SPV wallet. Bread set the standard in which numerous blockchain protocols have since forked their open-source code to create their blockchains native SPV mobile wallets.

DigiByte Android & iOS Wallets

Forked initially from Breadwallet code, the DigiByte Android and iOS wallet are taken to a whole new level. Because of DigiBytes quicker block timing (15 seconds vs. 10 minutes), these wallets have been highly optimized in numerous ways.

Several parts of the codebase have been rewritten and highly optimized to allow for rapid syncing when a new user downloads the wallet. DigiAssets is also getting added to these wallets, and we recommend these wallets as a quick way to get started with DigiByte. Because it is an SPV wallet is does not depend on any centralized backend daemon core wallet to support it.

Multicurrency Platform Wallets

A platform wallet is a software wallet that is designed to get installed on a mobile device or a computer that stores cryptocurrency, digital assets, tokens, or stable coins. While there are many different wallet providers in the industry today below, we have listed a few that we have experience with and have personally tested. These wallets are often dependent on backend centralized core wallets or API's to function. This reliance can lead to centralization problems or central attack points, but this is compromised in the interest of speed and ease of use to allow for better blockchain adoption worldwide.

Exodus Wallet

Exodus is a beautifully designed desktop web wallet that supports 100+ cryptocurrency assets. Exodus includes a built-in exchange feature, live charts, and portfolio management on Windows, Mac, or Linux. They also provide an iOS and an Android wallet.

Coinomi Wallet

Coinomi allows you to store, manage securely, and exchange more than 1,500 blockchain assets. Coinomi is available on Mac OS, Windows, iOS, Android, and Linux. Coinomi was founded in 2014, which makes it the oldest multi-asset wallet available, with millions of active users. Most importantly, no Coinomi wallet has ever been hacked or otherwise compromised to date.

Jaxx Liberty Wallet

Jaxx is a multi-currency wallet available for Android, iOS, Mac OS X, Windows, Linux, or Google Chrome extension. With Jaxx, you can easily send, receive, and even exchange 80+ cryptocurrencies right in your wallet. View balance, see transaction history and view detailed coin information.

Ownbit Wallet

Ownbit is a secure multi-coin wallet that gives you more control of cryptocurrencies: offline creation, SegWit, private-key export and import, UTXO customization, cold Wallet, offline Signing, multi-sig, and more.

Edge Wallet

With Edge Wallet, you can buy, store, trade, dozens of cryptocurrencies in one app. Edge is available on iOS and Android.

Atomic Wallet

Atomic Wallet allows you to secure, exchange, and buy over 300 cryptocurrencies and tokens in a single interface. Atomic Wallet is available on all major operating systems.

Guarda Wallet

Guarda allows users to receive, send, buy, exchange, stake, and do whatever you want with many different coins in one secure, noncustodial, multiplatform wallet. Guarda is available as a web wallet, desktop wallet, mobile wallet, and chrome extension.

Hardware Wallets

A hardware wallet is a separate physical device used to store cryptocurrency, digital assets, and secure your private keys. These devices are typically considered to be more secure than software Wallets as they have reduced attack surfaces, and the hardware is only designed to store cryptocurrency and digital assets.

Trezor

Trezor is a multi-asset hardware wallet providing a high level of security without sacrificing convenience. Trezor can sign transactions while connected to an online device. That means spending cryptocurrency is secure even when using a compromised computer.

Ledger

Ledger is a multi-asset hardware wallet created by Ledger SAS, Ledger Technologies Inc. As of this writing, over 1.5 million Ledger hardware wallets have been sold worldwide.

BitFi

BitFi is a very innovative multi-asset hardware wallet that, unlike other hardware wallets that do not physically store a private-key long term on the device. A key is only generated for a second when a user enters their passphrase, and then the key gets wiped from memory. Its often described as a private-key calculator that creates the private key only at the moment it is needed. We believe this approach to wallet design is game-changing and as some profound applications in the future.

KeepKey

KeepKey hardware wallet is a part of the new ShapeShift Platform launched in 2019. KeepKey is multi-asset and connects to a web-based interface that consolidates your many crypto tools into one, beautiful environment.

Initial Coin Offering (ICO's)

In 2017 and 2018, ICO's became the wild wild West of the blockchain and cryptocurrency industry. These "initial coin offerings" are most often launched on top of Ethereum as an ERC-20 token, though not exclusive to Ethereum. Thousands of ICO's have launched on top of many blockchains since 2013. At some point, a whole book could get written on the subject of ICO's, which we believe will slowly find their niche in the marketplace, but the cold hard truth is that 95% of projects that conducted an ICO have either failed, were scams or were nothing but rebranded vaporware.

Over 95% of these thousands of projects have failed within a six-month window after they initiated the ICO. Many launched in such a fraudulent manner they even falsely claimed government backing and partnerships that never existed. Anyone selling an ICO should instantly get met with extreme skepticism, and an investor should thoroughly vet the project and the founders.

To safeguard potential investors, we have included what we call the 2035 Rubric for evaluation of new blockchain projects in Chapter 11, which we hope you find it useful. Now let's give you some insight into the largest ICO's as of the writing of this book in 2019.

The name ICO is a play on the term IPO or initial public offering. Giving the very high barrier to entry for young companies to ever IPO and raise public funds, it was conceived even as early as 2012 that issuing initial crypto offerings could be a viable way for projects to raise funds to grow and develop.

Tokens

The term token often gets misapplied to every blockchain project and protocol. For instance, people often label DigiByte a token. This label is incorrect, as DigiByte never launched as an ICO on top of another blockchain protocol. The term token gets applied to any asset issued on top of another blockchain protocol and is most often associated with Ethereum. There are two specific types of ETH tokens.

ERC-20

ERC-20 is a technical standard used on the Ethereum blockchain protocol for issuing fungible tokens. Meaning each token is the same and fully interchangeable with others. The majority of tokens issued on Ethereum ar ERC-20 tokens. As of September 27th, 2019, there were a total of 215,725 ERC-20 compatible tokens found on the Ethereum blockchain protocol.

ERC-721

ERC-721 is an open agreed-upon standard that describes how to build non-fungible or unique tokens on the Ethereum blockchain. While most tokens are fungible (every token is the same as every other token), ERC-721 tokens are all unique. The most successful non-fungible ERC-721 token known is Cryptokitties, which at one point overloaded the entire Ethereum blockchain in 2018, highlighting Ethereums scaling challenges.

To date, there have been thousands of ICO's worldwide. Some of the largest include EOS, which raised $4.2 bill, and on September 30th, 2019, had to pay a $24million fine to the US SEC over an unregistered security offering. Another massive ICO recently halted by the SEC in October 2019 was the TON token backed by messaging app Telegram, which raised over $1.7 billion in private offerings.

Initial Exchange Offerings (IEO's)

Beginning in the fall of 2018 and through 2019, a new form of ICO, this time called initial exchange offering, has become more prevalent in the blockchain industry. The idea is instead of a project raising funds directly from consumers, the project gets instead launched on a centralized "trusted" exchange, and the exchange begins trading and selling a token while the founders retain a certain percentage of the token to fund growth and development.

An exchange will handle all AML/KYC (anti-money laundering, known your customer) and act as a trusted intermediary that has vetted and verified the project conducting an IEO. While this is a much-needed improvement over the ICO madness of 2017, IEOs still can scam and defraud investors, so it's highly advised to do your due diligence on any of these projects.

BitTorrent (BTT)

The BitTorrent IEO was held in January 2019 on the Binance exchange and was the very first "IEO" ever conducted. Users from most western countries were blocked from participating in this IEO. The *BitTorrent* Token is a TRC-10 utility token that is issued on the TRON blockchain. TRON bought BitTorrent for $100 million in December 2018.

Gatechain Token (GT)

GateChain is supposed to be a blockchain dedicated to blockchain asset safety and the creation of a decentralized exchange. Chinese cryptocurrency exchange Gate.io held the IEO and claims they had almost $3 billion worth of orders for "Gate Points" placed during the first phase of its in-house GT token sale in April 2019. Gate.io was founded in 2013 under the name Bter.com.

Armor Labs

Armor Labs IEO'd in April 2019, raising $40 million on the Bgogo exchange. The token had dropped to a $600,000 market cap as of this wring because little information ever got released about the project.

BlockCloud

Blockcloud labels itself as "A Blockchain-based Advanced TCP/IP ArchitectureProviding Constant Connectivity for Dynamic Networks." BlockCloud launched on Malta (Chinese owners) based exchange OKEx in 2019. The IEO sold out in a single second after the original sell was planned to last a maximum of 30 minutes. Blockcloud's token (BLOC) surged 1,600% after launch.

VeriBlock

VeriBlock was an initial exchange offering project launched on Bittrex in April 2019. VeriBlock touts itself as "Securing the world's blockchains using Bitcoin." *VeriBlock* uses what they call a "Proof of Proof "consensus protocol, which utilizes an independent blockchain protocol to secure the blockchain protocol of an inferior blockchain. It might be considered a secondary blockchain protocol.

BitPanda (BEST)

BitPanda allows you to invest in Bitcoin, gold, and over 20 other digital assets on your phone or desktop. It conducted an IEO on its own exchange.

Notable Scams & Ponzi Schemes

Since its inception, the blockchain industry has run rampant with scams, lies, and fraudulent uses of blockchain technology. It is of the utmost importance that readers of this book take the time to educate themselves on the dangers of investing in or supporting any new or many existing projects. Here are a couple of blatant outright known scams or Ponzi schemes.

OneCoin

OneCoin is a well known Ponzi scheme promoted as a cryptocurrency running on a "private blockchain." Ruja Ignatova created OneCoin, and Sebastian Greenwood acted as the public face of the company. They formed two offshore companies to run OnceCoin, OneCoin Ltd (Dubai), and OneLife Network Ltd (Belize) in 2014. Many people involved with OneCoin were previously involved with other Ponzi Schemes.

According to OneCoin, its main business was selling educational material for trading. Members can purchase educational packages ranging from 100 euros to 118,000 euros. Each kit includes "tokens," which are used to "mine" OneCoins. OneCoin supposedly is mined by servers at two sites in Bulgaria and one site in Hong Kong.

US prosecutors allege the scheme brought in $4 billion worldwide from victims. Chinese law enforcement recovered 1.7 billion yuan (US$267.5 million) while prosecuting 98 people for the scam. Ruja Ignatova disappeared in 2017, and her brother Konstantin Ignatov replaced her as the leader of OneCoin around the time a US warrant was issued for her arrest.

According to an assistant US attorney: "[OneCoin] "It is a fraudulent cryptocurrency that does not have, as far as the investigation has determined, a true blockchain, and most investors have not been able to recoup or take their money out of the scheme once they invest in these coins."

Konstantin Ignatov was arrested on March 2019 at Los Angeles International Airport and charged with conspiracy to commit wire fraud while Sebastian Greenwood got arrested in Thailand in 2018. US Attorney Geoffrey Berman said that "these defendants created a multibillion-dollar 'cryptocurrency' company based completely on lies and deceit." Currently, there is no way to exchange OneCoins to any other currency.

Bitconnect

Bitconnect (BCC) was a cryptocurrency running a high-yield investment program ran through the website bitconnect.co.

Bitconnect guaranteed investors could earn up to a 40 percent total return per month on their investment or 800 % annually. BitConnect followed a four-tier investment system based on the sum of the initial deposit. The more cash you put in, the more profit you could make. They promised a 1% daily compounded return on your money.

One of the first public voices to declare BCC a Ponzi in 2017 was Ethereum founder Vitalik Buterin. He stated: "Yeah, if 1%/day is what they offer, then that's a Ponzi."

On January 3rd, 2018, regulators from the state of Texas, as well as North Carolina, issued a cease and desist order to the company, calling it a Ponzi scheme.

The Bitconnect lending platform closed on January 16th, 2018. Loan values got distributed to users in BCC and not the Bitcoin they had initially invested. As a direct result of the closing (exit scam) of the platform, the price of BCC went crashing down, and liquidity evaporated. BCC plummeted to below $1 from a high of nearly $500. The collapse is one of the largest in the history of cryptocurrency.

Now that we have finished an extensive survey of numerous blockchain projects, let's discuss some ways for you to properly evaluate existing and future projects. We want to give you the tools and tips to avoid some of the vaporware, scams, and fraud we have seen in the past as blockchain adoption continues worldwide. In the next chapter, we will discuss what we call the Blockchain 2035 Rubric for measuring and assessing the merits of a blockchain protocol or project.

Chapter 11: Vetting a New Blockchain Protocol or Project

"In the short term, the market is a popularity contest. In the long term, the market is a weighing machine."

- Warren Buffet

"A good decision is based on knowledge and not on numbers."

-Plato

Not all blockchains protocols or blockchain projects are anywhere near the same level of quality or decentralization. Not all "blockchains" protocols are even really decentralized blockchains in the real sense of the word. The term has often been used indiscriminately, deliberately misleading users into a false sense of safety and security with a potential investment. It is quite common for development teams to label a protocol or a project as a "blockchain" - even when, in reality, it is a highly centralized operation controlled by a single company or handful or individuals.

The purpose of this chapter is to break down the marketplace and provide a useful set of tools we call the Blockchain 2035 Rubric for analyzing and evaluating various blockchain projects and protocols. We'll start where most people new to blockchain and cryptocurrency start: market capitalization and how misleading this metric is in the blockchain industry.

The Market Cap Fallacy

Quite often, the first metric people use for evaluating a blockchain when they are new to this space is the simple US dollar amount associated with a projects' market cap valuation. They go to CoinMarketcap.com and look at the top 10 or 20 projects thinking they must be the best projects to invest in and start there. While this approach seems simple and straightforward, it is a massive blunder for newcomers to make.

The simplest definition of the market cap fallacy is the belief or assumption that projects that are most 'valued' by the market (i.e., whose market capitalization is the highest) are the most valuable technologically or commercially. This idea is far from the truth. Market cap is calculated simply by taking the price of an individual token or coin and multiplying it by the advertised total amount of coins or tokens that have been or will ever be created.

There are multiple levels to the flawed thinking here. First, the market cap metric can be extremely misleading to new users. This is in part because many of these market caps are artificially inflated and distort the actual value of the project considerably. This is true, especially among blockchain projects and protocols where a handful of insiders or founders holds a majority of coins or tokens.

True Circulation Value vs. Artificial Inflation Value

Let's consider a simple example where a Token, Stablecoin, or Cryptocurrency pre-mines or issues a maximum of 10,000,000 tokens that are printed all at the start and controlled by the project's founders or a central company. The project founders/company then releases 10% of these tokens to the marketplace at launch.

This distribution means only 10% of the tokens are tradeable and in circulation for the general public to buy and trade. Let's say the token then achieves a price of $30 in the first few weeks giving the newly created project a market cap of $300 million. This valuation then puts it well ahead of other truly decentralized protocols that are not controlled by insiders or a centralized group.

While this sounds great, its not a genuine indicator of long term viability or real accurate market cap value. Because 90% of the remaining tokens are not in public circulation, the price is artificially inflated as well as the market cap because the token price established by the market gets based only on 10% of the total supply and not the full 100%.

The market cap is calculated by taking 10 million tokens and multiplying it by the market price of $30. This calculation is very misleading. If 100% of all the tokens were actually in circulation, the market cap and the token price would be upwards of 90% lower if not even lower do to the oversupply flooding the market.

So in the above-mentioned example, if 100% of the tokens were in circulation to the general public, there would be a roughly 90%

increase in the amount in circulation, which one could argue could lead to an overnight 90% decrease in individual token price as the market gets flooded. So in our example, the token, which once traded for $30, would now be selling for $3, leaving the token a much more accurate market cap of $30 million.

This valuation is a far cry from the $300 million established earlier. Unfortunately, this is the norm and not an outlier for the majority of projects nowadays. Many new projects are locking up 20% to 90% of new tokens that are held by founders or insiders artificially inflating their market caps.

There are many projects listed on CoinMarketcap that are either 100% premined, pre-issued, or where 20% or more of coins and tokens are held by founders and insiders artificially inflating their market caps. Hundreds of times, we have seen projects overnight jump into the top 50 on CoinMarketcap.com only to drop down into the 500-1000 range as insiders dump on uneducated investors. There are only a handful of blockchain protocols and projects that have remained in the top 50 for the past five years. DigiByte is one of them.

Decentralized Protocols vs. Centralized Projects

In a truly decentralized blockchain like DigiByte, where 100% of all DGB, which has gotten publicly mined so far, is tradeable to the general public, there is a much more accurate market cap valuation. Even Jared, as the founder of DigiByte, has a tiny fraction of less than 1% of the total amount of DGB in circulation, which he mined or bought himself on the marketplace.

Compare that to the almost 1 million Bitcoins still held in Satoshi Nakamoto addresses, which ends up being practically 6% of all BTC in current circulation.

It is not fair or accurate to compare truly decentralized protocols like Bitcoin, Litecoin, or DigiByte to stablecoins like Tether or 100% premined projects like Ripple (XRP) and NEM (XEM) or tokens issued and entirely controlled by corporations or inside groups making back door deals. DigiByte is one of the (if not the most) equitably distributed and decentralized blockchain protocols in the world today, and should not be idly compared to the market caps of stablecoins and centralized projects where there is an artificial market cap inflation by insiders.

Centralized Vs. Decentralized Assets

Second, the market cap fallacy also fails to grasp the value generated by true decentralization. All things being equal, if one assumed two tokens or coins were mutually fungible in every characteristic with the sole exception of decentralization, the decentralized token would naturally be more valuable. Decentralization means that a coin's value cannot be diluted or destroyed by the actions of a few select people, groups, or governments, where centralized platforms are vulnerable to redefinition.

This characteristic is important because it directly defines the durability of the digital asset as a store of value. It is this centralization of holdings that has led the US SEC to judge that centrally controlled and distributed tokens resemble securities as they resemble stock in a company more than they do a decentralized digital asset. This decentralized nature is why Bitcoin and Ethereum and other truly decentralized blockchains are being deemed commodities and not securities.

Functionally, the value of the technology at play in a blockchain project or protocol and the outstanding market cap are non-correlated. There are several projects in the top-100 of market capitalization rankings that are entirely derivatives of other projects and whose trading value is more affected by PR and hype than they are by providing useful technology or real-world uses cases and applications.

The Blockchain 2035 Rubric

To set a new baseline for investors who are starting to analyze blockchain protocols and projects, we have written what we call the **2035 Rubric**. We hope this is a useful tool in understanding what's out there and filtering out what you should pay attention too and avoid.

This Rubric is written on the principles of what we believe Satoshi was trying to achieve when he created Bitcoin. These principles include decentralization, mathematical scarcity, and absolute security. This Rubric is also written as a guide to detail all the ingredients we believe are necessary for a project to survive and thrive into the year 2035.

There are five fundamental categories of information you should evaluate when analyzing any Blockchain project or protocol. These five categories include:
- Economic Model & Vision
- Consensus Algo & Tech Stack
- The Number of Full Nodes
- Age of the Protocol/ Project
- Governance Model & Team

Answers to these questions will help inform you of the project or protocol's true potential and whether it shows signs of being viable in the market long term.

Economic Model & Vision

The first category of information that you should look at when evaluating a blockchain protocol or project is what kind of economic model is being laid out in the system and the vision and purpose behind the project. You could have the most decentralized protocol or project on the planet, but if the economics do not make sense, and there is no clear vision and purpose, then the rest of the criteria presented are irrelevant.

The blockchain titans of 2035 will be platforms that use the blockchain to scale solutions in the same way that Amazon was a bookstore with a better selection. Are there existing competitors or products that could be obsoleted, disintermediated, or improved by the use of the blockchain in the specific way the founders are seeking to pursue? These are good signs.

How is it funded?

The first aspect of looking at a project or protocol from an economic perspective is how are the tokens, coins, or digital assets distributed. Is the project pre-mind? If so, how much? Is the asset supply inflationary or deflationary? Is there a max supply cap mathematically enforced, and if so, how many assets will ever be created, or is it uncapped? Then we should ask at what rate are new coins or tokens coming in the circulation in the system? How is the project funded otherwise?

Pre mining/Pre-issuing

One of the oldest scams in the blockchain industry occurs when a new blockchain launches and the developer or group of people helping to launch the blockchain pre-mine (or pre-issue) a significant proportion of the coins, which in some cases can be as high as 100% of the potential tokens. Engaging in this kind of behavior is profitable because it creates an artificially high market cap that benefits the original issuers, who have incentives to "dump" their tokens once a peak valuation point arrives.

In effect, this is the set up to a classic exit scam: issuers premine or pre-issue as many tokens as possible without building any technology to add value to the tokens or give them utility, then the scammer offloads these tokens on speculative investors on an exchange. Pre-mine and pre-issue tactics are controversial because they are an almost 100% guarantee of some form of exit scam.

Some fraudulent exchanges have created a business model around this, demanding exorbitant listing fees in exchange for access to their platform, allowing scammers to gain liquidity, offload their tokens in a speculative environment, then exit at a profit. This practice is a core pillar of the exchange known as Binance's business model.

Premine/ Distribution

There are a few cases where pre-mines can be carried out successfully and ethically to help fund and support the beginning of a project. If this premining is clearly revealed and explained to the public, and these premined funds are properly accounted for, it can be a viable source of funding for a project. The danger becomes if a project pre-mines a large amount of a project's total coins or tokens, the premine effectively undermines the true decentralization of the project.

Capped /Uncapped

A huge and often overlooked part of a blockchain project or protocols coin/token distribution is whether the amount produced gets capped or uncapped. Capped meaning like the case of Bitcoin, there will only ever be 21 million Bitcoin created, or with DigiByte, there will only ever be 21 Billion DigiBytes produced. Many projects do not have a cap, and are, therefore, inflationary currencies long term.

Inflationary/Deflationary

Typically capped supply projects and protocols are in theory deflationary systems and currencies that should appreciate over time. But this is not always the case. Due to short term inflation, some projects and protocols may be highly inflationary in the short term. It is imperative to look at what the rate of production is to determine if a supply curve for a project will be inflationary or deflationary in the short term.

Rate of Delivery

It is essential to determine how fast new coins or tokens in a system are going to get minted into circulation. Some projects do 4-year "halvings" where the block rewards where every four years the blockchain cuts block rewards in half. Bitcoin and Litecoin do this. Other projects like DigiByte have a gradual monthly reduction in mining rewards. Some projects have been known to have high early distributions for a few weeks or months to attract miners or investors, while others have attempted to scam users this way.

How else is it funded?

Venture Capitalists

Traditional VC fundraising is generally a good sign precisely because it means that the company has gone through at least some degree of due diligence and that the founders are legally responsible to a third party, implying good faith that their technology and team are legitimate. Obviously, this reality isn't always the case, as many VC-backed companies still fail, and companies like Theranos have successfully defrauded investors in the past, but the outside investment is generally a good sign.

Many VCs use the assumption of each other's due diligence as a shortcut to their own, meaning a company can slip by the radar in a frenzy of speculative interest. To quote Ben Horowitz, himself immensely successful as a venture investor, "what do you get when you cross a herd of sheep with a herd of lemmings? A herd of venture capitalists."

One red flag is when a "venture capitalist" is insistent on the company issuing an ICO and being issued tokens *instead of* equity, or in addition to ownership. Some so-called "advisor groups" and "blockchain societies" are just trying to get in on an exit scam - if not run one themselves - and are actively pushing young companies to execute token sales that are not part of their business strategy.

This behavior is not only morally wrong; it's economically dishonest, as the founders will take the brunt of the legal cost when and if the token sale is declared illegal, while their "blockchain advisors" in the "blockchain society" have long offloaded their tokens on unwitting consumers.

Equity Crowdfunding

USA JOBS Act Crowdfunding - most serious crowdfunding platforms have legal standards and conduct due diligence before allowing a business to list on their platform, albeit the regulatory requirements for crowdfunding can achieve independent of any platform, though they are generally costly and administratively burdensome. As useful as crowdfunding can be, its disclosure requirements can create new forms of risk to the company, so from an investment standpoint, it makes sense to ensure that the company still has some "secret sauce" left to distinguish it in the marketplace.

CSO/STO - Crypto Security Offering/Security Token Offering.

Most CSO models take advantage of the JOBS Act of 2012 and leverage blockchains to reinforce existing crowdfunding legislation and protocol. A company's stock (a real portion of ownership in the company) gets tokenized, and that token behaves as a legal claim on a piece of the company. We feel this area of blockchain tech will experience a rapid explosion of growth in the next three years. The DigiByte developers and DigiByte community are focused on positioning the DigiAssets protocol as a platform for secure STO/CSO launchpad under properly regulated oversight in the future in a decentralized manner.

Bootstrapping

Independent financing (bootstrapping) is a good sign and shows you that founders have skin in the game with their idea and are willing to put up personal resources to make it a reality. Bootstrapping is where a project's founders use their own money and resources to fund and build a project or protocol initially outside of a premine or token sale.

Consensus Algo & Tech Stack

The next most important category of information to evaluate a protocol or project is which consensus algorithm is being used to secure the blockchain protocol or if a project in which consensus algorithm is used in the underlying protocol the project is being built upon.

Is the consensus algal proven, or is an unproven? Is it an experimental consensus algorithm, or is it a proof of work system which is considered to be the gold standard. Not all consensus algos are made alike, and not all are secure or unproven. There are many theoretical and new consensus algos that are often overhyped before vulnerabilities are found and flaws found.

Finally, is this a private or a public chain relying on something other than a decentralized consensus algo. The question then becomes how much central control is exerted over the network. Often systems not using a decentralized consensus algorithm are a wolf in sheep's clothing and should be met with scrutiny.

Can it be built upon? And will those applications be stable and scalable?

There exists a long-running debate in the crypto community between two schools of thought. On the one hand are the financial maximalists, who argue that the blockchain is only useful insofar as its purpose is to host Bitcoin or some other fungible asset on it to the exclusion of other assets or use cases. People in this camp are known for believing that Bitcoin will eventually replace fiat currency as a means of transactions in our everyday world.

One of the most intellectually vibrant exponents of this school of thought is economist Saifedean Ammous, whose book *The Bitcoin Standard* outlines several hundred years of classical financial economics and underlines how Bitcoin is effectively a natural hard currency alternative to physical gold. Ammous closes his book by being utterly dismissive of the potential for blockchain outside of anything but Bitcoin, which we have recreated here for context:

"...all the 'blockchain technology' applications being touted as revolutionizing banking or database technology are utterly doomed to fail in achieving anything more than fancy demos that will never transfer to the real world because they will always be a highly inefficient way for the trusted third parties that operate them to conduct their business. It is outside the realm of possibility that a technology specifically designed to eliminate third-party intermediation could end up serving any useful purpose to the intermediaries it was created to replace."

Dr. Ammous' position is not uncommon and reflects what most call a "Bitcoin maximalist" ideology, where every system that is not

Bitcoin is unjustly robbing Bitcoin's glory as a hard cash store of value and inherently doomed to fail.

The fact of the matter is that decentralized blockchains allow applications to be built upon them - even Bitcoin. The primary purpose of building apps upon a genuinely decentralized blockchain is to leverage the technology that we have outlined in this book to do any number of things, whether that is issue assets, secure data, or manage permissions for digital goods.

Some platforms are better than others at accomplishing this, with Ethereum offering better tools and infrastructure for developers than Bitcoin does, yet still suffering some issues of scalability at peak volume. What we're talking about here is not just the chain as it is and how the project will interface with it, but whether there is a sufficient pool of developers to improve that chain over time.

The Number of Full Nodes

Next, we need to determine how many full nodes are helping to secure and decentralize the project. After all, blockchain is and should be synonymous with decentralization by now. If this is an independent protocol, is it open, so anyone can run a full node, or is it limited or federated or closed off by corporate controls?

Independent/ Anchored/ Private

If a project is run within a private network, it is far from decentralized, and you should look long and hard at how secure the network really is. Instead, if a blockchain project or protocol is to be run in a private network, it should be anchored into a more decentralized public protocol for much greater security. Some private blockchains have been run by a single validator node. This single point of failure is dangerous and offers few benefits over traditional infrastructure systems.

Federated/ Limitless

A federated blockchain system is where there is a predetermined and limited number of nodes, such as EOS, which only allows for 21 validator nodes.

Active Nodes

Active nodes are considered blockchain nodes that are online continuously and actively working to help transmit and validate transactions in real-time. Measuring nodes on a 24-hour rolling cycle is a great metric to analyze the health and decentralization of a blockchain protocol and the security of the projects built on its blockchain. We refer to this as "Daily Active Nodes."

0-21 Daily Active Nodes - Fragile

Blockchain projects or protocols relying on 21 or less active nodes open the door to the possibility of centralized control by a single entity or group of people that collude.

21- 300 Daily Active Nodes - Vulnerable

This range is more decentralized but still could still possibly be attacked if enough resources or people conspire to do so.

300- 1000 Daily Active Nodes - Healthy

This range is a very healthy range for a truly decentralized blockchain. Projects should aim to be built on protocols with at least this many active daily nodes.

1000+ Daily Active Nodes - Thriving

This range is the gold standard for truly decentralized blockchains. Only a handful . of blockchain protocols have been able to achieve this level of true decentralization.

Is It Truly Decentralized?

Quite often, projects in the industry are touted as 'decentralized blockchains' but are running on only a handful of servers paid for and controlled by a central authority or company. In our opinion, this is no different from running a clustered SQL database, and is the opposite of innovative, and offers none of the actual technical advantages of a UTXO blockchain.

There is also an ongoing legal debate regarding whether or not Privately Issued Scrip is, in fact, a security alongside ICO tokens, as the valuation of these tokens is tied to business use cases, and the businesses managing these assets hold a treasury, much as if the currency were stock in a company that had undergone an IPO.

Decentralization is not strictly an ideological point. There is a strong correlation between a project's decentralization and its long-term survivability. Dogecoin started as a humorous fork of Bitcoin but still exists in the top cadre of cryptocurrencies. Dogecoin managed to decentralize to a sufficient tipping point that they stuck in the market, where coins that get centralized around a few stakeholders or a corporate treasury have so far not fared well and often died after a year or two.

Just as one could index and analyze the cryptocurrency market by how long a blockchain has been around, and how it behaves relative to the market, one could also evaluate the technology's value and durability by establishing: 3) how many node downloads have been committed and how many nodes are running at any one time. Node downloads and hashrate are a far better indicator of durability and stability for a network than the market cap is. Taken in unison with other factors will be illuminative of what kind of future that blockchain can expect.

As a reverse of this, let's run a quick intellectual experiment. We'll call it the *catastrophe rule*. How great of a catastrophe would have to happen to a project for it to fail? Would one core developer crash his or her "Lambo" kill the project? Would a plane crash that kills the founder and two developers? Alternatively, would the project continue unabated, even in the face of a tragedy affecting the core team? In cases with an extensive, running UTXO system, the founders and core developers could all disappear, and the blockchain could keep running unabated, even though that may affect future development.

The same survivability does not apply to centralized projects, whose fate rests on the talent, funding, and legal entities that they are operating out of. This fate doesn't mean that everything should always be completely decentralized, or that centralized applications cannot get built on top of decentralized UTXO platforms, but it does illustrate that decentralization generally improves a project's survivability. Which brings us to our next point:

Age of the Protocol/ Project

The fourth major category of information we should look out is how old is the protocol or project. The longer a project has been around, in general, the more trustworthy and secures it is.

Non-Existent/ Whitepaper Only

Projects or protocols that are non-existent and only contain a white paper and some fancy graphics on a webpage should be met with extreme skepticism. Many scams have been conducted in this stage. Many more projects have made tons of optimistic claims also at this stage only to fail to deliver a working platform on time or at all.

0 -6 months

Often working blockchain protocols or projects experience much turmoil in their first six months as this is when most bugs and flaws are discovered in a system.

6-18 months

By this stage, most projects and protocols have ironed out significant bugs and weaknesses and have become more stable. Often if the founders of a project were attempting to scam investors, it would be apparent by this time.

18 months -4 years

Projects and protocols in this stage of their existence are reasonably well established and reliable and should be given greater credence.

5+ years

Only a handful of blockchain protocols and projects have existed in the industry for this long. These should be considered the most reliable and functional in the industry today.

The Lindy Law

The **Lindy Law** is not at all unique to the crypto world, or technology generally. It is a simple heuristic for inferring how long something will continue to survive based on how long it has survived.

The Lindy Law originated with the practice of comedians in New York conducting postmortem analysis of their success in comic circles at the eponymous Manhattan diner, using the metric of how frequently their colleagues appeared on TV, at clubs, and how long they had been in the game. The Lindy Law is a rule of thumb that states: *if something has been around for a certain amount of time, it will likely continue to be around for that amount of time in the future.*

To borrow directly from Taleb:

"If a book has been in print for forty years, I can expect it to be in print for another forty years. But, and that is the main difference, if it survives another decade, then it will be expected to be in print another fifty years. This, as a rule, tells you why things that have been around for a long time are not "aging" like persons, but "aging" in reverse. Every year that passes without extinction doubles the additional life expectancy. This is an indicator of some robustness. The robustness of an item is proportional to its life!"

The wheel, various religions, and the human race all could be put on this timescale, as could Snapchat or Amazon. Even the name itself ironically ended up embodying the rule: when the Lindy Effect first appeared as a term in the *New Republic* in 1964, Lindy's Delicatessen was 43 years into its 97-year lifespan. Using it as a heuristic for gauging the survivability of blockchain projects follows the same basic logic.

The longer a system has been surviving, thriving, and contributing, the longer you can anticipate it will continue to exist into the future. The Lindy Law applies to blockchain projects (and other startups) in the same way: if a decentralized project has been around for a decade (like Bitcoin as of this writing), then there is a rational expectation that it will be around for another decade.

Conversely, if a project has been around for a month, spends massively on drumming up business, and doesn't yet do anything markedly better than another already existing project, then it can only rationally be expected to survive for another month. Borrowing again from Taleb:

"With human projects and ventures, we have another story. These are often scalable... With scalable variables ... you will witness the exact opposite effect. Let's say a project is expected to terminate in 79 days, the same expectation in days as the newborn female has in years. On the 79th day, if the project is not finished, it will be expected to take another 25 days to complete. But on the 90th day, if the project is still not completed, it should have about 58 days to go. On the 100th, it should have 89 days to go. On the 119th, it should have an extra 149 days. On day 600, if the project is not done, you will be expected to need an extra 1,590 days. As you see, the longer you wait, the longer you will be expected to wait."

So, say if a blockchain project raised an enormous amount of money, yet faced technical issues forestalling launch, you could develop a rational window of expectation for how long until it would launch based on the Lindy effect. Useful, right?

Governance Model & Team

The fifth and final category of information we need to look at is how all our updates and that the project the protocol itself governed and what team is behind it/.

Do volunteers build the blockchain protocol or project, or is it being built by paid employees of a centralized company that has control over the project or protocol? What is the prior experience of the team or individuals behind the protocol or project, and how consistent have they been in the past?

Onchain/ Off-chain Governance

Another important factor to consider is that governance can occur on-chain or off-chain. Is there a way for decisions to be voted on through a blockchain protocol itself? And if so, who are the beneficiaries of such a voting system. Some systems appear to have on-chain governance when, in reality, only a small group of insiders control the majority of votes on-chain.

Paid/ Unpaid

Another important factor in analyzing is are team members and contributors paid or unpaid. Blockchain tech, in its purest form, has largely been built by unpaid volunteers and contributors who are motivated by the vision of a decentralized future where they take power back and make their own ownership and financial decisions. Developers and team members only interested in financial gain should be met with skepticism. From our experience, the best developers and brand ambassadors in the industry are not easily bought or paid for. They are far more committed to building a brighter future for humanity than short term financial gain.

Corporate/ Decentralized/ Foundation

An obvious but often overlooked fact is if a blockchain protocol or project has a "CEO" and "Board of Directors," its definitely not decentralized. Yet there are many companies in this space masquerading as a decentralized system. This is far from reality.

Consistency of team

Has the team been involved with successful blockchain protocols or projects before? Blockchain is such a new technology that's vastly different from other industries, so previous tech experience does not translate as equally to direct success in a decentralized landscape. Nevertheless, prior proven experience from blockchain entrepreneurs should not be discounted.

Are there real blockchain developers on the team?

It is said by many pioneers in this industry that true blockchain developers that really understand a protocol are as rare as pandas. From Jared's experience, even this status is somewhat rare: during the ICO boom of late 2017, only one in ten so-called blockchain projects also had secured a developer on-staff. Many were simply contracting ERC-20 token developers to set up their ICO in the course of a few hours, with the rest of their efforts devoted to graphic design, slick websites, and unethical methods to pump their price once they recognized that the only way to make money was to offload the tokens they just paid to have created.

As a rule for investment, if the team you are looking at doesn't have a developer with chops (or if they only have someone fluent in making ERC-20 tokens for their ICO), you should be casting a jaundiced eye in their direction, because they don't actually have anything more than a white paper and a slick website. If there is a blockchain developer who can attest to their chops in working on a UTXO blockchain and has some degree of proof of work (pun not intended) using that chain, then the business has potential, at least from a technical perspective.

Legal and fiduciary responsibility

At this point, ICOs continue getting conducted to the most absurd degree of legal arcana that it defies the imagination or any business logic. In many of the late ICO boom examples we looked at, the companies domiciled their token sale on the Rock of Gibraltar, disbarring sales of tokens to anyone in the "**United States of America, People's Republic of China (except for Hong Kong, Macau and Taiwan), South Korea, Cuba, Iran, North Korea, Syria, Crimea Region**" - all for tokens notionally intended for American consumers to use on their platform! In effect, these company's ICOs sold tokens to anyone but the end-users who would be able to value the tokens on their platform.

These legal gymnastics are an effect of regulation designed to protect American investors, but it is also an indication of the perverse economics at play in ICOs generally, where companies and individuals are raising money in ways that are not economically honest or offer a realistic means for the ICO token to get valued by the market.

As a much more critical flaw in the ICO architecture, the very process by which many ICO tokens get released to the market is manipulative, involving the use of "presales" that progressively increase in price round by round, such that early investor's tokens are valued by manipulated fiat and not by market pressure. This presale is simply a way of leaving the later buyers as "bag holders" - people who bought a worthless asset because of the hype and have no more suckers left to come in and trade them. Typically, this is all done in a timeframe not correlated to the "roadmap" of goals laid out by custom of habit in ICO-model businesses.

Hence, there is no valuation process. Participants are being taken for suckers because they're paying more for the same token as somebody buying later without any core development in the business or technology. By extension, ICO's valuations are naturally irrational. At the time of purchase, there are zero mechanisms in place to provide for a reasonable estimate, and there is no accountability should the enterprise not even attempt to follow their roadmap. If everybody can get into the next big thing, speculative pressure will always exceed market demand in a bull market and fail to reach it in a bear market.

This speculation gets to the heart of the fact that the entire ICO logic is perverse. Think about what the great successes of the early web would look like if they had raised funding with this model. If Amazon, Facebook, Apple, and Google all started by doing ICOs, they never would have had the incentive to become great companies, because everyone would be so fixated on the token price and ambivalent to the actual technology. Worse yet, as we argue elsewhere in this book, building the technology and revenue model would represent a *net loss* from the treasury of the company, as would accepting the tokens for services as they get advertised.

What is the Track Record of the Founders?

Integrity matters. The founders and people involved in a project should have some form of credibility that can be measured, and conversely, many of the scammers engaged in this space are not first-time crooks. Past criminal or fraudulent behavior is a disqualifier, as is being a serial quitter who passes on to the next endeavor as soon as they incur a cap gain only to move on to start and hype a new blockchain project or protocol.

Centrally Controlled Blockchains

These are the worst bastardization of blockchain technology, to the point that the projects cannot in good faith call themselves "blockchains." These involve permissioned ledgers where a central party has complete control over a network. This approach is the antithesis of the original invention and purpose of decentralized blockchains, which do not rely on a single party to continue their existence and cannot be edited post hoc to suit the needs or desires of any particular party.

Readers must commit to doing due diligence to understand whether a single company has complete control over a particular blockchain. Numerous projects in the top 100 market cap ranking are 100% centrally controlled and issued, in effect undermining their value proposition, as they cannot rightly claim to be resilient to censorship, re-editing, or transaction reversals.

With permissioned "blockchains" run by centralized companies, the chain has, in effect, has already been 100% attacked - the developers can do any degree of damage they want to, whenever they want to, and that damage will be permanent.

Conclusion

Overall, this chapter was most concerned with using common sense. Ultimately, blockchains in their purest form are about honesty and accountability in a system that eliminates the requirement for trust. The use of hype surrounding "blockchain" for projects that do not embody this principle is a bastardization of the very ideology the technology is meant to represent. In a way, it's blasphemous.

We encourage every investor or enthusiast to do their own research. We are considering launching a public ranking of blockchain protocols and projects using the Blockchain 2035 rubric once this book is out. If we do, it will get located in the future on *Blockchain2035.com*. In the meantime, now that we have talked about the proper evaluation of a blockchain project or protocol, let's move on to discussing future use cases of applied blockchain technology in the coming chapters.

Chapter 12: Financial Blockchain Applications

> "The one thing that's missing, but that will soon be developed, it's a reliable 'eCash.' A method where buying on the internet you can transfer funds from A to B, without A knowing B or B knowing A. The way in which I can take a 20 dollar bill and hand it over to you, and there's no record of where it came from. And you may get that without knowing who I am. That kind of thing will develop on the Internet."
>
> - Milton Friedman, *1999*

> "I don't believe we shall ever have a good money again before we take the thing out of the hands of government, that is, we can't take it violently out of the hands of government, all we can do is by some sly roundabout way introduce something they can't stop."
>
> -Friedrich Hayek, *1984*

Upon mention of Bitcoin and blockchain, most people's minds *immediately* gravitate to money and cryptocurrency at the expense of any awareness of the technology and its potential. In truth, dozens of different financial applications can occur on a blockchain. This chapter is meant to provide some examples, as well as dispel some misconceptions about blockchain and finance.

Many of the blockchain projects out there are focused strictly on the financial upside that the creators might receive from creating their own money. Today's various forks of Bitcoin (Bitcoin Cash and Bitcoin "Satoshi Vision") represent inefficient debates regarding whether cryptocurrency is a form of payment ("peer-to-peer cash") or a store of value, as Bitcoin Core and other cryptocurrencies have evolved to be.

Initially, when we started writing this book, many of the people we talked to thought the entire book would be about financial applications and the complete reinvention of money by the year 2035. From Jared's experience in the early years of talking about the blockchain, the last thing he ever wanted to do when introducing the subject to someone is to start talking about money and ignoring the technology. One would immediately get hit with questions about problems like money laundering, terrorist financing, online drug marketplaces, and other criminal activities.

It is human nature to attack and criticize something we don't understand, but now that blockchain is increasingly being adopted and accepted, the exact opposite is true, but it is also human nature to be blindly trusting about things we only partially understand, and because of this many have been taken advantage of by hucksters and charlatans. That's why we have worked to explain the true potential of blockchain in the first part of this book, so the reader can grasp its origins, how it mirrors nature, the impact that it will have on rearchitecting the internet, structuring artificial intelligence, governing the Internet of Things, and changing the balance of power between people, corporations, and governments.

Now that we have talked about all these subjects, it is time to discuss financial applications and implementations of this beautiful technology in its most well-known use case.

Payments

It is already possible to pay merchants or employees anywhere in the world in a matter of seconds with cryptocurrencies like Bitcoin or DigiByte. This payment occurs directly and instantaneously, with no need for any middleman, bank, or central authority to ever be involved in the transaction.

This straightforward application can improve upon and potentially replace existing business models such as Western Union and Venmo, which are focused on interceding between customers and drawing rents from the process. This disintermediation is especially crucial for remittances across large geographic areas and between different currencies, where the exchange fees usually eat even more of the transaction between two people.

Real cryptocurrency and digital assets have the added benefit of not suffering the limitations that the traditional banking infrastructure does. Transfers on-chain are fast and point-to-point. Instead of a multi-day verification process until settlement, cryptocurrency can instantly transfer any value wallet-to-wallet without substantial fees or lag. Additionally, such payments can be private or anonymous. The data these transactions generate can remain between two parties, instead of resulting in surveillance of the user by a centralized platform.

Point to point settlement can substantially improve merchant's returns in environments with fluid markets, and where the time value of money imposes costs. Faster payments with sound money are better than slow payments with fiat currency. When payment is instantaneous, a merchant can turn around and use that capital to purchase more inventory, cover running costs, or address other expenses.

In effect, point to point payment on a blockchain can increase the velocity that money moves around an economy, because that capital is free of the large, centralized institutions who have the incentive to slow the process and "borrow" from the economy by treating money transfer as a service and suspending payments to gain a short-term deposit. Even if a stablecoin representing a fiat currency transfers through a blockchain, the velocity of exchange is substantially improved.

Store of Value Vs. Payments

One of the primary questions for scarce versions of cryptocurrency is whether they are a store of value or a means of fast payments. They are capable of both; the real dilemma is whether they are ideal for both.

In a setting where the price of a currency is highly volatile, there is a risk that one party in the exchange will lose out. This imbalance is real both when one is exchanging goods and services for money, as well as when one is exchanging various forms of currency for one another. Just as the value of the good or service might fluctuate, so too might the value of the currency. Imagine selling your car for Venezuelan bolivars and not getting rid of the bolivars - it would be as though you gave away your vehicle for free. Alternatively, the person who got your car is the big winner in this transaction.

The volatility of cryptocurrency is one reason many have argued against using it as a form of payment. One can draw lessons from Laszlo Hanyecz, a programmer who spent 10,000 Bitcoin on two large Papa John's pizzas on May 22, 2010. At the time, 10,000 Bitcoin was worth about $30. Today as we write this, that amount of Bitcoin is worth about $85 Million - a fortune in cash, and likely worth even more in the future.

Because of the longer-term prospects for an appreciation of cryptocurrencies like Bitcoin and DigiByte, which have built-in scarcity, it makes far more sense for companies and individuals to take profits in Bitcoin or DigiByte than it does to use them as a direct payment at the user level. Additionally, the person receiving crypto gets to avoid onerous fees for wire transfers, credit card fees, and other financial friction associated with the legacy system. There are good reasons to be paid in as an alternative to traditional banking methods. Imagine if Papa John's franchise who received the 10,000 Bitcoin just held them for the long term and 'ate' the cost of $30 in pizza. That's a trade we'll make all day.

Conversely, the incentive to pay with a cryptocurrency is very different from the motivation to be paid in cryptocurrency. Generally speaking, those who want to pay in crypto have to buy it first for fiat, which may involve some fees.

For payment to be cost-effective and appealing financially, customers need to experience appreciation before spending the currency or receive a discount from the merchant for paying in crypto.

As we cover later in this chapter, there is a real cost to moving money, with many cards charging a not-insignificant amount for the service of running a transaction. While Bitcoin is generally too expensive and slow to manage commercial transactions on-chain, with fees larger than most debit and credit card services, the Lightning Network offers an off-chain way to batch and scale small transactions. There are still open questions of whether or not the Lightning Network is a "money transfer business" and subject to additional regulations. DigiByte requires no such secondary layer, as it is fast and efficient on-chain, with most transactions taking only two or three seconds (as fast as Visa or PayPal) and with negligible fees.

This cost of moving money is not insignificant, and often you will see different prices for goods depending on how you pay, with a money order being less expensive than a credit card or PayPal. For this reason, it makes sense for merchants to discount payment in cryptocurrency, especially efficient ones like DigiByte, where the fees associated are negligible and the payment instantaneous. In the future, when you buy something online or in a store, you may expect a lower price for being able to pay with digital sound money, rather than fiat - albeit we expect prices to remain denominated in fiat for a long time to come.

A prompt payment could significantly improve transactions for goods generally. Imagine selling a car that has been financed, but has equity in it to a dealership. Today, many dealerships, at least in the U.S., will take almost a month to close the transaction, taking a full ten days to send a check to the bank holding the loan, all the while interest is accruing. On a blockchain, the act of transferring payment and a title could take seconds, not a full month. The existing process is grossly inefficient for all parties except the bank, which makes a nominal amount on interest by delaying transactions and adding fees.

Instead of this exploitative and antiquated system, titles could be kept on a blockchain, verified instantaneously, and transferred in the course of a few minutes, with the dealership paying the seller in crypto or fiat on the spot.

This increase in speed could also apply to houses or any other asset class. Because the transaction fees involved take so much out of the profit for buyers and sellers, using cryptocurrency can increase the profit margin, as well as prevent merchants who choose to hold crypto from having to buy it from a third party.

Using blockchains for payment doesn't come without risks and responsibilities. At this point, multiple people have bought real property with cryptocurrency, with a substantial risk that buyers and sellers gain or lose a significant amount of value due to price volatility. Imagine buying a house for bitcoin in 2016, before the late 2017 run-up. Alternatively, imagine accepting 20 bitcoin for a $400,000 home in January of 2018, only to see the value of your bitcoin plummet to $66,000 in late 2018. Price volatility is and always will be a hindrance to crypto transactions unless buyers and sellers can reach a level of comfort with a broader ecosystem or hedge their bets.

One popular argument for this is the adoption of "stable coins" like Tether (USDT), with the case being that since these coins ride on a blockchain, they can avoid many of the fees and inefficiencies that moving money through traditional channels requires. While this is true in concept, there are some drawbacks to using stablecoins as a store of wealth, since they are only representations of a fiat currency - really, they are a more efficient way of transferring fiat money from point to point, and one can quickly trade most established stablecoins for scarce digital assets like Bitcoin or DigiByte, which unlike stablecoins have the potential to appreciate in value. In effect, stablecoins serve as a bridge between assets, not unlike fiat but represented on a blockchain so that they are more easily transferrable.

Conversely, blockchains can be used to store value because their assets are scarce and not subject to a separate centralized authority that can undermine their value. This approach means "being your own bank" - taking power back from institutions and keeping your wealth outside of that centralized system. The long-term market price of Bitcoin and other digital assets is an argument for this. A user might be able to gain returns for saving in this setting, as opposed to saving cash in a world with long-term negative interest rates.

Being able to have control of your money is enormous, as we were writing this book, the nation of Australia banned large purchases in cash. While this might have been well-intentioned and designed to limit money laundering and straw purchases, there is no reason the government should be telling you how much money you're allowed to spend or make.

Using crypto as a store of value also makes you responsible; key storage and other details become essential because there is no entity to roll back transactions if you make a mistake. Effectively, treating crypto as an asset means you are making a bet against the value of one or more currencies in the fiat system, which is an application in and of itself.

Microtransactions

One of the best use cases for cryptocurrencies is that of microtransactions. In truth, it's costly to send money, especially in small amounts. Have you ever wondered why gas stations have a minimum sum that you can spend with a debit card? That's because the actual cost of the transaction (sometimes well over $0.40) is more than the value or at least the profit margin of, say, the pack of gum that you want to buy. If fees outstrip profit margins, the merchant gets punished for doing commerce.

Extend the problem of microtransactions to AIs and large, automated systems. If a value has to be exchanged by machines, it does not make sense to go through an antiquated system that charges fees. It makes even less sense if those transactions are occurring in fractions of a cent.

In 2011 it was estimated that running a debit card cost roughly $0.44, which took a full 1.15% of the median transaction value. By comparison, DigiByte's transaction costs are less than 1/2000th of a cent, compared to this 44 cent figure, the relative advantage of 88,000% per transaction.

With more efficient microtransactions, buyers and sellers can engage in much more discrete, real-time transactions. Active exchange of value is a significant innovation, especially for media and software sales, where small transactions often make up the bread and butter of a company's profit margin. If users make a series of $1 purchases, the seller can stand to lose nearly half their profit, as they are expected to "eat" the cost of running a credit or debit card. Such small transactions are the bread and butter of many apps, especially those distributed over mobile platforms.

Blockchain opens up a new arena for payment for small app developers and enables popular apps to break out of the "freemium" model that relies on in-app purchases, advertising, and sale of user data to make ends meet. The impact of this financial friction is even worse in instances where companies distribute their software over centralized platforms that charge hefty fees for access to the market, in effect leaving the user with very little in the way of profit.

The argument for embracing blockchain to improve micropayments has straightforward economic roots. As transaction costs go up, the number of transactions and the velocity of the economy go down. The reverse is also true - if it is easy to move money, the money will change hands faster, increasing the rate of exchange of the economic goods and services. By lowering the price floor for transfer, new forms of economic exchange can emerge.

Decreasing the cost of transactions matters to large corporations even more than it does to individual consumers. While an individual consumer might be numb to the extra cents here and there on every transaction, and those additional costs might become included in the price, the inefficient exchange of money costs large corporations billions of dollars per year at scale. If a corporation can hypothetically save fifty basis points on their year-end expenditure through adopting blockchain for micropayments, that could have significant follow-on effects.

Imagine the "olive jar" parable, where an employee discovers that by removing one olive from each jar, the company could save millions of dollars yearly. Instead of eliminating olives, blockchain microtransactions are banishing fees and lost time value of money, giving corporations more nimble control over their assets.

KYC/AML and Identity Management

Anti-Money Laundering/Know Your Customer Laws reflect a body of practice in banking where the party facilitating a transaction is held responsible for accounting for who their customers are. In the United States, this responsibility was codified by the 1970 Bank Secrecy Act (BSA), which made banks responsible for both recording and reporting transactions above a certain level.

At the time, both traditional banks and the American Civil Liberties Union (ACLU) challenged the BSA as unconstitutional under the Fourth and Fifth Amendments, arguing that the act constituted an unlawful search and potential seizure of assets without cause and circumvented traditional due process. It should be telling to us in the present day that up until the early 1970s and the collapse of the gold standard, people expected to be able to transact privately in both cash and through banks.

Both banks and the ACLU argued before the United States Supreme Court that the BSA created a scenario with *compulsory self-incrimination* since individuals engaged in nefarious activity could not use the banking system without tipping their hand.

In *California Banker's Associate v. Schultz*, it was ruled that the Banking Security Act was by in large constitutional. Reasoning by analogy, the reporting requirements pertaining to a centralized system are not much different from monitoring motorist's speed and driving on a highway. The BSA effectively serves as a State Trooper hidden behind a billboard and watching financial transactions with a radar gun.

By analogy, Treasury and the Department of Justice only have cause to investigate further when a report indicates some form of wrongdoing, much like a motorist swerving recklessly or driving 30 miles an hour over the speed limit.

This Supreme Court case was not without controversy, with Justices Brennan, Marshal, and Douglas dissenting on the constitutionality of various aspects of the BSA. Effectively in the four decades since, the financial system has become an extent of state power, with the United States using its influence over the movement of money to stop terrorists, clamp down on money launderers, and more frequently, chase tax evaders and prevent hostile states from accessing the banking system.

When it comes to purchasing cryptocurrency, AML/KYC laws sit on the edge. Within the traditional banking system, purchasers of crypto must identify themselves (often to centralized exchanges) to legally complete the transaction. This policy monitors what funds go into and out of the crypto ecosystem, preventing money laundering and also aiding taxation.

AML/KYC does not, however, apply to purchases made in crypto. Though some states have flirted with the idea of enforcing AML/KYC for all crypto transactions in a way that is much more draconian than the BSA requires, such a measure is technically impossible, as anyone can generate a wallet in a permissionless system.

The AML/KYC dilemma applies especially to privacy coins, such as Monero and ZCash, part of whose value proposition is that they facilitate a return to classical forms of financial privacy. If your wallet is private, but the government knows how much comes in and comes out, then it knows what is in your wallet. While privacy coins are a more purist approach, payments classical decentralized exist outside of the bounds established by the BSA, and governments have not yet come to terms with how to relate financial surveillance to stateless money other than by governing how the banking system interacts with the cryptocurrency ecosystem.

AML/KYC also has the potential to be a negative externality when it comes to security. As Binance's early August 2019 AML/KYC database hack exposed, exchanges and bank's practice of demanding identification from their customers does not necessarily mean that critical data remains protected once gathered. This centralization and poor security create issues for user's privacy and create avenues that persons holding cryptocurrency could get targeted by in the future.

One element of AML/KYC blockchains stands to improve over the existing banking system is demonstrable AML/KYC. Because existing AML/KYC only requires an image of a driver's license (and occasionally a social security number) without further checks done on the authenticity of those documents, there is still substantial room for fraud and fake IDs. By adopting a provable ID, or validating an existing ID as authentic, the AML KYC system can become more secure.

Blockchain innovations for AML/KYC also include the matter of identity management; secure ID should remain between the parties involved. There is no rational reason for personally identifiable information to be sitting on a database somewhere, waiting to be hacked. With a blockchain-backed anti-money laundering policy, these negative externalities might be avoided.

Smart Contracts

Smart Contracts are effectively an "if this, then that" statement. They are the cornerstone of programmable money. If payments tie to smart contracts, we can begin to model exchanges of value among people and machines or between machines and other machines.

Imagine a scenario where failing to meet your car payment meant your electric car would turn off or drive itself back to the dealership, or where home appliances and industrial machinery included subscriptions that the manufacturer drew rents from, on top of the cost of purchasing the asset itself.

Smart contracts also have immense positive potential, as well. Pay early and unlock more features of a product. Manage all of your subscriptions, expenses, and services from one wallet. Interact with all global markets from a single interface, where all purchases are instantaneous and linked to a worldwide supply chain. For this reason, smart contracts on a blockchain are a key to integrating payments in digital currency with the broader economy, including providing economic rules for how we interact with machines and across borders.

Assuming the pace of automation continues, smart contracts will dovetail nicely with the rise of automated manufacturing platforms, where exchanges of value can be automated seamlessly around the world.

Remittances

Remittances are the transfer of money across borders, typically among family and friends. In 2019, the World Bank estimated the global remittance market to be $715 billion annually, with much of that value flowing back to the developing world.

For remittance to occur, the value in question must be sent from point to point, and usually changed into a new form of currency. The transfer is generally subject to fees, and the exchange rate is typically managed to include a much more robust spread than one would find in foreign exchange (FOREX) markets. Western Union, one of the oldest money transfer services, charges immense fees for access to its network, sometimes as high as 10%. Money changers in ports and border crossings charge even more exploitative rates, often using an even broader spread on exchange rates between local and foreign currency.

Beyond fees, existing remittance infrastructure revolves around offices and kiosks. These networks with physical locations require a degree of density and commerce to sustain themselves, which means they can be difficult to maintain outside of major cities. If you are a migrant worker supporting your family in another country, this means you and your family both have the added stress of traveling to an endpoint in the network to send and receive money. This is known as *the last-mile problem*, and it affects all businesses that rely on physical logistics.

For the user, the alternative to using these networks is either mailing cash that can be stolen or getting on a flight with bundles of currency that can be confiscated by authorities and criminals, despite a lack of nefarious intent on the part of the user. It's telling that since 2014, government asset seizures have outstripped burglaries by value, with over $5 billion confiscated by state and local governments just inside the United States.[15]

---

[15] Christopher Ingraham. *Law Enforcement Took More Stuff From People Than Burglars Did Last Year*. Washington Post., 23 November 2015.
<https://www.washingtonpost.com/news/wonk/wp/2015/11/23/cops-took-more-stuff-from-people-than-burglars-did-last-year/>.

In the last five years, this campaign has expanded to seizures of cash amounts above a set amount - often in the low thousands - without any proof of nefarious intent on the part of the person holding the cash. In 2019, Australia banned purchases of over $7,500 in cash. Advancing restrictions have the effect of forcing everyone onto the existing, centralized systems for banking and money transfer, and have destroyed the freedom and privacy of individuals.

Additionally, most remittance systems take weeks and do not adhere to AML/KYC laws in the same way as the banking system, since no one can prove the authenticity of an ID on the other side of the transfer.

Blockchain remittances will revolutionize this space. Instead of a transfer getting milked by a centralized system and slowed down by an antiquated rent-seeking network, value can be sent around the world instantaneously and point-to-point, without risk of theft, interception, or exploitation. By sending money from wallet to wallet on a decentralized network, there is no last-mile problem; instead of two parties traveling to money transfer kiosks in different countries and then losing a significant amount on fees and exchange rate, they can send cryptocurrency from one wallet to another with minimal costs. With DigiByte, almost any amount can be conveyed around the world for a fraction of one U.S. cent.

Cryptocurrency is simply a better way to transfer value around the world than the existing system.

Banking the Unbanked

According to the World Bank's 2017 "Findex" report, an estimated 31% of the world's adult population remains unbanked. In practical terms, one-third of the world does not have access to a savings account, credit, or other financial products that might be able to improve their lives and empower them to save and buy assets.

As cryptocurrency exists outside of the existing financial system, it is naturally appealing to those who do not have access to traditional banks. While many jump to conclusions and assume this category is just criminals and terrorists, in truth, much of the world cannot reach a bank, or cannot trust the banks or the national currencies that they can access.

In this setting, many have more access to mobile phones and the internet than they do to an ATM. A cryptocurrency is a superior tool in this setting since the user is not subject to third world banking policies, confiscation, or required to apply to a banking system that is either corrupt, politicized, or too far away to visit physically.

The New Attention Economy

In the old attention economy, your access to goods and services online comes at the expense of your attention. These Web 2.0 platforms reserve the right to surveil your tastes and subject you to advertisements to fund their platforms, and many are willing to pay for your attention. Paid content involves a monthly subscription which exceeds the cost of the content, software, and licenses.

A new middle way for services is possible with blockchain. Micro-transactions allow for goods and services to be purchased based on time, requirements, and bandwidth. Based on the way the financial system works, it wouldn't make sense for you to pay for YouTube videos like you are paying ride in an Uber or Lyft, but with a blockchain, those small transactions are entirely feasible. Discrete sales like this would be better for the user, fitter for the platform, and more desirable for the content creator.

If a video posted online could create just a fraction of a cent per view for the producer, he or she would be able to sustain themselves far better than if he or she is dependent on a middleman and an algorithm that can become politicized or can push down his or her compensation by its monopoly power over distributing content. Would you pay half a DigiByte to watch a YouTube video without ads while supporting the content producer?

Content creators could also better engage with their audiences, creating content that the audience values without having platforms in the middle arbitrarily decide what content is capable of being remunerated.

Equities: T-0 Settlements

Have you ever traded stocks and wonder why it takes upwards of three or even five days for your trade to settle? On a blockchain, this can be done almost instantaneously in real-time, and without relying on market open times or third parties that take holidays. Much more value and equity would be tradable by allowing for real-time stock settlements. Everyone in the industry knows this, and there are multiple efforts to make stocks marketable as tokens on a blockchain as we write this.

Today's markets are automated and have been for decades. There is no rational reason for equities markets not to be open 24/7. If those stocks were operating on DigiAssets, trades could close within seconds. Pricing in this setting would be much more transparent since every equity price could react to news in real-time.

An added benefit is that with the instantaneous settlement and discrete amounts of stock available, practices like "naked short selling" are impossible. Naked short selling involves creating notional shares beyond the number of shares on the market. This practice forces the price of a small-capitalization stock down.

Seamless Trade Auditing

Because a blockchain is a perfect, immutable ledger, we can also dramatically reduce the amount of fraud and insider trading in the stock market. In 2014 around 20% of all trades and transactions occurred off-exchange in what are known as "dark pools." As of 2018, this number has risen to well over 50 to 60%, alongside the rise of high-frequency trading algorithms that make human-directed trades less competitive and take advantage of extremely discrete differences in market price without adding any productive value to the price or the market.

Lending

Companies like Unchained Capital and BlockFi are exploring the use of Bitcoin and other digital assets for collateral in traditional loans, leveraging smart contracts, and real-time visibility to inform margin calls and lending limits. There are several ways to execute this, but the simplest is using a smart contract tied to a specific wallet address as a means of guaranteeing collateral.

In this system, Bitcoin or another currency can be held in escrow as a collateral deposit on a loan, not unlike you might have with property in a bank. This loan can be tied to fiat valuations of the digital asset and can trigger a margin call or a warning if the value of the relevant currency in the wallet dips below an acceptable level defined in terms of service.

From the lender side, since cryptocurrency is a discrete digital asset and is also programmable, there is a substantial benefit for using crypto as collateral on loans, as the guarantee is readily accessible and can get called in the case of default. From the borrower side, ease of access to collateral means that borrowers can bargain for lower rates since the guarantees of secure collateral lower risk to the creditor.

"Initial Crypto Offerings" (ICOs) and "Tokenomics"

ICOs are mostly fraudulent. This reality is often conflated with blockchain and cryptocurrency generally, although ICOs are one small aspect of the technology, much like tire fires are affiliated with the automotive industry.

Much of the ICO boom and bust is the result of Ethereum, which made ICOs possible in the first place with its ERC-20 token. In layman's terms, an ICO is effectively a private sale of a token based on the presumption that the token in question can be exchanged for goods and services from a company in the future. These tokens can get defined in a myriad of ways, but usually, they are devoid of any underlying value. Companies executing ICOs didn't have profit margins, didn't have boards, and in some cases, the people conducting ICOs didn't even have a legally incorporated company in the first place.

Sometimes, as we cover below, these scams didn't even have programmers, or their programmers only knew how to set up the system to conduct an ICO but had no blockchain chops beyond that required to execute the scam.

Let's imagine that I am an aspiring coffee company, and I want to fund my company. I can't seem to find investors, or I can't tolerate the dilution or oversight that taking on investors might bring me, so instead, I opt to conduct an ICO, which I will call "Beancoin."

Instead of selling stock (i.e., equity) in my company and enduring the scrutiny and expense that might entail, I opt to sell future cups of coffee for a set amount of Beancoin. The public can purchase these tokens in advance, effectively signing up for cups of coffee in the future.

There are multiple ways I can arrange this transaction. This practice of legal gymnastics is sometimes known as "tokenomics," as it is an attempt to define the utility or value that a company's token represents.

In the case of Beancoin,

1. I could choose to accept a Beancoin as a one-to-one exchange for a good or service. There is also an open question of what a Beancoin gets me in terms of goods or services. Does one Beancoin buy me a regular cup of joe, a frappuccino, or a bag of seasonal roast?
2. Alternatively, I could choose to treat Beancoins received for services in the future just like cash, in which case someone would effectively need enough Beancoin to buy whatever product I have on offer at the fiat equivalent price. If a Beancoin only reaches $0.0025, then I'll need about 1600 Beancoin to buy a cup of decaf.

In Example 1, I am exposing my customers to risk that I might never open the coffee shop, as well as exposing myself to the risk that the token sale would not cover the cost of providing coffee (goods and services) to those that hold Beancoin.

In Example 2, my project is a self-licking ice cream cone. Why am I buying money to buy coffee? Why can't the consumer buy coffee directly?

Weak Incentives of Successful ICOs

There are two additional core economic problems with the dynamics created by an ICO if it's even successful. In the first scenario, If I am successful in having established my company through the ICO, I have effectively robbed myself of all my profits. It costs money to start a business, and if an ICO is successful in raising funds, then the incentive is for the founders to immediately cash out of the ICO rather than spend that money on building a business.

In scenario 1, either a Beancoin is worth less than a cup of joe, in which case I am losing money as a business, or it is worth more than a cup of joe, in which case the user has no incentive to use it for its intended purpose, since they can just buy a cup of joe in fiat currency and take their Beancoin profits to the bank. In an entirely liquid market, then maybe the price of a Beancoin becomes the equivalent market value of a cup of joe, but that raises a question: why are we doing this parallel process in the first place?

Even with vast infrastructure, the pricing for plane tickets and other similar goods cannot be completely optimized, so it seems strange to assume that such an outcome would ever happen for an ICO token, whether it sells coffee or compute credits. Further, in those commodity markets, there are such things as futures contracts, which denominate the asset in currency and establish a time that they mature, which an ICO does not. However, we digress.

The better of the two outcomes in scenario 1 is for me as an entrepreneur to have the token be worth *more* than a cup of coffee and take on a life of its own entirely apart from any real-world value or use case associated with my business. One can and should question the utility of an ICO for a start-up, especially a cost-sensitive startup because, in the best-case scenario, Beancoin has just made money, not a coffee business.

Alternatively, in scenario 2 I have created a system that requires so many middlemen and exchange rates as to be absurd: my customer has put money into Beancoin using another crypto platform (again, probably Ethereum) to gain a Beancoin, which I will have to translate back into Ether, then back into US dollars, so I can pay for my coffee beans, rent, and staff, creating serious transaction friction for what could be a very brisque transaction in the traditional financial system. Alternatively, I can go to my suppliers and ask if they accept Beancoin, in which case they will probably laugh at me and then evict me when it becomes clear that I am serious.

We're getting way ahead of ourselves. What steps must I complete if I want to launch Beancoin in the first case? Other than setting up an ERC-20 ICO issuance, the rest of my ICO has nothing to do with technology. ICOs are a social engineering exercise that has absolutely nothing to do with building a business. You might (and most do) post a white paper online and some slick graphics where you explain how innovative and revolutionary your idea is, but a working economy that does not make.

Because of the ICO's money-like characteristics, its value is directly proportional to its rate of adoption; because the economy for it doesn't exist that rate of adoption yet is driven entirely by speculation. What drives speculation? Bombastic, ungrounded, and unsubstantiated hype.

There is a fundamental logical disjunct here, which is essential to point out. Not all ICOs relate to ideas as rock-solid as Beancoin. Most ICOs are actually for companies that claim to be building a product or protocol for the blockchain and crypto world. So the irony of ironies is that many of their programming skills stop with the ability to use an existing blockchain (Ethereum) and blockchain protocol to issue tokens without adding any utility protocol or innovation on top.

From our perspective, it is utterly ridiculous for firms to be raising money for a technology that they do not genuinely understand. Worse yet, the crypto economy is still maturing, so many of the on-paper "good ideas" such as building an app store for the decentralized apps built on the blockchain are not and will not be viable until well into the future. There is a massive difference between selling iPhone accessories in 2002 and 2012, and one's preparedness to sell accessories for devices that do not exist yet does not predict their success in actually doing so when the time comes.

In most circumstances, the issuers of the ICO retain a large portion of the tokens through pre-mining and attempt to inflate the price of the tokens through a series of pre-sales at different fiat valuations for tokens. In layman's terms, ICO's are manipulative shenanigans are just frauds wearing the lipstick of a few slick graphics and "roadmaps."

The good, the bad, and the ugly of this for our hypothetical entrepreneur is that he or she has given away no equity, and got funding to start their business, and got to do so without the friction that compliance with existing Securities and Exchange law would require.

While the ICO method may be appealing to some honest people, in our observation, the shortcomings for ICOs far outweigh the potential benefits. Not only is the party doing the ICO basically running a multi-level marketing scheme that has nothing to do with their alleged core business, they are doing so in an environment where their exit (to fund the company, or to fund "Lambos") will effectively collapse the value of the coin with the sudden increase in supply. In our opinion, ICOs by themselves are textbook fraud and are not structured to produce good outcomes for investors or healthy businesses for that matter.

We believe that founders should have skin in the game and that the blockchain should be used to support that skin in the game rather than avoid it or to externalize risk to credulous investors. As we've summarized, the first tilt of an ICO is away from the interests of investors, and away from the success of the actual proposed business, since persons doing an ICO have limited to zero incentive to lose money building a company so that they can lose money accepting crypto tokens from their early supporters.

This judgment broadly reinforced by the historical data from the brief time ICOs have been in vogue: according to a study conducted by Boston College titled *Digital Tulips? Returns to Investors in Initial Coin Offerings*, almost half of ICOs went bust within just four months of their inception. From Jared's experience, less than one in ten ICOs or crypto projects even have a single meaningful developer on staff to build their actual platform beyond the ICO.

This fact has not kept dishonest brokerages and individuals from participating in the multi-billion dollar ICO craze, as there has been money in the "pimp, pump and dump" strategy that emerged in and around late 2017. Many crypto exchanges especially have been guilty of being complicit in providing markets for ICO exit scams, wittingly or otherwise. One firm, Binance, managed to create a business out of charging for coin listings, in effect creating a profit mechanic for scammers to offload their ICO tokens onto unwitting consumers, if only they pay the listing fee.

Binance is by no means alone in participating in this, as dozens of exchanges have followed suit or insisted on receiving tokens free as part of a listing deal. With minimal exceptions, including Brave Browser's Basic Attention Token (BAT), we are extremely skeptical of the ICO practice. Now that we've explored ICOs, let's move on to a safer alternative: Crypto Security Offerings.

ISO's - Initial Crypto Security Offerings

As a better alternative, we recommend the concept of a Crypto *Security* Offering - the issuance of a digital asset on a blockchain that represents real, distinct stock of ownership in a company. Rather than participating in the pump-and-dump mechanics of an ICO, a CSO can exist within the bounds of securities laws and norms generally, including the USA JOBS act of 2012 that allows for equity crowdfunding outside of the limits of traditional institutional and accredited investor circles.

What a CSO does is enable a transparent, liquid, and a regulated exchange of stock in a funded company, 24 hours a day, with the rules defined by the protocols of the blockchain system and subject to the filing and fiduciary requirements of traditional issuances of stock. CSOs can empower various classes of equity, as one has in a modern C-Corporation. If a CSO includes voting or supervoting shares, those shares could integrate with online systems of governance and permissions.

If a stock split occurs, that is merely an issue of doubling the number of tokens in each respective wallet. CSOs are a logical evolution of securities, and within the next ten years, we may well see the US and other stocks traded on a T-0 market empowered by a decentralized blockchain.

Government and Private Bank's Adoption of Digital Currencies

Governments and banks are beginning to issue their digital currencies. While there can be many forms of this, including using scrip models involving only a few servers, we believe it is best if a government-issued currency occurs on an existing, proven blockchain.

To a degree, some U.S. states, such as Ohio, have embraced accepting Bitcoin for taxes, enabling the country to gain digital assets on their balance sheet and enjoy future appreciation in the asset as demand increases.

There are many other ways to go about this, which we will go into later in this book. The core point here is that the cat is out of the bag. Sates are going to embrace blockchain and digital money in their various forms, and every entity in the world can now create a currency of its own.

Digitized Real World Physical Assets

The most exciting and fascinating area we see in the financial realm is the ability to represent and exchange unique assets through what some have called "non-fungible tokens." Especially when it is electronic, the dollars in your bank account don't have serial numbers like the physical cash in your wallet or purse does. What makes a non-fungible token unique is that it is unique - it has its own body of contingent characteristics. It is digitally atomic.

Cryptokitties, which we mentioned above, is one such system occurring entirely in the realm of crypto. Every digital cat has its own "cattributes" and can contribute to its crypto kittens in a different, permutative way, much like biological DNA and much like a real cat. While it may be a fun game and intellectual exercise, non-fungible tokens are also capable of representing real-world assets just as they emulate them in being atomic and unique.

At a philosophical level, most real-world things are non-fungible - people, places, and things are all unique, and it is this diversity that gives them their exceptional value in different contexts. Take the example of a car: while every new vehicle is functionally identical to every other new vehicle (of identical make, model, and skew), that fact changes after driven off the showroom floor. After that point, each car has a unique history - whether the driver rode the clutch, smoked American Spirits, got in a fender bender, or changed the oil on time affects the real material value of the asset.

In this sense, the car could be a non-fungible token, tracked as it lives its life, changes hands, and is maintained. We already do this with a vehicle's VIN - a unique serial to the car and represents it throughout its lifespan. A non-fungible token can act like a VIN for so many other goods and applications, especially in systems where there is a means of exchange or a complex system. Continuing our analogy, this could be the serial number of every major component in the car, improving the manufacturer's ability to recall faulty parts or to support the supply chain needs of existing vehicles.

The innovation of non-fungible tokens and the blockchain writ large is *not* that the parts have unique identifiers already, but that the blockchain can serve as a representative system that empowers new forms of analysis and efficiency. Relational databases in computing evolved to capture a vast ontology of characteristics (both fungible and non-fungible) in a computing environment - non-fungible tokens represent a logical evolution of this logic in a way that is verifiable and tied to the progression of time, decreasing the "garbage in, garbage out" challenge of a relational database. Additionally, non-fungible tokens allow for ontologies [categories] to be mutually exclusive, mitigating some of the duplication of data and the conflicts that arise from managing multiple relational databases.

It is this unique representation of assets completely discrete from others that makes the applications for non-fungible tokens so exciting. Non-fungible tokens are ideal for real-world assets, such as collectibles, real estate, or access to a system with limited space. Imagine season tickets to specific seats at your favorite team's home stadium, and being able to rent those tickets out on nights when you and your family are out of town and can't make the game. This example starts to grasp the discrete divisibility of unique assets over time that the non-fungible system is capable of enabling.

This system of management extends not only to stadiums but to traditional issuances of equities on the open market, such as stock in a publicly-traded company. Each class of stock bears with its different rights and permissions, as well as various kinds of risk. Some forms of stock offer preferred dividends that have liquidity preferences or voting rights within the company. One could call this a *semi-fungible asset*.

Semi-fungible assets are effectively a blockchain take on the concept of stock. As with stock, the system that semi-fungible assets are issued on determines the rules by which they operate. Is there a lock-out period for trading? Conditional fees? Is the stock capable of being diluted or divided into fractions? All of these characteristics can feature a semi-fungible asset issuance on a blockchain.

One of our favorite examples is the division of a great work of art. Imagine Picasso's *Guernica* were on auction. He isn't exactly making any more of them - in fact, *Guernica* is the only painting of its kind in the world, so it is entirely non-fungible. However, if the art were to come up for auction, one could theoretically buy semi-fungible stock in the painting, participating in its value while not owning the whole picture outright. I could, for example, buy a fraction of the final auction price, or commit a certain amount of money to the purchase as part of a group of bidders with the scale of my share calculated out post-sale.

Additionally, there could be a secondary market for my claim on *Guernica* - if I am willing to part with my claim on the final value, should the piece ever be sold to another buyer, I could set the price I am ready to part with my claim, allowing for arbitrage and informing market demand for the underlying asset. This system is not that dissimilar to the way equity markets publicly, and private companies work. The advent of the blockchain opens a vast world of new markets that previously would have been too centralized, inefficient, or cumbersome to exist.

Conclusion

Finance is the lifeblood of our economy and societies. It governs the ways value flows through human societies, and how that value is stored, represented, and transmitted. Now that we've talked about the myriad of ways that blockchain can change finance, it is time to address how blockchain changes the rules for government.

Chapter 13: Government Blockchain Applications

"The strength of a nation derives from the integrity of the home."

-Confucius

"...the question we now have to ask technologically is if it is possible to make an impenetrable device or system where the encryption is so strong that there is no key, there is no door at all. Then how do we apprehend the child pornographer? How do we solve or disrupt a terrorist plot? What mechanisms do we have available to do even simple things like tax enforcement? If in fact, you can't crack that all, if the government can't get in, then everybody is walking around with a Swiss Bank account in their pocket. There has to be some concession to the need to be able to get into that information somehow."

-Barack Obama, March 2016

Blockchain started on the fringes, meeting considerable skepticism by most governments, but today blockchain as a technology has been battle-tested, just as much as any information technology since the beginning of the internet. As we've discussed earlier, it is the evolution of decades of cryptography and information theory. We believe that it will become a critical component of cybersecurity strategy and other government applications in the future.

There are three core elements that the blockchain will impact in government by 2035. These are cybersecurity, auditability, and accountability, and finally, the prospect of state-issued cryptocurrencies and the policy options such a shift would create.

Cybersecurity is a requirement for every government on the planet. If you don't control your data, if you don't have command of your information, if you don't have some degree of privacy or secrecy, your adversaries can and will take advantage of you.

Control is even more poignant in the world of geopolitical and economic competition. One could also argue that companies and states cease to be companies and countries when they are unable to keep secrets. Imagine trying to innovate when every discussion you have gets scraped by a competitor or the People's Republic of China. You wouldn't be able to keep any of the value you created. If you think of value as a liquid, information security measures are the walls, dams, and containers. A "leak" is a loss of value.

Even if the information gets duplicated, losses diminish trust in the process since the authority of the data was compromised. To give a simple analogy, the key to your house or apartment is a form of information and embodies this principle. Even if you don't lose your physical key, having the whole world know what your key looks like and where you live reduces the value of the things in your home because they are much easier to steal. They are going well beyond mere theft, to malicious hacking and interference designed to break infrastructure and hurt people and programs.

Today's governments are sprawling enterprises. The U.S. DoD is the most significant organizational body on the planet by economic resources spent, and the broader U.S. Government is four times that size by budget. Governments touch everything, and for this reason, we think advances in cryptography, discrete permissions, and key distribution possible with real blockchains are likely to become a cornerstone of how nation-states protect classified information and critical infrastructure by the year 2035. Blockchains can help secure the democratic process and ensure that citizens cast the maximum number of valid votes and counted by governments, expanding participation and security simultaneously.

Further to the point of cybersecurity, economies are not separate from the nations and the laws that they operate within. Nation-states have stolen intellectual property from each other since time immemorial to gain the upper hand in trade and warfare.

The cybersecurity advances of the blockchain and Web 3.0 will be critical for countries to protect their intellectual property from theft. Web 3.0 will also protect elections from hostile influence, preventing hacking and dissemination of propaganda over social media. More on this later.

Second is the potential for blockchain to create new efficiencies in government. As a tool, blockchain will be progressively adapted to identify and combat waste, fraud, abuse, and inefficient markets for public or controlled goods. These shortcomings and fraud plague every single nation on the planet, and they are often a feature and not only a bug of government spending. Governments, by their very structure, are subject to waste, fraud, and abuse. Highly regulated markets, such as those that govern the distribution of controlled substances and critical dual-use technologies, will also be revolutionized by Blockchain and Web 3.0. Delivery of benefits such as social security and healthcare (both of which have been subject to massive amounts of fraud) and the maintenance of records such as drivers licenses, electoral data, and ownership titles will be turned on their head by this new system.

Third, we expect blockchain to be used to support state-issued and state-utilized cryptocurrencies that exist as an extension of states' national and economic strategies. As with everyday people, states have been beholden to banks for centuries for capital. Blockchains offer states an opportunity to renegotiate this balance in a way similar to the emergence of central banks in Europe in the late 1600s.

Government use of digital assets like Bitcoin is the most controversial projection in this list, with the present orthodoxy being that all states must use a form of inflatable fiat currency currently utilized by the international financial system. We believe countries that innovate first in this space will probably define the next era of fiscal policy. In some respects, individual states will inevitably rebel against the current system to get ahead, especially if they do not feel they are benefiting from the existing global financial order.

As we'll discuss later in this book, Venezuela's experimentation with cryptocurrency (both state-sanctioned and otherwise) sets a precedent for such testing. It appears to have been backed by more considerable state powers that stood to gain from the introduction of forms of economic exchange outside of the global order led by the American dollar. These experiments are likely to continue until they are successful. Just because non-democratic countries are experimenting with crypto today does not mean that democracies cannot, should not, or will not do the same in the future. Government-issued or government-accepted crypto may be the key to rescuing pensions, state bonds, infrastructure investment, and public works.

These three core disciplines overlap and intersect, both with each other and with the private sector. So it's essential to be specific and focused when it comes to defining the problems that are already part of the nation-state system, but also to be open-minded in approaching such a vast realm of possibility as the future.

Cybersecurity: The Surveillance or Security Paradox

As Susan Landau argues in her 2011 *Surveillance or Security: The Risks Posed by New Wiretapping Technologies*, there is a paradox that affects the architecture of the internet and how governments choose to interact with it. On the one hand, governments and corporations want their applications to be *secure*, while at the same time desiring the ability to monitor activity and *surveil* and monitor what may be hostile uses of their platform. As Landau pointed out nearly a decade ago, the insertion of backdoors and methods of surveillance ultimately tends to hamstring the security of an application. A hostile actor can use the backdoors just as easily as governments can.

This debate was embodied in the conflict between the FBI and Apple over the encryption, as the Bureau sought to unlock a phone used by ISIS members Syed Rizwan Farook and Tashfeen Malik to kill 14 coworkers and wound 22 more at a company Christmas party in San Bernardino, California. After the shootout between police and Farook and Malik, who had dropped off their six-month-old daughter with relatives before going on a shooting spree, Farook's iPhone 5c was recovered by authorities as evidence.

As a telecoms tool, Farook's device was his primary conduit to interact with ISIS overseas and was the key to identifying if Farook and Malik were in touch with other operatives inside the United States. Apple refused to comply with subsequent court orders to aid in unlocking the device because doing so would "compromise the security of their devices" and harm their brand - without apparent consequence. The FBI eventually withdrew its request upon establishing that the device was not secure in other ways.

While this example has a strong emotional pull for people on both sides of the political aisle, but it also demonstrates the core of the debate over encryption, with states still coming to terms with the wide-spread availability of encrypted communication and protections against surveillance. While the government can be ham-handed at times, the so-called "going dark" debate has been and continues to be a real issue for law enforcement and governments worldwide.

The tools to run an illicit organization have never been more available, and governments have never been more 'behind the 8-ball' than they are now, relative to private corporations and citizens. It is easy to sympathize with the FBI agent who is frustrated by large tech companies who seem to vindictively protect terrorists and murderers' correspondence over 'principle' - but there is another side to this debate, and that is Landau's point in *Surveillance or Security*. If the methods are available to crack encryption, for a government to compel software developers to compromise the security of their devices, then this exploit could be ported across their entire architecture.

What may have been useful in unlocking a terrorist's phone in one instance may be used by other parties (such as criminals and foreign intelligence services) to crack devices and accounts for their purposes. Encryption is a double-edged sword, so how will governments come to terms with it?

There are two stances to take. The first was already embodied by FBI Director Comey, who led what he called the "Going Dark" campaign, which documented cases within the Bureau that had been stymied or adversely affected by case subject's use encrypted messaging systems, such as Telegram. The second is the "cat's out of the bag" approach. If encryption is so widely available (which it is), governments will eventually either give up fighting it and learn to adapt around it and use different methods to accomplish their missions.

Trying to be as pragmatic as possible civilized nations can either; try to defeat civilian encryption with some degree of frustration by both parties, or embrace encryption as a means of preventing crime and intrusion. The worst-case scenario is to be simultaneously robbed blind while tech companies defend the principles of privacy for dead terrorists at the same time that their products are not secure.

We think the blockchain offers a better way. Instead of trying to hobble encryption and chase talent away to more welcoming countries, the government should embrace the blockchain for its cybersecurity characteristics. Nations will get more comfortable with everyday citizens having access and familiarity with widespread encryption, not because it is comfortable but because the other options have long-term costs. Instead of the government taking away your right to lock your front door and then poorly protecting you when someone tries to rob your house, we can have secure keys that are still auditable.

Properly deployed blockchain applications for cybersecurity will drastically improve how the internet works, which will have several positive externalities for civilized societies. Their citizens will be subject to less fraud; their economies will be healthier, their recordkeeping more robust, their national programs less subject to fraud and abuse.

Cybersecurity: Organization and Effort

Between 0.33% and .50% of the world's net energy production is being consumed by Bitcoin miners alone, with roughly 70% of those miners and mining pools located in China. China has undertaken an organized effort to become dominant in mining

Bitcoin, and this degree of organization belies the degree of organization involved PRC's other activities online.

The Western approach to cybersecurity is mostly corporate and scattershot. Many agency's security standards are dated. Those standards are not only cumbersome but poorly enforced and poorly understood by employees. Adopting a blockchain has the beneficial effect of getting relevant stakeholders on the same page when it comes to encryption, tools, and standards.

Cybersecurity: Identity, Documentation, and Decentralized Data

Governments should adopt blockchain for cybersecurity. As we were finishing up this chapter Defense Advanced Research Projects Agency (DARPA) was researching implementations of decentralized blockchains; not merely to monitor existing chains, but to leverage the technology for national security.

Cybersecurity is one of the primary implications of the blockchain. The building blocks of the technology were products of geopolitical competition and national security, and it stands to reason that governments and corporations both will begin to adopt blockchain technology to address the many challenges that they face in the 2020s and 2030s. There are already dozens of companies exploring the use of the technology for identity, distributed encryption, and direct applications that will revolutionize this space in the near term.

Identity

Just within the DigiByte community, we have the revolutionary application of Digi-ID, which provides a secure alternative to usernames and passwords, diminishing massive security exploits. With Digi-ID, you can log into a website with your DigiByte mobile wallet. Instead of relying on a password, which is vulnerable, a hacker would need access to your Digi-ID key, which is impossible without access to your wallet. Digi-ID is a paradigm shift in internet security. It combines the protection of relying upon something you know (a password) with something you have (your mobile phone).

This method is already in use by some governments. Digi-ID is an order of magnitude more secure than simple 2-factor validation and is compatible with validated identity in cases where it is required. Antum ID, a Belgian company, is currently adapting Digi-ID for use in government settings and is actively exploring pilot programs in Europe.

By the 2020s, expect to see other applications beyond just Digi-ID. Blockchains are the solution for private key distribution. The process of distributing keys is one of the most significant pain points with government IT and identity management. Sometimes employees and soldiers wait for over three months to get their accounts validated, with private keys and passwords exchanged piecemeal on Post-It notes after a long chain of administrative signatures. These antiquated approaches waste months of labor hours, both within government and in other institutions, where a blockchain could manage the process in a much shorter amount of time.

Documents

Government is nothing without documents; every action, every authority, every directive is subject to a paper trail. Many official documents get signed by 20 people or more - from the junior bureaucrat who wrote it up to the director of the agency or the president themselves. Once you have an identity in place, it is possible to use that validated identity to sign documents with your private keys. Signing with keys is already standard practice in government, though the private key distribution process is a security vulnerability and encumbrance.

By using the technology now available, officials can maintain proven, validated documents without the overhead and inefficiency of the old system. Standardization also has the effect of making fraud more auditable, as uses could scale across use cases with a lower cost of entry. Imagine signing your taxes or benefits with your private keys and validated identity, instead of waiting several months for a return. Blockchain could cut billions of dollars of fraud out of the benefits system in most countries, as people using false IDs to defraud taxpayers would be immediately identifiable.

The Power of Decentralization

Identity and documentation are critical for any government. Even more important is the principle of decentralization.

The most egregious hacks of government data have been the result of centralized and poorly guarded data. The government usually collects information systematically and in detail, but it doesn't appear to guard this data very well at all, as evidenced by the OPM hack of 2015.

The research and interviews it takes to grant someone a government clearance in the US is costly. Even the most basic investigation costs $15,000 and involves dozens of interviews of friends, family members, past roommates, a credit check, and other research. As of 2014, more than five million Americans were reported to have had security clearances, which included extensive personal data about the people interviewed, not just about the individual. The OPM hack represented a theft, not only of five million people's personal and private information but the identities of every person interviewed in connection with them.

Governments have kept all this data on centralized servers with dated protections. This policy allowed for the easy compromise of accounts and export of data, undermining the security of the United States and the people whose job it is to defend her.

Instead of centralizing data and data access, embracing decentralization could diminish the risk of such an outcome happening in the future. It sounds counterintuitive, but it's true. When accesses are limited to a need-to-know basis, and when more individual security checks are in place to access something, the barriers to entry and mass data exfiltration are higher. Even if files reside on a central server, the fact that different keys are required to access them diminishes the odds that an adversary could walk away with the whole enchilada.

Centralization of data increases the risk of compromise for everything, especially insider threats and the risk of a hostile penetration. Even though the data resides in one or two *physical* spaces, it can be *cryptographically* decentralized to prevent the outright theft of everything - in effect, decentralizing the information itself.

Blockchain: A Bulwark Against Propaganda

The 2016 election was a watershed moment in American history. 2016 stands out in part due to over meddling in the US election by information warfare professionals working for a foreign power, specifically Russia. Russia's Internet Research Agency, a political warfare wing of the government, leveraged Web 2.0 platforms like Twitter and Facebook to deliver "fake news" designed to divide the American electorate and cause chaos.

Covertly interfering in elections is nothing new, Russians have been interloping in European elections through what are called *Active Measures* (активные мероприятия) since well before the Soviet era. What was unique is the existing Web 2.0 ecosystem made this tactic that much more effective and scalable. Public knowledge and domestic politicization of Russian Active Measures changed our conversation with each other. Some on the losing side began publicly dismissing the political opinions of everyone not in their camp as foreign - a coup de grace Russia's Active Measures program. One might argue that the revelation of the formerly secret program did even more damage than the program when it was in operation.

In effect, *Active Measures* are a specific kind of propaganda, called *black propaganda* that is designed to sow distrust in an opponent's very institutions by spreading false information under a false flag. Black propaganda differs from "white propaganda" (official statements) and grey propaganda (talking points of clear affiliation but unacknowledged origin). When you're told by General Mills that you need to be "coo-coo for Cocoa Puffs," that's white propaganda. When CNN tells you everyone not in their political party is a racist, that's gray propaganda.

Black propaganda has historically included everything on the covert spectrum, from assassinations of journalists like Georgi

Markov with a ricin-tipped umbrella in London to the support of militant organizations like the Red Army Faction in Germany to the covert support of so-called "peace movements" opposed to US military cooperation with European nations. It's always plausibly deniable.

Many well-known conspiracy theories have their origin with the KGB's past propaganda and political warfare efforts, operated by KGB's First Chief Directorate (foreign intelligence and covert action arm, now the SVR). The claim that the United States created HIV/AIDS is just one example.

Not only does propaganda happen between countries, but it also happens within them in the form of "fake news." Individuals might fabricate stories to generate revenues through clickbait, or to attack a political rival in a way that has no negative consequences for the propagandist.

Over the past decade, *Active Measures* and black propaganda have focused on the cyber domain, where Web 2.0 has made dissemination easier and verification impossible. Not only does code and digital content scale better, but it is also less risky for the perpetrator since a well-executed attack can be non-attributable and hidden behind layers and layers of proxies.

To quote the US House, Permanent Select Committee on Intelligence declassified report:

"In the United States, Russian cyberattacks related to the 2016 elections starkly highlighted technical vulnerabilities in U.S. digital infrastructure and bureaucratic shortcomings that were exploited by the Kremlin. Russia's active measures campaign achieved its primary goal of inciting division and discord among Americans. For more than a year, U.S. politics have been consumed by bitter recriminations, charges, and counter-charges about the attacks. The reliability of the democratic vote-the bedrock of the U.S. republic-was widely and repeatedly questioned."

While there is no evidence that a foreign state actor successfully meddled in the actual counting of votes, the fact that a foreign nation had the gall to pollute our political discourse is issue enough. The Russian Federation's dissemination of false flag propaganda over unsecured social media networks demonstrates how vulnerable Web 2.0 platforms are by their nature. The powerful algorithms that Facebook and other systems used to optimize user's experiences were hijacked to push narratives (on both sides of the political aisle) designed to divide the United States' political discourse.

Further, this was successful in polluting the story, with many members of the losing party seizing on the accusation that the winning party in some way wittingly colluded with a foreign power. Two years and one thorough Special Counsel investigation later, there is zero evidence of collusion, though the accusation of a secret conspiracy between the Trump campaign and the Russian Federation has become a fixation of the party out of power.

Active Measures are designed to divide and humiliate. *Active Measures* tradecraft traces back the *Trust Operation*, run by Felix Dzerzhinsky's Cheka (the ancestor of the NKVD and KGB) between 1921 and 1926. During this operation, the Cheka ran a false resistance organization spanning much of Europe, intending to reel in as many supporters of the Romanov monarchy as possible. The Trust operation even included the staged assassination of Communist Party officials to build the *bona fides* of members and make the group more appealing, drawing in several Western intelligence agencies.

After half a decade, Dzerzhinsky publically rolled up the Trust, revealing that the entire resistance to Russian communism was thoroughly compromised. This public acknowledgment of a masterful intelligence operation was so humiliating to Western intelligence agencies that they covered it up themselves and shut down all future efforts to overthrow the Soviet Communist Party.

The eventual disclosure that the Russian government had successfully injected information into the United States political discourse is not much different. After the secret half of the operation ran its course, publicity accomplished the second goal of sowing doubt. This political hacking is possible, not just because of one company. It traces to the very structure of Web 2.0.

Web 2.0 is bottomless. It allows platforms to draw vast amounts of data from everyday users to build an advertising model, and to anticipate their tastes and habits. A culturally savvy adversary can write and disseminate propaganda abroad for a fraction of the cost and effort that it once took, and the impact of propaganda is higher by orders of magnitude. The West's open internet has been so greedy for data that there were no barriers to this exploit taking place, like a hungry sea turtle sucking down a plastic bag.

Identity and the chain of acquisition for information are essential to a Web 3.0 environment. Imagine maintaining your anonymity online, but being able to prove that you lived in your city. No one could call you a bot, or dismiss you. In the same vein, this would clear up a severe question of how our political discourse plays out since it makes the possibility of a political community online more feasible. Similarly, using blockchain to provide a chain of custody for media, authorship, and participation would rule out many of the approaches that opportunistic propagandists take, as meddling would be more identifiable without such criteria.

Censorious Tech Platforms and Fake News

Speaking of media, not every threat to democracy comes from outside. Many in media and tech have taken the position that it is their responsibility to "curate" coverage. Platforms that have

One of the more famous instances of this is demonstrated in freelance journalist Tim Pool's discussion with Twitter CEO Jack Dorsey on Joe Rogan's Podcast, which is listened to by millions of people. Pool briefly and succinctly outlined a myriad of instances where Twitter effectively took sides in cultural and social debates.

Among the most salient was the discussion over transgender bathrooms and "deadnaming" - whereby Twitter treated calling a trans person by their biological gender or birth name a bannable offense. This banning and deplatforming extend well beyond political discussions and hot-button issues to simple lifestyle choices. As we were finishing this book up, Facebook was banning Crossfit gyms and other pages for encouraging people to adopt a ketogenic diet. We have no idea what Zuckerberg or his employees have against cutting carbs, but banning fitness groups is a pretty good indicator that collectivist tech has become more potent than it should be, even for its wellbeing.

This problem cuts both ways; while conservatives are rightly angry about censorship, many on the left blame Twitter and Facebook for the election of Donald Trump. Companies have unintentionally become a victim in a tug of war, torn between taking sides with nation-states, individual political parties, and the preferences of their users, some of which create serious negative externalities. Just in the course of three years, Twitter went from being the primary PR platform for ISIS to deplatforming terrorists to being a conduit for black propaganda and political censorship.

That's not a fun position to be in as a company, but using the platform to shadowban anyone you disagree with represents a breach of the user's trust and does not combat the actual problem. Especially when it creates the expectation by both sides that capturing and controlling your platform is a logical approach to censor rivals.

Today and well into the future, there will be a crisis of truth in our democracies. Politicians lie, governments lie, and the media and collectivist tech are not a trusted source of truth either. There needs to be a decentralized, auditable record of reality if we are going to stay sane and maintain the integrity of our institutions.

Rearchitecting the Internet is decisive for the survival of Western Democracies. It is the only way to counter adversaries who are actively working to corrode the image and function of our democratic process.

Defending the Voting System

Every single vote counts. George W. Bush was elected in 2000 by a mere 537 votes in Florida, a pivotal swing state. As we wrote this sentence, Florida was yet again recounting votes, this time for the contentious 2018 midterm. Incidentally, it is rare for recounts in Florida to result in the same number of votes as were counted the first time, since many counties use a paper ballot. There is a rational concern over missing votes, uncounted, double-counted votes, or votes submitted fraudulently by people who do not have a legal right to vote in a given state or county.

Going back to Florida in 2018, there were reports that a provisional ballot box discovered in the back of an AVIS rental car in Broward County - an extremely evenly split district, where just a few votes could sway a statewide election. Either this report was fake news, or it wasn't, and in both cases, blockchain could rectify the problem. Absent any authoritative timestamping of the contents of the box and a transparent chain of acquisition; there are only three possibilities.

Either A) votes were legitimate but not legitimately counted; B) votes were illegitimate and being introduced by someone with a motive, or C) votes were real and scored, and the story itself is fake news. Having an immutable, decentralized ledger that only allows one vote per person would prevent much of this confusion and would support a more fair and effective democratic process.

A Better Way to Vote

By 2035, UTXO blockchains will become a critical technology for improving how our elections work. We would eliminate much of the voter fraud out there and have much more instantaneous (and more authoritative) elections within a blockchain system than we do with the current model. Blockchain voting is also much more reliable than the patchwork of voter ID laws across various states; many of the local governments that arguably should have stronger voter ID laws are incidentally the most resistant to implementing them.

Blockchain voting makes the election process itself unhackable. Beyond being resilient against external pressure, it would eliminate the costly recounts and the confusion present in our current process, which has difficulty counting and organizing the data and rarely comes up with the same numbers in each successive recount. Blockchain could also be used to verify other essential details, such as the voter's primary residence, their tax information, the absence of a criminal record, and their age - all of which are relevant to their standing to vote. Many do not exercise their democratic rights because they forgot to register or move their documents over to a new zip code; automating government identity would change this.

Those opposed to Voter ID laws often argue that the expense of procuring a trustworthy state ID is exclusionary. If identity can be verified online, the cost and accuracy of such procedures decrease substantially. This degree of verification makes remote voting by expats, soldiers, and those traveling for business much more feasible, as the unique identifier provided by a public blockchain nullifies many of the threats of double-counting or non-counting that we covered above, ensuring better participation in the election in question.

There are efforts underway to do just this. Startup 'Voatz' ran a pilot blockchain voting project during the 2018 midterm in West Virginia. The platform enabled users to create and validate an online account, much the same as one would follow through with AML/KYC compliance for a cryptocurrency exchange, and linked that data point to a blockchain ID that can only vote once per validated person.

Voatz was supported by Uber alum Bradley Tusk, who was responsible for managing much of the political campaigning that persuaded local governments to allow ridesharing companies to innovate and provide a better alternative to taxi companies. Tusk's experience in government inspired him to invest in technology that improves participation in elections.

Keeping State Secrets Secret

In June of 2015, the United States Office of Personnel Management (OPM) announced that it had been the victim of a massive data breach. 21.5 million records covertly exfiltrated by an "Advanced Persistent Threat." These records detailed the private lives of nearly every US person who had a "Secret" or "Top Secret" security clearance, as well as their relationships with friends and family interviewed during their security process.

This data included everything from social security numbers to names and dates of birth to the list of affiliations and family members that each person with a clearance had at the time their SF-

86 (security clearance intake form) submission. In terms of critical hacks of US infrastructure and data, the OPM hack was one of the most significant breaches of the US national security establishment in our history as a nation.

From an intelligence perspective, the data stolen in the OPM hack represented a "treasure map" of people, places, and accounts (such as phone numbers and emails) that an adversary could use to target US government employees. The OPM hack opened up American civil servants and service members to technical surveillance across their accounts, as well as human intelligence (HUMINT) targeting by foreign intelligence officers. OPM mapped every relation that government workers had and stored this data in an insecure setting, only to have it stolen by an adversary.

The OPM hack was a culmination of years of poor security practice by the US Government, with the Office both failing to prevent external intrusion and properly encrypt critical data. The House Committee on Oversight and Government Reform report on the breach strongly suggested the attackers were state actors due to the use of a particular and highly-developed piece of malware.

U.S. Department of Homeland Security official Andy Ozment testified that the attackers had gained valid user credentials to the systems they were attacking, likely in part by using the tactic of social engineering, gaining access by manipulating end users. The breach also consisted of a malware package that installed itself within OPM's network and established a backdoor. From there, attackers escalated their privileges to gain access to a wide range of OPM's systems.

Sources quickly identified the People's Republic of China as the culprit of the breach. Online blog *Ars Technica* reported that at least one user account with root access to *every* row in *every* database held by OPM traced as physically located in China. Another contractor contributing to OPM's database had two employees with Chinese passports, and the FBI subsequently arrested 36-year-old Yu Pingan, a Chinese national, in facilitating the attack.

The OPM hack by an "advanced persistent threat" (a government euphemism for Chinese public/private partnership in cybercrime) illustrates several of the critical vulnerabilities involved in government information technology, and also demonstrates the need for more broadly accepted standards in cybersecurity. That the USG was comfortable leaving so much vital information accessible and ready to be exfiltrated is a scandal in and of itself.

Second, security practices used by OPM had fallen into gross disrepair before the attack - OPM did not even use 2-factor authentication at the time the hack began. By the time OPM had adopted two-factor authentication, hackers had remote access to lists of usernames and passwords, daisy-chaining their efforts to maximize access across accounts.

Though access to records may not seem as catastrophic as the theft of, say nuclear weapons design, the OPM attack gave the PRC a persistent advantage in understanding the precise relationships of those who work with the U.S. Government. This data is an asset that will keep on giving when it comes to identifying people to recruit, technologies to steal, and risks to avoid when it comes to protecting counterintelligence operations.

The OPM hack is a masterclass in the strategic risk posed by the insecure, centralized internet that we have today. The vulnerabilities are significant, and the risks for running such a system are growing exponentially. By 2035, blockchains modeled on the UTXO system will be used by governments to distribute one-time keys, create atomic cryptographic identities, and store user accounts critical to accessing such databases as those managed by the OPM. In a blockchain-oriented cybersecurity infrastructure, user accounts could be locked or contingent on multiple other factors, such as access to independently delivered keys or user identities that are cryptographically locked to networks and hardware and thus cannot be run by proxy.

Security Within the Government

Advances in the blockchain will also presage advances in cryptography that prevent unauthorized access to critical data and programs. This development arc includes new cryptographic algorithms based on the increased interest in cryptography, but also an improved environment to distribute keys and a more robust marketplace of ideas for building innovative systems capable of utilizing cryptography and unique identifiers to protect information.

An excellent example of this is the blockchain's ability to execute a secure private key exchange between two individuals who seek to communicate in an encrypted environment. Another is the use of blockchains to replace the many passwords and keys required to access systems - as Andrew can attest, having a dozen different passwords and three times as many accounts to access can get confusing and inefficient. Worse, it disincentivizes professionals from using specific systems because the accesses and interoperability are cumbersome. This messy architecture leads to security issues such as reuse of passwords and storage of passwords on post-it notes. Often the first two to four months of a federal employee's career is spent getting accesses, and that process repeats every time they transfer jobs within the federal government.

Using a system like Digi-ID to validate accesses could save thousands of labor hours for governments, and enable a single discrete ecosystem that protects principles of both efficiency and need-to-know. Hitting this sweet sport is no small issue, and is critical in limiting the damage of an insider threat like that posed by Edward Snowden.

There are strong arguments that Snowden's public disclosures were both inaccurate and designed to cause harm and embarrassment to Western democracies. That Snowden provided detailed information to the Russian and potentially Chinese governments as a means of securing passage and safety (in turn worsening the U.S. position globally without doing anything for privacy or civil liberties) strengthens this argument.

Regardless of what one thinks of Snowden, his disclosures have popularized the use of encryption for messaging and other applications globally, and now we live in a new era in which encryption is the norm, not the exception. If you asked an FBI or CIA analyst in 2005 how they felt about a future where anyone can send any message anywhere, the content of which is immune to decryption, they would likely recoil in horror. The same goes for anyone having a "swiss bank account in their pocket." The fact of the matter is that these systems are not going away, so governments would be foolish to subject themselves to the handicaps that criminals, terrorists, and hostile state actors can now easily avoid.

Unless governments, law enforcement, and intelligence agencies wise up to the need for improved security architecture, both within their organizations and in private industry, they will be playing by a handicap that they can only wish their adversaries would adopt.

Protecting Critical Infrastructure: The Energy Grid

America, Europe, and the entire industrialized world run on electric power. Everything from our economy to our civic lives has a battery. According to the American Council on Foreign Relations (cited at length here, emphasis ours):

"Attacks on power grids are no longer a theoretical concern. In 2015, an attacker took down parts of a power grid in Ukraine... geopolitical circumstances and forensic evidence suggest Russian involvement. A year later, Russian hackers targeted a transmission level substation, blacking out part of Kyiv. In 2014, Admiral Michael Rogers, director of the National Security Agency, testified before the U.S. Congress that China and a few other countries likely could shut down the U.S. power grid. Iran, as an emergent cyber actor, could acquire such capability. Rapid digitization combined with low levels of investment in cybersecurity and a weak regulatory regime suggests that the U.S. power system is as vulnerable—if not more vulnerable—to a cyberattack as systems in other parts of the world."

The complexity of the existing power grid exacerbates its vulnerability. There are an estimated 3,300 utility companies that deliver electricity through *200,000 miles* of high voltage transmission lines - enough to stretch around the earth eight times, and *5.5 million miles* of distribution lines - enough to reach the moon 23 times over. Every level from generation to transmission and distribution is vulnerable.

Worse, any attack on the network would have cascading effects across the web. In one 2015 simulation conducted by UK insurance firm Lloyd's and the University of Cambridge Centre for Risk Studies, analysts calculated the second- and third-order effects of an attack on the greater Northeast (the area between Chicago, Boston, and DC).

Based on available information, analysts extrapolated that such an attack could result in as much as a trillion dollars in damages to GDP by the time power was restored, with only 4.2 billion in net lost electricity revenue.

Modern economies are all incredibly reliant on access to electricity, yet most Western countries are not securing their power grids against the kind of adversarial nation-state we've described so far in this chapter.

Most of the famous attacks on power grids so far have been conducted by Russia, but the most advanced and motivated publicly disclosed attacks appear to be Iranian in origin. Iranian efforts include the 2012 attack on Saudi Aramco and the subsequent release of the *Duqu* virus. Duqu is believed to be retaliation for Western cyberwarfare methods that had set back Iranian acquisition of a nuclear weapon, and directly emulates Western and Israeli cyberattack methods used against Iran's nuclear program.

Duqu was designed to scan for information that could be useful in attacking industrial control systems, such as those used to monitor and control the power produced by a hydroelectric or nuclear power plant. Duqu's established purpose was not to be directly destructive but to gather the information that makes it possible to mount an effective attack.

According to security firm McAfee, one of Duqu's core actions is to steal digital certificates (and corresponding private keys, as used in public-key cryptography described earlier in this book) from attacked computers to help future viruses appear as secure software. Exploits include capturing information such as keystrokes and system information, such that user accounts could be taken over to facilitate commands to break or disable the system. Blockchain can prevent precisely this kind of attack by facilitating private key distribution and encrypting the data that viruses like Duqu target.

Records Management

As we mentioned above, records management is a lynchpin for governments. The authenticity of information a government has ready to hand defines just how effective any policy might be. In this section, we'll give a few examples of how blockchain may be implemented to improve the quality of information that the government has in addressing disease, criminal history, and preventing waste, fraud, and abuse.

Tracking Disease

Tracking any disease, whether it is HIV/AIDS, Ebola, or Varicella, requires good records. Since diseases - like ideas - move from host to host, our best defense against epidemics is to quarantine subjects and to close off pathways of contagion. Quarantines require we map out the virus and understand its point of origin, how it has mutated, and what its unique characteristics are. Much like tracing a terrorist network, there are nodes and points of contact that explain the network effects of any viral process, which is ultimately a data structure much like a Merkel Tree that blockchains can map and model.

As various diseases fork off, mutate, and move from host to host. How better to track disease samples with a blockchain? One could hash and preserve samples, as well as track infected individuals. If something resembling the 2014 Ebola scare breaks out again (and it will), it makes sense to be able to track every traveler, log every sample, and verify every checkup.

Epidemics are one of the more significant risks to civilization in the modern era, especially as our cities have become more crowded, and our populations become increasingly mobile. Risk worsens in an environment where many "eradicated" diseases are being kept in cold storage and could reemerge. Better and more verifiable data management on a blockchain is the best method we have to make sure outbreaks stay contained and can be safely studied.

Criminal Records and an Auditable Justice System

The current infrastructure for criminal records owes much of its history to FBI founder J. Edgar Hoover, whose scientific approach to data is still the backbone of the agency. This proved revolutionary for law enforcement, as no national-level database of criminals, was available at the time. Criminals like Bonnie and Clyde roved from state to state, leveraging the speed of their cars against the lack of jurisdictional authority that any state police force might have to track them across state lines.

Even today, standard maintenance of criminal records is a challenge, as the entire system relies on manual entry. To this day, criminals are arrested by police who do not have full access to information or warrants from other municipalities or countries. Maintaining and sharing this data is a full-time job for many analysts, whose sole job it is to run records checks in dozens of databases to ensure that someone in custody doesn't have other outstanding warrants. Despite being critical, it is dehumanizing inefficient drudgery that is often subject to human error.

Blockchains can revolutionize criminal records by making the many databases work together and keeping a ledger of past activity and identity. It can also help in maintaining the privacy of the data through private keys, ensuring a person's past mistakes don't haunt them indefinitely by spilling into the broader world in a data breach. Each municipality can uniquely write to the database, and custody of prisoners is far easier to audit.

Beyond security, such a system could demonstrate what precisely courts are providing what sentences and could illustrate differences in justice systems across a country. There are few better ways to counter racial and classist bias in our justice system than to introduce machines and uniform data that point our when judgments are out of line with each other.

Preventing Fraud

Healthcare fraud was assessed to consume as much as $272,000,000,000 across the entire U.S. healthcare system as of 2014. The cost of the opioid crisis was estimated to be approximately $504,000,000,000 in 2015 If Blockchain helps mitigate even a fraction of this enormous cost, it will go a long way towards defraying the US national deficit, half of which is due to healthcare and entitlements spending.

Part of this will be the integration of cryptographically unique IDs for medical records, as well as to track drugs as they distributed across the marketplace. An essential element of this challenge is that fraud and corruption are so entrenched - if we could excise fraud and graft like a tumor, they wouldn't still be problems. We need systems that track inefficiencies and serve as a standardized record to identify just where waste and corruption are occurring.

As a vignette, let's take a moment to talk about the opioid crisis, which is an excellent example of the kind of problem that blockchain can contribute to fixing. According to the US Department of Justice, Purdue Pharmaceuticals (the manufacturer of highly addictive opioid OxyContin) has been aware of the highly addictive nature of its product since its launch.

According to the same source, Purdue is also very aware of the substantial black market for OxyContin. Instead of working to control the drug or limit its deployment to the most extreme cases, Purdue aggressively grew its sales of OxyContin to $1.1 Billion with an aggressive advertising and lobbying push. Purdue spent nearly $200 Million in 2001 alone to push the substance on the market, and by 2004 OxyContin abuse had become the leading form of drug abuse in the country.

Many small clinics serve as "pill mills" to distribute "Oxy" and other controlled opioids with prescriptions motivated by profit, ravaging communities across the country. Drug companies' deliberate overprescription of opioids that they knew to be addictive and lethal resulted in over 72,000 overdose deaths in 2017 alone, with more every following year. This level of destruction is orders of magnitude worse than 9/11, yet the crisis persists.

Addressing the opioid crisis is something members of the DigiByte community affiliated with Harvard Medical School are working on: a method of tracking opioids distributed across the US. Jacob Keteyan, a student at Harvard's School of Public Health, has identified blockchain as a critical element that may aid governments in tracking and regulating the flow of dangerous prescription drugs like OxyContin, as well as decreasing the amount of fraud and error in the medical market.

In an ideal system, prescriptions for controlled and addictive substances should be tracked and maintained on a decentralized blockchain. Purdue Pharmaceutical should not be allowed to "self-police" its distribution. Congress should demand that the prescription process for these controlled substances become more transparent, with full records of production and distribution occurring on an unhackable blockchain.

Finance and Fiscal Policy

It is now only a matter of time before nation-states successfully issue cryptocurrencies and national blockchains as assets in their own right. These processes might occur separately, or they may operate in tandem along with the same technical stack. For our purposes in this section, we will specifically focus on the fiscal policy aspects of states issuing national cryptocurrencies, and using blockchains as a specific instrument of *domestic* policy.

Fiscal Policy and Economic Competition

States cannot control decentralized UTXO-model cryptocurrency. They can crush corporations, defenestrate "distributed ledgers," and forbid trading of digital assets for their fiat currency within their borders, but they cannot stop people from finding ways to procure crypto assets.

Governments also cannot effectively prevent the triangular trade of their currency with crypto assets in the long run and outside of their borders. This matters even more in failing states like Venezuela, where cryptocurrency is a much more workable means of sound money than the ruined fiat currency.

Effectively, this dynamic cuts both ways. States have been beholden to central banks in varying degrees since the institution's inception in the late 1600s, in parallel with the evolution of the nation-state itself after the 30 Years War concluded with the Treaty of Westphalia in 1648. As we discuss in a later chapter, central banks evolved as part of the competition between these new political entities and gave the state the ability to borrow from the future to win wars and trade conflicts.

We live in a very different era: one shaped by runaway sovereign debt, massive deficits, and denominated in unbacked fiat currency. Everyone knows a sovereign debt crisis is coming, and everyone knows governments will be under the gun to deal with their debts in the 2020s and 2030s.

This situation creates the massive potential for states to innovate, and there is a chance that they may break away from old institutions and habits to embrace a new strategy that helps them capitalize on this disequilibria. Critical to this point is the fact that just as states cannot crush pure UTXO cryptocurrencies, they cannot crush *each other's* pure UTXO cryptocurrencies.

We believe that states will begin to issue cryptocurrencies of various technical stripes as a complementary asset to their fiat national currency. They will do so to supplement their national currencies and also as a means of exerting control over their economies and buffering their central bank's balance sheets. There are a plethora of ways this could play out, and it is important not to think of this process as some utopian or dystopian inevitability, but a natural product of evolution.

Banking and economics are already a competitive environment between nation-states for economic security and primacy, no different from the way states manage their existing fiat currencies, and blockchains offer new ways for countries to compete with each other.

In a democratic or open society, a national blockchain could run on an advanced decentralized UTXO model that maintains the transparency and auditability of the blockchain while being tied to trade, pensions, taxation, and all other sorts of applications. These are systems that are begging to operate on an efficient, auditable, immutable technical backbone, and blockchain is the right tool for the job. Alternatively, undemocratic countries will pursue highly centralized systems that empower surveillance and central control of the economy. In this scenario, transactions are whitelisted and occur only with revocable permissions.

Political dissidents could have their privileges (such as their ability to exchange fiat money for foreign currency) revoked. Such an approach might even be designed to lock users into using the national currency as a means of political power and isolation from the outside world, as North Korea's emerging system is. There are good reasons to think both Russia and especially the People's Republic of China dream of doing precisely this.

If we're good analysts, we should approach this problem from the mindset of governments themselves. It is the cadre of influential people that are typically risk-averse and slow to react that make decisions on these matters. They generally stay where they are at by being uncontroversial and not undertaking any initiatives that might consume political capital.

Only in a crisis do many innovations of this sort take hold. Because of this, state-issued cryptocurrency will likely come well after states have implemented the plethora of security functions outlined above in this book and are comfortable with the technology. Once blockchain technology begins to contribute to security functions in government and the private sector, the issuance of national cryptocurrencies will not sound that crazy.

Domestic and International: Legibility, Accountability, and Taxation

At a local level, there's more than just abstract fiscal economics that goes into this debate, and many in government were initially threatened by cryptocurrency by simple virtue of it not fitting within their existing mental model for how they expect to govern. The UTXO model means that a form of money already exists apart from the issuance of a state, and states by being sovereign generally exercise the right to tax their citizens to provide for the public good and secure order.

Countries naturally work to gain an information advantage over their citizens. Information advantage means governments know what assets citizens have, what they do for a living, and so on. To this effect, states pursue a national language, national rules for ownership of property, and national standards for transportation that make it easier to enforce taxation and governance, a dynamic anthropologist James C. Scott calls *legibility*.

Effectively, encryption and cryptocurrency prevent the state from enjoying this kind of easy readability, especially in a world with billions of people, devices, and the nearly infinite field of information that is the internet. Paying for goods and services in a currency that the state can't monitor (like physical cash) avoids this domestic surveillance. Some might also call this financial privacy, which many expect as a natural human right.

Crypto contributes to a libertarian school of thought known as *agorism* - where transactions are voluntary between individuals, with no intervening state. Since crypto completely circumvents the state, it lets individuals interact according to the principles of agorism, rather than relying on the state as a trusted third party.

Unless the government has a means of attributing, analyzing, and affecting transactions to enforce taxation policy on this new form of currency, crypto will be the new cash. Governments are emphatic about Anti Money Laundering/Know Your Customer (AML/KYC) laws because it affects their bottom line. Not only does AML/KYC help prevent illegal uses of cryptocurrency, but it also enables taxation.

On the other side of this equation is an entirely auditable tax system. Governments that overtax their citizens generally end up broke, and governments with clear, simple taxation and fees tend to attract capital. By using an auditable system for taxation, where wage and income statements are entirely transparent, it becomes possible to eliminate significant amounts of fraud and streamline the tax system. Instead of giving the government an interest-free loan every year by paying taxes, citizens could pay the exact amount of tax due through blockchain and automation. Refunds could be dispensed immediately and accurately, rather than work through a broken administrative jungle plagued by fraud.

Domestic: Pensions and Hard Currency

Fourth, we believe that states will come to recognize the utility of non-dilutionary UTXO-model cryptocurrency as a portion of their state pension systems and as a global reserve currency. US states such as Ohio already accept Bitcoin as a means of paying taxes, since Bitcoin is harder money than the USD. That local governments are acknowledging this is no small victory for cryptocurrency.

It is also logical to assume that local governments will adopt well-established cryptocurrencies as part of a balanced pension system, primarily due to the gold-like characteristics of crypto as a form of hard currency. Bitcoin and the UTXO model that goes with it have been battle-tested for more than a decade. As of this writing, thousands of attacks and attempts at hacking the core network have failed. As economist Saifedean Ammous argues in *The Bitcoin Standard: The Decentralized Alternative to Central Banking*, the deflative economics of a real UTXO cryptocurrency make it superior to gold as a hard currency.

Where the IMF and central banks have more or less monopolized gold ownership, UTXO cryptocurrency is money you own, and money that cannot be taken from you or diluted. This kind of asset can be rationally expected to *appreciate* as more and more users purchase it as a *consensus store of value*. For pensioners whose deposits are managed by large institutions, such as Blackrock, UTXO cryptocurrency is at least as good an investment as putting money into federal bonds. Crypto will only become more influential for pensions as negative interest rates destroy the bond market. Today roughly one-third of sovereign debt offers a negative yield after inflation. Pensions need a new way to preserve the fiduciary interests of their clients, and cryptocurrency is the best way to do so.

As a vignette, it is helpful to realize that the United States credit rating has been downgraded from "AAA" to "AA+" by the credit agencies. American sovereign debt has exploded since the conclusion of the Cold War. When Standard & Poors downgraded the world's most powerful economy, federal debt stood at 15 trillion dollars. This downgrade originated with "increasing doubt that the U.S.'s political system will reign in public spending to become sustainable over the long term." In the course of our writing this book, the same debt went from 21.5 trillion to 22.7 trillion.

If you have a pension or savings, this is a system you are betting your future livelihood on, by your own choice or by the compulsion of others, and it involves buying bonds at a meager rate. Worse, this form of economics spans much of the modern world, with large banks in Europe, Asia, and elsewhere operating very much under the same inflative standard. It is foolish to think that fiat cannot and will not face a significant crisis in the future that affects your ability to retire.

Nation-states and pension funds that adopt crypto as one of the many assets they invest in are hedging their bets, not undermining their nation's currency or their economy. A nation-state anticipating global instability (especially one as influential as the United States) may find it useful to be the first party to issue a state-backed hard currency. This currency could be globally available and act as a new hard global reserve currency, allowing it to float relative to all other assets. Such a pivot is nothing less than a reinvention of gold and central banking.

The Greenback is already a global standard for settlement, drawing much of its influence from the fact that the dollar backs global commodities markets (including oil) with those profits reinvested into US treasuries and companies. From a fiscal policy perspective, the credibility of a "GreenBlock" would likely compound with the credibility of the US dollar and system of laws with the added advantage of immutable code, drawing capital fleeing broken economies from the world over and allowing for a form of settlement in hard cash.

For members of the middle class, who expect to save for retirement and do not have the financial wherewithal to avoid the pensions system, ownership of such a hard currency is a far more sure bet than the fragility of being tied to bonds and equities markets. Adding the third pillar of hard cash would make the global pensions system more, not less stable, and whoever does it right first is going to reap the most significant rewards.

The National Digital Asset and Universal Basic Wealth

If countries are revolutionizing their banking system, it stands to reason that new policy options will come to the fore. One of these is a universal basic income, or UBI, which we discuss elsewhere in this book. In short, if a country is creating a deflationary UTXO asset for pensions and other fiscal purposes, it stands to reason that this asset that all of the country's citizens could receive an amount of this asset. The beauty of such a model is that this policy requires no new tax dollars, as a market would establish the asset's value in fiat terms, and the government adopting this could hedge against its own (and other countries) inflationary policies.

The first legitimate mover to do this will trigger a massive wealth transfer into their economy. Their asset will have a nation's economy behind it as well as global capital that becomes drawn to the path of least resistance and best returns. Just as the U.S. Dollar strengthened in economic downturns of 2008 when the broader world exchanged native currency for that perceived to be the safest, the introduction of a national digital asset will reshape the global monetary space. While these dynamics do apply to Bitcoin and other decentralized assets, they will likely also apply to any credible state-backed approach to a deflationary digital asset.

Conclusion

Cybersecurity, recordkeeping, and finance are all core functions of states, and these functions aren't going to disappear any time soon. Cryptocurrency and real blockchains are around for the long haul, too, so it is natural to expect their characteristics to intersect.

States are in a protracted competition with each other to be economically dominant. There are only so many jobs, resources, and productive endeavors to undertake at any one time, and they will explore blockchain technology as part of this process in the 2020s and 2030s.

It's one thing to anticipate how governments and companies might use the technology, but how does one vet the existing projects out there to find where and how these applications will get built? That's the goal of our next chapter.

Chapter 14: Commercial Blockchain Applications

> *"Once a new technology rolls over you, if you're not part of the steamroller, you're part of the road."*
>
> *-Stewart Brand*

One of the goals of this book is to provide the reader with actual, real-world use cases and examples of how applied blockchain technology will get used in our everyday life by the year 2035. Just like AI, blockchain will disrupt dozens of industries, especially those involving trust and value management, which are precisely where the blockchain shines.

Legal Applications

The World Economic Forum estimates that it costs the global economy trillions of dollars per decade, with litigation estimated to have cost the United States 1.66 percent of the nation's net GDP in 2011. According to the United States Chamber of Commerce, the direct costs to the global economy associated with commercial claims were roughly $870 Billion in 2012, of which the US accounted for $306 Billion.

Beyond the strictly monetary expenses created by litigation, legal disputes cost companies time and affect their ability to raise and borrow money, as time and money spent on litigation are not devoted to creating and selling better products. At an international level, the World Economic Forum highlights that the complexity of projects and international business arrangements, the diversity of domestic legal infrastructure, political and external factors that are beyond the control of both countries, and the distance between parties agreeing all militate against the clean and efficient management of legal agreements.

Beyond the strictly commercial, the U.S. legal system is estimated to be the world's most expensive, charging over 150 percent more than the legal systems of the Eurozone, and 50 percent more than the UK. This cost is a multiplier on the general litigiousness of US businesses, the largest of whom employ massive legal and compliance teams whose role is to defend the firm's interest from the administrative state and an ever-growing legal code.

Because of this, we believe that the legal profession is ripe for disruption with blockchain technology. More often than not, the inefficiency in our modern court systems is due to endless paperwork, poor records management, poor representation of agreements, and other issues that arise from the need to settle disputes among third parties in an environment where documentation and timestamping is paramount.

This inefficiency exists on top of the effects of bad faith by persons and companies, who might be motivated to change terms or renege on agreements, leading to the disputes in the first place. Since the law is basically about contracts and property, as we've discussed at length in this book, the unique cryptographic and timestamping characteristics of real blockchains will enable a new era in the legal profession, stripping out much of the inefficiency and doubt as regards contracts and the identities and standing of those who signed them.

Cryptographic identity is at the core of several legal applications for blockchain. Just as any IoT device or data set can have private keys associated with it, so too, can a signature or account. If you sign a legal contract with your private keys, that signature is as good as any wet ink signature with a notary. No one else could have signed it. As an immutable authority, that transaction is also timestamped and can be associated with other relevant circumstantial data. This immutability means that contracts could not get backdated, postdated, or manipulated after a signature had been committed. This undisputable trust is critical for legal applications where the consent of the subject is intrinsic to the validity of the legal contract.

Imagine signing the lease for a house only to have the landlord change the terms after the fact; with a blockchain contracts system, these sorts of manipulations will be transparent and easy to identify, as the contract document can be hashed and timestamped.

As we mentioned above, a signature through timestamped private keys on a blockchain can also obviate the need for a notary - insofar as the keys are distributed to an individual according to notary standards with a valid form of identification and verification, the use of those keys in the future can rationally get treated as a valid legal signature. Rather than relying on someone to check your real, government ID (which can easily get faked), you can sign documents with a universal assigned ID that has extensively gotten validated and which you conclusively own - remotely.

V-ID, a Dutch company that uses and develops on DigiByte, allows precisely this form of validation, such that users of the firm's technology have access to a digital notary. V-ID has developed dozens of exciting partnerships, but we'll name just three. First, V-ID's system is getting used by Baan Velgen, a high-end parts distributor for Ferrari, Maserati, and Lamborghini. This partnership allows these companies to validate invoices for parts and always be able to trust the quality of their supply chain. Second, V-ID has partnered with the Dutch Register of Architectural Inspectors to provide a blockchain-backed method of recording property valuations and inspections. Last, V-ID is helping preserve cultural treasures, including works by Rembrandt.

Healthcare Applications

One of the most important and critical areas that need and can begin adopting blockchain technology overnight is in the healthcare industry. Healthcare costs in the United States are entirely out of control, and our system is deeply flawed as most of us reading this know. No industry is quite as riven with inefficiency as the healthcare industry in the US, where multiple intermediaries drive up the price of care, prescriptions, and insurance. Worse, the US' quasi-statist "Affordable Care Act" mandates that citizens buy coverage from private companies, which has increased the expense of healthcare premiums substantially.

Persons receiving a tax credit due to a lack of income can lose their care, even their income has decreased, simply because "the documents don't match." At the care level, doctors often run patients through a gauntlet of unnecessary scans to pay off their expensive equipment, even when they know that the additional diagnostics are useless. On top of that, doctors tend to overprescribe drugs, and there is a near-monopoly within the US. The same drugs are significantly cheaper and available over the counter elsewhere.

The recent trial of "Pharma Bro" Martin Shkreli is one such example of this. Don't even get us started on medical records, which are kept in dozens of different files and not shared with the user "for their privacy" - despite the fact they get shared among multiple companies who have a profit interest in the individual.

Few things stick out to us as deserving disruption as much as the medical care industry. According to the U.S. Centers for Disease Control, American expenditure on healthcare topped $3.2 Trillion in 2017 or 17.8% of US GDP. Twenty-six cents of every U.S. tax dollar goes to support Medicare, Medicaid, and ACA subsidies, which are targets of massive fraud that provide vouchers to private industry and political constituents who profit from taxed and printed money being plowed into their industry by politicians.

Instead of going on a tear about just how corrupt and inefficient the healthcare industry is, let's imagine a world where healthcare gets revolutionized by a blockchain platform that streamlines the entire process.

Insurance and the Cost of Care

Insurance companies have more reliable data to work with, and they know whom they are insuring with the consent of the insured, who has shared their permissioned IoT data with their insurance provider. When a claim gets made, there is direct data to infer the associated cost, and the insurance firm and the patient are at less risk of being overbilled (which is a pandemic today, especially for advanced and lifesaving care).

Prescriptions

The high cost of prescription drugs is another issue that affects consumers and the cost of healthcare and may get improved by a blockchain system for distribution and fairer markets.

Today, there are effectively three markets for prescription drugs. There is the U.S., where many of the world's life-saving new medicines get produced, and where there is a somewhat statist architecture for how the cost gets covered by insurance; there are the regulated markets of Europe and elsewhere, where government boards enforce price ceilings for prescription drugs in order to keep the price down. This statist model provides a monopsony (single buyer and distributor), which allows the governments of each country to accept or deny a drug for distribution to patients.

This gets exacerbated by the fact that most pharma companies rely on patents for a near-term monopoly - in some instances there is a monopoly selling to a monopsony, either driving the price up or resulting in a situation where some go without not because they couldn't afford the drug, but because their government refused to pay what the producer demanded. As a result of this inefficiency, there is a third party - the broader market. While many go without lifesaving drugs because they 1) can't afford them or 2) do not have access to them within the bounds of nationalized healthcare, there is profit potential in fixing this inefficiency.

In this setting, drug producers in places like the U.S. attempt to capture their profits where they can, while making less handsome profits in markets where they must negotiate the price and where they would likely not have developed the drug in the first place. In effect, this means that American patients and insurance are subsidizing the medical development for the broader world, sometimes to the result of paying 10x for the same product, such as an EpiPen. This price gouging drives the general cost of healthcare up, as well as hurts consumers in both markets.

There are effectively two ways that the blockchain could improve this. First, by allowing for a more realistic market and bidding for drugs, buyers could acquire authentic medications at more transparent global prices. If someone could buy an EpiPen at

$30, why would they buy it at $300? If someone needs Hepatitis C medicine, why should they be disbarred from it when their government doesn't want to pay what it costs? In principle, this could enable arbitrage of goods while assuring their origin. Where the existing regulatory framework generally exists to jack up prices and defend economic fiefdoms, there could be a much more efficient global market.

Second, a blockchain could improve the progeny and integrity of drugs distributed globally. Counterfeit drugs are a huge issue, especially in less protected markets than the U.S. This is especially the case with Chinese exports, which account for a significant portion of the counterfeit drugs in circulation globally.

It's estimated 200,000 to 300,000 people die each year in China due to counterfeit or substandard medicine, and much of this gets exported globally. Nigeria's federal health agency (NAFDAC) in 2006 issued a public criticism of China's perceived unwillingness to collaborate against counterfeit medicines, as counterfeit medicines accounted at the time for approximately 68% of the domestic drug market in Nigeria, with the vast majority of those illicit products coming from China. If there is going to be a global market for drugs, the world should be able to verify its integrity.

Medical Records

Medical records are something we've mentioned at length so far in this book because they are one of the first areas that the blockchain will disrupt today's broken and inefficient system. You and I have medical records that span across every doctor, dentist, or optometrist we've ever been to over our lifetime. Every time we go to the doctor, at least in the U.S., we sit in a waiting room and fill out a form with questions from memory. Everything from past infections to broken bones. Also, each office keeps its own. When we go in for a treatment, the success or failure of that treatment often goes undocumented, as well as what drugs we took and what other symptoms we might have had.

Worse, the documentation that pertains to our very physical health is often poorly managed. Pharmaceutical and insurance companies have an interest in knowing what they can sell to us or might have to pay for our policies - your confidential medical data is being stolen and sold without your consent, often when you are not allowed to take your file with you when you switch doctors or move. The current industry is a wreck and ripe for disruption, and the blockchain is an ideal technology to accomplish that.

Instead of disparate files not controlled by you, practitioners could adopt a standard form of records management where the user retains their record for life and manages access with their private keys. As part of the healthcare process, the user would share the relevant aspects of their medical history with their provider, who would be able to temporarily review the records, as well as add new ones as part of the transaction.

The individual file could be stored by a company off-chain, with the unique address for the transaction on-chain. Your healthcare records could be a DigiAsset, one you keep with you, and interact with through a mobile app. This digitization would have the effect of improving the quality and speed of care, as medical professionals could rely on a thorough history of prescriptions, allergies, past issues, even genetics.

Now that we mention genetics, there is no better analogy (and no better use case) than genomic medicine managed on a blockchain. Why should a massive database control and repackage your most confidential data, which may be the key to your entire life's experience, without giving you power over it? If your doctor is treating you, shouldn't she know what diseases you're predisposed to, what diet you should have, your blood type, and everything else relevant to providing the right care that gets you back to full health as fast as possible?

In a world where AI medicine, advanced protein synthesis, CRISPR genetic editing, and constant IoT monitoring of health are possible, there are no better means to manage all of this precious data than on a blockchain where the user can control it all. This access is useful for practitioners and researchers too: imagine the depth of data that 23andMe has, except extending to your exercise patterns, your sleep cycles, and everything else that's relevant to making a diagnosis and developing a specific medical plan, both for preventive health and emergency care.

This kind of data management would be impossible without a universal system. Even more critical is the security required for this degree of data: because of the immense value, secure encryption is critical for any successful platform.

From a business perspective, blockchain medical records as a service could spread much like Facebook, or other social media platforms did. Both doctors and patients have an interest in better records. It's just a matter of time before business nails the formula develops the right partnerships, and changes how we manage our health for good.

Medical Devices

As medical devices become increasingly connected and complex, two primary domains will be affected by blockchain technology. Like other manufactured goods, medical devices and implants require substantial supply chain management and compliance that can be significantly improved by management on a blockchain system. This improvement can include an assurance that the correct device, such as a hip implant is delivered. This validation can assure that only the appropriate equipment has gotten issued, avoiding many horror stories about misfit or improper implants.

More interestingly, when medical devices become part of the broader IoT ecosystem, they must be secured. Some of us are old enough to remember episodes of *24* and *Homeland*, where the Vice President's pacemaker gets hacked. While this might seem like a far-fetched television trope, the reality is much scarier - in 2018, hackers proved that not just pacemakers, but a malicious hacker can manipulate insulin pumps.

Pacemakers could deliver an ill-timed shock, or deny one. Insulin pumps could do the same to a patient's insulin levels. Devices in this example, we're still operating on Windows XP, which as an operating system, is old enough to buy tobacco in most jurisdictions. This example might not seem like a massive threat for most people, who don't have a team of malicious hackers attempting to affect them - but what happens when influential people in business and politics have such implants?

This danger is not an unreasonable risk to game out in one's mind - imagine an executive with an insulin pump or pacemaker having that device manipulated in the middle of negotiations between two countries or companies, not enough to be fatal but enough to weaken them in the course of the ceremony. This vulnerability isn't far from the tactics of some countries; Vladimir Putin, in negotiations with Angela Merkel of Germany, was famous for introducing a large dog into the room while meeting her, knowing that she had been bitten as a child and had a fear of large dogs.

Manipulating an insulin pump to slightly lower ahead of state's blood sugar is much more subtle, but could have the same effect in a tense diplomatic exchange. Further, it would be difficult to prove, and the accusation of malice would likely sound ridiculous if levied on the world stage.

With a blockchain, this data could be encrypted and delivered point to point with no more fear of hacked medical devices; even if their code becomes obsolete, the encryption provided by a blockchain creates a defensive barrier.

Aviation Applications

Aircraft Maintenance

Routine aircraft maintenance is one of the most critical parts of the aviation industry to maintain the absolute safety and performance of aircraft. Often aircraft maintenance logs serve as the primary source of investigative materials to examine following any aviation fatality or incident. In some cases, these logs have not been correctly filled out or kept up to date. In other cases, these maintenance logs have even been fraudulently altered or changed after the fact. By anchoring and recording maintenance logs into a blockchain, many of these issues can be resolved.

Pilot Log Books

The essential metric used to govern pilots in the aviation industry is how many flight hours they have. How many flight hours a pilot has is used to determine everything from which certification they are eligible for to which jobs they are qualified to fill. All pilots maintain a logbook where they record every flight they make and what type of aircraft they flew and in what kind of conditions.

This process has to date mainly been done in an on your honor type system. It can be very easy for pilots to fake and add in a few extra hours of flight time here and there. By recording pilot flight hours on a blockchain, there would be no question how many flight hours or on what type of aircraft a pilot flew.

Aircraft Parts

Another area of aviation where blockchain would be useful would be for tracking and quality controlling aircraft parts. By tracking the origin, chain of acquisition, and age of every aircraft part on a blockchain, the aviation industry can become even safer. In the case of an accident or crash, there would be no question as to how old a part was or where it originated and when it was installed or replaced.

Supply Chain & International Trade

Blockchain has a massive potential to decrease fraud and empower platforms to sharpen their logistics process and is already in use by IBM, Maersk, Wal Mart, and others in their supply chains.

Blockchain technology dramatically improves supply chain management, which is a multi-trillion dollar industry. To this day, many merchants do not trust their supply chains and much of the world's commerce is still a matter of reputation and a handshake. By leveraging blockchain technology supply chains can become more efficient, reliable and trustworthy while preventing large amounts of fraud and abuses.

One of the first blockchain applications to focus on international trade and supply chains was DiguSign. DiguSign allows users to cryptographically sign and track documents involved in international trade with unique, immutable IDs. This helps to prevent fraud and backpedaling on supply chain contracts, which is common in Asian manufacturing and supply chain management.

Conclusion

Now that we have discussed many of the commercial applications for blockchain technology in the next chapter, we will talk about the gradual implosion of the fiat back system.

Part IV: The Future

Chapter 15: The Gradual Implosion of The Unbacked Fiat System

"Most of what people think is money is really credit, and credit appears out of thin air during good times and then disappears during bad times."

-Ray Dalio

"Deficit spending is simply a scheme for the confiscation of wealth. Gold stands in the way of this insidious process. It stands as a protector of property rights. If one grasps this, one has no difficulty in understanding the statists' antagonism toward the gold standard."

-Alan Greenspan

"A government that robs Peter to pay Paul can always count on the support of Paul."

-William Gladstone

"The farther back you can look, the farther forward you can see."

-Winston Churchill

The fiat system is the lifeblood of the modern economy. Almost every mode of exchange today occurs in currencies whose value ties directly to nation-states and their central bank policies. Fiat currencies interact with each other as vessels for the broader economies that they are part of, both inside and outside the borders of the nations who are responsible for issuing them.

In this chapter, we will cover significant arguments for why the long-term health of economies using unbacked fiat currency are questionable, and how decentralized cryptocurrencies offer a means of retaining value in a future deleveraging cycle. In doing so, we will draw strictly from major economic thinkers, academic economists, and policymakers, all of whom are deeply experienced in and intertwined with the operation of the world's current monetary system.

This chapter goes far beyond covering broad philosophical issues like the Keynes/Hayek debate, which is an intellectual exchange over what governments *should* do. Instead, we'll focus on the rational models put forward by actual banking and investment practitioners alongside thorough historical accounts that define what governments *can* do and *will* do. We do this to contribute to *descriptive* and *predictive* analysis, not just a normative debate over how things should be in an idealized world.

Relevant sources drawn on here include Bridgewater Capital founder and CEO Ray Dalio, whose systematic case study on massive debt crises details the policy maneuvers available to central bankers and governments. Dalio's work draws on several centuries of data and case studies. Also cited in this chapter is the detailed historical analysis of the emergence of central banking and its impact on cyclical credit crises by Professors Charles W. Calomiris and Stephen H. Haber (of Columbia and Stanford universities respectively). We also cover the political forces that exacerbate the bad issuance of debt. Raghuram Rajan, as well as Nolan McCarty, Keith T. Poole, and Howard Rosenthal, have all highlighted the political impacts of a credit-driven fiat monetary system.

Even though the plurality of those cited here are academics first, many of these scholars also have done tours in central banks and major financial institutions. Rajan is the most prominent, having served as the equivalent of the Federal Reserve Chairman of the Bank of India for three years following the 2008 financial crisis. Dalio served as an emergency advisor to the Federal Reserve and government during the 2008 financial crisis.

These sources are incredibly intellectually rich and host healthy disagreements between them, but the most important fact is that they all come from influential people who are not "bitcoiners." In other words, they represent the self-aware thinking of people who understand and drive fiat currency to this day, and as serious studies, they are uniformly well-intentioned in addressing the problems posed by politically captured central banks and fiat currencies.

What is Fiat?

There is a natural, historical arc that applies to money and its relationship with the state. In almost, all historical settings, states have eventually attempted to seize, debase, and regulate the money supply as an extension of state power, even if they initially started from sound money. This process has generally been done to gain an adversarial advantage in a broader geopolitical setting, something we will go into in subsequent chapters.

Together, these sources reference a standard set of monetary and fiscal policies that emerged in different societies going back to the Roman era. They demonstrate the commonality of the problem posed by sovereign debt cycles, and the near-universal drift towards debasement and borrowing from the future to pay for present-day political needs and desires.

There is a reasonably clear and consistent pattern of pressures that drive the state's actions when it comes to money, regardless of the central bank's degree of enlightenment to history or freedom in choosing a monetary or fiscal policy. This history also highlights just how revolutionary Bitcoin and other decentralized currencies are. As we said in our chapter on data and ownership, cryptocurrencies are a return to the primordial form of property, one which had been diluted many times over the last 2000 years of human history. Unbacked fiat currencies are the result of this long, politically driven process of dilution.

They tend to exacerbate the degree that political action can distort the long-term value of the currency. Since there is no overt "cost" or constraint to printing unbacked fiat currency, different political parties fight over who gets the reins, since having control means that you can create money for your own goals and patrons. In effect, the growing economic inequality, growing debt slavery, political toxicity, and increasing fragility of our current system are all direct effects of the unmoored nature of fiat.

The fiat system has led to a scenario where existing stakeholders in creating currency, credits, and debts have fed off of each other in a cycle and externalized the costs by moving that debt to the next generation through bailouts and massive government deficits. It is the fundamental economic injustice of our times, and if unchecked, this process will threaten the existence of our democratic processes and our financial wellbeing for generations to come.

The dynamics affecting today's fiat currencies are a matter of old rules of human nature operating in an environment with 'new' rules. Fiat currency is not something new. It is the evolution of the state's relationship with money according to clear, observable principles. Understanding the separation between money and the state created by pure cryptocurrencies requires understanding just how the state has thought about money historically, and what purposes control of money has for the country and those who make strategic decisions for the nation. Today, we have witnessed a massive policy drift in the United States and other economies towards unsustainable debts and negative interest rates.

Many have argued this is due to the political capture of the Federal Reserve and the broader banking system by political actors that either believe in a free lunch or don't give a damn about who picks up the tab when they are dead. Today, fiscal policy is dictating monetary policy. The balance sheet of the state is expanding without apparent regard for the cost, the impact on everyday people, or the destructive force that such a wealth transfer has on society and politics.

Let us be crystal clear here - we don't want to see a global financial collapse, and we wouldn't be citing so many serious economists if we did. Such a failure in a global credit crisis would do irreparable damage to our civilization, as credit crises have in the past, and would lead to substantial lost opportunities for innovation, progress, and human flourishing.

What we want, and what we think blockchain might help with, is helping create balanced, healthy economies that run on meaningful budgets, low taxes, ample opportunities for young people, and reliable means of engaging in commerce, saving, and planning for the future. We also believe that real, decentralized cryptocurrencies are a great safeguard and alternative to the dangers involved in fiat currency, which we will outline in detail in this chapter.

Fiat's Intrinsic Tie to the State

The cornerstone of fiat currency is that it exists by dictate - as we noted above, *fiat* comes directly from the Latin word for a *state decree* and is traditionally used to indicate that something was permitted or undertaken on sovereign authority. What this means is that fiat by its nature is an extension of state power - if it can be *fiat* one way on Monday, it can *fiat* another way by Friday. Because it exists by dictate, there is no set limit to how many individual units of fiat currency are in circulation.

By its advocates' admission, fiat currency has no intrinsic value other than being a tokenized, fungible medium of exchange. It might be "currency" as a medium of exchange and unit of account, but it is not as adequate as "money" - which is also a reliable store of value.

There are several anthropological narratives regarding how the abstraction of value evolved. While familial organizations do not need an abstract value-system between parents and children, the need to transact with people outside of our families requires some form of an agreed system of value.

Some had theorized that money naturally evolved as a symbolic system when tribes became big enough that there was not the same certainty of trust and reciprocity between people exchanging assets. David Graeber's book *Debt, The First 5000 Years* outlines a general theory for credits and debits *predating* the evolution of physical, agreed-upon currencies.

We are not trying to provide a comprehensive history of money here, but it is essential to note that money's first purpose is to serve as a means of a settlement. Money's value derives from parties' *mutual consensus* that the note in question is indeed something that can serve as a medium of exchange. Even when credits and debts get defined in a given currency, the value of that currency is almost always contingent on other factors.

Much of what people think is money is a series of credits and debits, and much of what sounds like good economics in prosperous times is incredibly fragile when the underlying performance of credit contracts fail.

Skipping forward a few millennia, what we think of as fiat currency evolved directly as an element of state power, with today's central banks beginning at roughly the same time the modern nation-state did. With the 1648 treaty of Westphalia - which revolutionized the political organization of Europe and established the status of a sovereign nation-state - states were imbued with sovereignty and the ability to plot their destinies in competition with each other without oversight from any higher authority. Westphalia didn't put an end to warfare, but it did provide a new means for the game to be played out, which put enormous stresses on kings and their financial systems.

Here is a critical point, and one we'll come back to later: rulers seeking to survive conflict domestically and internationally must be able to finance their positions and pay their armies and supporters. Kings who do not pay their troops tend not to remain kings - nor can they create value out of thin air, so they must resort to other means to pay the piper.

In classical feudalism, this amounted to direct taxation, extortion, and raiding - all executed by force, as well as by extracting value from serfs taxed in grain and other agrarian goods in exchange for the privilege of working on the lord's land.

In times of peace, this model limited the scope of any individual's influence. The administrative requirements to operate vast empires became increasingly burdensome with scale. As a king or duke grew their domain, they had to compel the obedience of an increasing number of people over a growing amount of space. People do not like being taxed, and that even includes people who are doing the taxing.

In this scenario, there were significant limitations to the economic wealth that a ruler could capture and maintain, especially in a war where his or her lands were under siege, and labor was not available to be taxed in the first place. Feudalism put rulers in a weak political position.

To pay for armies and mercenaries, rulers resorted to debasing their currencies, replacing precious metals with less expensive metals. Debasement meant trying to pass off coins as equally valuable, even though they were less intrinsically valuable, and stretching the same amount of precious metal over more coinage. In every case, this was an instance of counterfeiting by the state. Even if a nation started with ample precious metal reserves, its rulers faced incentives to debase its currency over time.

This trend dates back to the Roman era. The Denarius, minted near the time of Christ and equivalent to roughly a days wage, began with nearly pure silver content. One Denari was progressively diluted to 60% silver in the 200's, less than 5% silver content in the 300's, and finally down to trace amounts of silver by the fall of the Roman Republic in the 400's.

Interestingly, the move to silver itself has been a historical trend when countries are expanding, as expansionary monetary policies are desired to fund armies, navies, and new businesses that require access to credit. As an interesting historical side note, many have complained that cryptocurrencies utilizing 'proof of work' mining are contributing to climate change, as miners are today using the same amount of energy as small nation-states like New Zealand and Bulgaria. Climate change because of mining is not a first in history. Traces of Ibearan lead from Roman silver mining exist as far away as Greenland's ice caps.

Much of the pressure to dilute a currency was the product of military conquest. Paying soldiers is both expensive and generates limited immediate economic returns, and the institutions required to tax recently conquered lands take time to establish and are typically inefficient when they do work. It is a perfectly logical strategic decision to create standardized currencies and then debase them if you are in this position as an emperor.

It is this intrinsic link between the political goals of sovereign states and their currencies that is the most critical pillar in understanding the present-day risks posed by and towards fiat systems. Because the political dynamics affecting the value of money goes back as long as the written word, we can draw on well-established patterns when it comes to predicting the future. Money is a human technology. Even though it has changed substantially within living memory, observing the logic that has affected it throughout history is our greatest tool to inform what it will look like in the future.

The First Central Banks and the Gradual Shift to Unbacked Fiat

Classical fractional reserve banking generally involved a wealthy family, such as the Medici of Florence, providing a haven for depositors and profiting off of the interest generated by loans made against deposits, in effect creating money by issuing credit. "Banknotes" were precisely that - notes and certificates that represented credit from the bank and could exchangeable for goods and services as a substitute for exchanging physical, hard currency.

Up through the renaissance this was a primary means of banking. It extended up to the state level, with rulers taking out massive debts from private bankers to fund their military endeavors, and with banks and rulers occasionally breaking their promises to each other or withholding credit for political purposes. In a way, money was scarce, even to rulers, which diminished their power to execute wars of conquest with any staying power.

It was much easier for the king to overextend himself than it is in a fiat system. Desperate rulers would often default on their obligations to return payment due to their creditors, resulting in the failure or ruin of the private banks who had been forced to make the loan in the first place. Defaults on loans in hard currency were usually catastrophic to private banks. Lenders were forced to weigh different ruler's political fortunes and their ability to recover the gold lent to them by taxes, tariffs, or other mercantile measures like joint-stock companies and royal charters.

Insofar as states were subject to the credit of private banks, they could not be fully sovereign. If they strong-armed banks from outside their borders, they would ruin their reputation for credit. If they extorted the hard currency of their domestic banks and merchants, they would destroy their ability to borrow domestically in no short order, as the wealthy would flee to safer kingdoms.

Countries were also unable to debase debts in a currency that they did not control, meaning that they often had to bear the brunt of costs, not unlike modern-day nations who have loans denominated in foreign currencies. It was in this environment that the concept of a centralized national bank evolved.

Just as with the modern nation-state, the world's first major central banks emerged during the geopolitical upheaval of the Thirty Years War. The concept resurfaced most of a century later with William Patterson's proposal for an English central bank in 1691. The Bank of England was enacted into policy with a loan of 1.2 million pounds to the Royal Government just three years later.

In exchange, the bank received an exclusive charter that effectively made it an extension of state power solely responsible for issuing notes. This vested the Bank of England with the sole monopoly on the ability to issue loans to the British Empire, and importantly, the ability to issue notes to other smaller banks creating the money supply.

The first central banks still operated on a fractional reserve system backed by precious metals, though it did give the Royal Government one critical ability: to borrow from the future to fund the endeavors of the present. It was the origin of National Debt. Rather than a simple personal debt between kings and lenders, national debt occurred in a currency that the sovereign had some degree of influence over.

Calomiris and Haber describe this evolution as *privileges with burdens* - the still-private central bank gained the right to issue debts and print money, creating national rents, but the catch was that the central bank had to loan to the state. In exchange for being the source of credit to the crown, the Bank of England charter endowed it with the ability to control interest rates and compete at a substantial advantage against England's many private banks, who lacked the influence that comes with a royal charter and the ability to print notes.

Further, the Bank of England was able to profit by issuing debt contracts to private and commercial borrowers, effectively drawing rents as a benefit of being a "public-private partnership" between the state and private bankers. This position was mutually beneficial to the bank and the crown. The bank's constraints included an obligation to back the currency (and their credit and debt contracts) with gold, as well as a shared interest in seeing the state survive.

These rules did not exist in previous international banking arrangements, which operated independent of the nation-state and could withdraw their support if fortunes were not promising. In this setting, there was an essential new factor introduced: the central bank may be required to back their notes with gold, but they still were engaged in fractional reserve banking by issuing credit and notes.

The Break with Metalism

All banks that engage in fractional reserve banking while there is a gold standard face exposure to the risk of a bank run. If all depositors were to require their money at the same time, the bank could not pull in all its debts at the same pace, and could not settle all of the contracts outstanding in gold or another satisfactory precious metal or asset.

Asset pegs constrain the policy options of states and central banks by providing a floor, with liquidity to gold at the stated peg being a metric of trust in the currency and the bank. In exchange, the central bank's issuance of debt with interest allows the pricing of risk into government borrowing, with the caveat that the failure of the state in war or other forms of upheaval would also mean an end to the bank.

This system evolved progressively over the course of world history, but the principles remain the same from the inception of central banking in the late middle ages and the withdrawal from the gold-backed Bretton Woods system by Richard Nixon in 1971. Many overstate the so-called "Nixon shock" as if it was a single break from sound monetary policy. In truth, the U.S. dollar had been devalued relative to gold several times in the preceding decades, with the most egregious incident being Franklin Delano Roosevelt's criminalization of the private possession of gold in Executive Order 6102.

FDR was even reported to have dictated the exchange rates for gold from his bed based on personal conjectures involving his "lucky numbers." Monetary debasement has a long history, even in the relatively free United States. It's fair to infer that the criminalization of stores of value outside of the nation's sovereign currency has not happened for the last time.

Going even further back, the US had gotten to the gold standard progressively, having also used silver (from which we get the word *dollar*, borrowing from the Spanish silver dollar) in a bimetallic hard currency model. It is this model that is ensconced in the U.S. Constitution, not today's fiat model.

Fluctuations in the underlying supply of metals affected their respective prices, and one could readily observe Gresham's law in action concerning U.S. currency. Bimetallism began its decline with the Coinage Act of 1873, which was a response to the monetary damage that had occurred during the American Civil War. Bimetallism was later entirely abandoned in 1900 with the adoption of the Gold Standard Act by the McKinley presidency.

The Gold Standard Act fixed the value of the dollar at $20.67 per troy ounce 1900. FDR's actions undertaken just three decades later debased the dollar relative to gold from that steady $20.67 figure (a more valuable dollar in gold terms) to a final value of $35.00 an ounce. FDR's administration threatened jail time for those who didn't change their gold for paper money that was nominally backed by gold, something few today understand.

In perspective, Nixon's break from the gold standard as it was established by f the Bretton Woods system allowed the currency to float (that is, devalue) relative to gold and value relative to other countries. After Nixon's resignation, President Ford repealed FDR's mandate, allowing everyday citizens to buy again, hold, and sell gold as an asset independent of its relationship to fiat.

Perverse Incentives and Policy Options

That fiat currency floats is not necessarily a bad thing - it allows markets to find appropriate prices for goods in the near term to facilitate exchange. Slow, constrained inflation isn't necessarily a bad thing either, and the use of silver as an alternative form of precious metal currency is an example of this use case historically.

Inflationary currencies are also generally thought to be more conducive to the issuance of credit and broad economic growth, as investors seek a better return on their assets that outpace inflation and accurately price the risk of default. Again, not a bad thing.

The problem posed by unbacked, floating fiat currency is not merely that it is inflationary, but that it encourages the widespread use of these debts, especially by states whose politicians and policymakers have been demanding ways to cheat at money for millennia. It is the permeation of debt throughout an economy that makes it fragile, as non-payment of one debt can cascade to non-payment of another. This cycle is the root of credit crises.

Loose monetary policy progressively robs people of their wealth and allows states to live high on the hog, absent the accountability inherent in a currency's tie to a real, scarce asset like gold or another precious metal. This dynamic creates a setting where the system can print money to buy assets, rather than be forced to exchange money worth assets for other assets.

Within the unbacked fiat system, money creation occurs through credit created by the central bank. This credit is the key to money issuance into the broader economy, with private banks effectively serving as state-sanctioned distributors of new money through borrowing and lending of money created by the central bank. This process creates even more credits and debts to be repaid (to the bank) in the future.

Credit and debt existed long before fiat currency, but fiat currency is less constrained than hard money when it comes to issuing debt. We'll cover this in greater depth below, but the critical point to note here is that the central banking model represents a replacement of previous forms of money generation by separating the inputs that go into it. Instead of money being a certificate for a quantity of precious metal with one-to-one backing, much of today's currency derived through central banking is, in fact, debt.

Fiat is backed by credits and debts, with no set floor for value and a continually growing supply with every new credit issued. There is effectively no meaningful way to remove dollars from this system. The only way money slows down is for those dollars to be put in a bond - granting extra dollars - for parking that money as government debt. It is also misleading to call a roll-back of quantitative easing 'quantitative tightening' because selling assets you printed money to buy isn't changing the amount of currency in the system - it's merely offloading an asset.

Fiat currency is more useful in *transmitting* value than it is in *retaining* it because holding onto the money by itself results in infinite dilution to zero. New amounts of currency enter the same market by the second. Compounding inflation incentivizes those receiving fiat currency to move it as quickly as possible into some form of new asset or consumption, in theory stimulating the economy by increasing the speed by which value changes hands.

This model of a merged state and central bank who have shared political incentives but can offload risk on the population through their power to print money and tax creates a perverse series of incentives for the state and its banking infrastructure to:

- Overproduce easy credit, hence devaluing money faster than the rate at which economic growth is created, and generally creating waste and inflation.
- Create asset bubbles (people borrowing to buy assets with the expectation that they will go up in value, rather than based on actual market demand)

- Issue loans to the public that will end in default.
- Borrow from future generations by accumulating government debts undertaken for current political ends.

States, politicians, and banks seeking some mutual advantage in a competitive environment created this system. For politicians, that is usually the quest for power and popularity, for banks that is the quest for profits, for states that are the quest for survival in competition with other countries.

This new model has exacerbated the boom and bust cycles of yesteryear, in that the booms are getting bigger because states have a more exceptional ability to intervene in busts and defer the costs to later generations. Not much unlike an opioid addict taking ever-larger doses, knowing that the paramedics will show up in the nick of time to save the day. In effect, fiat currency is an expansion of the realm of policy by moving the economy from one that is driven by sound money to one operated by a giant web of credits and debits mediated through private banks. To that effect, we'll examine just what those policies are in the next section.

II. Options for Policy Makers and Central Banks in a World of Unbacked Fiat

In this section we draw heavily from Ray Dalio's new book *Principles for Navigating Big Debt Crises*, which provides an in-depth study of credit crises and shared dynamics going back to Roman times. What Dalio delivers is a very clearly written model of the options for policymakers confronting long-term debt cycles across multiple forms of money, not just the unbacked fiat currency we use today.

In a debt-focused model with a central bank, much of the money in circulation is part of a tangled web of credit and debt contracts between buyers and sellers, with each person's capacity to produce and borrow. Debt needs to be paid back in the future plus interest for an economy to work, and the upward part of a debt cycle involves money being readily available for lenders to seek productive applications of capital. As rules loosen; eventually, some fail to pay back the loan.

This failure might be due to a lack of productivity, or other causes like debtors not paying them due to a lack of productivity. When these ventures fail, they have a knock-on effect as the economic waste of lousy loans echoing across the chain of debts and credits. These drivers are what give us the boom and bust cycle in borrowing, which central banks and policymakers claim to manage through interest rates that regulate the speed that money flows through the system. The higher the velocity of money, the greater the inflation, as more dollars are chasing the same number of assets.

As Dalio points out, in truth, central banks often are guilty of encouraging a bubble. Instead of resolving it early, they accelerate bubbles for political purposes. To quote the text:

"In many cases, the monetary policy helps inflate the bubble rather than constrain it. This is especially true when inflation and growth are both good, and investment returns are great. Such periods are typically interpreted to be a productivity boom that reinforces investor optimism as they leverage up to buy investment assets. In such cases, central banks, focusing on inflation and growth, are often reluctant to adequately tighten money."

In effect, free money leads to bad economics, and central banks as political entities are often reluctant to take away the punch bowl when they should be minimizing the waste created by an economic bubble. In a bubble, everybody feels richer because their asset values and ventures are increasing in dollar-denominated value, and money is moving fast enough for demand to be higher. As money slows down, the credit cycle becomes vicious in the opposite direction, as credit dries up, and borrowers go without across the web of loans and debts described above.

When this bubble pops, there are only so many options for policymakers to try and undertake. By having interest rates too low, central banks create economic waste and damage in the future. Artificially low borrowing costs contrast with having interest rates too high, which prevents current economic productivity because interest is almost always a surer bet than any other investment. Bear in mind that none of this occurs in a vacuum - states are competing with each other and will "cheat" at banking if that means successfully procuring real value and productivity from a rival.

Currency manipulation and other geopolitical forces come in at this point, as states race to be the home of manufacturing and industry. Maintaining a healthy currency remains a matter of national security for nations. Central bank's purpose hasn't fundamentally changed since the founding of the Bank of England over 300 years ago.

Here is the most critical point: Each of these policies has a score of failure, and each aspect of failure drives policymakers and governments onto the next stopgap measure to try and resolve the credit crisis to a politically satisfactory point. This process isn't necessarily 100% linear, but the core issue here is that these are the only real tools in the toolbox. No savior is coming from outside the system rescue politicians leveraging fiat from the future impacts of their own decisions. Many are just hoping to be wealthy, dead, or retired by then.

The best modern-day policymakers can hope for is sophisticated management and skillful deleveraging in a time of crisis when it hits. Many savvy people, including Dalio, have expressed frustration at politicians' lack of urgency in dealing with ongoing mismanagement that will lead to predictably adverse outcomes in the future.

There are ultimately five policy options: changing interest rates, undertaking austerity in government spending, printing money, accepting restructurings and defaults, and engaging in massive wealth redistribution. We've arranged them here in order of severity.

Option 1. Changing Interest Rates

Classically speaking, adjusting the interest rate is a means of altering the money supply in the market by taking money out of the market in the form of bonds that have a higher interest rate. Interest rates are the day-to-day policy mechanism of all central fiat banks. Rate changes do not create value by making the currency more scarce in the long run. They reward investors for not using their money with, you guessed it, more money. Because bonds encourage parking money with more money, the long-term inflation of fiat currencies is inescapable even if the velocity of credit diminishes.

The impact of changes in interest rates is also contingent on how much debt (both sovereign and private) there is outstanding. If there is a huge debt but a low-interest rate, the economy might churn along for a while without noticing until it is too late that little productivity is backing the boom. As soon as interest rates rise, the burden of that debt becomes stifling. While this works in a tabletop setting where all the players are idealized, in truth, low-interest rates and political pressures encourage the government to borrow much like private consumers are encouraged to borrow money.

Cheap money leads to the accumulation of debt, often for projects and endeavors that have limited human value but do buy votes. In the long term, this means more and more debt is outstanding, resulting in pressure to keep rates progressively lower and lower - otherwise, the debt-fueled system will implode. This destructive spiral is a scenario we will cover later, but it is important to acknowledge here because it is this triad of forces that lead to long-term zero or near-zero interest rates.

The central bank is effectively stuck issuing free money indefinitely, at least until the more substantial moorings of the financial system break lose. Also, since the government and central banks can dilute the value of the currency but cannot make it increase in value by temporarily slowing or removing it through interest rates, this scenario means governments have to look to growth and austerity to deleverage successfully.

Option 2: Austerity and Increased Taxation

Austerity is when states tighten their belts and cease or slow down government spending. In countries where the government makes up a large percentage of gross domestic product, this is even more impactful, as it slows down the velocity of money circulating in the economy and can have second-order effects that leave the economy even weaker in the short term.

At the same time, austerity is generally a good policy when it is not apparent: states that do not overspend do not rack up the heaps of debt that cause debt crises. Increased taxation further damages economic prospects, as innovators either struggle to generate wealth or leave for greener pastures, worsening the downward spiral.

Historically, most debt crises are a result of war and conflict. When George Washington held shares in the Bank of England (through the American War for Independence), the business was booming, but the British national debt skyrocketed during the Revolutionary War and peaked at an all-time high of over 250% of GDP during the Napoleonic wars - only a few decades later. Britain took nearly a century to deleverage and did no incur so much debt again until the two consecutive World Wars a century later.

Present-day debt has been incurred not to fund wars, but to compete economically and to buy off voters in democracies who have effectively voted themselves other people's money. Austerity in the present era does not mean drawing down after a war, but reneging on contracts with people who have paid into the system (or not), and feel entitled to the promised benefit. In other words, present-day austerity is politically more complicated than post-conflict austerity.

Because government spending has grown as a percentage of the economy (including healthcare, retirement, and several other entitlements), a cutback at this level would substantially impinge on economic growth and several powerful lobbies who have enriched themselves in the short term.

Option 3: Debasement - "Quantitative Easing" and "Helicopter Money"

"Quantitative Easing" (QE) is the official euphemism printing money and buying assets with it to prevent the market from declining. QE is effectively a "buy wall" for the economy where the central bank serves as a buyer of last resort. Often, in a fiat system, these measures are tied to the money creation mechanism we described above, as money granted to banks through guarantees on their deposits and direct transfers. Dalio lists multiple reasons why QE occurs in credit crises:

To curtail panic and guarantee liabilities

QE purchases do what the Federal Deposit insurance on your savings account does, except for your stock portfolio. With the FDIC, Uncle Sam prints money up to a certain point to ensure liquidity and prevent a further bank run. This measure dilutes the damage that bad loans might have on an individual bank, but spreads the cost across the monetary system by inflating the overall value of the currency. With QE, the Fed facilitates the purchase of assets to prevent the market from imploding for a lack of demand.

To provide liquidity

If liquidity were to disappear, the market would crash in the absence of any buyers. One primary goal of QE is to prime the pump and keep money flowing, and the economy going, rather than allow for a progressively vicious cycle to play out.

To support the solvency of systemically important institutions.

More than just banks, QE can print money to purchase distressed national assets. This approach usually applies to strategically critical industries, such as automobile manufacturers, technology companies, major ports, and military contractors. QE does not step in to support everyday citizens, but might save the companies their employers and especially their employers' shareholders.

To recapitalize, nationalize, or cover the losses of systemically critical financial institutions

Since banks are the primary source of credit, QE prints money to cover the bank's losses and amortize toxic and nonperforming debt that the banks issued. Bailouts are a preferable option in such a scenario when the outright collapse of a bank would have even more significant economic effects. Having institutions that are "too big to fail" creates moral hazards, where the incentives are for executives to push the financial system to the limits and then leave the eventual adverse outcome to the taxpayers to clean up.

Institutional QE versus "Helicopter Money"

The short-term flaw with QE focused on bailing out institutions (what we'll call Institutional QE, where banks are "too big to fail") is that it is free money distributed through banks and large, state connected firms. Some of these firms are guilty of taking risks that led to failure in the first place.

While the institutions themselves may be systemically important, a paradox Dalio alludes to is that the productivity that this new money can buy is limited - leading to spending on investment in financial assets rather than spending on goods and services. To borrow directly from Dalio:

"QE benefits... those who own financial assets much more than those who don't, thus widening the wealth gap."

Effectively, this means QE gets captured in the stock market and assets such as real estate, not necessarily circulated in the general economy, where it would relieve broader pressure on the credit cycle.

Another problem with QE, which naturally stems from this, is the perverse incentive for stockholders and corporations to endlessly campaign for QE, since the net effect is positive for stock prices relative to the net economy, resulting in the potential for "crony capitalism."

Helicopter Money

The natural populist analog to Institutional QE is what the economist Milton Friedman called "helicopter money" - money distributed to everyone as if dropped from a helicopter. Exciting and simulative the first time, but if it happens every day, that money starts to lose its value. Helicopter money is not 100% analogous to Institutional QE since, in institutional QE, central banks buy bonds and other asset categories. Institutional QE pushes stock prices up in an asset swap that reinforces a price floor for equities markets (chiefly the stock market).

Like those who lived in the US over the ten years since the 2008 financial crisis can attest, there was significant political consternation over the fact that the stock market grossly outperformed everyday Americans' living wages and purchasing power.

Helicopter money is any policy that hands out cash to citizens to stimulate spending. It includes everything from transfer payments funded by deficits, to the straight debasement of hard currency in circulation (melting down drachmas to stamp out more drachmas with higher amounts of base metals) to writing down debt.

The only rule is that the money has to come from somewhere, whether it is from taxation or government bonds were taken out as debt and borrowed from the future. The only fundamental difference is that QE prints money to buy assets, while handouts stimulate short-run spending on consumption because people can spend beyond their means (i.e., above their current rate of productivity).

In a way, helicopter money is a regular part of the policy in almost all fiat economies, as money is being progressively debased to stimulate spending and consumption rather than savings. Inflation means that more money is coming into the system, and money held as cash (rather than assets) is consistently being diluted away by the growth in the money supply. If productivity and inflation were equal, there would be no inflation since the price of goods would keep pace with the value of the currency.

Existing policy results in a positive medium-term effect that makes those holding fiat currency more adverse than hoarding cash, effectively chasing that money into spending on consumption and assets in the broader economy. For nations that want to spur their economies to new levels of productivity, this has been a strategy, and many statist economists tout the "multiplier effects" of spending that are captured by the exchange of money for goods across the network of credits and debits that makes up the broader economy.

Multiplier effects are one of the more popular arguments for Universal Basic Income (UBI), which argues that instead of entitlements, people should receive a net transfer from the government to fund their consumption. With UBI, money is being taken from somewhere and granted somewhere else by the government, in effect redistributing wealth. Either UBI takes it directly from someone who created wealth (taxation), or by printing money that debases existing wealth and inflates the price of assets. The only alternative to this dichotomy is to engage in deficit spending, stealing from the future generation's wealth.

These redistributive policies already are policy. The United States has run up $210 Trillion in unfunded liabilities with Social Security, Medicare, Medicaid, the Affordable Care Act, and other programs leading the way. Fantasy proposals such as "free universal healthcare" are being proposed to redistribute wealth while making people more and more dependent on government handouts that cannot be taken away without causing great suffering.

Transfer payments suffer from a simple cycle. More money chases the same goods, pushing the price up, pushing the requirement to tax and print more money to provide adequate benefits up.

QE and Helicopter Money are Government Spending for Political Ends

Effectively, every aspect of the economy that government captures becomes a point to redistribute wealth, and every industry that lobbies for more regulation is ultimately arguing to set itself up as a defended cartel. These cartels come to count on money printed and consumers being forced to buy their product at whatever price the government supports. While there might be rational, honorable policies for governments to undertake, one would be foolish to ignore the perverse economic incentive that regulated enterprises pursue in the fiat system.

Take, for example, the issue of federal student debt in the US. Student debt has grown substantially since the policy was first rolled out, and the cost of tuition has grown more in inflation-adjusted dollars than any other service outside of healthcare (which is also subject to increasing government involvement). As we write this, there are approximately 1.6 Trillion dollars in outstanding student debt, which is crushing the financial hopes of the middle class, where education has long been thought to be a requirement for a middle-class job.

As an unsecured debt backed and issued by the federal government, graduates cannot even dissolve their debt obligation in bankruptcy, unlike private debts. When the high-interest loans are sold to private companies to collect, those companies have government assurances in the instance of default - effectively, being a student loan servicer is a rent-seeking enterprise backed by the government. The price of college has grown exponentially because more dollars are chasing the same goods with rigid demand.

Colleges are not incentivized to teach economically valuable topics and suffer no consequences for indebting students for useless degrees. By extent, students can borrow without regard for the economic viability of their major. While this is financially great for colleges, who milk students with federally guaranteed debts, they can never escape, in the long run, student debt is an example of the perversity of government spending.

Fiat tends to power crony capitalists and cartels who manage the system and government spending to their benefit and not that of society. With unlimited debt and the increasing price of tuition used to expand the quantity of state-backed credit, universities charge whatever they damn well, please. This price floor allows them to provide a substandard product without facing the consequences that would occur in a world without the state's politicized lending.

Student debt is an illustration of how the debt cycle can lead to a crisis with a *downward* cycle. The education market also shows an *unsustainable upwards* cycle in prices, as more and more debt pursues what is fundamentally the same good or service. We don't include this to go off on a tangent about the evils of the student loan industrial complex, but to illustrate the long-term toxicity of the easy money system embodied by the unbacked fiat paradigm.

The price of college has grown with the amount of money chasing it, and college is a market where debt has been used to massively increase the revenue going towards statist colleges and banks involved in student loan finance. This process is exploitative and conducted without regard for the health, wellbeing, or futures of the students.

The monetary system is much deeper than the simple value of money - it includes the governing philosophy and second-order effects of the entire civilization that it is a part of holding together. The more the role of government (and its fiat currency) grows in a society, the more the place of the individual shrinks.

So to summarize, QE exists to reinforce secular institutions considered relevant by the government - equities markets, manufacturers, and the like - by printing money to buy their assets, regardless of their underlying productivity. Redistributive schemes are designed to stimulate economic activity by giving people money to spend that is also not tied to their productivity.

Both are political endeavors that governments undertake as an extension of their desire to survive domestically (buy votes for their political party and stay in power), and sometimes at a strategic level, to survive in a setting of international economic competition. Even though governments resort to these methods more during a crisis, the cold hard truth is that they are actively using these methods even during much more comfortable times in the debt cycle. Serious deficit spending is now occurring even when the equities market is roaring, and unemployment is low.

Option 4: Defaults and Restructurings

Default is what happens when you can't pay your debts, and is the most extreme policy option available for dealing with significant credit crises. In simple terms, both defaults and restructurings represent a breach of the terms of the agreement initiated with the origination of the debt. These two options mean either canceling the debt outright, with the creditor counting it as a loss and the debtor having gotten something for free, or restructuring the debt by changing the terms.

Default generally ends the loan, though there may be other impacts that are adverse to the borrower. Restructuring is done to make the debt more accommodating to the borrower so the creditor can get *some* of their money back. Restructuring doesn't solve the crisis, but it does temporarily alleviate some pain points without resolving the debt itself.

Defaults and restructurings are extreme in an economy based on faith in fiat currency because trust is all that backs fiat currency. That faith is worth a lot - the US dollar is still the most influential fiat currency in a world of fiat currencies, primarily because it is backed by the nation's immense economic, military, and cultural power. Fiat currency also gains value from the rule of law in the country that produces it.

If you have a debt, then the value of the debt is dependent on the value of the currency. A default or restructuring is, by definition, a breach of that contract. Default on government debts threatens to initiate a fire sale of that nation's currency. This fire sale drives its value down precipitously, as holders exchange either one fiat for another, or fiat for assets that are believed to hold their value (gold, real estate, and yes, Bitcoin and other cryptocurrencies).

III. The Fragility of the Current System

Given that fiat is an extension of the nation-states that operate it, it is natural to ask how sustainable this system is in the long run. The engine that created the 2008 crisis is still running, alive and well, and the actions of those preventing the crisis from getting worse in 2008 did not fix the core problems that affect the system over the long run, especially when it comes to growing the sovereign debt. As we've covered above, national banks are an extension of governments, and even though they are symbiotically tied, they are a party to several incentives that lead to the long-term debt cycle.

Let's acknowledge this first: access to some degree of credit is beneficial to human growth and thriving in the modern economy. Being able to borrow wisely to afford a house, an education, and other essentials that increase one's productivity is critical in helping everyday people start their lives and begin to build wealth. A failure of the current system would be catastrophic for ordinary people and could send the broader world into a rapid downward spiral of sectarianism and political decay.

That said, we're not in charge - in fact, one might argue that no one, not even the president, is in charge. Both sides of the political aisle borrow from the future to buy votes in the present, often wasting that stolen money in the process. The government cannot and will not prepare people for the shortcomings in its design. Ultimately private citizens have to take it upon themselves to plan for the future based on the available information and resources.

The probability that the US and other advanced economies will eventually find themselves in a Japan-style debt trap is a mathematical fact at this point. If deficit spending continues unabated, there will be a substantial deleveraging at some point. This event will precipitously debase the currency, resulting in a massive contraction of credit. Deleveraging will also leave populations under crushing debts and taxes with no relief.

One can examine dozens of past examples of economic contractions from overborrowing in living memory, including Japan's lost decade, the Icelandic experience during the 2008 credit crunch, or the ongoing Eurozone crisis, which includes not one country but a host of lower-productivity countries who overborrowed a currency thinking somehow the basic rules of economics did not apply to them, while countries like Germany leveraged the financial system to build an export machine.

The U.S. has never defaulted on its debts. We brand ourselves as the Lannisters of Casterly Rock, though in truth, there is no gold left in the mines of Casterly Rock - and there hasn't been for a long time. When deficits reach a certain level, default and restructuring are a policy option even if they are disgusting and anathema at a political level, and every government will consider default and restructuring in the limited spectrum of existing options. Instead of defaulting, the U.S. has historically changed its monetary system, as it did during the Nixon Shock to avoid the cost associated with the Vietnam War.

What could this mean in the long run? If the US or another significant power eventually default on its debt, faith in their currency will break. People who are holding dollars (or Euros, or Yen, or whatever fiat currency) will race to exchange it for other forms of money that are more trustworthy, and those with the currency based on fundamentals will not want to sell. Because the US Dollar is so well respected relative to other fiat systems, American policymakers have gotten a more or less a free pass - money progressively printed has been soaked up by global demand for the dollar, with a "flight to quality" when economic contagion spreads.

In a way, advanced economies have exported their inflation by buying products manufactured elsewhere, the method of which has gutted industrialized nation's manufacturing base but has given the American consumer an immense amount of variety and cheap goods in the short run that is not necessarily backed by real economic value as much as it is the act of upselling foreign-made products to American consumers.

The Populist Capture of the Monetary System

The Populist Capture thesis is now orthodoxy among most modern-day bankers and scholars, who recognize that the post-Cold War order has experienced a pivot from central banks being insulated from populist demands and preserved for lending in times of war towards a world in which populist movements have borrowed money from future generations through bonds to finance present-day consumption, investment, and asset bubbles. This strategy has been politically popular in the short run and will prove catastrophically expensive in the long run, both in financial terms and in terms of the political impacts that it will have when the bill comes due.

Many attribute the first clear indication of populist capture to be the crisis of 2008, which had its roots in the issuance of subprime mortgages. Subprime mortgages were risky debt, which the financial system securitized (chopped up) and sold as an 'asset' across the financial system. This arrangement had its roots in the parallel shift from a strict fiscal policy by the U.S. government to the "monetization" of government spending by funding present-day consumptions with bonds.

As part of the money creation process, newly printed money moved through banks and issued as a credit for mortgages and other purchases. With the decrease in quality of underwriting and rating, banks took advantage of government policy and made revenue by creating and offloading bad loans. As the ease of borrowing pushed the price of assets upwards, more dollars chased the same assets. As people experienced the fear of missing out and chose to borrow to purchase those assets, the cycle continued. Dalio's observations on big debt cycles, which we outlined above, describes this process in detail. The financial crisis of 2008 was just 'another one of those.'

The Crisis of 2008 was a systemic issue, and we couldn't possibly do it justice in full here. Instead, we'll summarize established academic sources, all of which feature a consensus that the easy money policies of the pre-bubble 2000s were both politically fashionable and attractive to banks. This 'iron triangle' of borrowers and creditors relying on easy money sowed the seeds of an eventual implosion as the Fed increased interest rates in 2006 and 2007.

With the 2008 crisis, many banks visited the brink of failure, falling victim to a massive liquidity crunch as the underlying asset whose inflation was servicing successive debts failed. The cascade effects of bad debt quickly put the survival of the banks in question, with Lehman Brothers and Bear Sterns becoming insolvent.

Other banks were saved not by their own power, but by government and the Fed stepping in as lenders of last resort, effectively printing money to soak up the corrupt lending practices that the banks and government had collectively enabled in the first place, putting the burden of repaying bailouts on the public by adding the cost to the U.S. Government's sovereign debt and further debasing the currency (and the impact of the crunch) through "quantitative easing" which we discussed above.

While it is politically popular to criticize banks exclusively for the crisis, they are by no means solely to blame for the outcome of the financial crisis. The Fed and the U.S. Congress are as much to blame as anyone. Both had the power to prevent the fragility the led to the crisis in the first place. As Nolan McCarty, Keith T. Poole. and Howard Rosenthal demonstrate in their 2013 book *Political Bubbles: Financial Crises and the Failure of American Democracy*, the original conditions of the financial crisis are attributable to the political capture of monetary and fiscal policy, such that politicians 1) demanded artificially low-interest rates from the Fed, and 2) failed to grasp or enact regulatory approaches that would have popped or prevented the bubble from forming in the first place. There is cold, hard logic to this process: free money tends to be popular.

The authors attribute this drift to a handful of factors, which include the ideological bias of the political right towards deregulation of banks, and the political left to the redistribution of wealth. This bipartisan lovefest made easy credit uncontroversial. Regardless of its sustainability or long term effects, it has the value of the currency or the financial health of the country.

To quote the authors directly:

"Strong ideological commitments to markets and fears of moral hazard explain the behavior of politicians on the right, but the *egalitarian* ideology on the left was also crucial in setting the stage for the crisis. Specifically, egalitarianism fuelled some of the excesses in the mortgage market. Subprime and prime mortgage lending, especially to racial and ethnic minorities, was seen by many as an effective tool for redistributing income and wealth."

The authors then go on to demonstrate in extreme detail the voting patterns of American politicians on the left and the right, supporting their claim that the bubble involved a combination of political ideology and interest with the interests of banks engaged in subprime mortgages.

Raghuram Rajan's book *Fault Lines: How Hidden Fractures Still Threaten the World Economy*, fittingly titled "*Let Them Eat Credit,*" echoes this observation. Rajan, himself a well-respected financial economist and no stranger to the realities of service as a central banker, traces much of the political pressure for easy credit to the growing income inequality in the West, which intensified significantly after the world banking system converted to unbacked fiat currency in the 1970s.

Rajan cites McCarty, Poole, and Rosenthal's work demonstrating that inequality has contributed to greater polarization in Congress, but that both sides of this polarity had the incentive to extend easy credit, especially for assets such as houses, which are often American's most significant store of wealth.

To quote Rajan at length:
> "Politicians love to have banks expand housing credit, for credit achieves many goals at the same time. It pushes up housing prices, making households *feel* wealthier, and allows them to finance more consumption. It creates more profits and jobs in the financial sector as well as in real estate brokerage and housing construction. Moreover, everything is safe - as safe as houses - at least for a while."

To continue,
> "Easy credit has large, positive, immediate, and widely distributed benefits, whereas the costs lie in the future. It has the payoff structure, which is precisely the one desired by politicians, which is why so many countries have succumbed to its lure."

In effect, the political capture of central banks in democracies has created an environment where banks took risks issuing credit with the understanding that the Government and the Fed would bail them out, precisely because credit has become simultaneously so essential to the economy and thus within the bounds of political influence.

Governments have failed to "regulate" banks, not just because of the collective action problem of structuring regulation in a democracy, but also because the incentives are not aligned: Politicians want political credit for maintaining easy credit, banks desire easy money with low-interest rates, and the Fed answers to the political system, as well as to the influence of private banks that are themselves invested in equities (stocks and assets) that benefit from an easy money policy.

The untethered nature of the fiat financial system incentivizes various parties to work together to extend credit, in turn expanding the money supply and introducing significant risk to the currency and the broader economy. The Fed became politically captured, as growth in outstanding debt made it harder to raise interest rates without collapsing an ever-larger debt bubble that the Fed couldn't control without destroying the economy. As we've mentioned above, this means that the Fed is required to move ever further down the list of monetary policy options, from manipulating rates to engaging in debasement.

The complexity and perverse incentives of this system are increased even further by the sovereign debt issue. Government spending (fiscal policy) is used to take the edge off rising income inequality and buy votes in the short run with entitlements. These efforts are politically sacrosanct, immune to repair in the artificially good times created by easy credit, and untouchable in times of crisis.

Unbacked fiat currency has encouraged unsustainable borrowing and expansion of debt for political reasons. The government's fiscal and monetary policies have enabled politicians to pursue destructive, unsound, short-run economic pumps by embracing the endless dilutability of unbacked fiat currency, racking up massive debts that they don't intend to pay back with dollars or yen of the same strength.

The income inequality created by a debt-based system has led to greater and greater division, as political parties unmoored from the constraints of sound money have pursued massive spending campaigns and easy credit. This has resulted in weaker and weaker currency, stagnant wages, a financial system that has trapped much of the benefits of QE in Fed-connected banking institutions, and a political system that borrows massive amounts of money to fund entitlements programs to take the edge off the fact that economic growth in the fiat economy has become less and less beneficial to everyday people.

This malaise finds its worst embodiment in a school of thought known as Modern Monetary Theory (MMT). MMT takes the approach that government spending and taxation of fiat currency are inherently and uniformly stimulative. In effect, this model recommends permanent stimulus as the "new normal." Instead of a deficit, states' debts become miraculously repackaged as a "Net Spending Achievement" - a term just as Orwellian as it sounds.

MMT subjects the entire economy to a government's ability to tax and spend with no check on deficits. MMT has nothing to do with productivity - it is merely a reflection of an ideological commitment to bring all things monetary, financial, and economic under the heel of the state. MMT's comfort zone should be assumed to be massive debasement and inflation since there is no precedent for positive outcomes from similar past policies. The United States has been a spendthrift nation since the end of the Cold War, yet real GDP has stagnated between one and two percent per year, while Americans are now more indebted than ever before.

This ideological position and its less-radical antecedents are natural evolutions of the magical thinking involved in unbacked fiat currency, and while they may not be palatable to most, the last decade of U.S. monetary and fiscal policy (as well as that of other nations) has progressively followed the same ends. The only thing that MMT does that existing policy doesn't is to continue promoting the current system into the future indefinitely.

To borrow again from Dalio, this time speaking to CNBC at the tenth anniversary of the 2008 financial crisis, the next major debt crisis will be the result of unsustainable levels of sovereign debt and will be accompanied by massive political upheaval and division. Based on the above, as well as Dalio's reputation as one of the most insightful investors of the last 30 years, we believe this to be a well-informed prediction of just how the fiat economy will evolve.

The Progressive Debt Slavery of Fiat and the Crisis of the 2020s and 2030s

As we covered in the last section, the modern financial system while successful in spurring economic growth and Western financial influence has also given us bloated, inefficient spending and massive losses of value through fraud, misappropriation, and government-induced asset bubbles like those that occurred during the financial crisis of the 2000s.

As several respected scholars have pointed out, the current combination of representative democracy and fiat currency has resulted in a world where populations have effectively voted in representatives who manipulate monetary and fiscal policy to achieve populist ends, instead of adjusting budgetary policy (taxes and spending in the present) to remain sustainable.

Both the left and the right in the United States are guilty of pursuing policies that have borrowed trillions from the future to fund near-term asset bubbles and unsustainable financial economics. In the present day, it is debatable whether or not the Federal Reserve is sufficiently independent enough even to accomplish its policy goals, as the U.S. national debt has ballooned to the point that raising interest rates to levels sufficient to prevent future hyperinflation has become effectively forbidden.

We are living at the end of a decade where raising interest rates on nearly $22 trillion of the national debt in an economy with a GDP of $19 trillion will create a new recession. The incentive structure created by this addiction to debt leaves fewer public policy options in the future should that debt continue to grow unabated.

America's swelling sovereign debt is an issue in the arena of defense, as well as with the nation's entitlements programs (chiefly Medicare, Medicaid, and Social Security). It is also an issue in much of the European Union, Japan, and other economies whose sovereign debt burdens now create friction to economic growth, with more and more of the economy taxed to service the interest on sovereign debt.

As we write this, the service on the US national debt is projected to cost $1.05 Trillion per year by 2028, assuming, of course, no rapid change in current fiscal policy and spending. According to the Debt Clock, which is available online, the 2018 debt translated to $65,402 per US citizen, but $176,321 per actual taxpayer. By 2020, the US Government is on track to spend more on servicing the nation's debt interest than it spends on Medicaid. By 2023, that figure will outstrip what the country spends on national defense, and by 2025 servicing the debt will have overshadowed every single nondefense discretionary federal program combined.

An entire generation is expected to pay the interest and not the principal of the loans racked up by their parents and their peers.

This debt is the result of money borrowed from future generation's labor in the form of government bonds to fuel present-day spending and consumption. This figure is enormous, but it <u>does not</u> include the trillions of dollars in additional unfunded liabilities created by the United States' entitlements system, where obligations for future benefits are politically guaranteed regardless of whether or not Congress has a means of funding them.

As of this writing, unfunded liabilities were estimated to be 116 *Trillion* dollars, including medicare, social security, and the U.S. federal budget deficit - adding up just less than 1 million dollars per taxpayer ($949,556).

In traditional banking there is a measure known as the *Texas Ratio* - a bank's ratio of non-performing loans (money loaned out that is not being repaid) divided by the bank's common equity, plus the bank's loss reserves (that small pool of cash that the bank cannot loan out in the fractional reserve system).

The lower the Texas Ratio, the better. A ratio of 1:1 would mean that the bank's non-performing assets are worth more than the bank is, bringing life to the adage "when you owe the bank a thousand dollars, you have a problem; when you owe the bank a million dollars, the bank has a problem." To use a crude analogy, (Texas oil pun not intended), we could take this model to countries who have made loans to present generations by selling bonds to support present-day spending.

How much a country digests stimulus and turns it into real economic productivity, versus how much becomes squandered could be added together to make the Texas Ratio for that country - including the country the Republic of Texas voluntarily joined in 1845. When we do this with US citizens using the above figure, we get $949,556 divided by what the average citizen is going to pay in income tax over the same timeframe. Using numbers dated from

2018, only about 46 percent of Americans paid income tax, with the top 20% paying 87% of that tax.[16]

In effect, the United States' Texas ratio is a million dollars over every citizen, including the masses who do not contribute meaningfully to paying for that debt. If the U.S. government and economy were a bank, it would be forced to confront the problem sooner, but with an unbacked fiat system, greater debts can be taken out to cover the non-productive loans distributed through the system over time.

Even if the Texas Ratio is not 100% analogous to a nation-state wasting money on entitlements, the truth is that negative interest rates mean banks will continue to loan out money at interest rates that seem sustainable, but create mounds of debt that cannot be paid back over time, increasing their own ratios should rates ever normalize. Even if rates never normalize, there is the risk that non-performing debt becomes such a drag on the economy that the system implodes for other reasons, regardless of the interest rate. In effect, long term near-zero rates create a free money trap, fueling nation-sized debt bubbles.

The problem of unfunded liabilities extends to local municipalities. According to Truth in Accounting (TIA), a non-profit public accountability thinktank, no less than 63 of America's 75 most populous cities are functionally broke, with unfunded liabilities including city pensions totaling in the hundreds of billions of dollars by the end of Fiscal Year 2017 for several cities.[17]

New York City, Chicago, Philadelphia, Honolulu, and San Francisco all received "F" grades, while the City of New York has set aside just over $4.7 billion to cover $100.6 billion in public sector pension liabilities. In Philadelphia, every citizen would have to contribute $27,900 to square out the city's outstanding debt, on top

---

[16] *Top 20% of Americans Will Pay 87% of Income Tax: Households with $150,000 or more in income make up 52% of total income nationally but pay large portion of total taxes.* Wall Street Journal, 6 April 20

[17] Report: 2019 *Financial State of America's Cities.* Truth in Accounting. https://www.truthinaccounting.org/library/doclib/2019-Financial-State-of-the-Cities-.pdf

of the $950,000-plus measure attributed to the same figure at the federal level.

Even though some economists tout the benefits of giving people "helicopter money" to sustain themselves to create "multiplier effects" as that money is circulated through consumption, few of the applications of this free money are productive or support innovative technologies. Despite the underperformance, debt sticks around long afterward. The goal of politically captured fiat policy is to promote consumption by the less productive to keep them quiescent and buy their votes.

Often, these expenditures are paid for by taxes and progressive dilution of salaries. As a portion of income, the bulk of taxes to support this system falls on the middle class. With this and wage stagnation, many now see diminished opportunities to move up in life. Today that is innovators and large companies, but this burden does not entirely rest on their shoulders. Much of this consumption borrows from future generations in the form of bonds.

The cost of servicing bonds diminishes every country's ability to build infrastructure, educate children, defend the national security of their nation, and support the health and wellbeing of their citizens into the future. Effectively, the fiat system, when combined with a form of democracy that allows citizens to "vote themselves other people's money," has empowered the most significant intergenerational theft in world history.

Where past ideologies like communism and fascism destroyed the national legacies and wealth of the most productive, populist governments powered by unbacked fiat currency have led to a boom in present-day spending that eventually will become a burden to everyone trying to continue to produce in these systems.

This dynamic is only exacerbated by central banks that have effectively become trapped at long-term zero or near-zero interest rates. When the Fed and others cannot raise interest rates without collapsing the entire economy, they effectively can only debase the currency through QE, meaning that the wasteful applications of debt grow on both the sovereign and private side of the market.

The massive reservoir of money borrowed from the future and sloshing around in the global financial markets has led to enormous amounts of fraud and inefficiency, which millennials and Gen Z will be paying for well into the future, if not into our deathbeds. Add entitlements to more than $1,600,000,000,000 in student loan debt, which debtors cannot escape even in the case of a bankruptcy.

Many of those loans were taken out for degrees that are not capable of providing the income necessary to pay back the debt taken out to acquire them because there frequently is no connection between what skills colleges accept loans to teach and the real economy. Recently, the Federal Reserve concluded that student debt is suppressing homeownership among young people, representing some degree of self-awareness by one of the core institutions involved in creating the problem.

As a knock-on effect of this, young people are also delaying marriage, family formation, settling down, and community engagement, which is having a litany of toxic impacts on cities whose middle class has been eviscerated by the evolution of the financial system over the past 30 years.

These are effects of an unbridled fiat system that has given rise to intergenerational theft in an environment where those in power felt comfortable lining their pockets at the end of history, not contemplating the fact that history might repeat itself. The impacts of this system aren't confined to the Western world, either. Fluctuations in global currencies affect asset prices the world over.

Many have pointed out that the so-called Arab Spring, in which populist movements overthrew or sought to overthrow Middle Eastern Autocrats, was, in fact, an unintentional impact of inflation created by "stimulative" policies elsewhere. Stimulus drove up the price of commodities, including food, creating enormous frustration among populations making only a few dollars a day. Egypt is one such unintended consequence, where much of the urban population in that country is dependent on government subsidies for food and gas. With global asset price inflation, Egypt's political economy broke in 2011.

This general malaise is not the effect of some unknown conspiracy - it is a direct consequence of the economic lifeblood of the nation gradually being diverted to support wasteful ends, creating a cycle of rising inflation, debt, and the taxation required to sustain it. It is a gross violation of human liberty and is not politically sustainable in the long run.

Based on the growth of existing debt, we can reliably infer that the U.S. and many other economies will face substantial deleveraging pressure during the 2020s and the 2030s. This dynamic will significantly impact politics since it is diluting away much of everyday people's quality of life, their wellbeing, and their sense of belonging in the world. It also brings more and more people under the heel of further government dependence.

IV. Blockchain: The Backbone to Fix the Slouch of State

If you've gotten this far, it might sound like we have a pretty dystopian view of the entire financial system. That's not entirely true - the modern economy is still a miracle of creation and innovation, but in many ways that are in spite of government and dilutionary monetary policy, not because of the easy credit that the two provide.

What is objectionable is the progressive slouch of state. This economic drain is the enormous waste and second-order effects built into this system. Including where banks get richer, states get more overweening, and productive citizens are subject to endless debt and taxation. This trend continues to the point that they stand to have every ounce of equity and wealth squeezed from them by a system that exists for financial ends only, not to support human flourishing.

We don't intend to get political here, but we're pretty sure this isn't how healthy democracies (or even autocracies) work over the long run. As Americans who believe in the values espoused in the Constitution, as well as in the potential for technological progress and innovation, we believe that the Blockchain can radically improve the efficiency of our current system of financial governance at the domestic level.

In principle, we would like to hope (as we imagine Dalio and others do) that the fiat system does not implode - that states get wise to the impact their policies are having, and they find sustainable ways to operate their currencies without putting themselves in unsustainable positions where they slide into default or dilute away their citizens savings, or even worse endure a catastrophic collapse that upends the entire global economy.

It would be nice to imagine a world where wise and insightful policymakers could prevent such devastating events. Such a conceptual sustained fiat system would involve low government debt, with a surplus generated as well as financial elbow room to issue bonds in the event of a war or some other contingency, but based on the factors in the last chapter this is empirically not the world we live in today.

With the triumph of populism and "free lunch" ideas in democracies, fiat systems cannot survive indefinitely. They will continue to wrack up greater and greater debts, tax burdens, fragile systems, currency printing, and progressive economic weakening as a result of the increasing friction created through debt. The national deficit in advanced fiat economies is growing at a clip that future generations are unlikely to keep up with, regardless of whether the Left or the Right is officially in power. Our 'mature' global monetary system will have more overt political effects, as populations become more frustrated with the amount of wealth they are losing to the state and the financial system.

It is critical for the survival of our nations and our values that states begin to understand their monetary and fiscal policies in generational terms and as part of the great game of competition between themselves and other countries for primacy and, in some cases, outright survival. Many of the points in this chapter are incredibly orthodox from an economics perspective, and we're sure you could get on YouTube and find many of the same arguments encouraging you to buy physical gold, or guns, or canned food, or all three.

It's also important here that we not lose sight of the fact that this is a predictive exercise. In answering what the world will look like, we believe that unkillable, decentralized blockchains like Bitcoin and DigiByte get a vote too. Real blockchains will have demonstrable use cases both in improving the health of democracies as well as rebalancing the financial system and offering a way out of the destructive policies where they are pursued, at least for individuals.

In this section, we'd like to list a few innovations that come to mind, and which we think will become increasingly common into the 2020s and 2030s as the world becomes more and more fiscally and politically unstable.

Cryptocurrency for Individuals and Accountable Monetary Policy for States

"Who is John Galt?"

-Ayn Rand, Atlas Shrugged

There will never be more than 21,000,000 Bitcoin. There will never be more than 21,000,000,000 DigiByte. Real crypto assets are non-dilutable, other than the new coins scheduled through validation of the chain, which is part of the above numbers. Conversely, no one can tell you how many dollars there are or will be.

Decentralized cryptocurrencies will always be independent of states. They will run on global networks that are too expensive and complex to hack or alter. Decentralization makes them appear suspect to central banks and governments, who have become acclimated to being able to borrow or print their way out of a tight spot. Even though central banks gave a survival advantage to nation-states who were able to borrow money to wage warfare through raising war bonds, this dynamic has morphed considerably in a world where central banks have been politically captured to support crony capitalism.

The system has bailed out private banks, only to empower stock repurchases and issue additional debt to the public, financializing every sector of the economy. What cryptocurrency offers is an asset class for everyday people to store value outside of this banking-industrial complex, where moth, rust, lack of personal control, over-taxation, and infinite dilution destroy. Only the owner of the private keys can decide where the currency goes, and that is a return to the balance of power between the state, the financial system, and the individual.

Real decentralized blockchains will continue to run well into the future. They will get progressively stronger, scaling with the quality of computing power directed to validate them. They will outlive the banking systems whose mismanagement prompted their creation in the first place. Such a blockchain's assets will exist regardless of government's fiscal and monetary policies, and likely increase in relative value compared to the unlimited sums of fiat currency being issued by the second, especially when that system begins to show its age.

People who want to retain their wealth will leave countries that overtax them, and if they put their money in cryptocurrency, there is nothing the state can do to stop them, other than arrest and torture or extort them until they give up their private keys. Cryptocurrency restores the human right to preserve wealth.

Capital will flee oppressive countries, and this is precisely why states like the People's Republic of China enforce controls on everyday people purchasing Bitcoin and other digital assets. If taxation becomes too noisome, if wealth confiscation becomes malicious, then people with assets will trade them into cryptocurrency and will flee to the nation or state with the most welcoming policy and working laws.

For this reason, we believe cryptocurrency will eventually prove to be a check on reckless fiscal and monetary policy by states, and a limitation on the progressive wealth confiscation and dilution of the present system. There is already real-world precedent for this in failing fiat economies. While Bitcoin and others are not well known or as commonly held as we write this, recognition of the value represented by truly decentralized cryptocurrencies will evolve, especially as populations lose faith in the current monetary system.

If cryptocurrency can serve as money better than fiat currencies in crisis, people and institutions will eventually shift to it for transactions and payment. In the long run, this may form a check on the monetary system, where "full faith and credit" isn't accepted at the printed value. The total collapse of the financial system is something threatened by bankers during the 2008 financial crisis, and the world is only more indebted now. The longer the economy is bailed out, the more violent the correction will be.

The National Digital Asset as a New Analog for Gold

We're talking about a broad realm of possibility, so it's important not to get tangled up on the most extreme options and ignore much more immediate likelihood that the technology may impact. At the much more likely end of the spectrum, we believe that states in economic and geopolitical competition with each other will discover that being the first to issue a trustworthy crypto-backed monetary policy will create a substantial competitive advantage vis-a-vis other states. Fiat currencies are obsolete, and we are overdue for a new paradigm shift as countries compete with each other to attract capital, investment, and wealth at a global scale.

This strategy will involve the issuance of what we call here a *National Digital Asset*. The most effective approach is to adopt a minable and decentralized UTXO blockchain as a state's analog for gold. This blockchain embodies strict rules that cannot be affected by political drift, restoring trust in the monetary system, as well as international confidence in the asset's fundamentals. Such a model could be deflationary or inflationary at a set rate - say, the 2% target set by the Fed. Such an approach could involve a partial premine by the government, establishing a treasury.

Further, a National Digital Asset needs not to be a replacement for the currency. Much as the gold standard created a peg and final form of settlement, the core purpose of the NDA would be to constrain policy to healthy norms outside of the political morass. Open-market trading of the currency against the asset by the central bank would normalize prices and provide a medium of international settlement.

Alternatively, the cost of the asset could appreciate relative to the inflationary fiat currency and global demand for it. In effect, this would value the pre-mined portion and enable states to pay down or pay off their existing fiat debts and return to more stable fiat systems. A scarce National Digital Asset allows for deleveraging without resorting to QE, redistribution, and debasement of people's wealth.

Such an asset must be 1) legally recognized as having no future duplicate, and 2) that it be a minable UTXO-model cryptocurrency, regardless of whether it had an inflationary or deflationary bias. After all, the trust in Bitcoin and other assets is in the code: No one needs to know who Satoshi Nakamoto was to trust Bitcoin. If a state operates a bastardized model of the National Digital Asset, as the

People's Bank of China plans to, there will be no rational expectation that the code will not be changed or transactions whitelisted or rolled back.

Such centralization will rob the asset of any credibility at the international stage. National Digital Assets running on centralized servers are a sovereign-level scam. The only honest way to execute this strategy is to use a minable UTXO model, and preferably one with Proof of Work, as a Proof of Stake model would grossly advantage any premine, again diminishing trust in the asset.

This asset could also facilitate international trade settlement - much as dollars are redirected back into treasury bills. Citizens might each receive a small, equal amount. The wide distribution of the NDA would enable Universal Basic Wealth, rather than Universal Basic Income. Each citizen could receive an amount that was allowed to appreciate over time, rather than a check in the mail that exacerbates the country's monetary and fiscal position.

More on this later, but for now, we'll take a moment to consider two blockchain-powered innovations that may help prevent or blunt risks that the current system has created. These are the asset revolution and the ability to better audit and govern the dangers and complexities posed by the derivatives market.

The Asset Revolution and Political Stability in a Faltering Fiat Economy

"Saint Peter, don't you call me 'cause I can't go: I owe my soul to the company store."

-Tennessee Ernie Ford

In a world with growing income and wealth inequality, populism poses a threat to the state's ability to pursue a sustainable fiscal and monetary policy. The financial and monetary policies of advanced economies have, over recent decades, vastly benefited the wealthy and generally eroded the middle class. Stagnant wages and rising inflation have squeezed the middle class.

Along with regressive income taxation, these forces have had and will continue to have a political impact well into the future as more and more citizens become dependent on government and resentful of the nation's increasingly centralized wealth. Those who believe in growing the entitlements system to take the edge off inequality make one of many critical flaws: just because a state gives a citizen a handout does not mean those citizens miraculously come to love the country or the political system.

They merely become dependent as they acclimate to receiving a transfer payment. Often they will even be resentful of needing this assistance in the first place, despite the fact they feel entitled to it.

If capitalist democracy is going to be healthy, a new means of sustaining the middle class has to emerge, rather than the oppressive regime of endless taxation, dependency, private debt expenditure to maintain standards of living, and inflation.

Traditional models of distribution favor underclasses and those with enough resources to pay for goods, no matter what the cost against the industrious middle, and that is a net negative for the political, economic, and spiritual health of a nation. It is this progressive consolidation of financial and political power that drives much of the angst and division we see in our modern world, and this is not sustainable.

Large tech companies are progressively replacing much of the preexisting business infrastructure that people once relied on to make a living. We have improved products and services, but also large concentrations of wealth and limited room for advancement for those at the bottom of the economic food chain.

While we will always be fans of innovation and love the products that Apple, Amazon, Lyft, and other companies provide, it is vital to recognize the political impacts of such systems on domestic politics, primarily as they affect the labor market. These forces will be even more intense in an age of AI, where machines replace skilled and unskilled human labor with even better products - but employ even fewer people.

Many in the middle class benefit from these platforms in the near term, but they will forever struggle to keep up economically as a result of the effects created by these massive platforms. They often feel dependent on these platforms for their income much in the same way one might be dependent on government. While the government is continually diluting the value of its entitlements, making them unsustainable, tech platforms are actively (and much more transparently) trying to maximize the economic value that they can absorb from the people who use their platforms. The only ceiling on this process is their competition with other platforms.

Every private enterprise has every right to do this. We'd still be using hand-operated looms to make our clothes if the Luddites of the 1810's England had their way, all to preserve the place of labor. However, this doesn't resolve the problem - people are being and always will be displaced by newer, more efficient technologies. Economic displacement of new technologies is of direct importance to a nation's entitlements and social safety net system, which will be progressively strained - if not broken - by the forces outlined in this chapter.

States that care about how this trend impacts their nation's economic health can and should look to the same private sector for innovation and solutions that enable people to increase their ownership and build wealth. Blockchain offers the means for such democratic issuance of assets, such as ownership in small companies, distribution of profits, and auditability, all of which will be a net benefit for social health as technology and the fiat system progress into the 2030s, becoming ever more centralized. Blockchains will be the backbone for a more distributed financial system, one that enables new and more discrete forms of wealth for everyday people.

At scale, new asset classes created by blockchain may even put downward pressure on inflation - a net positive for investors and the broader economy. The stock market acts as a place to park money where it can be used productively, with shares acting as an asset. Share capitalism has seen the most exceptional boom in human economic efficiency and productivity ever recorded.

By making this system ubiquitous in daily life (and by providing access to sound money), a revolutionary new economy could emerge. The revolution in asset issuance by truly decentralized blockchains will be the backbone of a new middle class, resulting in fewer people falling into government dependency and less strain on social programs, as well as more efficient uses of capital across the economy.

We predict that governments that *do not* allow for and even encourage this form of wealth retention using blockchain technology will suffer more considerable social, financial, and political upheaval as a result of the progressive middle-class displacement built into the current system. An added benefit is combatting the increasing popularity of toxic political ideologies, such as socialism.

Such ideological positions assume that wealth must be taken from some and given to others by force, with no recourse for those who cannot escape the extortion of the state. We do not believe that socialism and its ilk are sustainable, just, or in the national interest of any country that cares about its long term economic, social, and political health. We implore those that believe otherwise to study the financial decay of Venezuela or any other fiat economy captured by such a movement, not just for economic, but also for fundamental social and human rights.

Blockchain-enabled wealth retention will be the new paradigm. The most surefire way for healthy economies to avoid drifting into destructive envy and class warfare is to allow for and encourage wealth retention by the middle class, who are the largest group of producers, consumers, and innovators in any economy. A universal economy of shareholders gives a nation a broader base for innovation, supports greater social cohesion, and more importantly, it gives people a sense of hope. Blockchain is the best way to go about creating the asset classes that do precisely this, as measures that are centralized on a single bank, government, or social program are damned to fail.

The Geoeconomic Turn: Financial Survival at the Macro Level

We end this chapter close to where we began it. The monetary system has been captured by the state to serve the purposes of the nation, and governments have at least historically made decisions regarding the financial sphere with regards to survival. Historically this was to allow the state to survive in warfare. In a post-Cold

War/end of history world, spending on military expenditures has continued, but the state has morphed to use unbacked fiat systems to borrow to support unsustainable entitlements programs as well.

This bloat has caused significant overspending, which has encouraged a loose money policy that gradually traps policymakers in an environment with massive sovereign debt, low-interest rates, and a significantly indebted and fragile society, with limited policy options to escape. Blockchain rightly applied will be strategically pivotal for countries, companies, and people the coming sovereign debt crises of the 2020s and 2030s.

This chapter has focused on blockchain and the domestic political economy. In our next section, we return to the fundamental premise that drove the state and banking together, and which we believe will drive the state and blockchain technology together. That force is the state's desire to thrive and compete with other countries for economic and military primacy and long-term survival. This field is known as geoeconomics.

Chapter 15 Bibliography & Further Reading

Ray Dalio. *Principles for Navigating Big Debt Crisis: The Archetypical Debt Cycle, Detailed Case Studies, and a Compendium of 48 Cases*. Bridgewater Press, 2018.

Charles W. Calomiris & Stephen H. Haber. *Fragile By Design: The Political Origins of Banking Crises & Scarce Credit*. Princeton Economic History of the Western World. Princeton University Press, 2014.

Carmen M. Reinhart & Kenneth S. Rogoff. This Time is Different: Eight Centuries of Financial Folly. Princeton University Press, 2009.

Richard A. Posner. *The Crisis of Capitalist Democracy*. Harvard University Press, 2010.

Nolan McCarty, Keith T. Poole, & Howard Rosenthal. Political Bubbles: Financial Crises and the Failure of American Democracy.

Raghuram G. Rajan. Fault Lines: How Hidden Fractures Still Threaten the World Economy. Princeton University Press, 2010.

Ralph Foster and Paul Myslin. *Fiat Paper Money: The History and Evolution of our Currency*.

Chapter 16: Blockchain, The New Geopolitical Arms Race

The last chapter focused mainly on the origins and long-term impacts of unbacked fiat currency policies, especially at a domestic level. We left one fundamental question unaddressed: the international aspect of finance and the role that finance, economics, and financial technology play in the competition between states for scarce resources.

This competition is a contest that involves both attack and defense, and blockchain fits into both sides of this equation. As states seek to wall off their economies, intellectual property, and spheres of influence, they will require more secure internet and banking infrastructure. As countries seek to explore new monetary policies in a world with negative global interest rates, blockchain will fit into how states (and companies) evolve their financial systems.

The individual gets a vote too, and blockchain also changes the classical equation in this contest, since it adds personal sovereignty and freedom to those who get caught in the crossfire between governments and large corporations - a first in human history.

As we covered above, central banks evolved as a policy response to competition between countries, especially for use in wars. Throughout modern history, central banks have been instruments of state power that have facilitated borrowing from the future to survive the demands of the present. Fiat systems have also mutated to serve present-day consumption and political patronage networks over and above the long-term national interest, often subsidizing private industries and special interests.

In a way, this is unavoidable; every country is doing this, and the country that doesn't protect itself economically is sure to get taken advantage of on the international stage. At the same time, this process opens financial markets to an ancient political force: cronyism and competition over who gets to use the central bank for their own political and economic purposes.

While it was fun while it lasted and enriched one generation at the expense of future generations, the long-term effects of untethered monetary and fiscal policy have eroded most government's abilities to defend themselves and exercise their sovereignty. As Ray Dalio points out in the works cited in the last chapter, sovereign debt has grown to the point that governments are working with a smaller and smaller body of potential policies to correct course.

Many states abdicated their fiscal responsibilities in the first place in favor of buying votes in the short term. While some might argue that this degree of public indebtedness will make states think twice before going to war, that's because it only makes war even more financially catastrophic than it already was. That a financial "doomsday machine" exists is no reason to presume no one will ever \ pull the trigger, or that no accident will happen to result in a similar catastrophe.

Untethered fiat currencies are difficult to sustain over the long run. The increased service requirement created by growing sovereign debts has divided society into a financial elite and a broader population that is increasingly dependent on that elite for access to government programs. Many in this growing underclass get taxed in ways they cannot avoid while demanding a standard of life that the government cannot subsidize long-term.

This system is gradually fueling more considerable resentment and political division, bringing into question the long term health of our societies, especially those whose legitimacy rests on their ability to support high levels of income, growth, and personal freedom.

Part of this dynamic has its origins in domestic political forces and stimulative spending, which we outlined above. An equally important factor is the fact that states are in *geoeconomic competition* with other nations. This chapter will examine the blockchain's potentially multifold role in this process, both from the perspective of statists (large governments) and from the perspective of individuals and companies who are subject to the systems that states create, for better or for worse.

Bear in mind; this isn't an endorsement of any of the policies outlined. It is a forward-looking analytic estimate based on the potential for blockchain technology's impact on the broader world, and it is an attempt to be realistic about the many ways the technology could be embraced (and is already being embraced) in the competition between states. Whether this leads to more openness in trade, a feudal internet, or a replacement to the global reserve currency is still an open question. This question depends on how states, corporations, and individuals choose to embrace the technology, and it's our goal to analyze these topics in-depth in this chapter.

What is Geoeconomics?

Edward Luttwak, a preeminent geopolitical strategist[18] with an extensive focus on classical grand strategy, coined the term *geoeconomics* for the intersection of geopolitics and economics.[19]

Generally, grand strategy means *the purposeful employment of all instruments of power available to achieve a goal.* By extension, geoeconomics is the use of a variety of economic and financial pressures across several domains to gain control and security in a geopolitical setting. It is the overlap of administrative and commercial areas. Within our scope here, we will draw on classical

---

[18] Readers with past military service will be familiar with the notion of strategic, operational, and tactical levels of warfare - and this is one of Luttwak's many contributions to western strategy and military doctrine. Luttwak is also responsible for the world's first handbook for analyzing Coups D'Etat, and has written two comprehensive manuals on the grand strategies and survival tactics of the Roman and Byzantine empires.

[19] Edward N. Luttwak. *From Geopolitics to Geo-Economics: Logic of Conflict, Grammar of Commerce.* The National Interest No. 20 (Summer 1990), pp. 17-23

minds in geoeconomics and orthodox scholarship, much as we did in the previous chapter on fiat and central banking.

There are three core purposes to geoeconomic competition, all of which are strategically critical for states at the international and the domestic level: They are the *competition for productive economic capacity and advantage*, the *protection of critical technology and infrastructure,* and *capital competition*. Blockchain will revolutionize all three, for reasons we'll go into below.

Competition for Productive Capacity and Influence

First and foremost, states are states because they can muster some degree of consent or submission of the governed. This 'submission of the governed' can be from a sheer economy of force, as in an authoritarian system, or it can be a matter of consensus among a diverse hierarchy of stakeholders, as it is in a feudal system. Alternatively, it can be a matter of limited government where the state draws its legitimacy from performing a delineated set of critical tasks well, as in a constitutional republic.

Regardless of structure, every functioning state draws legitimacy from the economic health of its subjects. A failing economy means lower tax revenue and less ability to pay armies and police to protect the nation from internal and external threats. Because of this, countries compete for economic resources that they can use to build wealth, defend their positions, and secure the support of their citizens.

This competition can involve access to natural resources, such as oil, or the economic advantages in inventing, manufacturing, and assembling goods. From the state's perspective, the more economic value that can be created and successfully absorbed, the better.

This value dovetails with the need for nations to be able to manufacture or otherwise acquire weaponry and pay soldiers in the instance of conflict. Even if its central bank has plenty of options to borrow money for war, a state without a steel industry cannot make the ships and guns required to project power. A country with a limited tech industry will struggle to resist the influence and advantage of states with healthy tech economies and platforms.

Such a nation would fail to resist domination from other state's technology companies. Imagine being confined to using Chinese or Russian-made cell phones and tech services, and you start to get the picture. It is for these two reasons (domestic stability and international competitiveness) that states compete with each other to gain economic advantages and absorb each other's industries, as well as defend their own.

Further, as is demonstrated by Russia's use of Gazprom in Europe, Chinese use of foreign investment in Africa, and the American use of the Marshall Plan to rescue Europe from the influence of Soviet communism, these *networks of value creation* are also *networks of influence.* People's livelihoods are inextricable from the nation's economic health as a whole, for better or for worse, and the use of measures such as tariffs and trade deals function as an extent of state power.

Geoeconomic policies create influences that diplomatic exchanges cannot. Take the recent use of non-tariff barriers by the PRC to halt Philippine agricultural goods from being imported to China during competition over islands in the South China Sea as an example. By leaving bananas and pork to rot at Chinese ports of entry, China has influenced Filipino farmers in critical voting districts by making them suffer direct financial losses.

This maneuver incentivized farmers to pressure their government to back off on its territorial claims that competed with those of the PRC. China then used its centralized state power to buy up Philippine products as an incentive to edge out Japanese advancements in the same contest.[20]

This kind of influence is much more useful than any "strongly worded letter" from some milksop in the Foreign Ministry because

---

[20] Cliff Venzon. Nikkei Asian Review. *China Uses Banana Diplomacy to Edge Out Japan: Fruit exports to China help economy but reflect Beijing's growing sway.* 26 July, 2019. Available at.
https://asia.nikkei.com/Politics/International-relations/China-uses-banana-diplomacy-in-Philippines-to-edge-out-Japan

they leverage the interconnected web of economic activity to affect domestic politics and livelihoods in other countries. These policies can be targeted or general. They can focus on individual citizens (as US sanctions often do), or they can be enacted to protect politically influential sectors and industries to the detriment of other producers.[21]

This form of competition can extend to tech platforms, which America's economy excels at creating. Facebook now has more citizens than any nation on earth, estimated at 2.2 billion people as of Q4 2018.[22] It should be no surprise that America's two geopolitical rivals have created social networking clones of their own that are beholden to their respective national governments.

In Russia, this is VKontakt, which is directly accessible to the FSB.[23] In China, this is a series of services, including WeChat, Renren, and Weibo, which are Facebook, Twitter, and other Western social networking services. Like VKontakt, Chinese services have a direct tie-in to the Ministry of State Security (MSS) as well as China's Orwellian "Social Credit" system, which ranks citizens and issues privileges based on how compliant they are with official policy. It should also not be surprising that foreign actors have leveraged the openness of American social media to create division and "fake news" in efforts to destabilize Western democracies.

---

[21] As US farm subsidies do, making other nation's farmers less competitive and unable to sustain and be sustained by their agricultural output, in turn fueling illegal immigration into the US.

[22] Statista. 9 August 2019. Number of monthly active Facebook users worldwide as of 2nd quarter 2019 (in millions). Available at https://www.statista.com/statistics/264810/number-of-monthly-active-facebook-users-worldwide/

[23] The post-Cold War name for the KGB, where the First Chief Directorate was broken off to form the SVR. Since the rise of Vladimir Putin in Russia the FSB has increasingly reclaimed its role in foreign intelligence operations and economic plundering within Russia. For a detailed account of this process, we recommend reading Andrei Soldatov and Irina Borogan's great book *The New Nobility: The Restoration of Russia's Security State and the Enduring Legacy of the KGB*.

While this extends to espionage and influence operations, it also relates to the productive capture of much of the world's supply chain. As we cover later in this chapter, Chinese supply chain attacks targeting U.S. critical infrastructure have become immensely sophisticated. The most egregious public example is known as the Big Hack - where Chinese suppliers implanted tiny chips in circuit boards to engineer a back door to systems used by the U.S. Government. Allegedly, this attempt at intrusion went undetected for years.

Such supply chain attacks are even more critical in a future where warfare and military competition feature drones, space satellites, autonomous defense platforms, and other high-tech weapons systems. The capture of productive capacity for hardware in peacetime makes these weapons easier to produce and allows the dominant party to control or compromise the export of these technologies as they see fit.

Competition for Critical Technology

As we've argued at length in this book, much of the existing internet is insecure to its very core. Cyber insecurity has resulted in a pandemic of data exfiltration, both at the domestic and the international level by large companies and by governments. All of these data aggregators are the targets of rivals, who seek to steal or scrape data for their purposes, without the work or good faith of having earned the data themselves.

At the domestic level, Facebook, Google, and others are aggregating data and using it for advertising and influence purposes. The attention economy's customers pay for these platform's centralized ability to target users with advertisements that are maximally effective and discreet, and in some cases, even measure the effectiveness of their ads in influencing consumer behavior. At the international level, this is foreign states using the same insecure internet to exfiltrate data from their competitors.

Chinese theft of American intellectual property was estimated by the United States Trade Representative to cost the American economy between $225 billion and $600 billion annually as of

2017.[24] That's is on top of and roughly equal to the amount of the United States' annual trade imbalance with that nation, which reached an estimated $375 Billion in the same year.[25] This theft isn't just a loss to America; it is a loss to America's trading partners in Europe, Asia, and the broader world who would have been the beneficiaries of that economic activity happening in their orbit, rather than captured by the PRC.

Competition for critical technology is a natural extension of the state's pre-existing desire for productive capacity. While using state power to capture more traditional industries such as steel mills and automobiles often relies on state subsidies and dumping practices, much of the competition for technology includes data and IP theft and espionage on top of the subsidy-oriented industrial strategy.

Middle Kingdom Mercantilism is often facilitated by the PRC's intelligence services, whose skills in exfiltrating national secrets works even better against an open market where innovators are enthusiastic about sharing their ideas and approaches. This low-effort heist has created real economic benefits for those participating in it.

In a world of geoeconomic competition over data, AI, internet of things, and the blockchain, this extends far beyond the designs for the latest chip. China has undertaken multiple efforts to capture the blockchain industry, both by state-backed efforts to dominate mining as well as PRC-backed "blockchain" projects that have attempted to centralize economic activity occurring on the blockchain under the PRC's umbrella of influence.

These reflect a similar strategy approached for AI, which focuses on supporting a critical mass of AI research within the

---

[24] Paul Goldstein. *Intellectual Property and China: Is China Stealing American IP?* Stanford Law School, 10 April 2018. Available at https://law.stanford.edu/2018/04/10/intellectual-property-china-china-stealing-american-ip/

[25] The Balance. US Trade Deficit with China and Why It's So High: The Real Reason American Jobs are Going to China. Available at <https://www.thebalance.com/u-s-china-trade-deficit-causes-effects-and-solutions-3306277>

borders of the PRC and its universities.[26] China's blockchain strategy, like their AI strategy, is focused on centralizing influence over the international network within Chinese territory, and has involved barring the exchange of the decentralized currencies by citizens, but encouraging miners such as BitMain to attempt to corner the market on the mining process and formally exploring the cryptographic properties of the technology for communications security.

This attempt at dominating Bitcoin through several prominent state-backed projects in support of pursuing a sovereign internet, much like Russia's, that is opaque to outside companies and governments. Since blockchain is a backbone to facilitate trade and exchange of value, many of these projects appear oriented towards capturing and centralizing trade and the transfer of value under Chinese-operated companies.

Examples include WanChain, Neo, NEM, WaltonChain, and others that lack the "digital gold" properties of UTXO chains and brand themselves as explicitly designed to track the exchange of goods and services among identities, rather than serve as a stateless, trustless system. Recognition of the importance of blockchain does not stop with China.

Other nations are beginning to explore adopting a national strategy for blockchain and AI. Chief among these is Great Britain, which was the first to announce blockchain as critical technology as early as 2015. National governments such as Australia, Malta, South Korea, Italy, and others all have announced some degree of formal support and initiative for welcoming blockchain projects and focusing on the impacts the technology will have for governance and trade.

This race for technical primacy is ultimately a defector game. Regardless of whether the world "needs" a super AI or any other technology, nation-states share an incentive to be the first to

---

[26] Future of Life Institute. *AI Policy: China.* Available at <https://futureoflife.org/ai-policy-china/?cn-reloaded=1>

construct it, just as they had a clear incentive to create nuclear weapons seven decades ago. Governments who do not participate in this race will face significant economic and perhaps even military costs for their failure to embrace innovation sooner than later.

Just as the Rosenbergs and Klaus Fuchs stole the plans for the Manhattan Project on behalf of the Soviets, so too will states attempt to steal and exfiltrate IP for advanced AIs and other sensitive technologies.

Monetary Geoeconomics

The present global monetary regime is primarily dominated by the U.S. Dollar, which serves as a global reserve currency and a medium of exchange for much of the world's international commerce and credit. This centrality is also what makes U.S. Treasury sanctions sting, as being unable to transact in the dollar substantially downgrades countries and individual's ability to do business in the broader world.

Like any tool, the repeated and single-use of the US dollar to support sanctions has created an environment where many political and financial powers have an increasing interest in subverting or replacing the international monetary order. Russia, China, and smaller players like Venezuela and Iran have all expressed their frustration with the dollar-dominated international financial order and have put forward institutions to oppose the primacy of the World Bank, the IMF, and the Fed.

Russia and China also both have an interest in pursuing monetary policies associated with their spheres of influence, where their central-bank issued currencies serve as a regional reserve currency for settlement between countries in their geoeconomic orbit.

In comments delivered at the BRICs Summit in July 2018, President Vladimir Putin stated that the U.S. Dollar's role as a global reserve currency had become a problem for the world economy. This statement is consistent in comparison to Putin's past remarks: in 2009, while visiting Davos, he called for an end to the

Dollar's role as a global reserve currency and its replacement with a more regional monetary order.[27]

China has been only slightly less transparent in calling for an end to the dollar. In the same setting as Putin's comments, Chinese policymakers are well known to desire an eventual replacement to the US dollar as a global reserve currency. As the Financial Times columnist Geoff Dyer noted in 2013:

"Among Chinese officials and scholars, there is a widely held view that the U.S. has been abusing its position as a controller of the main reserve currency by pursuing irresponsible economic policies. Nor do they hide the underlying geopolitical objective of the currency push - to place limits on the control of the dollar in the international monetary system."[28]

This desire to "de-Americanize" the financial world has also arisen from Xinhua, China's official press agency, which in 2013 called for a new global reserve currency devoid of American influence.

Especially notable in Xinhua's argument is the position that

"what may be included as a key part of an effective reform is the introduction of a new international reserve currency that is created to replace the dominant U.S. dollar, so that the international community could permanently stay away from the spillover of the intensifying domestic political turmoil in the United States."[29]

Given the gravity of such a proposed shift, China has instead opted for a "build and wait" approach with the introduction of the Asian Infrastructure Investment Bank (AIIB), which issues Renminbi-denominated loans to countries in China's sphere of influence. The AIIB is a logical extension of the "One Belt, One

---

[27] UA Wire. Putin Calls for Alternative to US Dollar. 29 July 2018. Available at <https://uawire.org/putin-calls-for-alternative-to-us-dollar>
[28] Blackwill & Harris, p. 78
[29] Commentary: US Fiscal Failure Warrants a De-Americanized World. Xinhua. October 13, 2013.

Road" initiative, which focuses on Chinese investment in infrastructure on its geopolitical periphery. Its objective is to reinforce the PRC's economic influence in foreign countries and enable Chinese corporations to establish monopolistic advantages in construction and commerce abroad.

Russia and China are both exploring methods to use digital currency and blockchain technology as a means to build a post-American monetary policy. Smaller experiments, such as Venezuela, are a technical and economic Petri dish for these more significant players. We'll go into all three of these topics in greater depth later in this chapter, but first, we'll focus on defining the spectrum of geoeconomics in the present tense and how blockchain will affect this domain of competition in the near term.

II. Domains of Geoeconomic Competition

Blackwill and Harris' *War by Other Means* outlines the core methods that states can and have used to pursue geoeconomic policies, which are contingent on what resources the country has as endowments and also depends on the state's political structure and governance of the domestic economy. It's helpful to outline them here, as blockchain will affect each of these strategic endowments, as states embrace the technology.

Trade Policy

Trade Policy is the traditional domain of states and relates to government negotiation of the terms by which countries exchange goods and value. This domain covers everything from the "most favored nation" status, and free trade deals with the implementation of tariffs to protect domestic industries or punish past breaches of faith.

A blockchain-oriented trade policy focuses on the management of identity and chain of acquisition. Not only do such policies dovetail with the nation's plans of protecting and encrypting critical technology, but such approaches may also rely on blockchains to track the legitimate export and import of goods. Blockchain-tracked trade policies could provide immutable details on prices and tariffs, as well as facilitate greater reciprocity in trade through standardizing the massive slew of data states generate as they exchange goods.

Such approaches will give policymakers more unified data sets to evaluate the strategic impact of trade deals. Such transparency could empower other strategies, such as an integrated trade AI that guides policymakers to maximize their country's trade advantage.

Conversely, depending on the detail involved, producing such an acute level of detail could improve the impact of other geoeconomic policies, as the region dependent on import and export of certain goods could be targeted explicitly with sanctions or incentives. Imagine targeted sanctions on a specific product that twists the arm of a local politician critical to a foreign policy objective.

Alternatively, imagine retaliatory economic measures designed to exacerbate unrest in a province already experiencing instability. These policies already occur elsewhere. China and Russia have manipulated imports and exports to impact foreign rivals' domestic politics. Technology will only make such strategic gambits easier to model, recognize, execute, and counter.

From a Western perspective, universal import/export standards that account for the chain of acquisition can also decrease fraud and crime by insisting on the issuance of identities and the maintenance of data. Not only does this improve national capabilities in preventing the sale of goods based on stolen IP within their sphere of orbit, but it also encourages transparency and reciprocity between nations acting in good faith. If good fences make good neighbors, respectful trade policies make even better ones.

Investment Policy

An investment policy is simply the rules and infrastructure for how money is allowed to move between countries. It determines how much of a company foreign buyers can own, the terms of their investment, and whether the state can (or will) confiscate wealth and ownership as leverage against the investor's home country.

China's 51% domestic ownership rule is an excellent example of this, as the state implements limits on foreign investor's ownership to bar investors from having full control over their assets inside China.

This approach also relates to investor's liquidity when invested abroad. If an investor cannot control the company in question, he or she can also be squeezed to sell for a lower price without much recourse. Local Chinese governments work to support local companies; foreign firms have been made to feel welcome initially, but in the end, most get ripped off once the locals believe they have sufficient resources and know-how.

Investment policy cuts both ways: the relative ease by which foreign investors can deploy their capital inside the US draws wealth and supports asset prices and domestic investors. Blackwill and Harris cite economists Benn Steil and Robert Litan's observation that "forty years ago, 90% of cross-border flows were trade, but in the 2010s, 90% of cross-border flows were financial."[30]

Cryptocurrency and blockchain-based assets can work both ways; by not being controlled. Control of capital flows through banks is a substantial instrument of state power. Agencies directed to combat fraudulent activity in domestic markets play an essential role at a geopolitical level. The strategic value of control over capital flows is even more relevant when you control the world's reserve currency, which denominates trade between third parties.

Economic Sanctions

Sanctions are the most relied-upon tool of geoeconomic statecraft by the US. Because the U.S. dollar is the global reserve currency, for now, this has contributed to natural hostility by Russia, China, and smaller actors who seek to escape the international hegemony of the dollar. The power of sanctions is directly proportional to the influence the currency has - if someone

---

[30] P. 53; Benn Steil and Robert Litan. Financial Statecraft: The Role of Financial Markets in American Foreign Policy. Yale University Press, 2006.

were to bar the United States from using the Iranian Rial or the Iranian banking system, there would be a minimal effect on American investors. The same does not apply to Iran, whose inability to use the dollar and Western banks adversely affects the nation's ability to settle trade and sell its oil worldwide.

That is not to say that banks necessarily follow their nation's geoeconomic policies. One might note HSBC's well-known skirting of sanctions to launder "at least" $881 million in profits from Mexican drug cartels, as well as deliberately skirting sanctions against Hamas, Hezbollah, and Iran. HSBC was fined $1.9 billion for the malfeasance in 2012. This kind of mischief does not stop with HSBC - smaller Dutch firm Rabobank was fined $369 million in 2018 for similar violations, as was now-defunct bank Wachovia, which was fined $160 million in 2010.[31]

The United Nations Office on Drugs and Crime (UNODC) estimates that $2 trillion worth of fiat currency gets laundered annually.[32] Almost every major bank faces fines for lack of oversight in this field. When opponents to Bitcoin and other cryptocurrencies pillory them as tools for "illicit transactions on the dark web," one should take this with a grain of salt. The very banks that such critics often work for have been fined repeatedly for much larger-scale cases of illicit activity, many orders of magnitude above the present-day market cap of all cryptocurrencies combined according to the UN's estimate.

While we have covered privacy coins in-depth in the technical chapter and they are an outlier, all genuine blockchains are fully auditable. They may not be directly attributable to a person, but large transactions do occur in the clear, and using blockchain analysis techniques is much faster than getting a subpoena from a

---

[31] Greg Farrell. Business: HSBC Sued Over Drug Cartel Murders after Laundering Probe. *Bloomberg*. 9 February 2016. Available at <https://www.bloomberg.com/news/articles/2016-02-09/hsbc-sued-for-drug-cartel-murders-after-money-laundering-probe>
[32] https://www.bloomberg.com/graphics/2019-dirty-money/

bank, especially a foreign bank like HSBC. Even if a subject of sanctions were to use privacy coins, this is not fundamentally different from using paper dollars.

States addicted to sanctions could learn a thing or two about adopting a different approach as their power diminishes relative to cryptocurrency and foreign banks whom they have limited or no influence over. While criminals and hostile states do and have adopted crypto, there is no way for other countries to stop it. The cat is out of the bag.

Cyberwarfare (Both Offense and Defense)

Cyberwarfare is the most critical geo-economic initiative of the early 21st century. We have cited elsewhere the estimate that intellectual property theft represents between $250 billion and $600 billion, leaving the American economy every year. Like any form of economic growth, that figure compounds with time. Technologies stolen ten years ago have fuelled growth and innovation by competitors, like a mob boss investing ill-gotten gains in a legitimate business.

IP theft is a national industry in the PRC and elsewhere and is formally backed by the nation's resource-rich intelligence services, closely tied to the public sector through the Communist Party of China (CPC). Cyber Attacks are reported to comprise 15% of global internet traffic on any given day: that figure plummets to about 6.5% on October 1, China's National Day.[33] Doing the math, roughly 57% of professional cybercriminals take Chinese federal holidays off.

Cyber is the most critical present-day conflict between sovereign states, and the countries that embrace blockchain and cryptography for cybersecurity implementations will gain geopolitical advantage. That doesn't mean that we will "put everything on the blockchain" - far from it. As we've outlined in our

---

[33] Tony Capaccio. *China Most Threatening Cyberspace Force, U.S. Panel Says.* Bloomberg Business, 5 November 2012.

earlier chapter on the evolution of the technology, blockchain provides substantial approaches to fix enduring cybersecurity flaws. The technology can help us move towards an internet that is not fundamentally insecure and inclined towards theft.

Economic Assistance

Economic assistance comprises most forms of international aid, but it can also serve geopolitical ends. The Marshall Plan was one such example, with the U.S. footing the bill to reconstruct much of Europe after WWII. The Marshal Plan was not done strictly out of the goodness of American's hearts. It made solid strategic sense to stymie the advance of destructive communism.

It also made sense to prevent economic grievances from fuelling the formation of another extremist party, as the draconian treaty of Versailles did by destroying the German economy through war debts. The Marshall plan also benefited exports to Europe, helping American manufacturers and aiding the European economy in recovering its industrial might.

While there is substantial non-strategic aid, many of the US's existing policies did initially have a geoeconomic edge to them. As an example, USAID built Cairo's sewer and sanitation system in the late 1970s, decreasing the filth and human misery that affected millions living amidst Egypt's urban sprawl. This aid took some of the tension out of the hot peace between Egypt and Israel following the Yom Kippur War and the Camp David Accords.

In effect, international aid took the pressure off politicians' domestic concerns long enough to change the focus away from war and internal strife. The Gulf's more recent support for Egypt's two post-Mubarak presidents, with the Islamist Morsi receiving money from Qatar, and former general Sisi receiving economic backing from the Emirates and other Gulf countries, is another salient example.[34]

---

[34] As we've covered elsewhere in this book, much of the instability in Egypt had its roots in food prices, which had inadvertently been driven up by the Fed's Quantitative Easing regimen during the 2008 Financial Crisis.

China and other country's pursuit of economic aid within their desired sphere of influence is a much broader topic. There are arguably applications for blockchain in making the systems installed by foreign powers only operable insofar as the nations receiving the aid toe the line on their benefactor's policies. Imagine a world where water treatment plants and communications systems answered to foreign-installed permissions. You can start to see the potential for the technology in a more sinister setting. Not your keys, not your power grid.

Financial and Monetary Policy

As we covered in the last chapter, fiscal and monetary policy are among the most critical geoeconomic tools that blockchain threatens to change. This coming revolution applies both for everyday people who can break away from the state-controlled banking system and for states that pursue financial and policies in the interest of their elites and geoeconomic policy. In broad strokes, states' use of fiscal and monetary policy includes printing their currency, buying gold and other assets such as equities (stocks), and buying other government's money in the form of bonds.

Blockchain and cryptocurrencies are a new evolution of this dynamic, and central banks are likely to acquire decentralized currencies in much the same way that they already purchase stocks, bonds, and precious metals.

National Policies for Energy and Commodities

Energy and commodities policy is probably the least likely to be directly affected by blockchain and cryptocurrency, as they are defined by hard commodities that are often controlled by states and statists. That said, the use of a blockchain to verify possession of oil or other products and exchange certificates as a substitute for paper money is an idea in present circulation, as Venezuela's failed experiment with the Petro shows.

State efforts so far are impotent relative to cryptocurrencies running on real blockchains, as most rational investors will prefer to trust Satoshi over an Ayatollah or dictator. We're not saying these strategies are doomed to fail, or that they will never be a threat to the existing monetary order, but that centralized efforts face challenges of legitimacy as it stands. The value proposition for "commodity credit" currency is only as good as the off-chain settlement process, which is questionable in most states pursuing this strategy in the present. There's no way around scarcity created by code and decentralization.

A second angle that blockchain may provide, somewhat on the fringes of geoeconomic competition but directly related to private markets, is a global market for commodities not directly tied to states' local markets and investment banks. Such a market would provide 24/7 trading and the ability for commodities futures to be locked in as smart contracts and settled in a variety of other assets (fiat, crypto, other commodities). In such a market, participants could validate that products purchased had been consistently delivered in the past, enabling trust-based exchange through repeated, attributable use of a trustless system.

This strategy becomes essential when a commodity-rich state wants to exchange its national export without resort to the existing banking system, which in turn would impact the current monetary arrangement that uses the US dollar as a means of settlement.

III. Cryptocurrency in a World of Fiat Competition

It's impossible to separate the currency issue from blockchain in this domain. Bitcoin began as a criticism of global fiat economic policy. We will address how blockchain and cryptocurrency might fit into currency competition. Bitcoin and other UTXO systems are pro-individual and self-sovereign, but states and banks have an incentive to emulate or eventually borrow these features.

Decentralized cryptocurrency is an escape valve for the effects of fiat competition, and it also provides a new strategic move for the existing players in that competition. It is both a check on the state-led financial order and an inspiration for how that order will evolve.

Central Bank's 'Beggar Thy Neighbor' Competitive Devaluations

Monetary policy is endowed with many objectives in the United States and elsewhere. The Fed, for example, has the dual mission of minimizing unemployment and inflation, which some have pointed out, is a mutually exclusive set of tasks. As the economy runs hotter and employs more people, prices raise both for labor and goods. The value of the nation's currency and its systemic role determines its competitiveness in producing and consuming products on the global market.

"Currency manipulation," despite being used as an epithet, is nothing more than the act of having and using monetary policy. "Policy" is not a sterile territory - all nations with fiscal policies are manipulating their currencies because any policy action will change outcomes in the marketplace. By definition, using a strategy to alter the currency is "manipulating" it. That said, there is a point at which everyday policy stops and dangerous manipulation starts. In the realm of fiat currency, there are three basic positions that a nation can take as its trade balance fluctuates: to allow the currency to float relative to other currencies, or to peg the currency high or low.

A high peg artificially overvalues the currency. This strategy is popular among small-state politicians with weak economies and limited exports. It allows local elites to effectively print money that they claim to be a fraction of a global reserve currency (usually the US dollar) and fuel consumption and foreign investment. High pegs have the effect of increasing the amount of expenditure that people transacting in that artificially valuable currency can engage in, but it makes value-added industries like manufacturing and technology more expensive.

High pegs also make labor less efficient, as labor and commodity prices become inflated above their market worth. This policy is harder to maintain, as the inflationary nature of fiat monetary policy places downward pressure on the currency, and trade imbalances build up over time as a result of artificially strong capital fleeing abroad. For this reason, high pegs often fail to catastrophic effects.

The opposite side of currency manipulation is a low peg. The low peg is the position taken by the People's Bank of China, where an artificially suppressed currency harms the consumption of imported goods and gives local manufacturers an advantage in exporting. In this scenario, it is cheaper to export, and the trade imbalance created can be translated into capital abroad. The low peg of the Renminbi has successfully deployed as a strategic tool to gut the U.S. and other advanced economies of manufacturing over the past twenty years.

This mercantilist approach is not without precedent - the Japanese Yen was historically undervalued relative to the US dollar during the first three postwar decades. Eventually, Japan's peg broke during a massive boom in Japanese manufacturing and export markets, as China's likely will in the future. Low pegs are naturally more sustainable, as the central bank can effectively print money to devalue the currency and maintain its peg, but they create a scenario where the pressure is too high for the administration to sustain.

Even in a monetary environment defined by floating fiat currencies, there is a defector's benefit in cheating by devaluing. This dilemma results in competitive devaluations by central banks relative to each other's currencies to gain a manufacturing advantage and is known as a "beggar thy neighbor" monetary policy[35] since it creates economic harm through devaluation.

Further, competitive devaluations like those engaged in by the PRC naturally lead to trade wars, as a country's balance of payments and domestic economies suffer from the death of manufacturing and the inability to competitively export to the country with the artificially low currency. Low pegs and beggar-thy-neighbor policies are not without tradeoffs. President Trump's pressure on the Federal Reserve to cut rates amid America's trade war with China is a natural outcome of this tension; the United States must compete

---

[35] Term originally attributed to Adam Smith in his discussion of mercantilism.

with the Chinese policy of inflation, at the expense of risking domestic inflation.

Geoeconomic Forces and Fiat Competition

The impacts of 'beggar thy neighbor' policies do not stop with simple trade imbalances. They are a direct tool for use in the modes of competition we outlined above, chiefly for a nation's procurement of critical technology, productive capacity, and domestic tranquility through satisfying their citizen's economic needs. If people's jobs evaporate in a globalist world that seeks to optimize trade value, then those who cheat at the currency game will always win.

Two intellectual worlds are colliding. On the one hand, policymakers usually pursue the positive impacts of trade, seeing how commerce diminishes tensions and gives cause for cooperation. In an honest Ricardian[36] model, all producers find a mode of domestic production and currency valuation that best reflects their absolute and relative advantages. Ricardian thinking is reinforced by what is known as Kaname Akamatsu's "Flying Geese" paradigm of trade.

Akamatsu's model describes how currency and capital appreciation resulting from having a productive economy makes manufacturing more expensive locally, but also allows for more costly and complicated industry and value creation to occur. When nations move from doing a low cost/low skill organized production, such as that of textiles, towards mechanical and digital value creation that requires more expensive capital, they move up in the hierarchy.

As this plays out, the innovations of the leading economy trickle down to less developed countries as the leader advances, lifting the fortunes of all. This thinking is appealing not just because it is poetic but because it offers hope for human development and the benefits of free markets.

---

[36] David Ricardo is the father of international trade theory, one of the fathers of classical economics, and demonstrated mathematically how the pursuit of trade focused on absolute advantage enriched all participants.

The other side is the geoeconomic approach, where countries and governments don't play fair and seek to gain advantages through the theft of intellectual capital and the creation of a financial edge through means of artificially cheap currency. This approach, far from being a free exchange in spirit, is focused on the aggregation of productive capacity, human capital, and intellectual capital.

It is mercantilism with state support for strategic enterprises, even if they operate at a loss. Chinese steel dumping and other strategies designed to compromise the financial viability of Western businesses are one such example. Neomercantilism has centralized steel production in China, gutting foreign economies' infrastructure devoted to steel production. Oil production in the Gulf is another example, which demonstrates the limitations of the strategy for commodity exports as compared to technology and manufacturing sectors.

Even though OPEC sets quotas to establish a price, there is a strong incentive for every OPEC member to defect, in turn lowering the market cost of a barrel of oil, but increasing the amount of capital flowing into their coffers. Overproduction is reportedly the strategy taken by the Gulf, as Texas and Canadian fracking have increased global supply.[37]

By increasing production and lowering the price, Gulf states temporarily suppressed oil production in East Texas and elsewhere, where the cost of production per barrel is higher than it is in the Arabian Peninsula. This strategy was unsuccessful in the long run, in part because oil is always localized, where manufacturing requires substantial human and technical capital that can be either built upon or undermined. You can't permanently steal oil production, but you can capture and transfer manufacturing capacity.

If jobs at the steel mill disappear, so will the skills, communities, and equipment that the mill required. This dynamic is

---

[37] The Economist. Saudi America: The economics of shale oil. 14 February 2014.

even more pivotal in fields like semiconductors, which require substantial human capital to design, produce, and distribute.

Both the classical free trade model and the geoeconomic model capture realities about international trade and commerce. Trade agreements between nations who trust each other can lean more Ricardian, trade between countries without trust must naturally lean more adversarial. It is when there is an imbalance or deceit that significant policy frictions and trade wars arise. It is this disjunct that is behind the current trade imbalance between the US and the PRC, with the PRC embracing a long-term geoeconomic strategy while the US embraced policies focused on free trade.

US consumers benefited from incredibly cheap consumer goods, and Chinese manufacturers benefited by acquiring much of the world's productive capacity for electronics and other high value-added products. The realization of these fundamental facts is at the root of the trade war between the two countries.

Populism and Upheaval as an Effect of Geoeconomic Policy Failure

Geoeconomics is not merely a government-to-government relationship. It directly involves the peoples and economies involved competing with each other to create and capture economic value. Because the US is a relatively open democracy and has the benefit of the dollar's position as the global reserve currency, American consumers have effectively allowed themselves to be bought off with artificially cheap goods. This purchasing power is subsidized by debt spending and entitlements, as the most economically valuable jobs have evaporated.

As we covered in the previous chapter, a natural reaction to the economic displacement in the current order has been populism. As the average citizen's security and relative income have decreased, local wealth inequality has massively increased as money flowed into assets through quantitative easing and currency debasement.

In democracies, this is increasingly unsustainable spending by the government to buy off and pacify a population that is naturally sensitive about the demise of their livelihood. Competition for control of fiscal policy (government spending) has led to gross division and the politicization of the economy, reducing human freedom in the long run. Wealth redistribution and taxation are increasing in popularity as a result.

This drift is especially critical, as populist policies make the very production required to survive geoeconomic competition less viable. High taxation and redistribution are flatly adversarial to business and investment. In such a "death spiral" scenario, taxes are raised to support more unproductive consumption, and citizens become more reliant on government. Private enterprises that cannot be profitable elect to move operations and profits abroad.

Capital flight has already happened to a degree. Several tech companies domicile their US dollar profits outside of the country because they face tax penalties in repatriating them. The transaction from an Uber ride in Seattle flows through several tax havens outside the United States, even though it is an American company operating in America.

Many companies have moved their manufacturing infrastructure outside of their home countries because of hostile regulation designed to protect incumbent industries, many of whom achieved that position through lobbying for laws that bar new market entrants through cost. This feudal capture of the economy has created a self-perpetuating cycle in many industries, as victims of hostile regulation and taxation of advanced economies have moved to more accommodating shores.

Over the long run, special interest-driven stagnation will affect the value of the dollar as the global reserve currency. Eventually, currencies with sound monetary rules will not need an overplentiful dollar to serve as an intermediary in international trade.

In this scenario, the trillions of U.S. dollars held abroad have nowhere to go but back home, potentially resulting in hyperinflation as the glut of new money pursues a diminished pool of goods in a significantly smaller economic orbit.

This collapse is the ideal strategic state for the West's rivals, who are exploring digital currency in tandem with more traditional economic policies to unseat the dollar and Euro and to pivot the world back to competing spheres of influence. What is critical is that state use of blockchains provides a means to lock out competitors. Just as blockchain makes digital goods atomic, it provides a source of immutable authority for transactions and smart contracts. States and large corporations are naturally interested in doing just this, locking down their financial systems and networks of commerce.

There is a better edge to this double-edged sword. Blockchain is also a means of defending against the very predations that have occurred and will benefit a first mover who adopts a national strategy whose focus is on fixing cybersecurity threats and increasing the reciprocity of trade. Instead of reams of paper and conditions that get progressively circumvented, states could plan their geopolitical engagement with the world through a blockchain-powered trade dashboard that makes all exchanges visible and enables a more programmatic approach to trade. Such an "Eye of Sauron" approach has several advantages, in that contracts and commerce could be directly built and attributed.

Imagine a smart contract that ties trade to withdrawing a hostile currency peg, and proportionally links tariffs on goods to the economic policies of the country seeking to do the exporting. Just as there is an Internet of Things, there could be a national policy of things, where the policymakers use asymmetric leverage across domains.

Better yet and far more likely, embracing blockchain to protect intellectual property and pivot the internet away from its present-day insecurity will help rebalance an order that is currently predominated by an attack, hacking, and IP theft. By embracing encryption, rather than fearing it, economies will be able to protect their intellectual property and productive capacity from hostile threats, both from competitors and nation-states. Violations in IP could result in sanctions and barring that stolen product from the market, encouraging greater respect and reciprocity among nations whose incentive to trade in good faith is increased by the consequences of trading in bad faith.

Reciprocity extends to monetary policy. Though beggar-thy-neighbor approaches to devaluation do work at the international level, long-term devaluation hurts the local population's consumption and exacerbates income inequality, increasing populist sentiment in democracies. A return to sound money or at least an embrace of sound assets on a state's balance sheet may be a critical strategy in the geoeconomic competition of the future.

There are two basic approaches to this, which we have alluded to elsewhere: the National Digital Asset and national purchases of decentralized cryptocurrencies. In the first case, countries issue cryptocurrency of their own as an analog for gold and a means of settlement. In the second scenario, central banks purchase of pre-existing (and more credible) digital assets with the understanding that those assets will act as a store of value, again as an analog for gold.

Efforts to Replace the Dollar and the Global Banking Order

Russia and China, as geopolitical rivals of the United States, both have logical strategic reasons to replace the dollar over the long term in favor of a more balkanized international financial system. That said, both countries are too large and too prominent in the global order to endure the risks of sudden monetary movement, especially when employing an element of surprise in making fundamental changes to their financial systems.

For this reason, the more *avant-garde* approaches have been taken by smaller authoritarian states who also suffer from in the US-led global order, but are in positions of crisis enough to have the incentive to experiment with new forms of currency. Chief among these is Venezuela, which has attempted the issuance of a digital currency fictitiously tied to the country's oil reserves with the Petromoneda project.

While Venezuela failed to successfully roll out such a massive monetary product due to the Maduro regime's unblushing incompetence, the project itself began with Russian and Chinese involvement. Both government's interest stems from a credible strategic interest in replacing the U.S. dollar as the global reserve currency. In Venezuela's case, intentions appear to orbit the issuance of a digital currency allowing the Maduro regime to transact outside of the existing banking order, circumventing U.S. sanctions.

Further, the Venezuelan Socialist government's efforts to tax cryptocurrency transactions while providing a less sound public coin echo the paradox of corrupt states trying to have it both ways. The Venezuelan government is simultaneously confiscating sound currency and Bitcoin mining rigs while attempting to force the public onto a centralized, technically unsound system controlled by the same people.

Iran has recently indicated an interest in a similar approach. As we write this, the Iranian regime is openly exploring the issuance of a "crypto rial" with the same ends and grievances, focused on replacing the U.S. dollar as a medium of exchange and settlement. The Iranian approach also echoes the Venezuelan effort to decriminalize and then seize citizen's decentralized currencies.

Both the Petro and the Crypto Rial embody efforts to replace the dollar as a means of international settlement. Both projects are getting examined quietly by more significant players with more considerable technical expertise and interest in issuing a new reserve currency outside of the Western-dominated global order. This observation draws on clear public statements made by policymakers in Russia and China, and we believe the next wave of innovation will occur around the future sovereign debt crises of the 2020s and 2030s, which we detailed in the last chapter.

These new digital currencies will be put forward as an alternative to dollars and euros that are facing severe inflation, as Western governments attempt to print away their critical debt loads. It is also rational to infer that rival sovereigns want to beat both the US dollar hegemony and counter the freedom offered by Bitcoin and other decentralized UTXO blockchains. This strategy could involve endorsing a statist digital currency while attempting to seize, punish, or at bare minimum tax into submission those who use real cryptocurrencies.

Sovereign Cryptocurrency and Global Economic Competition

Nothing defines the post-Cold War world better than economic competition and development. Many in the early days of this era had utopian visions, exemplified by Thomas Friedman's "The World is Flat" and Francis Fukuyama's "The End of History and the Last Man." In both books, these thought leaders assessed that democracy and capitalism had won the global ideological race with communism, feudalism, and every other ideology of governance.

9/11, the 2008 financial crisis, the Euro Crisis, the rising geopolitical competition between Russia and the United States, and Europe, as well as economic competition between the U.S. and China and the political collapse of the Middle East, have led most cosmopolitan optimists to recant. Some academics and political figures refuse to accept that cosmopolitan globalism has failed to achieve its promises, and cling to the ideology as a moral and not a realistic political issue.

Worse, the West has become politically divided to the point that it is difficult to unify around shared goals and a vision for the future. Many working in government today feel as though they are under siege. Even though the world has enjoyed a period of protracted peace, sovereign states are competing from all angles to try and sustain their functions at a domestic and international level, and many of those functions are becoming antiquated with advancing technology and straining monetary systems.

Above, we discussed how states embracing blockchain over the next two decades would underwrite security and administration, two of their core sovereign functions. The third contest over money and finance. Economic dominance is the holy grail in this new era of post-Cold War competition. Geoeconomics is also the domain that the West's geopolitical and economic rivals are well on their way to reinventing in hopes of overthrowing the existing American-led international order.

Why are we discussing sovereign states issuing their cryptocurrencies? For the simple fact that neither is going to disappear. The unstoppable force and immovable object will need to come to terms with each other. Even more importantly, just like advanced AI, there is no avoiding this eventuality. If things don't develop as we would necessarily imagine or hope, we must undertake the intellectual exercise of examining what courses the future may hold.

States are already beginning to embrace blockchain and cryptocurrency, and eventually, a government will see the benefits of being the first to undertake endeavors in the examples we cited above. Government policies may include accepting crypto as a means of payment for taxes, purchasing digital assets for federal pensions, or issuing a nationwide digital currency. It also could encompass using blockchains to exert influence, and tax, monitor, and secure domestic and international trade.

These efforts will likely occur in tandem with the cybersecurity regulatory measures outlined above. There considerable cybersecurity effects to running a national blockchain, which we've described elsewhere in this chapter and book. There are also financial upsides and an intellectual legacy in most Western countries, which have at least historically been accepting of multiple forms of currency. As we mentioned above, the debt-based fiat system naturally generates progressive magnitudes of debt and worsening inflation.

Fiat has a middling track record stimulating economic growth in the short run, as young fiat systems make everyone race to be more productive than the "risk-free rate of return" provided by government bonds. It is misleading to presume that this is the indefinite status quo. As we've covered, fiat contains the seeds of its demise, as the system encourages governments to rack up substantial fiscal expenditures to buy off their populations while pushing those debts onto future generations.

Satoshi ostensibly created Bitcoin as an alternative to fiat and said as much in the genesis block by forever linking the currency to bank failures in the 2008 Financial Crisis. The fact of the matter is that these crises are not going away - they are a feature and not a bug of state-backed fiat systems, and states compete with each other for capital and economic growth in these money markets.

A nation can print as much money as it wants, but that doesn't mean that it will create value - money is just a medium for the rest of the economy to transmit and ideally store value. Servicing the interest on sovereign debts is an ever-increasing challenge for governments, and will be much more so into the 2020s, and 2030's as debt payments outstrip public defense and entitlement programs.

It stands to reason that sovereign nations will see the benefit of embracing forms of sound money. The Euro Crisis, in part attributable to unproductive levels of sovereign spending and debt, as well as the 22 trillion dollars of American sovereign debt, are not merely going to "go away" at the snap of anyone's fingers. To quote the University of Chicago economist Herbert Stein, "What can't go on forever, won't."

It is a rational inference that if the existing monetary system is showing its age, then states will begin to experiment with new forms of money. Bear in mind, there was a time when paper money was new, too, and it is not historically unusual for states to have more than one currency. In the not-too-distant past known as 'bimetallism.' The United States and others operated with both a gold and a silver currency, including a notional scale at which gold could get exchanged for silver, and vice versa.

Bimetallism was actually ensconced in Article I, Section 8, Clause 5, the Constitution delegates to Congress the power *"To coin Money, regulate the Value thereof, and of foreign Coin"*, as well as Article I, Section 10, Clause 1, which imposes upon the States the duty not to *"make any Thing but gold and silver Coin a Tender in Payment of Debts."*

At the time, Alexander Hamilton proposed a 15-to-1 ratio between silver and gold. Only with the Coinage Act of 1873 did the United States abandon bimetallism for a single standard - the Gold Standard - which lasted until the Nixon Shock of 1973 and the US Dollar becoming a free-floating fiat currency. Americans who are resistant to the idea that the United States will eventually find it useful to issue a cryptocurrency are ignoring 200 years of the nation's history in exchange for the last 45.

We mentioned Gresham's Law above, which describes the tendency of lousy money to chase out good. Gresham's law already applies to the crypto market - people are more reluctant to spend cryptocurrency than fiat. Other scholars have argued that bimetallism can be a stable form of currency insofar as the two currencies are allowed to float relative to each other instead of operating at an artificial peg. Fiat floats and is inflationary; floating for a credible nation-state backed digital asset may result in a rapid bubble but would find a point of equilibrium over the long term as the new currency finds goes through the process of price discovery.

A future hybrid Fiat/Crypto model would not necessarily that of 'postmodern bimetallism.' States may elect to embrace sound money, or they may have a blockchain-issued representation of their inflationary currency in the form of an official stablecoin. While there could be arguments for such a system for a tracking perspective and it could ride on a real blockchain, we think that this model is a bit superfluous.

Since there is limited monetary upside for those who use such a system, it is far more likely to be an implement of surveillance. A hidden upside, though, is that such a system may decrease the friction of moving money and diminish rent-seeking behavior in the banking system.

Pragmatically speaking, if you have more money in the bank than you have in paper cash in your wallet, your money is already digital. Gold is not an excellent medium of exchange precisely because it is physical, hard to precisely divide, and expensive by volume. It would be ridiculous to buy a cup of coffee in gold flakes, and historically people used silver or gold-backed notes as a more flexible medium to represent smaller quantities of gold. Crypto is already digital, can be divided to a micro fraction of a cent, is universally auditable in its pure form, and obviates the need for complex systems of banking to support a transaction.

Is the advent of a credible state-backed cryptocurrency a threat to those states' fiat systems? Yes and no. The motive for current experiments in sovereign cryptocurrencies tends to be adversarial to the dollar-denominated global order, though that will not be the case indefinitely. The competitive nature of the international financial economy, as well as the dynamics that happen within states, creates a strategic incentive for countries to remodel their monetary systems. Motives can be domestic or geopolitical because, at the financial level, there is not much distinction.

Such an approach could likely involve a large pre-mine as a national reserve; rather than the inflationary dynamics of a central bank and traditional fiat currency, which is used to stimulate exchange and growth. States will probably treat the deflationary mechanics of digital assets as a piggy bank and national reserve.

If the system is credible enough, states may even be able to sell and trade assets within this zero-sum reserve to fund public works projects and pay off debts, stimulating the economy and improving the sustainability of the nation. Rather than having to buy and store a gold reserve in fiat currency, states may find it more efficient to support a resilient blockchain and issue their digital gold.

This method also has a credibility curve, not unlike fiat. Nations like Venezuela will continue to lack the credibility for capital to flow into their coffers, and their attempts at a national cryptocurrency will probably be stillborn for lack of demand, at least as they get executed now. Nations with established governments, working systems of law, and a non-Marxian conception of the future will fare better because they can conceive of the responsibility they have to provide for the long-term economic health of their nation.

As governments become comfortable with cryptocurrency and come to recognize that the technology is not going to disappear or go to zero, the next logical step is for states to try to win the race to establish their own. From a political perspective, this is not without motive. Such a blockchain would cease to be anonymous but could be used globally for payment and exchange. We can't imagine the government issuing an asset that it can't tax.

There is a high likelihood that state-backed digital assets would be used either for taxation (in democratic countries) or to control the finances of the elite who have been cleared to transact in this currency. Some core paradoxes will not go away.

Regardless of how profound a technology like a cryptocurrency, AI, or nuclear power is, the technology by itself is amoral. The morality of its outcomes depends entirely on how it gets used, and to this effect, cryptocurrency could play a part in a dystopian future just as easily as a utopian or pragmatic one. Americans and other westerners are often blithely ignorant of how taxation and national security get organized in other countries, especially undemocratic ones. It would be profoundly naive to ignore this as a possible motive in states that are now experimenting with state and corporate-issued cryptocurrency.

Just as Mao used his equivalent of the Secret Service to monitor political rivals while being their "bodyguards," so too would a national cryptocurrency become an instrument of party power.[38] This motive is precisely the People's Bank of China's current purpose in issuing a national digital currency - to enable the state to monitor transactions and make it that much harder to hide or move money without the approval of the central state authority.

There should be no surprise to anyone familiar with the evolution of the People's Republic of China's technical state. Money in non-democratic countries is a means of control, and states can just as easily repurpose technology to do things that are antithetical to its original purpose, including locking people, foreign companies, or even political competitors out of the economy.

Similarly, the Communist government of Cuba has a dual model with fiat. The incredibly weak Cuban Peso, which everyday goods' prices get pegged to, is used domestically. The "Cuban Convertible Peso" (initially pegged to the Russian Ruble) gets used for trade outside of Cuba. In effect, this walls off Cuba's domestic population from the wealth brought in by naive Western tourists and confines that wealth to the ruling class.

Readers in democratic countries should get over the notion that non-democratic countries will play fair in financial economics, especially with their populations. As UTXO purists who believe in

---

[38] Xhuezhi Guo. China's Security State: Philosophy, Evolution, and Politics. Cambridge University Press, 2012. Pp. 106-137

the power of decentralized blockchains, we could elect to gloss over this possibility for fear of "seeding the idea," but the fact of the matter is that this already appears to be a logical goal of some existing experimentation in sovereign cryptocurrency.

Centralized sovereign digital currencies should get recognized for what they are: an attempt at greater surveillance and manipulation. That said, sovereigns do not get confined to using centralized models; they could as quickly embrace decentralized assets that are publicly trusted, and capture the upside from doing so.

If open-source technology like blockchain is available, it is only a matter of time before governments recognize its utility and turn it to their advantage, for good or evil. The personal desires, mores, and predilections of any individual state or civilization do not matter when there is an ongoing contest for advantage, and in this contest, the software is open-source, not classified like the nuclear bomb, advanced AI, or stealth technology.

National Crypto Reserves as a Strategic Financial Maneuver

The logic is clear. If Bitcoin and other true UTXO cryptos are understood by states and central banks to be stores of value, it makes strategic sense for countries and central banks to purchase them as an on-balance sheet reserve and a hedge against their policies.

Nation-states are not subject to insider trading rules. They can do what they want and can hold Bitcoin and other currencies, exchanging them much as they trade different currencies and gold on the open market. This investment can be made by central banks, by sovereign wealth funds, or any number of actors with the capital to pursue it.

This strategy works best for decentralized cryptos that are globally distributed and available for the world to access. For centralized projects operating on a Privately Issued Scrip model, the value proposition for state purchase is not there, as no party has a logical reason to trust the software company involved, especially if they are outside of their sphere of influence.

No state other than China has cause to buy a Chinese digital asset operating on a private ledger inside China. Conversely, a globally minable UTXO could be a store of value in multiple countries, significantly increasing its value to governments as an on-balance sheet asset and as a medium of exchange.

The first mover in this strategy will have a natural advantage, as they will be buying Bitcoin and other cryptocurrencies as cheaply as it will ever get offered again. The natural scarcity involved means this may be a sound method for a state's banking institutions to profit, vastly expanding their hard currency reserves and allowing for a new medium of exchange between countries, not unlike settlement in gold. Better yet, states using fiat currencies could print money to buy Bitcoin, turning unbacked paper into sound money. While not necessarily ethical, it's not a wrong strategic move.

This move is not a certainty, but the strategic logic for large institutions to embrace Bitcoin and other assets is airtight should they chose to pursue it. Even though gold has historically been the source of scarcity in currency, a truly decentralized UTXO cryptocurrency embodies scarcity even better than gold. It is available to acquire and store absolutely, where gold has much more demanding storage requirements and cannot get relocated in a time of crisis.

Instead of a multimillion-dollar vault and guards (sometimes outside of their country and difficult to liquidate in times of crisis), all a state needs is a cold storage wallet and parties willing to buy and transfer crypto, which no other sovereign state can ultimately stop. If crypto is more sound than gold by greater availability and greater scarcity, it may even push the value of existing gold reserves down as a substitute should such a pivot occur.

There are, of course, natural limitations to the execution of a crypto reserve policy. States will have to reach some consensus of just what cryptocurrencies are worthy of inclusion in their portfolio.

Despite the messianic tone of some Bitcoin Maximalists, there are several good reasons for this not to be Bitcoin. Beyond Bitcoin's technical limitations, there is also the problem of distribution.

States will naturally debate why they are enriching and empowering those who held the currency initially. American policymakers will ask why the US Treasury or Federal Reserve is enriching the Chinese Bitcoin billionaires like Li Xiaolai or Zhou Dong, who hold large chunks of Bitcoin's supply.

Otherwise, the economy will fracture among states and banks' various forks, as well as the nations who invest in private ledgers and proof of stake models that cannot be trusted any more than their issuers can. Because of the vast number available and the valuation mechanics involved, it would be better for states to hold the same cryptos, rather than different ones, but this is a prisoner's dilemma.

Worse, trust in a currency, even if it is decentralized, may suffer if a single state is known to hold too dominant a position in it, such that it would be cheaper for rival states to purchase a competing cryptocurrency. For this reason, we believe it makes strategic sense (in the hypothetical) for coordinated purchases and systems between states, such that aligned countries would share a decentralized cryptocurrency that is multinational and not controlled by a central bank.

This strategy also includes a technical paradox. States doing the due diligence will need to validate the technical characteristics of the UTXO chains they adopt, especially when it comes to the algorithms involved mining. It is a logical inference that purchasers would have a natural interest in cryptos that are ASIC and quantum-resistant, open-source, and have robust mining characteristics.

The ability to hack or whipsaw a blockchain with mining pressure could impact another state's holdings and liquidity, gutting the nation's reserves. In the present setting, if the PRC could dominate an ASIC-minable chain (such as Bitcoin), countries purchasing that asset could be beholden to PRC pressure and coordinated action at the domestic level. While trust is still building in blockchain, some blockchains are more robust than others, and this can be roughly modeled based on the assumptions involved in the chain and its record of behavior over time.

IV. Protecting Economic Capacity: Countering Economic Espionage

As we've covered in this book, the internet evolved as an insecure forum, whose insecurity is leveraged by large companies and nations to support their commercial and political ends. The TCP/IP protocol model used today remains fundamentally insecure, and most existing internet business empires operate by using highly centralized technology and services that leverage the internet's lack of security to track users and monetize their data.

This fundamental insecurity extends to espionage - as Bruce Schneier has noted in multiple books, at the geopolitical level, all actors seem to be focused on the attack while living in glass houses. The current architecture supports significant hacking and gross violations of privacy, as well as the wholesale theft of data, mainly by competitors to the US, who have found efficiencies in investing in espionage rather than investing in conducting their R&D.

Supply chain attacks on critical hardware manufactured abroad are an example of the successful economic capture of productive capacity. The latest case of Chinese government insertions of chips into servers used by Apple and Google - which broke as we were writing this chapter - should come as no surprise to readers.

The "Big Hack" represents a massive breach that leverages the insecurities built into the existing internet and supply chain. The same goes for the (again Chinese) hack of Facebook accounts and user passwords, which broke the month before the chip scandal and involved the theft of more than 50 million user's data.[39]

This effort is simultaneously political and economic. As Elizabeth Economy and Michael Levi point out in *By All Means Necessary: How China's Resource Quest is Changing the World*,

---

[39] Jordan Robertson and Michael Riley. *The Big Hack: How China Used a Tiny Chip to Infiltrate America's Top Companies*. Bloomberg Businessweek, October 2018.
https://www.bloomberg.com/news/features/2018-10-04/the-big-hack-how-china-used-a-tiny-chip-to-infiltrate-america-s-top-companies

global hacking statistics against governments and corporations drop *precipitously* during Chinese government holidays. There is even a smaller but still measurable dip during Beijing's lunchtime on workdays.

According to the Washington Post, in June 2018 example, China stole an immense amount of highly sensitive military data. This theft included: "614 gigabytes of material relating to a closely held project known as Sea Dragon, as well as signals and sensor data, submarine radio room information relating to cryptographic systems, and the Navy submarine development unit's electronic warfare library."[40]

In his recent book, *Dawn of the Code War: America's Battle Against Russia, China, and the Rising Global Cyber Threat*, former U.S. Department of Justice Prosecutor and Chief of the National Security Division (NSD) John P. Carlin substantiate this point. Chinese and other state actors have been so successful in stealing American and European technology and selling it back to us that they have "entirely given up on trying even to conceal it." according to Carlin.

In an interview with Benjamin Wittes of the Brookings Institute, Carlin cited former FBI Director Comey's quip to Congress that "Chinese economic espionage is like a noisy gorilla rummaging around your house." Brazen is too polite a word - nation-state backed hackers in China don't even feel the need to cover up their activities.

China's industrial IP theft can get directly tied to the PRC's massive geoeconomic effort to seize productive capacity. In his book, Carlin also cites former NSA Director Keith Alexander and ODNI Chief Dennis C. Blair's calculation that Chinese IP theft represents "the greatest illicit transfer of wealth in human history."

---

[40] Ellen Nakashima and Paul Sonne. *China Hacked a Navy Contractor and Secured a Trove of Highly Sensitive Data on Submarine Warfare.* Washington Post, 8 June 2018. Available at https://www.washingtonpost.com/world/national-security/china-hacked-a-navy-contractor-and-secured-a-trove-of-highly-sensitive-data-on-submarine-warfare/2018/06/08/

Damages from IP theft range as high as 600 Billion U.S. Dollars per year by Blair's estimate.[41]

This statement represents the nation's chief cybersecurity official's understanding of the current operating environment, and it provides a concise diagnosis of the problem at hand. We recommend you read it in full at your convenience, but because it is such a helpful object lesson, we have included excerpts here as a vignette to address how blockchain would specifically aid in confronting this massive challenge:

> "Chinese companies, with the encouragement of official Chinese policy and often the active participation of government personnel, have been pillaging the intellectual property of American companies. Altogether, intellectual-property theft costs America up to $600 billion a year, the greatest transfer of wealth in history. China accounts for most of that loss.
>
> Intellectual-property theft covers a wide spectrum: counterfeiting American fashion designs, pirating movies and video games, patent infringement, and stealing proprietary technology and software. This assault saps economic growth, costs Americans jobs, weakens our military capability, and undercuts a key American competitive advantage — innovation."

Chinese companies have stolen trade secrets from virtually every sector of the American economy: automobiles, auto tires, aviation, chemicals, consumer electronics, electronic trading, industrial software, biotech, and pharmaceuticals. Last year U.S. Steel accused Chinese hackers of stealing trade secrets related to the production of lightweight steel, then turning them over to Chinese steelmakers.

---

[41] Dennis C. Blair and Keith Alexander. *China's Intellectual Property Theft Must Stop.* New York Times Op-Ed, 15 August 2017. Available at https://www.nytimes.com/2017/08/15/opinion/china-us-intellectual-property-trump.html

We've already discussed how copyrights and digital goods like music and entertainment can be protected on a blockchain to make these goods atomic again at a domestic level. While this doesn't stop someone from videotaping a movie in the theatre and sharing that file, it does provide a means to cryptographically lock media such that only those who pay can consume it, either by renting or by buying.

Regarding proprietary technology and software, the same approach can get made. If technology is vulnerable, it should be encrypted. Better yet, it should get integrated into a permissioned environment where its export is barred by cryptographic locks limiting what devices and circumstances it can run on, or how many instances it can have at any one time.

The same goes for the core code - if calling a blockchain for its rights to operate is intrinsic to the function of an application, then stealing it would at a bare minimum require the added work of retooling it for another blockchain.

This idea isn't that far-fetched an example. In 2011, American Superconductor discovered requests for software updates delivered to its servers were coming from Chinese windmills not manufactured by the company. The Chinese firm had stolen the company's design and software to such a tee that the code still called back to the company's servers for software updates.

Worse yet, the Chinese competitor (SINOVEL) employed classical espionage techniques, offering an insider at American Superconductor large sums of cash ($1.7m) an apartment in Beijing, and access to prostitutes to compromise the company's intellectual property. Losses to the firm are estimated at greater than $800 million in revenue and over a billion in corporate market value.[42]

---

[42] *Chinese firm payed insider 'to kill my company,' American CEO says.* NBC News, 6 August 2013. Available at https://www.nbcnews.com/news/world/chinese-firm-paid-insider-kill-my-company-american-ceo-says-flna6C10858966

To quote American Superconductor CEO Daniel McGahn, "They were out to kill my company... We thought we were playing by the Chinese rules. We didn't anticipate outright theft as part of their business model." Notably, the espionage tactics (bribes) that SINOVEL paid were explicitly used to get an unencrypted copy of American Superconductor's core code, which had been centralized and was easy to duplicate with such an insider.

Blockchain and Strong Encryption as the Answer to Protect Critical IP

As we've made the case above, in an environment where IP matters, protection, and encryption matter. The present national strategy of the United States as we write this is to pursue tariffs against nations that succeed through brazen theft. This strategy hits the economy generally and occasionally fails to be nimble or proportional, especially in complex supply chains where several different systems need to interact at once.

Tariffs are still far better than free trade policies with a competitor who brazenly cheats, but their sweeping nature is still unwieldy. There are two solutions to trade wars that the blockchain could be used to pursue.

First and foremost, the representation and timestamping of an invention on a public blockchain can be used to prove who innovated first, and makes the IP contest more than a matter of "he said, she said." If a nation or company deliberately violates IP by stealing it and selling it back to the country that hosted that innovation, the aggrieved party should be able to identify the corporation or persons involved for specific retaliation.

If a corporation or product deliberately violates international norms, its theft can be recognized on the blockchain, too, and the smart trade systems of the future can embrace a new form of reciprocity where that specific innovation is challenging to sell outside of the nation producing the knock-off.

Second, and more importantly, blockchain can enable the distribution of strong cryptography to prevent intellectual property theft and exfiltration in the first place. Countries already use encryption for national defense, but often the most critical files are easy to export because they have not gotten adequately protected. Nowhere is this more evident in the defense industry, where the plans to most major U.S. Military systems have gotten stolen. To quote the diagnosis of Alexander and Blair;

> "Perhaps most concerning, China has targeted the American defense industrial base. Chinese spies have gone after private defense contractors and subcontractors, national laboratories, public research universities, think tanks, and the American government itself. Chinese agents have gone after the United States' most significant weapons, such as the F-35 Lightning, the Aegis Combat System, and the Patriot missile system; illegally exported unmanned underwater vehicles and thermal-imaging cameras; and stolen documents related to the B-52 bomber, the Delta IV rocket, the F-15 fighter and even the Space Shuttle."

Carlin echoes Alexander and Blair's point in *Dawn of the Code War*: the technologies that are getting stolen from the West, day in and day out, are the very technologies that could be used to kill our service members in the event of a conflict.

From an economic perspective, this theft is also impoverishing the American Middle Class, robbing the nation of the value it creates in harboring innovation and production.

> "For decades, successive American administrations have concluded that some level of exposure to China's depredations against our intellectual property is simply the cost of doing business with the world's now second-largest economy. This is not acceptable. Although China is an important trading partner with the United States, it is imperative to establish a fair and level trading environment.
>
> Driving down intellectual-property theft by China and other countries is vital for America's economic well-being and national security. We urge American companies, as well as our allies abroad, who share these interests, to work with the administration through this process.

> *The government should lead in this effort, but it can't go it alone. A broad, sustained campaign bringing together the government, the private sector and our allies is the only way to halt this hemorrhaging of America's economic lifeblood."*

It is difficult to overstate the importance that a new architecture for security will have for the government and the private sector. Today the internet is being used for wide-scale exfiltration of proprietary data from the very nations the built the internet. Blockchain offers an opportunity to begin to restore order to what has been the most significant driving force in civilization for the last 20 years, and begin to protect the livelihoods of democracies and capitalist economies over nations who do not adhere to the rules and norms of international trade.

V. Blockchain and the Battle for Sovereignty

Sovereign Internets and the Balkanization of the World Wide Web

Today, the internet is the lifeblood for the exchange of information and commerce, but many Westerners fail to understand just how separated and balkanized; the internet has become over the last twenty years. This balkanization is both at a surface level, with major tech companies trying to box out competitors to dominate the internet, as well as at an international level, with nation-states working to exert control over the use of the internet within their own country and sometimes well beyond their borders.

Just as the modern-day internet has become dominated by a few giants in every major country, the global internet will continue to be increasingly dominated and walled off by states who can resort to force to seize and protect the internet within their borders from foreign companies.

From a sovereign perspective, this is best embodied by "The Great Firewall of China" and Russia's "Red Web," though it extends to most non-Western nations who exert control over what services and content can be connected to by their citizens. This control is both a matter of espionage and concern of social control. Since the internet is a searchable connection to the world that can get attributed to the end-user, it plays a critical role in domestic governance for several non-Western powers.

These powers have rejected Western companies, not Western technology, building local clones that are beholden to their restrictions and censorship laws. VPNs and other tools are sometimes available, but vast swaths of the populace go without questioning or being able to challenge the information they have access to inside their own country. In China, this means that questions about Tibet or the Tiananmen Square protest of 1989 are undiscoverable.

In Russia, that means all national web traffic flows through a SORM box for surveillance purposes. When people try to talk around an issue with coded language, centralized censors have the power to recognize and edit that, as the Chinese government did when portly Premier Xi Jinping was referred to in code as "Winnie the Poo" on China's Weibo, a domestic Twitter clone.

Google's nascent expansion into the Middle Kingdom in the early 2000s failed, with state-backed and private local competitors soaking up much of China's market. Some of these competitors went so far as to run identical "Google" branded services on different servers.

The same applies to Russia, where Western firms seeking to expand into Russian markets get coerced with demands by the Russian Federation to domicile all data available within the Fatherland and make it available to the state for surveillance and censorship purposes. While Google still has a ".ru" service, it has lost significant market share to Yandex, a Russian internal search engine that fully complies with Russian censorship and surveillance law, and offers many services analogous to those provided by Google.

Weibo, Yandex, and others represent the insulation of the Chinese and Russian internets and economies from outside influence and competition. They are direct exercises of sovereignty by those nations in excluding Western companies, products, and ideas from their marketplaces. These domestic competitors often get cloned from working American and European business ideas but are used to reinforce the control of the respective states that host them.

This repurposing of business models represents a balkanization of the internet, dividing the world's information highway up into fiefdoms captured by local elites that seek to dictate how money and information flow into and out of their countries. In the anarchy of international affairs, nation-states will always opt for their domestic tech giants over those of their rivals.

The process of internet and commercial balkanization does not just get confined to the usual suspects. The European Union's "General Data Protection Regulation" (GDPR), which is well-intentioned but written based on technical standards from the mid-1990s, represents an attempt by a meta-state to govern the internet in a way that transcends individual states.

One can infer from the EU's pursuit of American Web 2.0 data giants like Google and Facebook that the intentions of the law are similar. One might conclude the EU seeks to punish companies from outside its sovereign orbit, and potentially exercise sovereignty over the internet, much as Russia and China already have done.

This trend is an embodiment of geoeconomics in a world that relies on the internet. Not only are states subverting an open web for censorship and surveillance, but they are also pursuing domestic regulation to attempt to limit the influence and tech wealth that goes to companies outside of their borders. Some companies, such as Google, have tried to adapt to this by developing sovereign-compliant products.

In Google's case, this is rumored to have been the "Dragonfly" browser project, which Google reportedly designed for a Chinese market that demanded government access and censorship. While companies are free to pursue this strategy, they still have no recourse when sovereigns support the progressive theft of their technology and kick them out once a domestic competitor is in a position to gain market share.

With the progressive drift to a less open internet that is divvied up among states and large corporations, we believe that blockchain will have geoeconomic impacts in the three-front battle between censorious sovereigns, large corporations, and individual users. From our perspective, the shift from a top-down Web 2.0, which fits naturally into states and large corporation's competition towards a decentralized and resilient Web 3.0, should be a more important focus for policymakers and cybersecurity professionals.

The Web 2.0 competition for sovereignty over the domestic internet naturally extends to independence (or at least influence) over other user's experience of the internet. By adopting robust encryption and more resilient, decentralized systems, nations, companies, and individuals can become more resistant to outside influence, including having their data and intellectual property stolen, compromised, damaged, or halted.

Web 2.0 gave us sovereign internets, where each state and company sought to leverage the insecurity of the internet to make massive, top-down empires where they have complete legibility of their citizen's use of the internet. To paraphrase Schneiner, Web 2.0 has been fundamentally an attack-inclined architecture. Governments and corporations live in 'glass houses' with potent cyber weapons but have held off on using those weapons based on the mutually assured destruction that would occur in any conflagration.

Web 3.0 provides defensive tools that we believe states will adopt in line with their geoeconomic policies. It's important not to get wrapped around the axle here - the U.S., China, Russia, the E.U., and the broader world all have slightly different approaches to the internet.

Ultimately, we believe Web 3.0 will be as vast a break from the present paradigm as Web 2.0 was from the original. It is difficult to make predictions of just how it will play out at the national level, but it's a genuine possibility that we will see the world fork into fundamentally different internets. To continue the balkanization metaphor, this is the equivalent of a Web 2.0 Yugoslavia becoming a Web 3.0 Croatia, Serbia, Bosnia & Herzegovina, Montenegro, and

Kosovo, with different technical makeups, different rules, and different interoperability for people and companies from each smaller fiefdom.

More bluntly, two core models will emerge autarchic sovereign internets and decentralized self-sovereign internets. From a currency perspective, this is the difference between a nationally issued coin that runs on a state or bank-operated ledger and a UTXO coin that runs on a globally decentralized and unkillable network. From a technical perspective, this strategy involves nationalized encryption and top-down power (as exemplified by the Great Firewall of China), where encryption is used in commercial terms to lock 3rd party states into permanent dependency and vassalization.

Imagine being a Southeast Asian government and not being able to control a Chinese-installed and financed dam that provides a third of your country's power and could flood an urban center when compromised.

The second model is a distributed, open, individualist (vice *statist* or *corporatist*) model with substantial property rights that extend to the user's data, identity, and freedom of association. We call this concept *Blockchain Democracy*, and it is the topic of our next chapter. The opposite of Blockchain Democracy is a concept we call *Blockchain Tyranny,* where the principles of the technology are leveraged by large states and corporations, in tandem with AI, internet of things, and a "sovereign internet" approach to claim top-down power.

In effect, this is a contest between three parties in play: states, companies, and individuals. Because blockchain is a way of representing identity and property rights, each will pursue uses of the blockchain to their ends, in a way that empowers them vis-a-vis the other two parties. Naturally, there are three approaches to Web 3.0; statism, corporatism, and individualism.

Statism: One Belt, One Road, One Chain

China is the best example of a state that has progressively geofenced its internet and commercial infrastructure, effectively defining user permissions for who gets to be somebody online. This approach makes access to industrial and commercial products impossible for those who do not consent to the state's dominion over corporate dominion over the individual.

The statist approach to blockchain technology means that external products and services can be subjected to a controllable set of terms, barring foreign companies from doing business by making (or giving the option to make) their software and hardware inoperable within the Chinese sphere of influence.

In the case of the PRC, this is a logical strategic extent of the "One Belt, One Road" initiative at the infrastructural level, and of the Asian Infrastructure Bank (an institutional rival to the World Bank) for monetary policy. As we've made the case in this book, blockchains can support both.

The PRC's involvement in several blockchain projects indicates a clear interest in creating a blockchain that is operated by the Communist Party of China and capable of unifying commerce within the PRC's broader sphere of influence. The PBOC's digital currency is an extension of the PRC's infrastructural strategy, as communications infrastructure is just as necessary economically as the ports and roads that the PRC is "loaning" to countries such as Sri Lanka.

Those vassal countries will eventually default on the debt, and sign 99-year leases over to the Chinese government and the corporations affiliated with it. The same will go for their information infrastructure.

At its most extreme, a statist Web 3.0 could be adopted across the spectrum of government and commercial applications we posed elsewhere in this book. This transition would allow central governments to enforce their control over the entire internet, becoming the sole issuer of permissions and identity online in a way that extends beyond its borders.

In a more futuristic setting, an integrated blockchain tyranny could use its permissioned control over foreign and domestic infrastructure to grant and deny permissions, to turn off overseas support, and even to delete people and events from a ledger that is both centralized and not immutable.

This authoritarian approach is antithetical to the ideological and moral position of real, decentralized blockchains, but it is the natural statist course. A statist Web 3.0 focuses on depriving individuals of rights and ownership through the consolidation of all the private-keys in the hands of the ruling party. Not your private-keys, not your country.

Corporatism: Venice in the 21st Century

Elsewhere in this book, we've discussed the natural bent of large corporations to use Web 2.0 approaches to profit from customers, avoid government intervention, and maximize profits. Corporatism tends to cater to human needs rather than the absolute dominance of a state or a statist elite, but it too has its limits.

Corporatism is the de facto position in the United States. Free enterprise is still valued, but smaller companies exist in a food chain of large competitors who are trying to kill, eat, or absorb them, amoeba-like, lest the larger company lose its footing. Often, corporatists successfully hijack regulatory and other state bodies to secure their position, as they did in late medieval Venice, where influential trading families seized the republic and prevented new competitors or innovation from taking root. To this day, Venice is a museum of to the city's 15th century golden age, not a monument to modern innovation and industry.

From a tech perspective, this is a matter of modern industries, internet giants, and yes, banks, seeking to hold onto their positions and ensure their existence well into the future. If allowed to transition into an oligarchy, such corporatism can have highly corrosive effects on innovation, leading to intellectual capital flight.

Brain drain has already happened to a degree in the blockchain space, as the U.S. government and many corporations were at first hostile to cryptocurrency and blockchain. Many fled to more libertarian cities like Hong Kong - a trend that is slowly reversing.

Corporatist centralization still affects how large corporate entities approach blockchain technology. Ripple Labs and JP Morgan's recent forays into Privately Issued Scrip are excellent examples of this, as they adopted features of blockchains (atomic digital money exchanged on an electronic ledger) and assert themselves as the supreme authority. The drawback of this approach is that there is no barrier to competition. Many were expecting XRP to become a payments system for banks- instead, banks just invented their own instead of buying Ripple's XRP bags.

In another example, if Facebook's Libra launched as an international currency operated by an American company and banking network, many countries and customers would resist or ban Libra. France and Germany already have, arguing that the power to issue currency is a sovereign right not shared by private companies. It is this disagreement over who gets to hold the keys to a centralized system that makes decentralized networks so much more powerful and robust.

Decentralization gets around the Venetian curse on the general economy, and it is an alternative to being stuck in this competition. Such influence may prevent any innovation that threatens to upset the incumbent's profit margin, but when a system isn't about bagholders and centralization, it becomes more robust than these centralized systems. Instead of giving one party the keys again, or fighting over who gets to roll out a centralizing system, decentralization provides a third option where everyone can participate in a bigger network.

A corporatist approach to blockchain resembles the statist approach and fails for many of the same reasons. If this extends to networks, companies might tie encrypted systems into their terms and services, such that a centralized authority can add and rescind rights for popular products. A company might be motivated to pivot everything in its portfolio into a 'subscription model' - feudal rent-seeking - and govern the utilization of products and services well outside the halls of the company's headquarters.

We're also not seeding this idea, either. The fact that Microsoft Office and John Deere tractors run on a subscription model are living examples. Imagine a world where your car or your medical implants required a monthly payment to "stay up to date."

Not your keys, not your company.

Individualism: The Self-Sovereign Web

Blockchain has its roots in individualism, so this is where it is best positioned to shine and be its true self. In an environment of self-sovereignty, money and information are free from the influence of corporations and the state. You own your data; you control your money and your communications.

The challenge is that this form of Anarcho-capitalism is naturally atomizing and that cooperation breaks down at a large scale, resulting in inertia. Corporations and states are successful and continue to exist because they have collective action advantages and incentives that are absent in non-hierarchical lateral organizations.

At its best, this approach embraces personal freedom, responsibility, and productivity. At its worst, this is a Hobbesian struggle of all against all. There is limited recourse to third-party resources or justice, an no king or queen to defend rules not embodied in code. By pretending that no state or corporation is legitimate or can be justified, many take an ideological position over a pragmatic one who sees no utility in nation-states to provide order and corporations that provide for human commercial needs and desires. Such a hidebound approach is magical thinking, and probably shouldn't be relied on as a prediction of the future or as a moral yardstick in and of itself.

Web 3.0 and blockchain are a renegotiation of the balance between states, corporations, and individuals. Because blockchain and encryption exist and are available, it's possible to go off-grid, to escape broken systems, to transfer value without centralized banks and information without surveillance and third-party steering of what the individual is allowed to say or hear.

Serious blockchains are a Second Amendment for the internet: if states can trust their citizens with guns, they can trust their citizens with secure encryption and data security. Initiatives to take away and weaken an individual's information security are not unlike efforts to prevent citizens from defending themselves because a small minority abused the right to own a firearm — not your keys, not your data.

Conclusion: Blockchain Unifying the Trinity of Geoeconomics

The individualist ideal is more of an escape valve than it is a self-contained ideology. Each of the three pillars of the trinity (governments, companies, and individuals) has a vital role to play, and while they might take the technology a specific direction, they are much stronger when operating in harmony.

What the UTXO model is, compared to other models, is a simple approach whose terms enforce rules on participants and give the individual a renewed position vis-a-vis more significant players. We discuss this at such length because we believe the UTXO model has advantages for precisely this reason so that individuals, companies, and states can engage in a more productive exchange based on the equilibrium of forces, rather than domination.

The use of a decentralized blockchain to govern transfers and relationships among these parties represents a digital constitution for the modern era. We believe that UTXO blockchains can serve democracies well in the context of the geoeconomic competition between states. They are more amenable to individual rights and capital retention, and they are less likely to be used to dominate users, as more centralized systems are.

It is this new constitution and rebalancing that we discuss in the next chapter: Blockchain Democracy.

Bibliography & Further Reading

Robert D. Blackwill & Jennifer M. Harris. *War By Other Means: Geoeconomics and Statecraft*. Belknap Harvard, 2016.

Elizabeth C. Economy & Michael Levi. *By All Means Necessary: How China's Resource Quest is Changing the World*. Oxford University Press, 2014.

Robert Spalding. *Stealth War: How China Took Over While America's Elite Slept*. Portfolio Press, 2019.

Michael Pillsbury. *The Hundred-Year Marathon: China's Secret Strategy to Replace America as the Global Superpower*. Henry Holt Publishing, 2015.

John P. Carlin and Garrett M. Graff. *Dawn of the Code War: America's Battle Against Russia, China, and the Rising Global Cyber Threat*. Public Affairs, 2018.

Edward N. Luttwak. *From Geopolitics to Geo-Economics: Logic of Conflict, Grammar of Commerce*. The National Interest. No. 20 (Summer 1990), pp. 17-23

Edward N. Luttwak. *Theory and Practice of Geo-Economics* from *Turbo-Capitalism: Winners and Losers in the Global Economy*. HarperCollins Publishers, 1999.

James G. Rickards. *Currency Wars: The Making of the Next Global Crisis*. Portfolio Press, 2012.

James G Rickards. *The Death of Money: The Coming Collapse of the International Monetary System*. Portfolio Press, 2014.

P.W. Singer. *LikeWar: The Weaponization of Social Media*. Houghton Mifflin Harcourt. 2018

Robinson and Acemoglu. *Why Nations Fail: The Origins of Power, Prosperity and Poverty*. Crown Business, 2012.

Chapter 17: Blockchain Democracy

> "The real problem of humanity is the following: we have paleolithic emotions; medieval institutions; and god-like technology."
>
> -E.O. Wilson

> "For in order to turn the individual into a function of the State, his dependence on anything besides the State must be taken from him."
>
> -Carl Jung

> "Where you find the laws most numerous, there you will also find the greatest injustice."
>
> -Arcesilaus

In the last few chapters, we've covered a lot, economically, politically, and technologically. The world of the 2020s and 2030s will be dominated by competing nation-states, broken financial systems, destructive populism, huge corporations, and general economic upheaval. This future can be a dark vision and one that leaves many people uncomfortable. However, it doesn't have to be like that.

Blockchain is fundamentally a more democratic technology than A.I., advanced manufacturing, and the IoT are. These technologies all rely on centralized and hierarchical systems to produce and order them, where blockchain is decentralized and participated in by choice. In that vein, we believe that blockchain can ultimately become an open-source check on some of the excesses of these other systems. Just as blockchains with unhackable smart contracts can be checks on A.I. and IoT ecosystems, so too can they be a check on wild financial policies and economic theft, as we've argued above in the last few chapters.

In this chapter, we're going to imagine a Star Trek Universe, not based on utopianism but on pragmatic features that may come into the world because of blockchain. This is the world of *Blockchain Democracy* - one that still has sovereign states and successful private enterprises, but one that hasn't abolished foreign and domestic conflict. Blockchain will be a check on this world as a fundamentally democratic technology that is censorship resistant, an immutable record of truth, and brings accuracy in accounting to finances, trade, and politics.

New Economy, Old Constitution

The origins of the modern word *economy* go back to the Greek, and those origins have mutated over time to the meaning we know and use today. In the modern era, we use *the economy* and *economics* to represent a mathematized discipline around the exchange of goods and services, separate from the rules that society uses to govern itself and provide standards for conduct outside of the world of production and consumption.

In the Greek setting, the word *oikonomia* (οἰκονομία) meant "the arrangement of things" and the dynamics of managing a household. Where the modern economy relates to the production and exchange of goods and services, the ancient *oikonomia* involved the arrangement of different people and things in the most optimal order. As Catholic theologian Giorgio Agamben notes: in the context of the ancient Greek language that the gospels were written in, there was an *oikonomia* in a household, even for how utensils should be arranged at dinner.[43]

In Agamben's study, he expands this to Christian theological notions of the *Trinity* and ecclesiology (a conception for the right roles and functions of the Church concerning God and people). In effect, an *oikonomia* represents the rules and interactions of *different forms of value* with various parts that interact but are not mutually fungible with each other.

---

[43] Giorgio Agamben. *The Kingdom and the Glory: For a Theological Genealogy of Economy and Government*. Stanford University Press, 2011.

Real, decentralized blockchains can underwrite a new *oikonomia* of different parts working as a whole, including things that are not monetary in nature but relate to the relationships people have to the larger world.
This *Blockchain oikonomia* might include things like identity, voting, free speech, and the rights to privacy and free association.

There is no exact monetary value to these things, but as we have argued elsewhere in this book, they are valuable. Immensely valuable. Today these are extended as rights by constitutional forms of governments. Blockchain can be an extension of those constitutional values into our increasingly opaque and hierarchical world.

In the case of encryption and free speech, blockchain can and likely will support greater access to information as a direct result of not being censorable. On-chain, no government or company can undo what has been written to the ledger, and off-chain blockchain can be used to distribute strong cryptography without relying on centralized tech companies for distribution. Perhaps in the future, the internet will evolve beyond centralized DNS servers to something resembling a permissionless mesh network, in which case there will be no way to stop information from being distributed or exchanged.

Web 3.0 stands in stark contrast to the existing order, in which large but still private companies provide services where they reserve the right to govern and edit what grows within their walled garden as they wish. While this is critical in a world of property rights and free enterprise, it is also a liability, as there is no ultimately "fair" approach to censorship, and as the process of "combating abuse" is itself often abused and hijacked.

The same basic logic applies to states, who is serving as the highest temporal authority bear responsibility for making their governance sustainable and not burdensome to their citizens. Citizens aren't saints either - they often demand unsustainable things that they expect others to pay for, and use the government as a piggy bank with the expectation that more productive people are going to be taxed to pick up the tab. One criticism of American democracy is that it creates misaligned incentives.

By being decentralized at the state level, and centralized at the federal level, it accommodates a high degree of inefficiency, where everybody fights to "get theirs" and externalize costs through taxation and borrowing. This arrangement also allows individuals to take advantage of the openness of the system and cheat. As we've covered above, this is what has happened in our monetary and financial policy, with the U.S. crossing 22 trillion in outstanding sovereign debt as we wrote this paragraph.

It is the blockchain's revolution in providing a decentralized, unhackable backbone for property rights and ownership that underwrites its utility in providing the same value to other immensely personal qualities. It provides a system for different applications, and it is this characteristic that makes the technology such a powerful check on overreach by the state, political parties, and private entities. Blockchain can and will support specific applications in the future that make for a more verdant world, one with diversity, freedom, *and* security.

The DAO as a Constitution Embodied in Code

One such proposal for a new constitution is the Decentralized Autonomous Organization, or DAO. DAO Democracies were first proposed by Ralph Merkle, himself iterating on Vitalik Buterin's general concept, both of whom you will recognize from his work cited earlier in this book. By definition, a DAO is a system that has no unaccountable central node of power, operates according to a set of priorities that it optimizes for (usually the general welfare), and retains its integrity (has boundaries and acts as an organization).

Merkle begins with an indictment of the collective action problems involved in any democracy, where individual voters and centralized authorities struggle to get anything better than the minimum viable outcome, and where the right thing often goes undone for lack of consensus. This collective action problem gives us the results we discussed in our last two chapters. It is the driver behind bloated sovereign debt, cronyism in government, and broken states where conditions grind towards oblivion even though many have a solid grasp of what is going wrong.

Merkle's proposed solution is to allow for a predictions market. This market is a weighted voting system, where participants vote on policies that are estimated to create the most favorable outcomes. Members rate their welfare on a scale of zero to one, and this feedback drives the system. Because a decentralized network votes on decisions through a prediction market, there is an incentive to optimize for ideal outcomes. Decisions with externalities (such as human suffering in war or pollution from a factory) must be kept in perspective against the welfare of the system as a whole. Because the system might conclude that you are disposable, there is no way to renounce your citizenship in advance of being drafted or pressed into slavery.

Before getting up in arms, it's crucial to recognize this is already the case in democracies today. Present-day governments reserve the right to draft their citizens and don't offer their citizens rights to opt-out of hard collective actions, or of taxation, or any other costs associated with citizenship. The goal of a DAO democracy is to provide better incentives and minimize adverse outcomes for the individual.

In effect, a DAO democracy replaces a constitution with rules embedded in an unhackable network - by definition, one built on a blockchain. Instead of outlining institutions that rely on human judgment, execution, and judicial review, a DAO connects rules with a feedback loop and outputs.

As an idea, DAOs can provide a great deal of inspiration, since they are effectively code and machinery built around legal institutions and human communities. They are intended to take some of the crooked timber out of our political condition and can inspire solutions to problems that we face in our existing political systems.

For examples of just how this thinking can apply, let's examine how blockchain can make the voting system more representative.

Voting

You can't have a democracy without elections, and you can't have elections without a secure voting process that's representative. Today, this process runs on old systems and methods with neither standardization nor security. As we covered in our government applications chapter, this has been taken advantage of by foreign governments seeking to manipulate or undermine the integrity of our voting system.

The insecurity of our voting system has also become a political football, as domestic political parties and news outlets seek to control the narrative and capitalize on crises to their benefit. Ironically, the same partisans who complain that elections are being "hacked" (when they lose) also complain that voter I.D. is a violation of human rights and that the voting process needs to remain opaque.

Nowhere is this more evident than in the State of Texas' discovery of approximately 95,000 individuals inside of Texas who had illegally registered to vote, despite not having legal status as citizens. Of these, 58,000 persons were discovered to have illegally voted in elections for which they had zero legal standing. To cite the Texas Secretary of State's statements on the matter:

> "Through this evaluation, the Texas Secretary of State's office discovered that a total of approximately **95,000** individuals identified by DPS as non-U.S. citizens have a matching voter registration record in Texas, around **58,000** of whom have voted in one or more Texas elections. Voting in an election in which the person knows he or she is not eligible to vote is a second-degree felony in the State of Texas. Upon receipt of this information, the Texas Secretary of State's office immediately provided the data in its possession to the Texas Attorney General's office, as the Secretary of State has no statutory enforcement

authority to investigate or prosecute alleged illegal activity in connection with an election."[44]

In an environment where a single vote can sway a county or state election, 58,000 fraudulent voters are a significant threat to the function of a democracy.

Whether these individuals were non-US citizens, citizens of other states, or otherwise ineligible, their votes represented a violation of the terms that democracy works on, where voters bear the costs of the decisions the government makes with their consent. The same moral principle is in play here, whether it is a matter of illegal aliens voting in Texas or red-blooded Texans trying to vote illegally in California.

It is this process that blockchain can fix. By embracing validated identity and immutable records, those participating in elections can be confirmed in a much more uniform way, ensuring they are a real person who has skin in the game and standing to vote in the community they are voting in.

Identity validated on a public blockchain has other uses. Instead of having a dozen different I.D.s resting on a dozen different databases with several dozen laws applying, a blockchain could streamline the transference and maintenance of identity. Registering to vote and participate in a democracy can and should be faster, cleaner, and more available.

---

[44] Texas Secretary of State. *Secretary Whitley Issues Advisory On Voter Registration List Maintenance Activity. 25 January 2019.* Available at <https://www.sos.state.tx.us/about/newsreleases/2019/012519.shtml>

Transparent Taxation and Preventing Waste

Taxation today is fundamentally disordered and unfair. Many feel taken advantage of by the fact that their taxes often go to waste in bloated, ineffective bureaucracies whose only purpose is to expand personal and political fiefdoms while doing the minimum amount of work possible. From experience, roughly a third of the functions undertaken by government workers could be executed by a present-day A.I. platform and with a higher degree of consistency and quality.

This includes everything from administering Social Security to analyzing and prioritizing infrastructure spending, where human inefficiency and corruption waste billions of dollars a year. David Graeber put it best, saying many government jobs are "bullshit jobs" - employment without productivity or purpose, that creates unskilled and unmotivated people incapable of doing anything else in the real economy.

The management philosophy present in most governments embodies mid-20th-century organizational design confronting 21st-century problems and led according to 13th-century internal politics. Competition over who gets what incentive or exemption means companies have to increasingly court politicians. Investigative reporter Peter Schweizer describes this as an "extortion racket," with politicians demanding private companies kowtow to them and donate to their campaigns or otherwise face burdensome regulations and enforcement actions.[45]

In a world of expansive geoeconomic competition, where capital has many places it can go, blockchain management of identity, taxation, and terms of agreement flies in the face of this extortive model. If companies and individuals have a means of interacting with the state that is transparent to them and allows explicit expectations about costs and terms of engagement with

---

[45] Peter Schweizer. *Extortion: How Politicians Extract Your Money, Buy Votes, and Line Their Own Pockets.* Mariner Books, 2014.

state, local, and federal government, then the relationship between the state and the individual can be rebalanced. In a world where the government makes byzantine rules and governs by an opaque bureaucracy, rather than democracy, it is ultimately the citizens that pay the price.

It is important to note that states are not necessarily losers in this rebalancing. The country that can be most accommodating to capital will tend to attract that capital, especially if it is highly mobile, as assets on a decentralized network tend to be. There is a reason why people invest in the United States, Japan, and European countries: because they have some semblance of the rule of law and property rights. Imagine being able to visibly demonstrate this rule of law and transparency as a government in this global competition for capital.

Security and Privacy

Only a tyrant would insist that only a criminal would want privacy. Privacy, if not a right, is at least a basic expectation of being human. If you close your blinds at night, you believe this. As we've covered at length earlier in this book, data is being gathered continuously and hoarded by today's platforms, and they are not protecting your data in the same way they safeguard their I.P. or revenues.

Personal privacy isn't just about privacy from the state and corporations; it is about having freedom as an individual. If every step you make gets tracked, if every bit of information you receive is through a filter you are not aware of or do not control, you are not free. If we are going to perceive the same world, we cannot have an invasive force like modern collectivist tech telling us individually what to think, even if that process is well-meaning and designed to cater to our existing biases and interests.

Further, privacy is a natural right. In a past era, people could keep a transaction in physical cash (which is naturally private) and have a conversation in person (which is usually private). That our internet and banking system have both evolved to track our every financial and social movement is invasive in a way that many are coming to recognize, and the natural conclusion of this for those who own and control these networks is that we as users can and should be directed to spend our time, money, and attention as they see fit, not as we see fit.

Privacy is not a matter of preserving some criminal intent. It is a matter of safeguarding personal agency. Though many could care less, we would argue that you do not truly live in a democracy if you enjoy no real privacy.

A Borderless World for Decent People

With the collapse of the Arab Syrian Republic in 2011 into civil war, millions fled the country as refugees. As refugees, many lacked any form of official documentation or identity, meaning they arrived in Europe and the broader world with no possible means of vetting their claims. In these numbers, thousands of Islamic extremists, criminals, and others with ill intent took advantage of the chaos, infiltrating Europe, drawing social benefits, and engaging in mass casualty attacks. As of 2019, these attacks are almost too numerous to count, with attacks spanning from the Charlie Hebdo shooting to the Bastile Day attack in Nice that killed 86 and wounded 458, to the Bataclan shooting in Paris that killed 130 and injured 413 others, to the attack on a Christmas Market in Berlin in 2016 that killed 12, all just innocent families enjoying the holiday together.

These are only a sample, with dozens of knife, ax, and explosives attacks in addition to numerous shootings. Islamic terrorism is a massive problem for Western society, with European intelligence agencies and federal police completely overrun and incapable of tracking all but some of the most blatantly dangerous cases.

Many are reticent to correct for this mismatch between extremist savagery and Western values, which seek to uphold human dignity and freedom and allow for honest asylum for those persecuted in their nation of origin. At the extreme, some cheer for open borders, not knowing or caring that they undermine the character cohesion of their societies.

Borders are a controversial topic because most country's management of their borders is poor. In the case of Syria, there was no documentation to validate who somebody was or wasn't. If such documentation existed, was recoverable, and attributable, on a timestamped public ledger and using private keys that only the person in question could use, that would have alleviated much of the pressure in vetting people who claimed asylum.

There is a big difference between a professional with a family of four, who can show his marriage records, his relationship to his children, his prior residence, and his past professional affiliation, and someone who can't.

In this respect, the use of blockchain to prove one's past can be a defense to protect the liberties of decent people. By linking someone's identity to a publicly available ledger, which is decentralized and protected by private keys, we can preserve their identity in the instance of such a conflagration as war, famine, and mass migration. Without adopting such methods, each citizen is reliant on the state's centralized database, often collected and compiled without the citizen's knowing in police states like Syria.

Relying on centralized, statist systems of identification means the citizen loses their records when the state fails. Decentralized identity is especially important when the country is the party responsible for the persecution in the first place - there needs to be a separate standard. Further, such a system encourages the use of fraudulent documents - even by people who are not themselves criminals and terrorists.

Blockchain identity management is a better means of enabling people to transit borders and do business broadly and still protect the public from the dangers of terrorism and criminality. Some standards need to be written to ensure that private keys and identities are not exchanged, such as a hashed DNA sample, but in principle, such a system could protect human rights and enable a more functional international world.

Further, this could cut down on the substantial waste generated by the security state.

Anyone who has been through a TSA checkpoint knows how much time, effort, and money is wasted, preventing citizens from traveling with saline solution and nail clippers. Beyond the cost in time and money, this also affects the human dignity of the people traveling, with incompetent TSA agents confiscating pens from pockets and toothpaste but frequently missing knives, ammunition, and other articles supposedly in their mandate to stop. Anyone who has buckled down and committed to using TSA Pre-Check knows the difference between the long lines and ineffective surveillance theatre and how much better travel could be.

A critical pillar of such a validated blockchain I.D. would be that it is government recognized but not necessarily government issued. By being decentralized and timestamped, no nation could issue false I.D.s, as several corrupt states are wont to do for a sizable fee. Second, the failure of a state or its technical system would not affect the decentralized I.D., and the encryption (reliance on private keys) means that the I.D. would remain secret until it is needed to sign a document, cross a border, or validate a history. These are all crucial transactions for those who live internationally.

There are already much less comprehensive visa agreements, such as the agreement between the U.S. and U.K., which do not require advanced approval to transit from one country to the other. Such a system is not intended to diminish these forms of free exchange and transportation between friendly nations, but to give the world a standard that allows decent citizens to own and control their identification and proof of their history, rather than relying on centralized and often corrupt states to be acknowledged and able to travel and transact in other countries.

New Forms of Wealth

The most obvious impact that blockchain will have is a fundamental rearchitecting of how we track and exchange value. It is also a check on the systems that would deprive us of our worth and dignity and provides better means for societies to distribute wealth than traditional "tax and spend" policies have.

Real, Unhackable, Immutable, Timestamped Property Rights

Even for the denizen of Deir ez-Zawr in the last section, land rights are essential. Being able to validate past affiliation with land and property is critical for everyday people, especially in states that use coercion to confiscate land and wealth. Blockchain's capacity to represent ownership is part of why it is so fundamental for real estate, and why land deeds on an immutable, unhackable ledger are such a paradigm shift for the world, especially for people whose land is their primary source of wealth and livelihood.

Blockchain's revolution in ownership extends not just to land, but other forms of property. We both are descendants of settlers and homesteaders in the American West, and for many of our great grandparents, the threat of cattle rustlers and bandits was a real one. Historically, ranchers branded their cattle with hot irons - a process that is as uncomfortable for the cow as it is for the branding party's nostrils. Branding involves heating an iron pattern (often a crude stamp) and pressing it into the cattle's hindquarters once a calf is old enough. Then you can recognize stolen livestock when and if brought to market.

The same could be done with blockchain and extended much further into the product cycle. By hashing heifers, ranchers could not only brand their cattle, but they could also open up secondary markets for breeding and track their products well into the market, including both beef and leather goods. Such a data-centric approach both empowers ranchers by enabling timestamped property rights, and it helps inform markets and futures. We're very bullish on this idea.

The commercial chain of acquisition isn't just for cattle but extends to all forms of property. We've already mentioned real estate, but this can extend to intellectual property, collectibles, and any number of commodities and deliverables.

Universal Basic Wealth, instead of Universal Basic Income

We've spoken elsewhere in this book about the use of a "national digital asset" as a policy gambit to strengthen central bank's on-balance sheet assets, and as a means of paying down debts and sustaining a national blockchain that is also leveraged for cybersecurity and other functions, such as voting, identity management, and so on. An additional application for the technology is even more enticing; as an affordable, democratic way of approaching universal primary wealth as an alternative to the inflationary pressures of "universal basic income."

What is UBI?

UBI is very much in vogue as we write this. It is naturally a politically appealing response to the waves of automation that have occurred over the last 30 years. Automation is displacing many whose livelihood and ability to thrive economically has disappeared, which has been exacerbated by a monetary system that rewards those with assets and punishes those who are just starting out in life.

The desire for a universal baseline of income is even more salient as big tech firms like Amazon and Google have gained increasing power in the marketplace. There has never been a better time to be a consumer; assuming you can afford to consume anything, but incomes have declined relative to healthcare, education, and real estate.

Due to the fiat monetary system, real wages have been stagnant since the mid-'70s, around the time the gold standard disappeared. Instead of being able to save sound money, a large swath of the population has been converted into serfs who rent indefinitely, don't have families, and cannot afford to start new businesses.

The vassalization of everyday people has had severe social and political impacts. As more people feel their quality of life slipping, they seek a solution to protect themselves, their families, and what many consider to be an entitlement living in the Western world; the opportunity to do better than one's parents. It is this context that makes UBI politically appealing.

"Basic Income" can mean three different things; governments can:

1. Set a floor for how much someone can make, with or without means testing or the caveat that they need to find some level of income,
2. Provide conditional insurance, such as that already provided by the Social Security Administration, which makes up an enormous fraction of existing public spending, or
3. Provide universal payments to every citizen without regard to their income or financial ability.

Countries like the U.S. already have heavily subsidized incomes for certain classes of people: specifically seniors. Seniors are more likely to vote than any other demographic, are generally too old to "learn to code" or take up a new career, and often have the added advantage of having nothing better to do than protect entitlements that they have priced into their expectations for retirement. Social Security has mutated to become a national retirement program that provides transfer payments from the economically productive to those who are not. It is the third rail in American politics and makes up roughly 24% of the U.S. Federal Budget - 916 Billion Dollars in 2017.[46] Additionally, Social Security has joined Medicare, Medicaid, the Children's Health Insurance Program (CHIP), and subsidies under the Affordable Care Act (also known as ObamaCare), which consumed 26% of the Federal Budget in the same year.

That's roughly 1 trillion dollars, led by Medicare at just short of 600 billion dollars. In aggregate, almost 50% of the U.S. tax budget in 2017 went to entitlements programs. That's not counting other forms of transfer payments, such as farm subsidies to swing states, federal unemployment insurance, or the child tax credit.

The existing transfer payment programs already eat more than half of the United States budget, with defense taking 16% and all

---

[46] Center for Budget and Policy Priorities. *Where do our Tax Dollars Go?* Available at: <https://www.cbpp.org/sites/default/files/atoms/files/4-14-08tax.pdf>

other programs (federal workforce, retirement, research and development, education, et cetera), taking roughly 18%. This segment, which is mainly discretionary (and not an unfunded liability where people have priced the presence of government assistance into their spending and saving habits for a lifetime) is further squeezed by the service cost on the existing federal debt, which in 2017 was 6% of the Federal Budget and expected to rise indefinitely, squeezing out other programs.

Add the insult to injury that income taxes disproportionally affect the middle class. Net income tax and forced expenses (like mandated healthcare) in most U.S. states eats between a third and half of American's total salary, where capital gains tax from having assets is much less onerous. Many Americans feel as though they are being taxed to support others but have no hope of seeing any benefits themselves. In effect, many in the middle class feel disposable and resent the system that they perceive to reward rich and poor at their expense.

It is in this environment that politicians are proposing even further benefits, in the form of Universal Basic Income. In Democratic presidential candidate Andrew Yang's version, UBI means $1000 a month for every citizen. Yang's case naturally resonates with a broad group of people, many of whom feel threatened by the advance of self-driving cars and semis, the automation of legal and administrative work, and the stagnant wages and long hours required by today's gig economy. Further, because the economic upside from automation goes to a few tech behemoths, it is not distributed widely.

Even more, human labor today is taxed, while robots are not. When cashiers at McDonald's demanded a higher wage (as was recently the case in New York), the fast-food chain added touch screens to streamline the order process. Touch screens might be temperamental and covered with slime and germs, but they never take days off, they don't ask for more than their allotment of energy, and they don't get tired, unionize, or treat customers poorly. They don't cost as much as people by order of magnitude.

There is no policy option outside of a running a gulag that provides "room and board" that can mandate such employment. Instead of trying to mandate jobs with a living wage, which is counterproductive, UBI represents an attempt to tax innovators to provide that economic value to people who have been displaced by innovation.

What is generally not conceived or covered by those enthusiastic for such programs is the immense cost that UBI assumes to the national budget and debt.

Based on the 2018 estimated population of the US (327.2 million people), multiply $1000 by 12 months in a year and that comes out just short of 4 trillion dollars in new expenses (per year) to be either gathered in new taxes or printed by the central bank in the form of government debt. Fiat-based UBI would double the national budget at a time where the national debt is already higher than GDP.

Some might argue that the Keynesian "multiplier effect" of giving people helicopter money (a term covered in our fiat chapter) would spur the economy. Dollars circulating might result in new goods, and people newly able to afford a higher quality of life. If coupled with adjustments in Social Security and other entitlements programs, UBI may be a fairer way of distributing wealth than taxing the young to pay for the old. However, the major drawbacks to UBI are macroeconomic and unavoidable.

First, there is nowhere to source the funds for UBI other than by taxing, borrowing, or printing money, all of which have adverse effects on the natural economy. Second, because UBI offers a guaranteed payout and typically does not come back in the form of taxes, it is far more likely that governments embracing it would print the money, rapidly diluting the value of the currency. For perspective, if there were a guaranteed payout of $1000 a month in 1987, that same payout would only be worth $440 in relative value in 2019, and that's with historically low inflation over the past 30 years that is unlikely to repeat when debt is 120% GDP. Accelerating payouts and other macro headwinds would almost certainly inflate the currency and send asset prices soaring, in effect blunting its positive impact while generating debt and economic inefficiency. The expense would also crowd out other spending possibilities, such as the country's ability to invest in infrastructure, education, and defense, or emergency response, just as other entitlements have.

Further, this inflationary standard would naturally push the price of real assets and services, like housing, education, and healthcare, upwards. Imagine being a landlord where every single potential tenant had $1000 more to spend a month. If he is rational, he charges precisely $1000 more in rent per month. There needs to be a better approach to the problem UBI is trying to solve.

Universal Basic Wealth as a Sustainable Alternative to UBI

You're probably wondering how blockchain might fit into the conversation about Universal Basic Income. In truth, it's relatively simple. If a country were to adopt a National Digital Asset with sound technical principles (minable, decentralized, deflationary, and acknowledged as a valid asset by the government), then it is only natural to explore whether this asset can be distributed fairly.

If a nation were to adopt a National Digital Asset, it would not be difficult, at least at a technical level, to distribute an equal amount to all of its citizens and their validated wallets. These digital assets would not necessarily need any assigned value; they could float just like fiat does, but they would not rely on taxation, spending, and inflation. Instead, they would be widely dispersed assets with the same core attributes of Bitcoin or DigiByte, and the market would establish their value. The state could create a trust of assets for as-yet-unborn citizens and could use the cryptographic properties of the system for other users in a way that is more reliable than the existing Social Security Number model, which is riddled with fraud. Further, the state could maintain a treasury and liquidate these scarce assets to pay for infrastructure, education, and other essential spending priorities. Upon birth or naturalization, every citizen would receive a set amount, regardless of the market price. We call this concept Universal Basic Wealth or UBW.

UBW is a far better approach to the problems of UBI because it deals with assets, not an unsound currency or an overweening social state. It wouldn't crowd out other social programs or increase the debt. It would give everyone a shot at paying off their debts or purchasing other assets, such as education or homes. Savvy citizens could trade the market, improving liquidity. Non-citizens would have just as much interest in buying and mining the National Digital Asset, both adding security, and liquidity, and the value-added to the treasury could be the key to rebalancing the global monetary system and the country deleveraging its fiat debts.

A nationally distributed cryptocurrency is sounder than almost all existing social policy programs. We think it's a fascinating possibility for a more democratic financial order: one built on ownership, not infinite dilution.

UBW restores the concept of saving; rather than having one's savings diluted away through inflation, one can transfer fiat into real assets when they want to preserve value. Instead of relying on a corrupt government or political party that seeks to create oppressive dependency, UBW frees people while restoring monetary policy to realistic terms. It's simply a better approach to money and government.

A 24/7 Market for Everything

Real markets don't sleep. While the NYSE and others do have their closing times, the digitization of markets means that markets do not have to go down when the offices of the major exchanges do. Secure, modern crypto exchanges operate year-round - even on Christmas. In a tokenized world, we can begin to expect this year-round market to include billions of tradable goods and new markets. Blockchain is nothing less than an information revolution in markets, much like writing was 3000 years ago. Not only can these blockchain-enabled markets increase the time horizon that goods can get exchanged, but they will also increase the diversity of tradable products.

What is beautiful about a blockchain model "market for everything" is that it can incorporate data timestamped to the blockchain and validate the history of the good in question. If this is a luxury product (say, Yeezy sneakers when they were cool), then this product can validate that the asset is authentic, and not a counterfeit. If the good requires a chain of acquisition from the supplier, such as fair-trade coffee or grass-fed beef, then markets can incorporate validation into the supply chain and limit the good's ability to enter the market based on its point of origin being authentic.

Redefining the Wallet

The blockchain revolution extends to every form of asset. Today, ownership occurs through legions of brokers, databases, holding companies, and laws. Blockchain solves that, for home and car titles, for stocks, for delivered goods, for data, for identity. As a technology, it can be and will be the backbone of a new, more efficient, more transparent system.

Trust but Verify

As we were putting a bow on this chapter, well-connected sex offender Jeffrey Epstein died while in custody at the New York City Metro Correctional Center (MCC). While the circumstances of his death (an alleged suicide) are still not established as we write this, those who remember this incident in retrospect will recall just how much conspiracy theory and suspicion it brought about. Epstein's career in finance, whereabouts, affiliations, and the circumstances of his death are all shrouded in mystery. Many speculated that his associations went deeper than public sources identified.

While not a time to indulge in speculation, Epstine's actions and passing are an excellent illustration of the dynamics in the modern world. For the first time since 9/11 or the invasion of Iraq, conspiracy theories went mainstream. The inconsistencies in the public narrative spurred further and further speculation, some of which are likely to persist indefinitely.

Blockchain democracy is about verifiability, transparency, and timestamped records of transactions and events. Imagine a world where records of some of Epstein's actions were treated with this high standard. Also, imagine a world where the monitoring system, roster, and access to his prison cell gets monitored as uniformly. There would be so much less room for doubt and obfuscation.

That is the heart of blockchain democracy. A verifiable, fair, and transparent system open to both verification and security. Instead of trusting centralized institutions and authorities, blockchain allows us to verify evidence, ownership, and the overall record of the world. It may not catch everything - garbage in, garbage out, as they say. However, when it expands to the Internet of Things, to the management of data and identity, to financial transactions and ownership, to titles and records, blockchain makes the world a better place.

Chapter 18: The Quantum Leap

"There are known knowns; there are things we know we know. We also know there are known unknowns; that is to say, we know there are some things we do not know. But there are also unknown unknowns—the ones we don't know we don't know. And if one looks throughout the history of our country and other free countries, it is the latter category that tends to be the difficult ones."

-Donald Rumsfeld, White House Press Briefing

"If you can't explain something to the average person, you don't understand it well enough."

-Albert Einstein, 1922 Nobel Laureate in Theoretical Physics

"Hell, if I could explain it to the average person, it wouldn't have been worth the Nobel prize."

-Richard Feynman, 1965 Nobel Laureate in Quantum Physics

Quantum computing is the natural evolution of computer science, and represents a complete rethinking of the architecture involved in creating a computer itself, with bits (representations of information), logic gates (providing if-then rules), and other core elements mirrored in the much more challenging setting of manipulating individuals atoms and electrons, rather than physical gears, vacuum tubes, or transistors. Quantum computing uses the material world to exercise computation at a much more microscopic level, though many of the mechanics and rules remain the same.

This evolution is critical in many ways, but chiefly for the fact that working quantum computers will revolutionize computation just as much as the original classical computers did. Just as access to a computer in the days that Bill Gates and Steve Wozniak were young was scarce, so too is access to a modern quantum computer for students learning today. As this form of computing becomes more evolved, it may become more ubiquitous, though the physical and economic constraints for such systems will probably remain in play for a long time, just as classical computing moved from the room-sized ENIAC to your mobile phone.

To borrow from our earlier example of timekeeping, one can construct similar functions across a variety of mediums. An hourglass measures time by letting sand through a choke point at a set rate. A water clock measures time relative to the trickle of water out of a container, or into one. A mechanical clock executes the same function relative to its power source - usually a tightened spring. A quartz or electronic clock measures time corresponding to the rate at which electricity can move through a piezoelectric quartz crystal.

These are all different mediums for estimating the passage of time by putting power through a set constraint. Though telling time is essentially the same, the method has become more miniaturized and accurate. Analogous to changes in timekeeping, quantum computing is similar to classical binary computing, but in a new medium that can address more complex questions. Just as moving from hourglasses to wound mechanical clocks made new functions like stopwatches possible, quantum computing makes new forms of code and modeling possible.

This evolution is immensely vital for blockchains working in the classical computational setting that we have today. Some have already proposed that quantum computing will pose a threat to the cryptographic systems that blockchains use. There are many impacts this could have, such as if an attacker mustered the ability to create cryptographic collisions on a blockchain, gain control of other's wallets, double-spend assets, and other attack vectors. In the furthest sphere of possibilities, quantum computing is speculated to be capable of obsoleting existing blockchains.

We'll call this the *apocalyptic outcome for quantum computing*. In this scenario, an entity that is opposed to a blockchain network attempts to break it with the newfound power of a quantum computer. This attack might be done to ruin the blockchain's credibility as a record of truth or to attack a particular user or wallet address.

On the other hand, there is an optimistic scenario for quantum computing, where blockchains are critical in distributing quantum-resistant cryptography and defending people and institutions from the threat of such brute force attacks. Because we are so far away from generally available quantum computing (just like we are from general AI), we believe that this is a more likely scenario. The defensive characteristics of a decentralized blockchain will continue to develop as these other technologies come into their own, and in that respect, blockchain will be critical to how we respond to a world with advanced quantum computing.

Beyond adversarial applications, there will likely be some overlap, as well. For example, quantum computing might lead to a new era of blockchain mining. If decentralized computational processes continue to become more complex and more ASIC resistant, it stands to reason that miners will come to leverage quantum computers. The monetary reward might justify seeking the significant technical advantage required to pursue this strategy.

There are, of course, limitations to this - today's quantum computers are immensely fragile at the physical level, and they are not yet robust enough to be held in hand rest on a desk in your kitchen. That, and they're damned expensive. Access to a quantum computer today is usually in an experimental environment, though eventually nation-states and large companies will have quantum platforms of their own.

Much like the divergence between American and Soviet science, these different quantum computers may even be built on different architectures, as there are multiple ways to build and program the underlying hardware, which we will discuss in this chapter.

The first quantum computer involved the use of a chloroform molecule ($H_1C_1Cl_3$) in which nuclear magnetic resonance enabled scientists to manipulate and measure spin within the molecule as a makeshift logic gate. While this is, by definition, a quantum computer, the kind of quantum mechanics involved define how powerful it is. Many of today's quantum computers use isolated atoms and not whole molecules because they offer a larger and more efficient body of quantum states to observe.

However, before we get carried away in the realm of possibility, let's get back to the basics.

Quantum Basics

To provide a simple example of the possibilities of quantum computing, let's use license plates as a metaphor for the information possibilities in a quantum bit (also known as a *qubit*).

Imagine you are producing vehicle license plates for two municipalities; *Number County* and *Alphabet City*. Each license plate can be no more than eight assignable characters long; Number County is rural and uses sequential numbers, where Alphabet City is urban and uses a combination of letters.

In Number County, each slot in the eight-character string can have one of ten possible values, from "0" through "9." In Alphabet City, each slot in the string can have any one of twenty-six possibilities, "A" thru "Z," fitting more information into the same amount of space. Let's do the math.

In Number County, there are a total of 99,999,999 possible license plates that you can issue, with numbers from 1 to 99.99 million assignable within the eight-character spots. Once you reach this number, you cannot create a plate without duplicating a past plate.

In Alphabet City, one can calculate the possible plates by multiplying 26 to the power of 8 - that's 208,827,064,576 possibilities, to be exact. If you were to put these possibilities next to each other on a graph, the smaller range of possible plates in

Number County is exponentially lower than the number of possible plates in Alphabet City.

This effect scales as we add more slots to the license plate. At one character, the possibilities are just 26 versus 10, and at four letters, the plates in Alphabet City have more than 45 times as many options as a digits-only plate in Number County will have (456,976 letters versus 10,000 numbers, to be exact).

This principle is an essential pillar in information theory and compression, and something that was a conceptual cornerstone in engineering DigiAssets. To be information-efficient, the maximum amount of information must condense into as little representational space as possible. Bear in mind, the process in our oversimplified example here is only using 1) numbers or 2) capital letters, and still generates this massive range of possibilities. In a real computing setting, several more characters can be used, from hexadecimal numbers to lowercase characters, increasing the range of possible information substantially.

The beauty of information is that it is and can be truly infinite. If you calculate the possibility of randomly generating a long string of characters - such as this book - according to the same rules as the license plates in our example, you will get lost before you completed the first page. Just adding just one character to our epilogue would multiply that number by whatever the set parameter of usable characters is. We alluded to Jorge Luis Borjes short story *The Library of Babel* earlier, and this is the same effect. *Even constrained for space, information can be nearly infinite.*

In the license plate example, our eight characters are the bottom limit. In classical computing, each of the eight characters is stored and processed from binary, themselves being strings of zeros and ones known as bits. This on/off characteristic is the primary constraint for compression and dictates the smallest quanta of energy that can represent information, as the storage and processing cannot occur below the level of ones and zeros. A bit can be zero or one, a byte (8 bits) can represent up to 256 variable arrangements of ones and zeros.

486

Today's processors may be considerably denser than the first binary processors, but they are still subject to this ultimate physical constraint. This progress is still linear, just as John Harrison's huge marine chronometers were more significant than any modern mechanical wristwatch, which is not necessarily more accurate. This limitation becomes more and more evident at scale, as more massive amounts of data are simultaneously represented and processed in a deterministic system.

The use of quantum phenomena for computation expands the possibility for representation similar to how using letters in Alphabet City expands the possible number of plates. This higher density of information means that a quantum computer that has the same amount of bits as a classical computer is, by its nature, exponentially more powerful and capable of processing than the traditional computer is. Depending on the number of subatomic phenomena that can be measurably isolated, a qubit can provide a whole new set of characters to insert in our theoretical license plate - or quantum *byte* of available storage processing power.

What is especially interesting is that there is no fully mechanical standard definition of a qubit as we write this. There are multiple testing and working models, and even more untested theoretical models that leverage quantum phenomena to generate a qubit. Unlike bits that are on or off, there is no set limit on how many positions a qubit could have.

There is also not a set number of numbers or letters that a qubit can represent, where a classical computer is constrained to strictly binary possibilities. Different architectures of a qubit have various opportunities and challenges in manufacturing, usually defined by the number of available electron orbitals in the qubit. Naturally, there are some possible architectures for a qubit that make more sense than others, but there is no such thing as Orthodox quantum computing, and there may never be.

Like timekeeping, some may opt for molecular qubits, while others may opt for (likely more expensive) qubits made through isolating atoms. Because of this, any predictive exercise is better constrained to *principles* and *applications* in the context of a world still dominated by classical computing, rather than speculation about what specific course QC itself will take.

In a way, quantum computing mirrors our discussion of AI. We don't have general AI yet, and we don't know when or if we ever will. The same standpoint should get embraced in making predictions about quantum computing. What we *are* emphatic about is that blockchains will be a cornerstone in how these technologies play out and interact vis-a-vis the existing computer infrastructure.

Much like AI and blockchain, QC goes back to the foundational era of most general computing. According to most sources, Russian-German mathematician Yuri Meinen was the first to propose the basic idea of quantum computing in 1980, with physicist Richard Feynman positing a model for a Quantum computer just a year later. Feynman understood that the traditional engineering model of computing would not lead to a revolution, because it was stuck in the binary model that we still use today... 40 years later.

One limit of classical binary computing is that on a large scale, where a processor includes billions and billions of transistors, the system faces stresses and bottlenecks in its function. Even accounting for Moore's law, the execution of a supercomputer past a certain point runs into hard constraints, such as those imposed by time, heat, distance, and other problems of physics. Take, for example, our note on time earlier in this book, where two processes running in different spaces have space and time between them, resulting in computing that is not contemporaneous.

Distance isn't an issue for basic human applications, but in a machine trying to run extremely complex linear processes, it can become an error-inducing constraint. It also matters when the outcomes of parallel processes depend on each other, such as in calculating a stock price or adapting to multiple sources of new information.

We are already bumping into a glass ceiling for classical computing. As Dr. Talia Gershon, a materials scientist and lead researcher for quantum computing at IBM point out in a 2017 talk, today's conventional supercomputers still struggle with two core functions: optimization among complex variables, and modeling proteins for drug applications.

In the example of modeling proteins, a computer is required to account for the rules for hundreds of competing for electron cloud positions, potential binding sites, and permutations based on other factors such as temperature. Asking a computer to account for all these variables is immensely complex, and even our most advanced supercomputers struggle to model the everyday enzymes in our digestive system - which is sobering to consider.

This complexity also sheds light on our failed pursuit for a General AI. Without improving our hardware, the levels of parallel computation executed by the human mind will remain out of reach for circuit boards of classical bits.

Quantum Superposition and Cryptography

The evolution of QC is critical for cryptography. As we outlined above, with more significant numbers of qubits comes the increased potential for computation as the qubits are scaled together. While a 2-bit computer could analyze only two of four possible arrangements of zeros and ones, a two-qubit computer could simultaneously investigate all four possibilities.

At just 500 qubits, a quantum computer could analyze more positions than there are estimated atoms in the universe. Since SHA-256 and other encryption algos create hashes such that the likelihood of a cryptographic collision is as small as choosing the same atom in the scope of the universe twice, this figure maps nicely.

Quantum computers can be anticipated to obsolete several existing models of cryptography, and this is a big incentive for nation-states and large companies to develop them. Encryption is powerful, and being able to break it is even more powerful.

Not all Qubits are Made Equal

Up until this point, we have described qubits as being all the same. This idea cannot be further from the truth. There are several different approaches to building a quantum computer and adding qubits, just like there are different approaches to creating integrated circuits such as CPUs, GPUs, FPGAs, and ASICs.

Quantum Annealing Vs. Universal Quantum Gate Computers

There are currently two main leading approaches to building quantum computers. Quantum annealing and universal quantum gate machines. Think of a universal quantum gate machine as a general-purpose quantum computer that functions much as the CPU in your laptop or desktop that is good for performing a wide array of tasks.

Think of a quantum annealing machine as a specially designed quantum computer geared for specific tasks like a GPU or ASIC is.

Google Quantum Supremacy

On September 20th, 2019, the Financial Times reported that Google had achieved "Quantum Supremacy" with a 53 Qubit universal gate computer named *Sycamore*.[47]

This is a significant milestone in the development of quantum computers and can be compared to the first powered flight by Orville and Wilbur Wright in 1903. Sycamore undertook a task called a "random circuit sampling problem," where after a series of calculations each qubit outputs a 1 or 0. The aim of this test is to calculate the probability of each possible outcome occurring, similar to solving the solution to a random number generator.

Sycamore found the answer to the problem in 3 minutes in 20 seconds, while Google estimates it would take the world's most powerful supercomputer 10,000 years to get the same result. If true, this means Sycamore is logarithmically more powerful than existing supercomputers, at least at the task computed. It's difficult to overstate how critical this breakthrough is without these numbers.

---

[47] Quantum supremacy is considered to be achieved when a quantum computer outperforms the world's most powerful classical supercomputer at a specific task.

The paper for this experiment was released on NASA's website before subsequently being taken down. At the time of this writing, Google has yet to clarify further details around the claim and give more proof of Quantum Supremacy was indeed achieved.

D-Wave 5,000 Qubit Quantum Computer

On September 24th, 2019, D-Wave Inc. announced it had sold the world's first 5,000 qubit quantum annealing computer to Los Alamos National Laboratory (LANL.) This 5th generation quantum computer named *Advantage* includes D-Waves' new Pegasus topology. More about quantum annealing in a bit, but it's important to point out here that the qubits involved are less individually powerful than those involved in *Sycamore*.

Quantum Encryption

The reverse of quantum decryption is the potential for quantum encryption. Two possibilities stick out to us.

The first is the possibility of quantum generated encryption, which takes the innovations of classical cryptography and leverages discoveries in QC to make the process more complicated and secure. Quantum encryption is theoretical at this time, though many using conventional computers are experiencing success in building quantum-resistant cryptography as a defense.

The second topic is that of quantum entanglement as an alternative to transferring information between two points through a signal. In effect with quantum entanglement, a party could transmit information by manipulating the spin of a particle where the other entangled particle is in the physical custody of the second person.

While this isn't necessarily cryptography, it would represent the manipulation of the core information mechanics of the universe in a novel way, has been featured in science fiction, and has been proven possible in a lab at a distance of 10 feet. Imagine sending a message across the universe instantaneously with no potential interceptor or intermediary. Quantum entanglement communication would be a macro-level paradigm shift for the secure exchange of information.

Blockchains and the Quantum Breakout

It's impossible to discuss quantum computing without acknowledging the environment in which it is evolving. First and foremost, quantum computing is part of the national security race between democracies and non-democracies. Whoever gains the capability to conduct quantum computing at scale will have a substantial advantage over those who do not, much in the same way that the digital revolution in the West outmoded much of the analog tech that the USSR ran on during the Cold War.

Quantum computing will operate much in the same way at the strategic level, and whoever has it will have a substantial information advantage against their adversaries in military espionage, commercial intelligence, information security, and research.

Because existing models of quantum computing require the isolation of atoms or molecules in a near-absolute zero (zero degrees kelvin), near-perfect vacuum, and a vibration-free environment, it's natural to speculate whether the relative emptiness of space offers new opportunities for experiments in QC. Orbital computing labs might be a natural evolution of the technology, with problems beamed up from earth using more traditional methods. The expense for such an endeavor would be tremendous, as would the challenge posed by the severe G-force and vibration from a space launch.

However, if the raw tools for manufacturing qubits were sent skyward and assembled in place in geosynchronous orbit, such a possibility may be explored in the distant future. It may seem like science fiction, but it is not so far off. China's space agency already claims to have launched a quantum computing satellite into orbit as of 2017, using it to facilitate quantum-encrypted communication between Beijing and Austria, and this is only a public statement. More advanced experiments may well be underway.

Just like binary computing in the 1960s, quantum computing is expensive and will offer a substantial advantage to those who operationalize it first, but there are also limitations to how broadly this can scale. Because of the significant physical requirements (i.e., the near-zero temperature in a vacuum, discrete electromagnetic force to measure logic gates, sensitivity to vibration, et cetera), there are slim odds we will personally accessible forms of quantum processors as consumers out in the world anytime soon.

It is much more likely that quantum computers operated by large corporations and nation-states - entities that are not necessarily friendly to blockchains, but that have new priorities, such as gaining an advantage in protracted competition with each other.

The paradigm shift towards quantum computing means blockchains will become more critical for security. Mass adoption of blockchains is essential from a national and financial security standpoint if nation-states use their QC platforms to target rivals. Centralized institutions often operate with antiquated modes of cryptography that a quantum computer may be able to crack where existing brute-force techniques do not work.

Unless we elevate our cryptographic game, from commerce to government and personal correspondence, we are liable to lose control of our infrastructure.

Security isn't merely a matter of information theft through copying. Imagine if a hostile actor could retroactively change records, manipulate or suppress information, or if critical infrastructure could be run into the ground by a hostile party with an advanced QC platform

While it might be exciting to speculate, It's helpful *not* to think about QC as an exponential runaway technology that will necessarily result in some singularity.

It is much more likely that QC progress will be slow, and that classical computing (which is broadly distributed and has a worldwide development community) will remain competitive during much of the early quantum era. That said, this is not an asymmetric process. The entire idea of advantage, in any competition, is that there is asymmetry in capabilities or information. This matters in everything from chess to basketball, to financial markets and national economics.

Instead of a singularity, where the technology gives a company or country "one chip to rule them all," quantum supremacy is the state where a quantum computer can solve problems no classical computer can. Unlike tests for AI, which are ambiguous, quantum supremacy is easy to demonstrate. Give a conventional computer and a quantum computer a problem - two enter the ring, and one leaves.

Blockchains in a Post-Quantum World

As we've argued here, blockchain's cybersecurity benefits are coming into a world with several emergent domains – AI, IoT, competing nation-states, and QC. In this section we'll touch on specific algorithms and applications where blockchain and QC intersect.

Breaking Existing Encryption Systems

There is a future step known as the quantum advantage which follows the achievement of quantum supremacy by Google's *Sycamore* - a 53 Qubit universal gate quantum computer sourcing a random number. With quantum advantage comes several use cases and tasks which are better handled by a quantum computer than a standard computer. One of these tasks will be cracking and breaking existing encryption algorithms.

One might ask, "how will quantum computers break existing encryption algorithms?" Legacy encryption algorithms will most likely first get broken by one of two algorithms designed just for that purpose. Grover's and Shor's algorithms. Keep in mind these are only two of the known possibilities, to quote Donald Rumsfeld we still don't know the "unknown unknowns" or what other additional algos might be getting developed in secret.

Grover's Algorithm

Grover's algorithm is a quantum algorithm that is designed to search and organize data sets in a very efficient way. Grover's algorithm was devised in 1996 by Lov Grover. Think of this algorithm is an extremely fast way of searching through a massive unsorted database. Grover's algorithm could brute-force a 128-bit symmetric cryptographic key in roughly 2^{64} iterations or a 256-bit key in approximately 2^{128} iterations.

This ability to brute force is why currently widely used symmetric key lengths should get doubled to protect against future quantum attacks. One widely circulated calculation states it would take at least a 5,276 Qubit quantum computer with 15,329 gates to break SHA-256 mining with Grover's algo.

Schor's Algorithm

In 1994 Peter Shor invented what is now called Shor's algorithm, which is a quantum computer algorithm designed for integer factorization. To put it simply, it solves the following problem: Given an integer N, find its prime factors. This focus on prime integer factorization means Shor's algorithm is the one most likely to be used by quantum computers to break many encryption algorithms.

Many encryption algos get based on the complexity of prime factorization. For Shor's algorithm to break RSA, it requires 4,098 qubits and 5.2 trillion Toffoli gates for a 2048-bit RSA key. Some recent estimates claim it would take a quantum computer with 2,330 qubits and 126 billion Toffoli gates to break elliptic curve cryptography with a 256-bit modulus (128-bit security level) showing that ECC used in blockchains could be easier to crack than RSA.

Quantum Annealing & Prime Factorization

It has been widely theorized that quantum annealing computers such as the new D-Wave 5,000 Qubit much worse at integer factorization than universal quantum gate systems like IBM and Google are building currently in the 50-100 qubit range. Some recent research turns this belief on its head. Annealing quantum computers might, in fact, quickly become more powerful at cracking existing encryptions systems than universal quantum gate computers.

In 2019 researchers proposed a transformation that maps the integer factorization problem onto the quadratic unconstrained binary optimization (QUBO) model. They tested their algorithm on a D-Wave 2000Q quantum annealing machine, raising the record for a quantum factorized integer to 376,289 with only 94 qubits.

NIST - Post-Quantum Cryptography Standardization

On December 20th, 2016, the National Institute for Standards and Technology (NIST) initiated a process to develop and standardize one or more additional public-key cryptographic algorithms. This process is known as Post-Quantum Cryptography Standardization.

During the first round of this competition, there were 69 submissions to NIST. Of those, 26 have moved on to the second round, which got announced on January 30th, 2019. The finalists from this standardization process are still a ways off, but it is safe to say that the future algo that will get widely used across multiple blockchains is probably one of these finalists.

In the future, we believe almost every existing major blockchain today will have to update many of the subcomponent encryption algorithms within their core protocols. One such algorithm among the 26 finalists getting looked at closely by the DigiByte devs and Jared is SPHINCS+. This algo was created by a widely respected group of cryptographers and mathematicians and is even a favorite of Ralph Merkle himself.

Protecting Information in a Post-QC world

Massively powerful computers offer great promise for solving problems in modeling new medicines, creating powerful AIs or enhancing existing ones, engineering and discovering new materials, and hundreds of other applications that are yet even to get anticipated. The dark side of this reality is that some players' greatest innovations are in stealing, not in creating, as theft is much cheaper than R&D.

Blockchains that lock, timestamp, and protect information will become substantially more critical to support our technological ecosystem. As multiple parties have access to quantum computing, blockchains will be how quantum-resistant cryptography running on classical computers is distributed to protect from the overwhelming force of hostile quantum computers.

Running Quantum Blockchains

Quantum computing is not all bad for blockchains, either. If QC becomes more and more accessible, and quantum code becomes a more well-known skill, it's logical that we will see QC blockchains run between distributed computers. Quantum blockchains may even be a mechanism for researchers to build cooperation between disparate, competing, and even mutually distrustful labs working running QC platforms.

A "quantum blockchain" could work in multiple ways - perhaps a quantum-minable algorithm is integrated into classical blockchains, giving stakeholders an incentive to validate the chain. A strictly quantum blockchain may develop once the technology gets widely distributed enough this specific possibility becomes a longer-term possibility, as the QC platforms of today are as far from running blockchains as the ENIAC computer was from Genesis Block.

Quantum AIs, International Competition, and Security in a New World

As we pointed out in our chapter on AI, existing advanced systems require a massive amount of computing power to operate, and many of these systems run in RAM in a way that is substantially less efficient (and much hotter) than the human brain. Much of the challenge in today's AI research is the gargantuan amount of power and classical binary hardware required to operate these systems. Today's AIs work in long, parallel processes and struggle with modeling complex dynamic relationships due to the math that we outlined above, which even staggers at modeling electron positions in complex proteins.

If we as a species are going to focus on building a general AI or a superintelligent one, it stands to reason that QC will be a boon to research that hinges on modeling complex relationships as physical neural networks do. Use of superposition and exponential computing power may be the key to an entirely new embodiment of intelligence, and that intelligence may have its life, memories, and other characteristics mediated by a decentralized cryptographic network.

Turning the problem around, what happens when it is not your country that owns this technology? What happens when a foreign power can ruthlessly scan your internet, probe for vulnerabilities, and overload your networks? What happens when we face digital supervillains that answer to hostile forces? What happens when big tech firms and governments are the only authority in town, and we have no other option for news, finance, or freedom?

The only way to anticipate this threat is to focus on cybersecurity and new ways of rearchitecting the internet using existing technology. Decentralized blockchains can do that. If our companies, governments, and private lives do not get protected from this competitive global process, we will be a victim to those successful in these other fields. It may not be a quantum computer, a superintelligent AI, a dictatorial Internet of Things, or a quantum AI. However, it will happen, and we need to address the glaring flaws on the internet today, not tomorrow.

Conclusion

As we've emphasized in this chapter, quantum computing represents such a broad set of possibilities that we cannot rationally predict what it will look like, though we can speculate on use cases and applications. This future goes for all the technologies and concepts we've mentioned in this book, and we hope you've enjoyed reading it even half as much as we did writing it.

By 2035, our world will have changed substantially, and decentralized blockchains will have been a big part of that. Blockchains will serve for everything we use in our day-to-day lives, from being a source of trust for businesses to working as a check on advanced AIs. New monetary alternatives will impact governments, large corporations, and banks that blockchain provides, especially in an era defined by overwhelming debt and quantitative easing.

Blockchain technology is one of the pillars that will be key to how we forge our way forward as a species in this new era. Unlike general AI or ubiquitous quantum computing, blockchain is already here, and it's ready to be built upon to create a decentralized, secure future!

Epilogue - Introducing VESTi Inc.

> "The future is already here. It's just not evenly distributed."
>
> -William Gibson

> "The reason why men enter into society is the preservation of their property."
>
> -John Locke

We're pleased to introduce you to a project we've been working on over the last two years. This project is a practical, real-world use case for applied blockchain technology in the real estate sector. We are calling it *VESTi Inc.*

VESTi is the culmination of over seven years of blockchain development experience and countless conversations and discussions with business development people and developers in the blockchain industry. It is also a culmination of the frustration felt by our generation all across the Western world, as the financial pressures created by an increasingly unequal economy begin to crush the ambitions and finances of the urban middle class.

Affordable housing is the most significant domestic crisis America currently faces in the modern era and is exacerbated by dozens of other factors, some of which we have outlined above.

The average millennial today had spent over $100,000 on rent before the day they turned 30. The average person born after 1995 is expected to spend $225,000 on rent before they can put a down payment on a starter home - which itself is sometimes more than a starter home is expected to cost outright. A broken housing economy is a problem for everyone, and many are just one bad divorce or a lost job away from financial failure. Homeless rates are rising significantly, and advanced housing markets are contracting because no one can afford the exorbitant prices in today's highly inflated market.

Our grandparents' generation was able to afford and buy their first home early on and begin building wealth in an economy characterized by manufacturing and analog technology - in the present era, most economic growth is in our cities.

Rent is fundamentally a transfer of wealth from those who can't afford a property to those who can. Those holding land are getting wealthier, but the prospects for the middle class are rapidly deteriorating. We want to fix that. We're excited about the future, and we hope you'll join us.

Acknowledgments

We want to thank all the people that made this book possible, from research to writing, editing, publishing, and distributing it.

We'd also like to thank everyone in the DigiByte blockchain community, whose enthusiasm made this book so exciting to write, as well as all of the developers for DigiByte and other awesome projects that have made this space so intellectually rich (you know who you are).

We'd also like to thank our friends and families, without whom none of this other stuff would be meaningful.

Made in the USA
Middletown, DE
18 July 2021